Z 668 .M49 1985
Michaels, Carolyn Leopold.
Library literacy means
 lifelong learning

Library Literacy Means Lifelong Learning

by

Carolyn
Dennette Clugston Leopold
Michaels

The Scarecrow Press, Inc.
Metuchen, N.J., and London
1985

SIDNEY B. COULTER LIBRARY
Onondaga Community College
Syracuse, New York 13215

Acknowledgments of permissions to reprint begin on page v.

Library of Congress Cataloging in Publication Data

Michaels, Carolyn Leopold.
  Library literacy means lifelong learning.

    Includes index.
    1. Library education (Continuing education)
2. Library science--Philosophy. 3. Librarians--
Psychology. I. Title.
Z668.M49 1985   020'.7'15   84-10705
ISBN 0-8108-1719-5

Copyright © 1985 by Carolyn Leopold Michaels
Manufactured in the United States of America

To Bill, whose patient, good humored, concerned love-in-action has supported both this "knowledge package" and my own personal struggle toward freedom.

Wood engraving by Lynd Ward

ACKNOWLEDGMENTS

I am grateful to the following artists, authors, and publishers for permission to use their material in this book:

Chas. Addams, captionless drawing, "Mouse in Information Booth Maze," is used by permission of The New Yorker, © 1981 by The New Yorker Magazine, Inc.

Passages quoted from Mortimer Adler's How to Read a Book, Simon & Schuster, © 1940, are used by permission of the publisher.

Excerpts from the work of John Malcolm Brinnin, Paul Hendrickson, Henry Mitchell, Tom Shales, Jonathan Yardley, and Edwin B. Yoder are used with the permission of The Washington Post, © 1980, 1982, 1983.

Quotations from "The Effect of Art Work on Perceived Writer Stand" by Hugh M. Culbertson, Journalism Quarterly (Summer 1969), are used by permission of the author.

Sections of Frank Debenham's Map Making are reprinted by permission of the publisher, Blackie & Son, Ltd.

Excerpts from Arthur French's "The Comprehension of Pictures," Visual Education (June 1963) are quoted by permission of the author.

Excerpts from Animals and Maps by Wilma George are are quoted by permission of the University of California Press. Copyright 1969 by Wilma George.

Quotations from "Folklore and Cultural Awareness in th the Schools" are used by permission of the author, Dr. Byrd Howell Granger.

A passage from Mapping by David Greenhood is reproduced by permission of the author and of the publisher, The University of Chicago Press. Copyright © 1964 by the University of Chicago.

Passages from The Intelligent Eye by Richard L. Gregory are used by permission of the author and McGraw-Hill Book Company. Copyright 1970.

Passages from Pauline Kael's "The Current Cinema, Numbing the Audience," are from Deeper Into Movies. Copyright © 1970 by Pauline Kael. First appeared in The New Yorker. Reprinted by permission of Little, Brown and Company in association with the Atlantic Monthly Press. Permission also received from Marion Boyars Publishers Ltd., holders of the copyright for the British Commonwealth.

"The Dewey Decimal System of Classification" is used with the permission of the Los Angeles County Public Library.

The Foreword, "Go Forth and Be Useful," is reprinted by permission of the author and of the World Publishing Company from The Little Package by Lawrence Clark Powell.

Quotations from Principles of Cartography by E. Raisz, copyright © 1962 by the McGraw-Hill Book Co., Inc., are used by permission of McGraw-Hill Book Company.

Nonverbal Communication: Notes on the Visual Perception of Human Relations, by Jurgen Ruesch and Weldon Kees, was originally published by the University of California Press. Passages are reprinted here by permission of The Regents of the University of California.

An excerpt from Nightwings by Robert Silverberg is reprinted by permission of the author and his agents, Scott Meredith Literary Agency, Inc., 580 Fifth Avenue, New York, N.Y. 10036.

The wood engraving, "Prisoner," is used with the permission of the artist, Lynd Ward.

CONTENTS

Acknowledgments   v

Forewords

     Lawrence Clark Powell   ix
     Elizabeth W. Stone   x

Preface   xv

Abbreviations, Acronyms, and Initialisms   xxi

1.	We're Here--But Where?	1
2.	Thinking Like a Librarian	19
3.	The Library in Context	41
4.	Our Knowledge Environment	55
5.	The Library Map: How to Get There from Here	63
6.	One Librarian as a Professional	83
7.	Reading--for Librarians	107
8.	Materials as Method	135
9.	Our Ears as Channels of Information	149
10.	Reading Pictures	171
11.	Entry-Level Library Skills	197
12.	"Library" as a Textbook for Climbing the Knowledge Pyramid	207
13.	Determining Library IQ	255
14.	Our Public Service Responsibility for Education Toward Humaneness	265
15.	The Science of Who--Folklore and Festival	295
16.	The Science of Whereabouts--The Lore and Use of Maps	313
17.	Fact Is Not an End--But a Beginning	331

Bibliography   341

Index   351

FOREWORD

GO FORTH AND BE USEFUL

Go where? To a library where you can give, where what you are and what you have will be needed and wanted. This is the ideal to seek. If you fail to achieve such a situation, if you find yourself merely getting, in a job which does not tax you to your utmost, which is just a job, a salary, a day's work, without challenge or trouble or demands which make you give till it hurts and makes you grow by stretching; if, I say, you are not changed by what you do, then you are one of the living dead who haunt librarianship and make it sterile as a graveyard.

Go to work each morning, asking, What am I needed for? What is there for me to do today? Dress at home, then undress on the job. Walk naked. We have tried to toughen your skin. Be yourself. If called on to write, reach for Fowler and Webster. If asked to speak, bounce your words off the back wall. Write to be understood, speak to be heard, read to grow.

And if you are not already given to prayer, learn to pray. For what? Humility, and courage. If you stand for truth, sooner or later you will be called upon to defend it; and if you are called to the stand, remember you do not stand alone. For company you will have Milton and Jefferson, Thoreau and Emerson. Because you are a reading believer, a believing reader, they and all other defenders of truth will be there with you, far more real than today's shadowy, shady politicians.

This is not mysticism. This is reality--but only if you are a believer.

Try not to be snobbish. Remember that the hands are

also capable of learning. Let no day pass, regardless of your title or classification or responsibility, that you do not lay hands on books. Then let the eyes have them, followed by the mind and heart. There is no machine on earth can do what man can do.

Strive to be a librarian in whom the trinity of head, heart, and hands are co-equal.

Let your pride be no greater than your usefulness to others. Distinguish between service and servitude. Avoid fancy names. When asked who you are, reply with two one-letter words, one two-letter word, plus one longer word, which go to make the declarative sentence, I am a librarian.

Now that the cord is cut, go forth and be loving and useful, whether you be followers or leaders. Be librarians.

> Excerpts from a Valedictory Address by Lawrence Clark Powell given to the Class of 1962, School of Library Service, University of California at Los Angeles.

THE CHALLENGE OF LIFELONG LEARNING:

NECESSARY INGREDIENT FOR CAREER SATISFACTION

> The most important thing about education is appetite. Education does not begin with the university and it certainly ought not to end there.
> --Winston Churchill

We live in an exciting age--with change the only stable factor left to us. Librarians face opportunities and responsibilities far beyond those faced by their counterparts of only a decade or two ago. They not only have an obligation to keep up with the implications of new technologies and to gain control over the growing avalanche of information, but they also need to find wisdom and the sense of mission to guide them in judging how change can best be used to serve the wants of their clients and the overall needs of society.

What is the prescription to remedy the inertia that can result from fear of change--which can lead to professional obsolescence and, in turn, to unfulfilled aspirations? I believe it is persistence in planning and carrying out a learning agenda throughout one's life--an agenda determined by one's own career goals and aspirations. Personal career goals should be a major factor in determining how to select and intertwine the array of available learning opportunities.

As is true of most prescriptions, there are some assumptions and conditions that must be noted in order for this one to be effective. The following seem particularly important to me:

1. Accept primary responsibility for your own learning. The ideal of every profession, whether stated or implied, is that each professional worthy of the name should carry on his or her learning throughout a lifetime of practice. This requires an ability to diagnose every situation and see how creativity can be woven into performance at any organizational level. It means that the vigor and enthusiasm with which one enters a profession should be sustained throughout one's career. It means a willingness at intervals to take time away from the job in order to look at what has been achieved in order to return to work with a clearer idea of the service one is capable of giving. It means learning from other professionals through group activities in solving profession-wide problems. It means then, what Cyril Houle stated in his latest book, Continuing Learning in the Professions.

> Ultimately a major part of the real cost of continuing education falls upon the individual practitioner; the acceptance of this obligation is part of the price which he or she must pay to secure the status, privileges, and exemptions that the occupation provides. (Houle, p. 199)

2. Think of yourself as a performer of a role. Adult educator, Malcolm Knowles, has done all professions a favor by emphasizing that being a professional really means performing a role. This means that we need to develop for ourselves a model of the competencies we need in order to perform the role, or roles, we choose for our careers. A career role model must include three kinds of competencies: first, the

core competencies basic for the profession of librarianship; second, the competencies needed for a particular job one has or hopes to have; third, the stylistic competencies--so often overlooked in our self-development programs. Stylistic competencies encompass the attributes centered on our particular strengths and abilities; these are the personal peculiarities that afford an opportunity to develop the full potential of our distinctive selves. It is through the use of these that we can elevate routine jobs from drudgery to challenges.

3. <u>Identify gaps in competencies.</u> Once you have decided on your career goals, one of the best motivations for learning is self-assessment. How would you like to be performing, or how should you be performing, to be considered outstanding in your professional role? Here again Malcolm Knowles offers practical help: he suggests that we build models for ourselves which will lead to the levels of knowledge and competence that we would like to achieve. He suggests that we devise learning contracts for ourselves. Set up four columns, headed (1) What am I going to learn? (2) How will I learn it? (3) How will I know I have learned it? and (4) How will I prove I have learned it? The contract you design for yourself should contain a date after which to evaluate progress and then design a new contract based on prior accomplishment.

4. <u>Make use of a variety of learning resources and strategies.</u> What are some of the options open to you in filling out column two, once you have decided what it is you need to learn? I have, for convenience, grouped your options in four categories: course work, interaction, self-learning, and specialized opportunities.

We are all familiar with varieties of course work; often they are the most effective. But people learn in many different ways, and there are often constraints when it comes to taking courses, workshops, institutes, and seminars. But be not discouraged; there are other possibilities.

Consider interaction. Communication with colleagues provides valuable motivation and stimulation to sustain intellectual interest in your work. One such way is to attend professional meetings which offer opportunities for informal face-to-face interaction with people of the same interests. Other examples include practica, internships, leaves with pay, in-house lectures and seminars, and invisible colleges.

Then there are a whole array of self-learning opportunities. These include reading the literature, teaching others, writing for publication, engaging in personal research, and home study programs. These provide opportunities for life-long learning in a manner organized, but at the same time flexible in pacing and time.

Finally, there are specialized techniques to investigate and initiate if they appeal to you. These include continuing education centers for professionals with libraries following the model developed by teachers in Britain. They are particularly helpful as agents for change, as they facilitate the lifelong learning of participants in given locations through constant regular exchange of ideas and experience with colleagues. Another specific is the assessment center, designed to help people analyze competence and performance gaps.

5. Keep a record of your learning activities. Many people participate, but keep no record, or at best a haphazard account of what they have done. The Continuing Library Education Network and Exchange (CLENE) has developed a voluntary recognition service, one part of which provides a way in which your activities can be as a substitute for or supplement to your personal record keeping.

These are five suggestions for ways to continue a lifetime of learning, but many more opportunities will be available with the rapid development of new and potentially interactive technologies. Interactive television, video discs, cable television, computerized instructional programs, satellite conferencing will soon be readily available learning technologies.

Public service librarians are the ones for whom the present emphasis on library literacy as a vital educational competency has especial professional relevance. The formulation and tackling of the problems that arise as part of growth toward personal career satisfaction should provide exercises in critical thinking transferrable to other life-long learners that cross their daily working path.

Your present professional competency rests on a K-M.L.S. academic base. Where you are on your career ladder required a long learning-to-learn path, with each new step being built upon an already created knowledge rung.

To give an inner feeling of radiance and achievement through lifetime learning the essential element is to begin a learning experience that meets a specific immediate learning need. Once that is achieved, plan for the next experience, and the next, and the next.

>Elizabeth W. Stone, Dean,
>School of Library and Information Science, The Catholic University of America, Washington, D.C.

PREFACE

The morning after experiencing Lois Lowrey's lecture, "The Craft of Fiction," I was working on the manual level, readying the house for a party. On the "book" level I heard, "Your book is patchwork too, just like this eclectic collection of household 'things.'" To which I respond (I never ignore myself), "Of course--there's your analogy!" A revision should qualify, even if, "written" on a word processor, it would have no in-process physicality beyond the electronic. Mine is a true patching. Scarecrow sent me two copies of School Libraries Worth Their Keep and said, "Cut these up and begin the next edition." But, though divorce produced empathy, I am not MEDEA. I photocopied the text and began. The LLMLL manuscript created from the 5-1/4" by 8-1/2" photocopied pages pasted onto 8-1/2" by 11" sheets (mainly palimpsests from an earlier use of side one), then cut apart and re-ordered with both penned and typed new copy inserted, plus the decoration of word by word editing with correction tape and white-out displays craft--if not art. (Is there a bid from a literary archives?)

Patchwork also describes the intellectual content--a philosophy distilled from experience into a working paper on professional problems. Being mental, it is neither paper collage nor pieced fabric, but it nevertheless is a very real map of my feminine, marriage-directed professional odyssey. Family anecdotes used as examples--take them out, leave them in, or edit to reflect the present--a map of painful changes! Professional examples demanded further editorial decisions. The toughest, yet most satisfying part concerns overall content. The central design--my "philosophy plus strategies" remains the same, but borders must be added to reflect twelve "new" years. Thoughts and experiences, blessed with a publisher, will become alive to gain a reach beyond my spoken voice. A book, that perfect knowledge artifact whose only enemies are paper life and collections managers, is terrifying yet nutritious ego food.

Pauline Anderson of Choate Rosemary Hall, Dean of Independent School Librarians, dear colleague, when cornered at the American Library Association Conference in Philadelphia and asked for her comments on this revision wrote:

> Some of those schools to whom you addressed the book remain unchanged ... they are still on square 1 and need to start with SLWTK as square 1.... Most school libraries have changed between 1972-82--but if they have not they probably never will. Fewer and fewer librarians are teacher dropouts. Those who exist will continue "as is" until they retire--on earth or in the great beyond. The new breed--at least on the secondary level in both the public and private sector--are competent with a real sense of their abilities and intellectual worth.... I would prefer a sequel which addresses the new challenges and the problems. [Her bottom line]: I believe that SLWTK still fulfills its original purpose.

The thesis of SLWTK, enlarged, not altered in LLMLL, is that the public service librarian has a central role in the learning process, very different than has Marian, the custodian of books. That professional role is to use the library as a textbook to help humanity develop the ability to think critically--to locate facts in context, to avoid common fallacies of logic, to analyze arguments, and to formulate the differences between conflicting lines of reasoning.

In 1966, Richard L. Darling, then my boss and President of the American Association of School Librarians, now retiring as Dean of the School of Library Service at Columbia, confirmed this idea. He commented that indeed I was right--traditional print-based school libraries had never been fully utilized as a means of learning. "The task before us now," he said, "is to make our dream a reality in the new world of media technology."

In 1972 I quoted the old hymn, "Once to every man and nation comes the moment to decide." Librarians decided--for media technology, not for instruction in knowledge process. The flood of federal money brought record benchmarks of technology while leaving society's stragglers and information dropouts as beached as before. Now our channel carries a trickle of cash and the cresting data-base industry clearly means to keep the streams of information and knowledge separate. As Clare Boothe Luce has said, "The difference between an optimist and a pessimist is that a pessimist is better informed." The profession's consciousness of Bibliographic Instruction (BI) is at a cyclical high. What will come of this turn of the wheel? The finale of SLWTK hoped for the Cultivation of Consciousness Tall--for Teaching All--"a land whose citizens believe that what they studied to become credentialed practitioners of the Guild of Rememberers must be imparted to students--a daily encounter group with our untried craft of Teaching All."

This was my extrapolation from Charles Reich's The Greening of America.

A February 1971 Library Journal editorial adds this:

> Consciousness I librarians ... were the good ladies ... whom we remember from yore. To them librarianship was a test of the moral fibre as much as a practical affair ... there was no question as to one's role. One served to amuse the literate, assist the scholar, enlighten the clod, hush the rowdy, and preserve the books.
> Now Consciousness II is the ethos of the expert managers of society who run our businesses, churches, government agencies, things like ALA and the Ford Foundation, libraries, and library system. The II librarian ... learned personnel work, business management, public relations, architecture, systems design and computers. His libraries grew.
> The III librarian surfaced first in suburbia and at association meetings. He bugged the II librarians with his lack of reverence for the structures they had built, and proposed risking these beautiful things in a civil war against hitherto respectable social evils.... We submit that the III librarian may be the only one nervy enough to lead us to new organizational forms, forms in which power over persons is not the primary cohesive force." (Berry, p. 429)

Do we want to add a reverence for teaching knowledge process and become IV librarians?

At the annual change-of-command banquet of the District of Columbia Library Assocation in May of 1983, the D.C. Superintendent of Schools, Floretta Dukes McKenzie, delivered a witty, informative talk. One comment stood out for me, screaming that Dick Darling's "dream" was still over the rainbow, though the speaker heard something very different. "My school librarians just loved all subjects so much that they never could settle on one!" And then she went on to talk about high-tech library technology--on hand and on hope. Such a square-shaped wheel at this turn does not encourage me toward general optimism about prospects for "Teaching all!"

What does the patchwork in the new borders say? New professional fabric tells of adult learners in a continuing education university setting (including one whose mother was a distinguished President of ALA) who give as their reason for taking the class, "I want to feel comfortable in a library." There is some old-school-tie silk bearing a variety of organizational devices such as the yellow square of the National Geographic and the spinning wheel of the DAR. This fabric signifies more time spent on both sides of the Reference Desk--as researcher and Reference Librarian--demonstrating that process can be consistently taught either one to one at a Reference Desk or one to group at an impromptu requested lecture. The "more management experience" patches say that process teaching, not product delivery, if decreed, can be carried out.

My use of some terms needs clarification. "Academe" covers formal educational institutions, K-Ph.D. A denizen of academe is termed a student. "Learner" refers to library patrons beyond and outside of academe. Sick of the sticky wicket of "he? she?" am I. Should I adopt a formal, correct he-she; or affect the h/s of John Dewey? My choice is to eliminate all these uncomfortable pronouns wherever reasonable and then let gender fall where it may.

The words of two most special librarians create the patch labelled "Foreword." Lawrence Clark Powell's are my favorite excerpts from a graduation speech reprinted in SLWTK. Gracious and generous Dean Elizabeth W. Stone of Catholic University agreed to write a personal joining for my "philosophy plus strategies." Both these eminent, authoritative, very different spokespersons have materially influenced my library career. LCP early, when we both worked at the now LCP Library at the University of California at Los Angeles, and, for me, forever. The influence of EWS extends from a period when I worked directly under her in 1969 until--I hope--always.

* * *

Chapter One discusses our current "Moment to Decide." Chapter Two asks what we as professionals do that entitles us to a place in education, or why does the wheel of library literacy keep being invented? Chapter Three searches for "essence" and asks "What constitutes the 'order' that makes libraries meta-knowledge and produces the textbook for BI?" Chapter Four discusses how "collection" becomes ordered knowledge. Chapter Five charts organizational structure and discusses how this turns "collection" into "library"--the knowledge map. After all, isn't a good theory the most practical thing? "One Librarian as a Professional" announces the content of Chapter Six. The next four chapters deal with some of the specifics of the librarian's tools--old and new, print and non-print--in the context of now.

The following two chapters offer "how-to"--some of the promised "strategies." The skills comprising library literacy are divided between entry-level in Eleven and the library as textbook in Twelve. To assist action one must provide ammunitional specifics to those about to fight. Thirteen offers a seat-of-the-pants way to measure patron library literacy. Fourteen discusses "story" and places it within our teaching responsibilities.

Chapters Fifteen and Sixteen offer philosophy and strategies for "no teacher homework" library classes supported by two broad subject areas that interest all learners from entry to exit. Seventeen: "Facts are not an end but a beginning" closes my side of the dialogue.

Patchwork to the end, my "thank you's" go to old and new benefactors. Dale Brown whose title now reads Supervisor, Libraries, Media and Textbooks, has given again of his precious professional time to listen, counsel, and read all the patches. My debt to Edward B. Koren and Katherine Ferriter Parker must be reacknowledged as their illustrations again appear. Madelyn Fenstermaker, now, again, Madelyn Leopold, shares the illustration credit with my husband, Dr. William M. Michaels. Madelyn also contributed professional editorial skills in the service of this edition. I am also indebted, gratefully, to Lynd Ward for the use of his 1973 wood-cut, "Prisoner," which graces the dedication page and to George M. Barringer, Special Collections Librarian at Georgetown University for his help in turning the original into book copy. Kathryn S. Scott, beloved former DAR colleague, must be thanked for her gift of a most able ear and blue pencil. Anne Goodwin copy-edited and provided a solid, objective wall for idea bouncing. Continuity with Holton-Arms now takes the form of thanks to Joan Kuhn Thomas, a dear colleague and "just" former head of their Middle School, for her gift of the calligraphy in the chapter titles. Lastly, for a crucial skill of any manuscript, patchwork or word processed, thanks must go to my superb editorial typist, Cindy Rummell.

                Carolyn Dennette Clugston Leopold Michaels
                Charleston, South Carolina

ABBREVIATIONS, ACRONYMS, AND INITIALISMS FAITHFULLY EXPANDED

AAS	American Association for the Advancement of Science
AASL	American Association of School Librarians
ACE	American Council on Education
ALA	American Library Association
AP	Advanced placement
A76	Office of Management and Budget Circular
AT&T	American Telephone & Telegraph Co.
A-V	Audio-visual
BI	Bibliographic Instruction
BRS	Bibliographic Retrieval Services
CIJE	Current Index to Journals in Education (journal)
CLA	Catholic Library Association
CLENE	Continuing Library Education Network & Exchange
COM	Computer output microform
CRT	Cathode Ray Tube
CU	Catholic University of America
DAR	Daughters of the American Revolution
D.C.	District of Columbia
DCLA	District of Columbia Library Association
DDC	Dewey Decimal Classification
E	Easy book
EMC	Educational Media Center
ERIC	Education Resources Information Center
F	Fiction book
GRE	Graduate Record Examination
K-Ph.D.	Kindergarten through doctorate levels of education
K-12	Kindergarten through high school levels of education
LC	Library of Congress; its classification scheme for labeling books and arranging them on the shelves
LCC	Library of Congress book classification scheme
LIRT	Library Instruction Round Table (of ALA)
LLMLL	this very book
L.S.S.I.	Library Systems and Services, Inc.
M.L.S.	Master of Library Science degree
NCHE	National Commission on Higher Education
NCTE	National Council of Teachers of English
NGS	National Geographic Society
OPM	(U.S.) Office of Personnel Management
OV.	Oversize
PF	Pamphlet File
port.	portrait
RIE	Research in Education (journal)
SLWTK	School Libraries Worth Their Keep (earlier edition of this very book)
SOP	Standard Operating Procedure
U.C.	University of California, Berkeley

xxi

U. C. L. A.	University of California at Los Angeles
VF	Vertical File
VLA	Virginia Library Association
WHCLIS	White House Conference on Libraries and Information Science

Chapter 1

We're Here ~ But Where?

Whose service is perfect freedom.

Book of Common Prayer.

Destination is crucial to any journeying. "Here" implies having been somewhere else before and, for the library profession, that "before" is being questioned. Information Age is a major descriptor for "where." Some current items that have served as signage for my odyssey range from a recent double-page Bell System advertisement which begins its comments on Information with Plato and continues to Brattian, to the oft-quoted lumpy statistic that more people now work in Information than in agriculture and manufacturing combined, to the remarks of the stirring new force of the "First Librarian in Congress," Congressman Major R. Owens of New York. Information-related articles and national meetings proliferate, each with their own subject definitions and approaches. Library schools add "Information" to their titles--thus confusing further the already questionable legitimacy of our profession's use of science as a descriptor. That the information business is big business is not open to question. It is. That it includes wildly advancing and proliferating technology is not subject to question either. Our ability to rearrange and transmit information (manipulate/massage data), being a function of that technology, needs no further fertilizer than praise and purchase. Once anything enters a part of this system, it, like the space traveler, is on its way!

Way where, way why, way what? As Richard De Gennaro, Librarian of the University of Pennsylvania, states so skillfully, we are running two systems now. One is the print system from which the electronic system emerges and upon which most of it builds by transmuting published print into electronically republished something. Very little of the information that concerns librarians is born electronic. Magazines, novels, non-fiction works, reference tools, and ephemera begin as print. Even an institution's own archives that now commonly soon become microform, originate as letters, researchers' notes, or board and committee reports. The first cost is creating the printed item--the print system.

We're Here--But Where?

Then the second system, the electronic inputting, microreprography, etc. takes place and adds its cost to the original cost of print publishing. For argument, let us call the print system "library" and the second high or higher tech system "information." Then the library that was understood in Department of Library Science is De Gennaro's first system, and Information Science becomes the piggy-back layer.

Speed is the god served by electronically processed information. Felix Krayeski in his presentation at the 1982 District of Columbia Library Association/Special Libraries Association Spring Workshop, described "yesterday" when research (data) requested by a Congressperson was put in a manila envelope and delivered across the street or through the tunnel by messenger at foot or wheel speed. Now the page wanted can be copied photographically and transmitted electronically to a receiving machine which prints the page --speed of light! If the information need being met is speed-of-light, a medical emergency--for example--or a fresh legislative thought at almost vote time--the response is appropriate. But when there is foot or wheel or mail lead time, why not also continue to use the people-intensive technology? Extant hardware is paid for, and people already trained to walk or ride need such work to be self-supporting.

Long ago (1967) when Maurice Tauber was describing the wonders of library's forthcoming automation, I queried him as to its potential to affect clerical jobs. He responded that this was not his concern. An IBM TV commercial selling information systems for office management highlights one of its features which reminds a boss not only when it is time to leave for Chicago but also to check the CRT for his messages. The electronic employee says, "Remember the blueprints and your umbrella." Scene closes as he does just this. Is the broader message that the computer has replaced secretaries? After us, let them eat cake! But that solution serves the present and unemployment in South Succotash no better than it served Marie Antoinette. As Milton Terry of the Bell Labs said to a 1982 computer seminar at the National Society of the Daughters of the American Revolution, "Yes, a computer can be made to 'do anything' with data that you want it to." But, in the fine print read (find) this specific: "If you have the time and if you have the money!"

Congressman Owens presented it thusly at a May, 1983 program of the Library of Congress Professional Association: some "micro problems" which are 000 library funding in

Reagan's budget, A76 contracting out which lumps Federal library service with janitorial and guard service, and the OPM Reclassification threat qualify us to be a "profession under seige." The "macro problem" has two heads--to establish (note the absence of re-) librarians as keepers of the tools of decision making, rather than as keepers of the quiet place and, by doing this, force the information industry to include us in. He sees commercialism threatening to steal, hoard, and hold hostage our recorded heritage unless we librarians can take charge. Our choice then becomes the vanguard or the rear guard.

My descriptor for where we are is selfhood--a stance proposed, defined, and acted upon by such as De Gennaro, Owens, and Daniel Boorstin:

> As the Librarian of Congress I speak for a national fortress of knowledge.... Our relentless Jeffersonian quest tempts us to believe that all technologies ... were created equal.... I would like to focus your attention on the distinction between Knowledge and Information, the importance of the distinction, and the dangers of failing to recognize it.... The last two decades have seen the spectacular growth of the Information Industry.... A magic computer now accomplishes the dreariest tasks in seconds.... The Information Industries are a whole new world of business celebrity.... Our knowledge Institutions ... include our colleges and our universities --and ... our libraries. While the Information Industry flourishes ... our Knowledge-Institutions go begging.... They are sometimes called "philanthropic"--which means that they profit nobody except everybody, and their dividends go to the entire community. (Boorstin p. 113, 114)

We run the knowledge industry and we can still make the information industry serve us if we re-write the tune before we continue the dance.

What do we librarians want these machines to do for our libraries? A comment from the 1983 Catholic Library Association meeting to the effect that the term computer no longer adequately described their current activities in data manipulation makes me uneasy with what I guess has become a generic for hardware that is racing light years ahead of its software--ahead of its human direction. During ALA San

We're Here--But Where?

Antonio, over breakfast, Frank Pezzanite, the computer genius behind Minimarc (now L. S. S. I) provided detailed technical chapter and verse for such thinking. America's genius has always been her technical know-how and drive, and once again it has created a tool that intensely demands of society choices--a multi-faceted road, complex to the nth degree.

As information professionals, those choices rest squarely on library's front stoop. When the philosopher Mortimer Taube conceived information science and then, with the publication of <u>Computers and Common Sense</u>; "the Myth of Thinking Machines, delivered it fullborn, the first choice for us had arrived. Sadly, we did not recognize that babe as our own. Now, 22 real years--many light years-- later, though our choice is as different as such chronology would dictate, we still have one.

To reaffirm our societal role, let us search for the essence of a library. That its quintessence is greater than the sum of its parts stems from the organization which creates its order. Using this order, the human mind, once taught how to collect, evaluate, and apply information, has the skill for lifelong learning and rational knowledge. A library itself provides the key to and the textbook for the skills necessary to process information into knowledge. This, not a proliferation of academic degrees, is continuous, continuing education available freely to everyone. Humanity has risen from a primitive existence to a much more intricate one. The achievement of this complex society requires some way of storing accumulated knowledge so that each new generation may profit from what has gone before.

Man's first storehouse of knowledge was a spoken one (currently called audio or oral history). The long tales that were sung around camp fires became the <u>Iliad</u> and the <u>Odyssey</u>, <u>Beowulf</u>, and <u>Paul Bunyan</u>. Writing began with the hieroglyphs of the clay tablets of Assurbanipal and progressed through alphabets and languages to computer languages read from a microchip. Possessing the ability to transcribe, the record could be preserved so that each new generation could begin far ahead of its parents in culture and technology.

The method of information storage is really not important. Storage and retrieval are the vital supports for each new generation. To explore this in a personal way, what about our own storage of records and what would happen if these disappeared?

In 1946 I lived on the beach in Hawaii where there is always the danger of a Tsunami or tidal wave. Our arrival occurred not long after a very disastrous Tsunami at Hilo on the island of Hawaii where 200 people were killed. One morning my meteorologist husband telephoned me and said, "There's a Tsunami warning out. Get together everything you can carry with you. I'll call back in five minutes." After organizing my two young children, the things I decided to save were my jewelry, the family papers, and our photograph albums. Fortunately, when the call came five minutes later, the alarm proved false.

You might not, under similar circumstances, make the same decision as I did. Consider, however, where you would be without your Christmas card list, or your address book.

The number of records that any of us stores varies considerably, but their value to us depends in a large measure upon the way we have them organized. We organize to locate and compare data. Consider, for example, the usual family process when the Christmas card list is gone over for names and then checked against a more up-to-date address book into which entries are made all during the year. These two information sources serve as cross references to check the inclusion and authority of the data being used. Information theory stresses that we must organize to get the maximum amount of information with a relatively worthwhile amount of work. Our personal Christmas card reference directory is both noted with each year of sending and categorically color coded. Some adult children, tragically orphaned by an automobile crash, may find parental Christmas card lists the only record source for locating friends who should be notified of the tragedy. Others, on a happier mission, might use such a list to gather parental friends for a surprise, mega-anniversary celebration.

Assembled, such records form the collective consciousness of mankind from which he draws his ability to move forward on the basis of what the men who preceded him have learned. Along with the family Bible, Christmas card lists will form part of some children's inheritance. Man may completely disregard the wisdom in written records attending only to discrete facts, but it is imperative that it all be there for generic MAN to use. Over the long period of recorded history, the library has been the instrument to organize and make available this collective consciousness of mankind.

We're Here--But Where?   7

As it stands today, information scientists possess the field of advancing record/data technology. By ignoring these practitioners in the early years, librarians have allowed them to become prosperous while traditional collections suffer. When the mist vanishes, nothing, not even the book, may have escaped the tools of information technicians. Paper crumbles, microforms are new and cheap; information becomes bits to be counted and stored electronicially. By not being them (let alone joining them), librarians now face the financial, spiritual, and intellectual consequences of a house divided.

Librarian as teacher of "library" implies an institutional base. Any non-personal library either is an institution (public library) or is within an institution, school, college, church, business, or organization. It is a small business operating on its own or within a larger unit. Ideally the pupils/patrons would have learned the educational sequence of problem identification--problem solution--through the use of relevant information/knowledge materials within K-12 "school." Beyond that, instruction need only cover new technologies of access or introduction to new reference tools. Advising readers on matching fiction to seeker is forever. That interpersonal exchange cannot really be replaced by Book Review Digest and its like regardless of whether access to annotations is speed of computer or speed of print.

In the immediate post-sputnik era immense pressures were exerted upon the whole educational community to demonstrate new guises for saving America. From this panic came an opportunity to develop school library collections. In the golden sixties, Federal support brought the miracle of instant money to the whole school library picture. Francis Keppel, Secretary of HEW, was a major public relations figure instrumental in founding new elementary school libraries, as the grande dame, Frances Henne of Columbia, was for the school library profession.

Now, 25 years later, a related crisis is media fare. An apparent lack of hard math and science teachers and resource materials is threatening our scientific and technological supremacy. Educators and scientists alike see an empty human pipeline ahead. MacNeil and Lehrer recently devoted a program to this topic, pitting Secretary of Education Terrel Bell against Carl Sagan! Perhaps another sizable windfall to fatten school library budgets is ripening.

This "micro" alarm was almost immediately elevated

to "macro" with the cry of "A Nation at Risk," by the National Commission on Excellence in Education. We Americans are now hereby informed that the power of the educational gauntlet cast our way by sputnik has dissipated, leaving the young unready for our present and future world of hi-tech and one-worldedness.

Under the totem of education, inmates are taught. Our role as teachers of "library" may be oft rediscovered and redesigned, profiled, researched--and ignored, but in educational institutions one can be a teacher. Not so for the other two-thirds of the library pie. The Public Library Reference Librarian, whether teaching process or delivering product, is educating the patron--one to one--sans public role approval! Public librarians are not over noticeable in the ranks of the Library Instruction Round Table or Bibliographic Instruction. Heads of Reference Departments seem to be more interested in computer access than in library instruction--or so the notes and articles in American Libraries indicate.

The other third inhabits the hallowed halls of commerce and science where, though Special Librarians breathe lip service to education, most patrons still lack comprehension of the order called either information or library. Experience as a Special Librarian (in Education K-12, Higher Ed, and Genealogy) and, observing fellow researchers, (a librarian incognito) at the National Geographic insists that, roughly, no one is library wise. Good researchers must be information-able. Given the material, they can evaluate, criticize, and validly use it for their work. They avoid, however, seeking it in the library maze whenever possible, hoping relevant books and articles will land on their desk. For researchers at the American Council on Education and the Geographic, they did. For the others--teachers of Montgomery County, Maryland and searchers in the Genealogical Library of the DAR, the Reference Staff taught process and hoped motivation would enable those lessons to stick.

The idea which this book argues is that the organization and collections of libraries create a/the textbook for knowledgeableness and informationability. The common assumption that any large proportion of the educated population is taught by the school to use a library is a monmental myth. Unused, libraries are tidy book repositories to be pointed to pridefully when the administrators conduct visitors through their domains--institutions truly not worth their escalating price tags.

We're Here--But Where?

All librarians are being pushed toward new designs for service while the old designs, which never materialized, become ghostly relics. We must face the differences between need (what the doctor feels is good for the patient) and demand (what the patient will pay for). The people's demand is for factual information and help in their search for identity and employment. The credibility gap is one proof that the mass media are not the answer to America's demands for information. Library collections traditionally hear and give equal space to all voices. A balance upon which to build knowledge therefore equates with library.

If this is so, why doesn't formal education, generously equipped with resources, produce information-able people? Because the lack of education in library use negates their collections' potential to provide information.

Schools continue to be a prime focus of a disgruntled America--institutions broadly criticized for changing so much or so imperceptibly! Our coddled students are thorny, grubby, and generally anxiety-producing. If neither the immediate customer nor the taxpayer is happy with the product, it is good that the process remains under inspection.

A survey by questionnaire of independent schools made in 1965 showed an average library use of one-half book per student per month. Less than one-third of the students and one percent of the faculty made any independent use of the library. Except for the presence of warm bodies, flirting or doing homework, which study-hall use brings into the reading room, these school libraries were only expensive storehouses. Run the tape fast forward to ALA, 1980 to hear this; "In my school only one-third of the student body are readers and library users." And this, "Educators say the library is the heart of the school but act otherwise--putting it on the periphery."

If fine teaching can be considered an art, then media capability enables one to be a better artist. Competent use of these new tools gives a teacher/librarian greater means to reach every seeker. Not just the verbal, conscientious person that once we were permitted to consider the normal societal building block. Without such comprehension, multimedia teaching relates to true art as paint-by-number kits to a creative canvas. This exciting technology MUST provide more creativity than does a numbered painting kit.

Otherwise the educational community will have a more invisible new suit of clothes than ever did the Emperor. The knowledge function of library order is visible only when the cloth of gold glitters on the librarian.

The purpose of teaching is learning. The inquiry method asserts that learning is an experience in itself. It is a personal happening, in contrast to the syllabus or curriculum guide method which forces the learner's mind into someone else's patterns and substitutes the teacher's story for the learner's happening. Learning by questioning moves "library" into a dominant role as the incarnation of answers.

To be educated, in the sense of lifelong learning, requires not just a few specialized materials but access to the world's fund of knowledge. It implies knowing how to make a free choice among the possibilities, and how materials are organized so that what is chosen can be found efficiently. Only a library offers these facilities. What is lacking is, first, an acceptance of such a definition of learning; and second, the training needed to implement access to the fund of knowledge.

The first one who must see these goals clearly, if they are to be attained, is the school librarian. Their mission should be to enunciate and reiterate these goals, and to demand to be made part of the process of teaching both access and utilization. School librarians must be for real.

What is required if we are to make the thriving information industry our servant instead of our master? Servants serve by performing tasks set by masters. All right, what then should be the tune we call; how can data manipulation serve our knowledge industry? After twenty-plus years library automation has accomplished much that Tauber prophesied, but it has failed to fill its promise completely to substitute computer-based bibliographic systems for our manual ones. The software, or directive, lag is one effective restraint. The Montgomery County Public Library system is a recent local case in point. A multi-hundred-thousand-dollar circulation automation semi-black hole developed because the task of designing the software (which equates with defining the need and the solution) was assigned to the county's computer unit for fiscal and housekeeping services. Onto management error Number One was added the not-uncommon reality of the system selected being able to be characterized as an unborn pig in a poke. No professional should be asked to dance to someone else's tune.

We're Here--But Where?

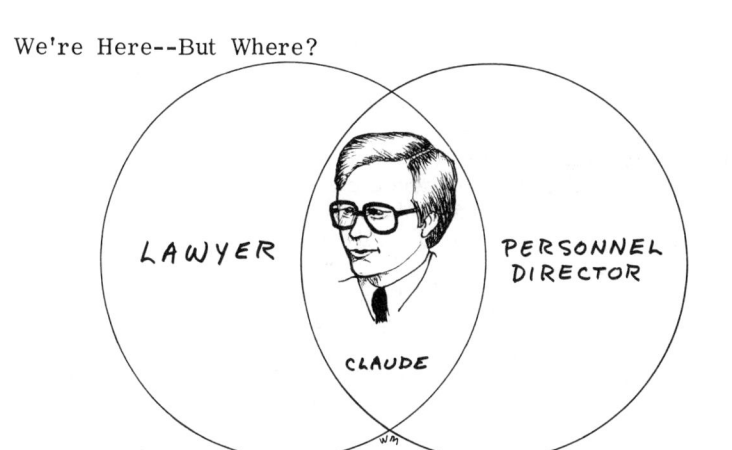

LAWYER CLAUDE PERSONNEL DIRECTOR

What need for public services can computers fill? The God of speed, combined with Boolean logic can do one whale of a lot for reference work. The on-line capabilities of Dialog, Orbit, BRS, Lexis, and the like, in the hands of a skilled searcher (which is not the average patron), when the main frame is not suffering from p.m. E.S.T. lag or a "wrinkle," produce magically immediate bibliographic results. Time spent in comparison with manual search is a clear trade-off, but the Boolean combination subject-linking capability comes by no known manual route presently in existence. All that such a search provides is a bibliography though--unless offprints are purchased. My practical spouse tossed aside a lovely search with a snort: "Where are the articles? What good is this?"

So, yes, we like technology's on-line database searches for our clients, but the cost? We like that piper's tune, but can we afford to incorporate it into our Reference Services? Thusly is raised the current "for pay" controversy. With Dialog connect time billed at an average rate of $45.00 per hour and offprints costing an average of $7.00, "for pay" is an apt phrase. Public libraries are free to the taxpayer, but that "free" shows no signs of being expansible to encompass on-line. Just the consideration of erecting within Carnegie's free university such a financial barrier caused a crisis of professional pride and intent. On the other hand, the verbalized intuition of some public library reference practitioners signals that the for-profit sector enjoys our immobility on this rung, because an expansion of our free services would threaten their sales of home computers. Thus another chapter in "As the Library Turns."

Detroit ALA, 1977 Eric Moon Message: 'I would hate to see librarians ... befogged or bedazzled by words

like information and data ... fail to emphasize the broader
things ... knowledge, ideas, creativity, understanding,
awareness of self and the world around us--even--by God,
wisdom. Or ... a way of becoming human." A society
in transition produces such a lack of value consensus that
most younger people are boats without moorings--adrift.
For lack of values, people drift, for lack of inner-directed
people, institutions drift, for lack of inner-directed institutions, society drifts towards--towards what?

Michaels' Message is to unfog and undazzle ourselves
by a return to our ROOTS as librarians, keepers of the organized collections of the carriers of knowledge and of the
skills needed to fully use these resources. July fourth, 1976
was a fine hour because we Americans pulled enough strength
out of our past to envision new values which gave us grace
to stand kindly and proudly together, albeit for only one day.
If the ghost of such a revolution can put so much starch into
us, what might live effort accomplish! Want to try?

"Dear Lord, help me to reform the world--beginning
with me!" By finding professional goals as expressions of
professional values, we know for what we fight. The purpose and the process of value determination are the same,
both for individuals and institutions. To find individual
moorings for humanity's present overload of aimlessly cir-
cling craft makes the awful demand of each of us that we
establish personal values clear enough to be found in a fog
and strong enough to be secure in a storm.

Our professional revolution supports that earlier one
because it can give each person access to fact upon which
to build personal truth. It is the essence of that freedom
Jefferson counted on, Adler warned us about in How to Read
a Book, and 1984 lays to rest. Our revolt would truly produce free thinkers--people who can determine unique personal
goals and obtain for themselves the facts by which to inform
or educate themselves into those goals. It is a heresy equal
to Luther's which could accomplish meaningful social change
by ending mental bondage in just one set of K-12 years and
guaranteeing to all the freedom of choice lifelong learnability
provides.

What is our revolution? It is to discover, defend,
and display one of our reasons for being more an educational
part of any institution than cafeteria or book store managers.
I say we are teachers--of the process of lifelong self-

education--individualized instruction--how to think--how to become human and stay that way!

When the subject is today's informationability, out of all the rhetoric, one need seems clear. Public service librarians must assume responsibility for ensuring that all who use libraries, everyone they can reach out and touch, becomes a comprehender of information organization. To enable these people to recognize the value for them in our costly technical processing is basic Marketing 101.

Our organized collections of the carriers of knowledge are the incarnation of the process of search or library reference work which applies the principles of critical thinking to the specific problem at hand. Our skills, the content of our M. L. S. training, make us the sole credentialed denizens of this particular piece of intellectual territory. This is our subject speciality. This is what makes us teachers. "Teacher" consists of an attitude toward people and an academic skill to teach. Our revolution lies in a convinced proclamation of our subject-knowledge process!

Today's America has an "old culture" and a "new culture"--both extremes crushing the middle path. The polarities which characterize the old culture over the new tend to prefer property rights over personal rights, technological requirements over human needs, competition over cooperation, striving over gratification, the producer over the consumer and secrecy over openness. Libraries as status quo institutions have become primary battle grounds for this war, because most institutional-type adults still prefer business as usual and a steady boat to anything else.

Inadvertently, the advanced placement courses became one of the first catalysts of the new culture. They brought together bright students and excellent teachers. Motivated brain-power, turned loose in cross-disciplinary courses, with individualized instruction and training in library research, freed enough minds simultaneously to make a noticeable impact. At the peak of their developmental idealism, this youth saw all the pieces of an issue fit together. Assumptions of the old culture became fully visible. What those students saw was the vision that helped to produce the social gains of the 1960's. Through influential parents they were able to materially affect a scene far broader than their own power to act would have provided. The case of the then Secretary of the Interior, Wally J. Hickel, illustrates this. In the letter he wrote to Nixon that brought about his dismissal by Nixon, he indicated his debt to his son for helping him change his assumptions. These able young minds were taught to understand the interrelationship of the fact, opinion, and value judgment, and past, present, and future data matrix. They used this power to find new assumptions with which to direct personal and societal growth. There is still a desperate need for Eric Moon's "Poor kid in Brooklyn" to possess the means to his personal ends.

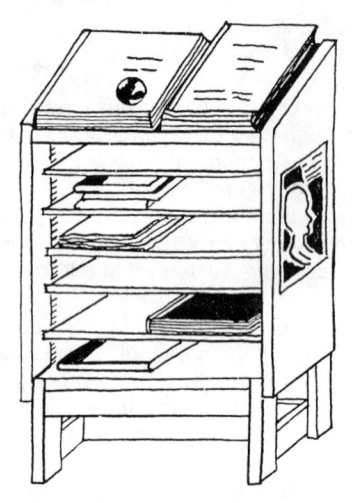

The problems that underlie our current recurrent institutional crisis--inadequate financial support, shifting educational objectives and sexual roles, professionalism vs. the OPM Standards, etc.--were and are and will be eternal, because they are the tough, "when push comes to shove," basic human situations which institutional man seems to resolve by continuously rediscovering the wheel rather than firmly putting the horse before the cart and driving on. These seemingly eternal issues swirl about us like snow in an old fashioned paperweight, or memoranda in a meeting. Acting as individuals--ignoring the troubled and cluttered institutional sky--the resources we now presently hold title to are more than adequate for a library revolution.

I sense that "fact" is ill considered today. My first glimpse of this in action came at a graduate seminar. The students listened to a scientist, a man of impeccable expertise who was presenting hard data. I watched and listened to them shrug off this documented presentation of fact. They didn't believe.

We're Here--But Where? 15

Over the luncheon that followed, to test this, I asked: "I had the feeling from what I observed that you doubted the factuality of this material." They looked a little sheepish, and said, "Yes, that was true." I asked why? "Well, we lived through the 50's, when there was the Cold War, and then in the 60's came détente, and Vietnam and the Domino Theory. So, if there is some absolute--some surety--where is it?"

While taking graduate courses at the University of California at Berkeley, I watched students react as if there was no way of checking what the professor or fellow students said. No mention was made of library resources. The comments were tossed around, as if each had equal value. Each man's word was coin of the realm. There was no way to bite it and find out if it really was gold.

On a cross-country flight just before the 1980 election, I engaged my seatmate in a devil's advocate discussion of the question of how we might determine the facts of military preparedness or Reaganomics before we cast our ballots. During our dialogue, he refused every touchstone offered as to how one could obtain facts. He lived and voted by unsubstantiated opinion--an Archie Bunker!

Recently, I was discussing with a practitioner the school field testing that the National Geographic Society does for *World* magazine. All the subjects are factual--expository. In that context, I asked what she sensed of student feeling about the existence of fact as an absolute. She replied that fact was often considered as an unnecessary restraint upon open-mindedness.

In current media parlance, a direct quote, spoken "live" and fed into a telephone bank to be used on a radio news spot is called an "actuality." Webster's defines "actual" as "existing in act ... in fact and reality." By contrast, what we know of the manipulability of tapes when compared with the sacredness of footnoted scholarly quotations shows us the predisposition of the electronic media to further fuzz exactitude and documentation.

A newspaper column on nutrition responded to a query about the "mayonnaiseness" of diet mayonnaise in terms of a "standard of identity"--which mayonnaise has. So, if you can tell what it is, you can tell what it isn't. Mayonnaise is a fact. So is the time of a basketball game. If the newspaper says one thing, the bulletin board another, and a friend yells at me to say the game has been called off--I'd better nail down facts.

Fact carries with it authority--authority upon which to build one's personal notion of rationality. Trouble arises when people lose respect for external authority without developing any internalized standards. To those with no prior commitment to the hegemony of reason, these discoveries implied that rationality itself is an illusion. Competing versions of reality make it hard to defend one and exclude others.

Such cultural relativism clearly produces disrespect for the worth of reason. Without the mechanism for testing and building personal moral moorings, a society opts for the simplistic succor--Hare Krishna or "Being Reborn" or for the mindlessness of surfing or motorcycles or cocaine.

For those who choose to remain librarians, intellectual support abounds, which, if taken to heart, could produce financial support. One powerful voice is that of John Berry, editor of <u>Library Journal.</u>

> It took Dennis Dickinson's "Library Literacy" ... to alert us to the national crisis in library instruction ... students entering college have an almost total lack of library knowledge.... More crucial ... is the probability that those who don't go on to college never learn how to use a library effectively.... We have built and maintained one of the greatest library systems in the world.... Yet we have neglected to build into the system the means and methods to insure that our citizens have the skills to use these libraries and networks.... It is time that we took urgent action to insure that our citizens have the skills and knowledge to gain access to the nation's libraries. To do less will only allow library illiteracy to persist, leaving many Americans wondering why they should spend tax money on more than <u>Pilgrim's Progress</u> and the Bible. (Berry, p. 831)

Or from another societal voice, Henry Mitchell, the "Any Day" columnist for the <u>Washington Post:</u>

> No easy answers. No ... human is as human does. You don't escape realities, you don't escape responsibilities merely by defining them

away or pretending they don't exist.... Flip a coin. Ask a star. Get it decided some the hell way or other ... that is the basis of modern decision-making. (Mitchell, F1, F4)

Mitchell was concerned over such as everything-anything-free colas that are still labeled as perhaps being injurious to health. Other Americans flounder trying to decide whether to sign an anti-nuke petition. Berry has cast down a gauntlet marked "Librarian's choice." So--librarianship needs patron financing and patrons need library literacy for lifelong learning if Jefferson's and Dewey's and Carnegie's views of an educated, decision-able, upwardly mobile democratic electorate are to survive. Being equated with God, motherhood and apple pie has preserved us so far. Now, the costs of keeping us housed, clothed, and fed are soaring and those with the cash adopt new roles and technologies which they feel may succeed where those of our "knowledge industry" are registering no growth. To paraphrase that hymn, Once to every trying-to-stay-a-librarian comes the moment to decide. That is where we public service people are--that is the "where." The rest of my odyssey that follows is full of hope--and challenge!

chapter 2
Thinking Like a Librarian

Skill and confidence are an unconquered army

—George Herbert

Twenty-five years post-sputnik, the educational world is still contemplating its navel--goaded by the hue and cry from its taxpaying creditors. A revolution in teaching mathematics and science was one result of sputnik. New methods and materials in the field of mathematics and science, however, are now considered by many competent people to have been a whirling dervish that brought change but not necessarily progress--heat, but not necessarily light.

    The mushrooming nuclear nightmare, the agony of Vietnam, Proposition 13, and 10-plus percent unemployment added to the upheavals, forced upon man's consciousness the same "all is not right with the world" feeling in the social purview that the Russian space success of the 50's did in the area of scientific technology. Crime in the cities, pollution, racial injustice, and the realization of young people's social and economic power, all contribute to the endless list of unsolved problems that turn our cities into battlefields. Some of us still wish that America had not picked up the challenge of the space race from Russia, or gone into Vietnam or, and what an or, decided to unleash the power of the atom in World War II. Each of us has his own candidate for 20-20 hindsight--based on factual occurrence. Therefore, difficult as it may be for the Archie Bunker hidden in each of us, we are forced to grant the same difference of opinion to those who feel that any present disorders should or can be ignored and, in due time, all again will be right with the world. "Progress is inevitable, and the ship will right itself" is their motto. To those who do not feel that there is any such automatic governor to society, the introduction of a crash program in critical thinking that will enable society to evaluate facts, sort out opinions, and make and act upon personal value judgments is a number-one priority for any one in the Knowledge Profession--as distinguished by Boorstin from the Information Business.

    Critical thinking goes beyond the traditional library

Thinking Like a Librarian

skills curriculum of meeting the need to find out how to find out. In 1982-83 the College Board's "Project Equality," for developing a plan of curricular reform, has distilled 35 academic competencies clustered under six headings: reading, writing, speaking and listening, mathematics, reasoning and studying. Under "competencies" they list the ability to organize, select, and relate ideas and the ability to distinguish between fact and opinion--another set of symbols to communicate the concept--critical thinking.

Thought is a brain product called "thinking." Criticism is hard, factual appraisal and evaluation of another's thoughts. We seldom are critical of ourselves. Over the years, as a teacher of library, my definition of critical thinking has become a pyramid, like this:

[pyramid diagram: UNSUPPORTED / VALUE JUDGMENT / OPINION / FACT / OPINIONS]

Every time I draw it, I am struck by the paradox that the identifying terms expand as the pyramid tapers.

To think critically, our minds must learn to problem solve in relation to these three categories of information-- fact, opinion, and value judgment. Within books, fact resides in a dictionary or the World Almanac; opinion embroiders itself into encyclopedia articles and overpowers most works of exposition; and value judgment glitters in such as the Bible and the Koran. Religion ultimately lies beyond fact, and the mystical content of its great books (as separate from historical context) place them outside of our pyramidal icon for critical thinking. In truth, works of exposition themselves generally contain the whole pyramid. Fact is a requisite--otherwise they should be in F for Fiction. Opinion goads the author's pen and tends to press on to the judgmental mountain top. In processing information in any area having two sides or two decisions, people seek data and a delineation of the multiple courses of action. Finally, based on their value judgment, they act.

A librarian thinks order--relationships, interrelationships, heirarchy, selection. On the job, order becomes one of those tasks, technical or public, that create generic library. To be a teacher of "library" means that you want to take the processes that create "library" and, by turning them inside out, enable patrons/people to use library order as a textbook in critical thinking which, beyond academe, becomes successful lifelong problem solving.

One hypothesis states that there are three kinds of skills necessary for content learning and storage, as opposed to motor learning--for program as separate from technology. These are the ability to cipher, to read, and to abstract, analyze, generalize, and utilize the material taken into the brain by means of these other two skills. Reflect on this for a moment with the help of the diagram on page 23.

This diagram plots the human brain against a computer. Omit the idea of man's soul--this enables the analog to fit. The program--mind set--mental map--is the major determinant shaping input into output. The database equates with the brain's stored content.

The languages for both systems must have inherent organic integrity. Both organisms are electronic circuits. Man differs from the machine in his ability to generate the electricity necessary to the brain's connections. Only death or massive brain damage can "pull his plug." Mental exhaustion and mental illness equate with computer downtime.

Numbers and their related symbols are a language called mathematics. The two basic languages of Roman alphabet and Arabic numbers make possible the process of general education which is the ability to construct from the information input that part of the human mind which controls cognition.

The work of Jerome Bruner of the Center for Cognitive Studies at Harvard supports this reasoning. He divides the phenomenon of perception into three factors. It begins with a hypothesis of what is to come. A child, drawing on past experience, assumes a stance for handling what he next expects. Input from the environment is the second stage in human perception. The third stage is confirmation or rejection on the basis of the first two steps. If regularities and relationships are discovered between ideas experienced, the learner has mastered the ability to relate and so construct a generalization. A structure of the materials of

{ Recognition of language of mathematics } ⇒ { Human brain (motor connections utilize abstractions and generalizations) } ⇒ Ability through thought process to function as a literate, deliberate person

{ Recognition of language of alphabet and words } ⇒

Input from all areas of information (disciplines) provided by mathematics, alphabet, and words

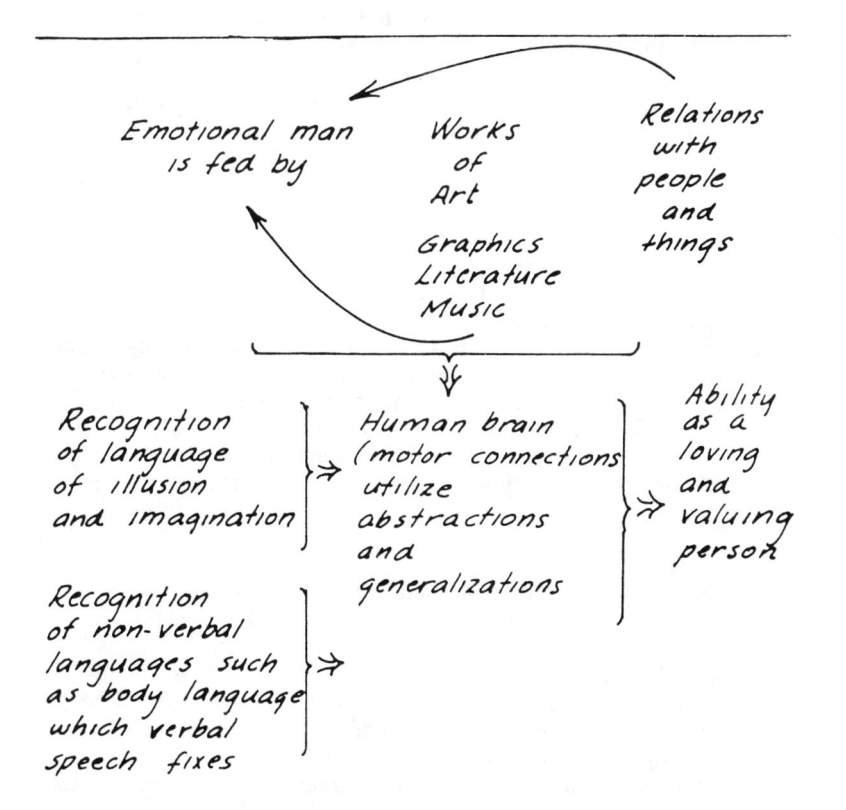

Emotional man is fed by Works of Art Relations with people and things

Graphics
Literature
Music

{ Recognition of language of illusion and imagination } ⇒ { Human brain (motor connections utilize abstractions and generalizations) } ⇒ Ability as a loving and valuing person

{ Recognition of non-verbal languages such as body language which verbal speech fixes } ⇒

information as a basis for sequential problem solving is required.

This ability to grasp significant relationships from a mass of material can be called critical thinking. It is problem-solving in an integrative not an additive way, using a conceptual structure to integrate information by means of classification, definition, and generalization.

If this simplification of the complexities of man's learning process has some intuitive truth, what does it mean for the educational library? It means, to me, that the school library in combination with reading instruction and the department of mathematics is the school. Robert Jordan and Louis Shores in the "Library College" have employed this argument at the college level. To state it for the grades seems only an extension of their intuition.

All definitions, like all lists, are out of date and open to question at the moment of conception, and if the Library College concept were going to come to fruition, it would have. But as a basis for discussion, such simplification has value in establishing a point from which to proceed. This definition of education is threefold: 1) the process of learning to read, 2) the process of learning to cipher, and 3) the lifelong process of learning to use these two language skills for the practice of education--i.e. to separate fact from fiction, to determine authority, to use the bibliographic network to locate information, etc.

An elementary school designed according to this definition would consist of reading and mathematics laboratories with the central and chief space the library. By whatever name it is known on building, this central core might be designated today as a Learning Media Center. In this LMC let us design offices for the subject specialists who are the advisors for the disciplines--geography, history, literature, chemistry, biology, etc.--and for the tutor-librarians as learning resource directors.

The traditionally accepted teaching tasks of the educational librarian are still honored more in the breach than in the observance. For the herein conceived main role of Bibliographic Instruction librarians--to teach the skills of critical thinking to each student in their charge--this library curriculum must be greatly expanded. To do this, they would use the abstract, philosophical level of Library Science. To teach the cognitive skills which underlie meaningful

Thinking Like a Librarian 25

reading, and to apply this learning to either subject disciplines or life's hurdles, would center well as the librarian's special responsibility.

Deafness has not come to me, as yet. I hear the reader's screams of "Time, time, time. I can't get my books out on the shelves, or back on the shelves, or my book lists out, or my bulletin boards done, or whatever, and here you are adding another 40-hour week to my job description." To these pleas I offer only my own experience. I taught--really taught--eight hours every week. The library routines got done. Perhaps you'll have to call for volunteer help--parents, students, or "liberated librarians." But for this there is both precedent and support. It is far more defensible and valorous to claim conscientious objector's status on grounds of personality and temperament than on grounds of no time.

This concept of education as a combination of the library and reading and mathematics instruction is not far from the vision of those who feel individual study should absorb a larger and larger part of the daily work of each student--kindergarten through grade twelve. The beginner must first acquire the basics of ciphering and reading. Once the student possesses these, the curriculum would consist of problems in various subject areas. There should be considerable freedom of choice for each individual. Problems, once chosen, would be unraveled by the seeker at his own pace, with the supervision of library and subject tutors. Provision should be made for continuous interaction and dialogue between students to guarantee the inter-personal contacts requisite for human development. Scholarly dialogue for the young is not an unreasonable assumption, and current experimentation is showing the value of peer teaching. Some creative school systems are using peer teaching to handle classes with a broad intercultural and language mix.

This school that print has just quickly built seems but the logical outgrowth of the Independent Study Program which evolved out of the concern for meeting the needs of the gifted in the post-sputnik era. The advanced placement program pushed bright young people in small classes to accomplishments that had formerly been considered college level. To do this, pupils needed free access to materials and the ability to use them. This combination of brains, motivation, and library skills are a way to waive many freshman-level courses for AP students.

But did and does the school administrator consider the librarian part of the team required to make Independent Study a reality? In my experience the answer is "no."

Individualized Instruction also developed from another level--the bottom of the ability range. It was seized upon to make teaching possible in a non-homogeneously ability-grouped classroom. This became imperative with the phasing-out of the track system of educational sectioning triggered by the Passow report.

No one objects to having his child or pupil put in a very bright track and learn at that level of homogeneity. The demurrer comes, and I think rightly so, from the parents and teachers of average children who feel that these students will lose by being consigned to a homogeneous grouping of their own level. With this method, the teacher handles a class with a wide IQ range by working with small homogeneously sectioned groups or individuals while the rest of the class is otherwise independently occupied. To handle this diverse group the teacher must have access to aids--teacher aides or technological media aids.

To carry on the team teaching program for my "print school" the subject tutor would carry the responsibility for providing authority and direction in the discipline itself. He would also accept partial leadership for the daily group interaction activities. The teaching librarian would be responsible for daily supervision in the skills necessary for choice of media among the Center's resources and the critical abilities necessary to learn from the materials selected.

To accomplish such an instructional design would require an about-face for our administrators and classroom teachers. As a headmistress said to me when I came in a cloud of subdued joy to present as a fait accompli a schedule of library classes I'd worked out for the middle school, "But, Mrs. Leopold, how can you talk about a library for a whole year?"

Support for school libraries has been late in coming because deep down in the hearts of our administrative superiors there lives the feeling that, as Emperors, our suit of gold is imagined. To them, the librarian is but a degreed clerk who serves to put things out where the customer can find them. Our records show us that if school librarians were functioning as part of industry, the administrator would be correct. School libraries are small businesses not in the black.

Statistics old and new corroborate any testimony concerning the continuing lack of mutuality between librarians and their bosses. In a roomful of 160 independent school librarians--elementary and secondary--from all over the United States, I gathered these data in 1971. One hundred and forty of these schools were departmentalized, with department heads. In response to the question "How many of the librarians from these schools hold the rank of department head?" only 36 answered yes. Thirty-two of these librarians were able to serve on curriculum committees. Forty are free to visit subject classrooms. After one secondary school librarian had described glowingly how valuable it was for her to be the one to check and grade preliminary and finished term paper bibliographies, the group wished to know who else did this. Three others raised their hands.

Reality for them sounded like this.

> Independent Study is here. But neither the librarian nor the student is ready for it.
>
> To keep on top of curriculum developments, I eat lunch with the faculty, though I could walk home and happily stretch out.
>
> Our English teachers hate to spare the time for me to give library instruction.
>
> I have children in the school. I keep up with what's going on in some courses through their dinner-table talk.
>
> To make my faculty library-conscious, I ask them, "Who am I responsible to? Students, parents, administrators, you?"
>
> In spite of my mimeographed, annotated book lists and my special shelving spot for new books, the teachers consistently manage to ignore them all. The students find them, though.

Responding to the one person who had multiple, regular teaching time--six periods, one a week during a special activity unit--another librarian said, "If I could only get this wonderful amount of time.   Gosh, a whole period to cover just geography--atlases and gazetteers. "

April 1983 and the Catholic Library Association meets in D.C. Since one financial fruit of unemployment is bargain membership, with relative painlessness I joined CLA, digested my professional bonanza of four months of <u>Catholic Library World</u>, and anticipated my re-entry update. The many notes on the margin of the manuscript for this book insisting "get a current reference" demanded attention. The Conference more than fulfilled my recognized needs and added the plus of a chance to observe Mr. Reagan in the flesh.

At a program presented by Mary June Roggenbuck of the faculty of the school of Library and Information Science at Catholic University, "The Librarian's Role in Curriculum Development," the currency blank regarding the self-perceived role of the school librarian was filled. The question and answer period cued the point I wanted to raise with a dialogue on "Let's not differentiate between teachers and librarians. We're teachers too. " I asked for some response to what they then would consider to be the subject which enabled us to call ourselves "teacher. " "Was it library skills which earlier speakers had had in mind?" They responded to this--by silence--until one almost aghast voice said, "Service is what we give. " In the hall outside the meeting room I had the chance to check my perception against that of the person whose comment had given me my opening. She agreed that we had witnessed an instance of professional self-preservation by denial. Confronted with the need to identify themselves, they joined St. Peter.

One thing that has kept BI forever on the looms of the Emperor's weavers is the conviction of the librarian herself that she does not have the competence to teach organized precepts in the name of the library. The idea that in the institutional order of a library reposes the primary text for teaching the skills of thinking may have crossed her mind but it has not taken root.

Therefore, the first Classroom Reality is the belief that you as librarian have something to teach with and about. The orderliness that is the library is our textbook and the intellectualism of our professional education is our curriculum. Let us look first at ourselves and our specific opportunities, restrictions and requisite skills. To me, one adequately timeless guidebook is Jack Delaney's <u>The School Librarian:</u>

Human Relations Problems. Some desirable professional personality traits are:

1. An outgoing personality;
2. A pleasant manner;
3. Doesn't easily get rattled;
4. Patient and compassionate;
5. Receptive to change;
6. Ability to meet deadlines;
7. A good housekeeper;
8. The instincts of a good interior decorator;
9. Distinct memories of one's own childhood;
10. Sort of flower child;
11. Loving in the sense of "make love, not war."

In addition to being this paragon, there is a further unique organizational hurdle for the school librarian. Though success demands classroom involvement, she has no authority beyond her own staff; all clout must be achieved through charisma.

Personal influence must reach out in three dimensions. It must go up to the administrator, for without rapport and support at that level, the game is nearly lost. Motivational outreach must be horizontal to the peer group, the classroom teachers. She must meet with them as an equal worker in the vineyard, but as one possessed of special skills in the field of education. And, finally, of course, outreach must be down to the students themselves. These three kinds of hierarchical outreach are all necessary in order to produce measurable success. The need for personal qualities amounting to organizational witchcraft provides another clue as to why the media specialist as librarian has not been an overwhelming professional success.

A brief exercise in logic may clarify the argument. Librarianship is considered to be a profession. Once most of us have secured this mantle of status for ourselves, the specific qualities which, taken together, constitute our professional status, slip out of our consciousness.

To refresh ourselves, here are some criteria for a profession, distilled from reading and old course notes:

1. The possession of a large body of special knowledge and an educationally communicable technique for transferring this knowledge to successive student populations.

2. A universally recognized curriculum to accomplish this transfer which culminates in a formal degree or degrees.
3. Learning that is applicable to practical ends.
4. A service- rather than a profit-orientation.
5. To be a professional implies working in an essentially intellectual operation with great individual responsibility.

How then can we be the equals of our teacher colleagues (we say we are--and some of them parrot agreement) and yet be accorded a place somewhere between a clerk and the head maintenance man. You're laughing, but can we, when the crisis generated by the current OPM standards so seriously threatens our professionalism?

A Library Journal article by Maurice P. Marchant provided for me the missing piece to this puzzle of the marshmallowy support which school administrators and teachers give to the intellectual aspirations of school librarians:

> Libraries provide access to books, both supportive of and threatening to the professor's position, and librarians control them. Thus they are in a position to challenge the professor's preferred monopoly over the minds of the students. Indeed, both her historical heritage and her professional education support the librarian's tendency to compete with the faculty. Librarians want to be considered as faculty and thus legitimize their role as part of the instruction process. (Marchant, p. 2887)

"Praise be and thanks also to the 'god' of serendipitous browsing!" My belief in cause and effect had told me that there was a missing clue that had escaped my mental rummaging. Widen this insight to cover all of school-- K-Ph.D.--and, for me, it is now clear why subject teachers reinforce our skills as book handlers while denying the content of our M. L. S. degrees as the basis for teaching skills in critical thinking. Our traditional role of providing the relevant universe of knowledge and the technical and cognitive keys to unlock it, being a threat to the intellectual fortress of the teacher in his closed classroom, has guaranteed our being maintained as harmless museum keepers.

This consciousness of the emotions which have produced the low esteem in which we are held, and of the role this has played in keeping our teaching a most costly myth may enable us to use the special attributes of this turn of

Thinking Like a Librarian

the wheel to break out at last. Critical or productive thinking is a skill that has been left to the cracks in the educational platform. Teaching it will involve endless "I don't know's," usually anathema to teachers, which our learners will answer from the library itself. Perhaps by cutting this elusive and controversial maverick out of the herd for ourselves, we can at last earn a place in the intellectual bunkhouse called lifelong learning.

The chief raw material for instruction in thinking is fact. As we consider the teaching role of the librarian, let us exert our personal critical powers on the concept embodied in the term "fact." Since Dewey's classification system separates Fiction and Nonfiction, what is the relationship between fact and the 000-900's? Between fact and nonfiction?

Fact is a commodity subject to the laws of symbolic logic and rationality. Fact is something that must be able to be touched, measured, and counted. Fact is something that can be proved, and this proof left in such a way that another person who so desires can follow the exact method of the first proof and achieve the same results. If the engineer uses the same unit of measurement and always measures accurately, the Empire State Building will always contain exactly the same number of units of measurement.

There are, of course, levels or degrees of demonstrable fact. It is a continuum from the most concrete of realities to a more tenuous conclusion stemming from a series of propositions or extrapolations. In a given case, we may draw the line at some place in the continuum and refer to conclusions stemming from that established place as "fact." Such an accepted fact may, in reality, be the result of a standard computation using an observed quantity, but the final accepted fact is not the observation itself but the computation from the observation or measurement.

To cite an example, the published values of the flow of different rivers are used in various engineering plans for the development of water supply. These values are published in the water-supply papers of the U.S. Geological Survey. In every court in the country these values are accepted as official "facts" or basic data because experience has shown the values to be consistent, reliable, unbiased, and derived by known methods. Yet these accepted "facts" are the result of combining a field observation of water stage or level with a series of disparate measurements of velocity by an instrument, computed to a given degree of precision in a formula expressing the law of physics known as continuity. The continuity equation is an expression of the Newtonian statement of the conservation of matter. There is a level of precision applicable to each part of the computation. The precision of the instrument, the current meter, is one percent. The precision of the readings of water level is one to three percent. The final result has a precision averaging one percent and an accuracy equal to or better than three percent. Yet the final result is considered by all concerned to be a "fact," even though it is not the original observed quantity but a derivation from several observed quantities.

Man is a non-rational creature, living most of his life on the level of emotion. Only when man is acting at a high, objective level will intellect and rationality govern his actions. To respect the rational and replicable as the only language of truth inhibits us in our necessary study of the non-rational--of the poetic, the mystic, the primary process, the dream-like. This dichotomy between the world of man's emotions and the world of man's rationality can be clearly seen in the order of the library. This is one of the teaching dividends from the process of cataloging and classification.

As librarians, imagination and emotion are as much our concern as is the factual information. The existence of these two categories and the library's clear identification of their separation is but another argument for the validity of library order and its worth at the center of the process of education. Order is the first law of heaven.

For such topics as the Federal budget and the nuclear freeze the great difficulty is in locating the facts on which to base opinions and then values and, finally, decisions. In a situation of such breadth, facts are hard to come by, and where much of the information is classified, they are-- almost--beyond normal intellectual reach.

A Revolution in Graphics has set the stage for today's vast, unheralded alterations in our media environment. In the last quarter of the 19th century, man's ability to create, preserve, transmit, transmute and disseminate exact reproductions of human events, pictorial events--images of scenes and people, the sounds of men and mobs--grew like Topsy.

Thinking Like a Librarian 33

Photography is one example. Dry plate photography came into use in 1873, the roll film in 1884; Eastman's first Kodak is dated 1889; motion pictures arrived in 1900; and television dates from 1941. Satellite transmission began in 1958 with a recorded Christmas greeting by President Dwight D. Eisenhower.

As the ways to disseminate information multiplied, each new technology exerted its own special demands for informational fodder. News--in infinite variations--is the demand for a 24-hour newsday. All of this is a millenium from the town crier of colonial America, or from the daily newspaper of Our Town and Main Street.

One facet of this is the fakery that man has been unable to resist using, once he had such powerful and demanding technical tools. Adam and Eve's eating of the apple provided us with the conception of right and wrong. Having knowledge, we are as Gods. But as Daniel Boorstin posits so well in the book Image: Or What Happened to the American Dream,

> ... the modern news makers are not God. The news that they make happen, the events they create, are somehow not quite real. There remains a tantalizing difference between man-made and God-made events. (p. 11)

> Nowadays the test of a Washington reporter is seldom his skill at precise dramatic reporting, but more often his adeptness at dark intimation. If he wishes to keep his news channels open he must accumulate a vocabulary and develop a style to conceal his sources and obscure the relation of a supposed event or statement to the underlying facts of life, at the same time seeming to offer hard facts. Much of his stock in trade is his own and other people's speculation about the reality of what he reports. He lives in a penumbra between fact and fantasy. He helps create that very obscurity without which the supposed illumination of his reports would be unnecessary.
> (Boorstin, p. 34)

To take the obverse of this and consider small interpersonal, intercommunity involvement, let us speak of individual neighborhoods faced with changes. A freeway is coming through or a road is being altered or a shopping center is planned and the affected community, objecting, has decided to take action. In this case, the facts are obtainable by walking out the door, by using the telephone, or by attending community meetings. The relevant facts are within the reach of these citizens. The first-hand records are available at the courthouse, if one knows how to find them. For mastery of both of these classes of information needs, the library is the best teaching resource.

The noted Episcopal scholar, Albert T. Mollegen, a former professor at the Virginia Theological Seminary, once remarked that man, when he puts himself seriously to lying, usurps the role of God. "When man denies reality and substitutes for a God-made event a Man-made event, he plays God--a supremely destructive masquerade."

Boorstin teaches through the metaphor of the "pseudo-event." This he describes as a happening that is not spontaneous, but is planned--primarily for the purpose of being reported--like an interview. It is pseudo in relation to reality, ambiguity therein being its charm, and tends to operate as a self-fulfilling prophecy. A celebrity is a pseudo-hero (legendary variety). A tourist is a pseudo-traveler. Television is pseudo-fact.

Much of thoughtful America now agrees that, more and more, what is being printed bears less and less resemblance to the actual happening, totally pseudo or not.

Throughout the newspaper there is more and more editorializing--far beyond the "editorial page." The television news, by simple selection, is editorializing. Haven't we all wondered just how the same face appears simultaneously on Time, Newsweek, and People. Furthermore, most people are so removed from the things covered by the mass media that first-handedness is terribly difficult to come by. This is perhaps an extreme example of the difficulty of gathering facts in order to form an opinion. Yet, if individuals are not aware that there are hard facts and do not know how to go about determining them, America will continue to be in the position of not knowing that it doesn't know--no situation for a democracy.

The process of education must build a base of critical communication and information skills which man can use to gather the facts on which to form his opinions and his value judgments. The library, in my opinion, is the place where this training must be acquired, and soon, if the democratic process is to survive. My value judgment is to become a practitioner and disciple of BI. The mechanics of the library and the skills of the librarian are the best tools for teaching this hard core of education--the ability to think critically. In outline form, the librarian's curriculum as the information center of the lifelong learning process would look like this:

<u>Fact--what is it in relation to opinion and fiction?</u>

Techniques for:

1. Location--isolation and identification:
   a. Determining authority;
   b. Classification into a relevant order including techniques for working out the hierarchical levels;
   c. Determination of the interrelationship between levels of fact from different "families."

2. How to locate a) an isolated fact, and b) the body of fact which surrounds the piece of information sought.

3. How to locate the opinions relevant to the body of fact under study.

4. How to locate, or devise, the value judgment needed as a prelude to action.

5. The history of ideas, or the subject background of the problem needing solution. In other words, how to avoid the continuous rediscovery of the wheel. (This might kill the committee.)

It is possible, of course, to argue that this curriculum is relevant for the scholarly only: All very well for the decision-makers in society, for the college bound, but totally useless for the majority of the human race who have a mind but aren't in touch with its existence. My contention is quite the reverse. If, in the democratic process, we are to continue the situation where there is one person, one vote-- where at the ballot box and on the committee, or aiming a gun, each human being carries the same weight--then each person is going to have to be taught to use the mechanics of the critical process so that he can arrive at an independent judgment on the things for which he is judgmentally responsible.

As part of the educated elite, we can look at this outline and think of everything from the identification of Shakespearian sonnets to the sexual revolution. The thought processes by which we decide how to vote rationally, which washer to buy, or how to get the best financing on a new house, are so subconscious as to make us feel they are innate. Not so. Whenever we function as rational minds we are using all the techniques of critical reasoning--induction, deduction, generalization, even symbolic logic and semantic symbolism.

The oft-quoted "Any nation that can put men on the moon can surely conquer illiteracy or eliminate crime and poverty" can serve to illumine America's error in confusing what can be done by man's rational side--science and technology--and what comes a cropper when emotion dominates the game plan. Yes, of course, positive emotions like national pride played a clear role in the success of our moon missions. But without a similar commitment of money and personnel, pride of country manages only to wave over a lip service land of Flag Waving, Motherhood, and Apple Pie, ignoring the front line where the fight against illiteracy and poverty is being lost.

Another group of humans, much larger than ours, is desperate to learn to perform problem-solving techniques needed to deal with unfair landlords, verify the bill presented by a hospital administrator, weigh the merits of one job over another, or make an intelligent choice at the polls. Such actions require all the thought processes of the "knowledge pyramid." For all Americans to have the chance to live "equal" each must have the mental training to enable him to get from here to there on all current information missions. That knowledge is power is a truism proclaimed by National Library Week posters, but not translated by librarians into on-the-job action.

In all the problems of today: water pollution, air pollution (the first forms of the crisis of ecology and conservation to hit the fan); Social Security (about the crisis in human relations and problems within the establishment and generations); the Pentagon budget (about politics, power, and aggression)--whatever the area, we see the need for value judgments. Those who march do so because of their own personal sense of values, a commitment to anarchy or humanity.

The <u>Pocket Oxford Dictionary</u> defines value as "worth

or utility; the amount of money or other commodities for which a thing can be exchanged; what is or passes as the equivalent of something. " And then, in a sub-definition, it refers to the field of painting and says: "The relation of one part of a picture to others in respect to light or shade. " Mulling over this definition, we find such things as "commodities for which a thing can be exchanged, the equivalent of something, what is denoted by a symbol, the relation of one part to another with respect to light and shade. " In order to adopt any value, we have to know what is light and what is shade, and what is an equivalent, and therefore an equal symbol. For what treasure will we barter our lives? We must know the basis of fact before we can make our own individual assessment of those facts and opinions which become the actions of an individual or a society. As librarians, perhaps our greatest contribution as we teach is to work toward patron attainment of the skills needed to rationally determine value. Value judgment is requisite to sane, rational action, but being an affective behavior, it is not truly verifiable. Value judgment is emotion in action. Who you are is compounded of two things: what you do and what you believe. What you believe dictates what you do.

Lifelong learning is an exercise in the ability to analyze, conceptualize, and abstract; whether it takes place in a classroom, in a library, or, at home, in front of a CRT or with a terminal. Education reduced to its fundamentals and separated from either developmental psychology or motivation is the procedure by which a person can determine, first, that there is something he needs to know; second, what it is he needs to know; and third, how to go about acquiring that knowledge. That understanding may be the hard knowledge called fact, or the in-between of opinion. It can be in the realm of human interpersonality, or of the imagination, or of values and belief. Wherever or whatever the content sought, this totality of order can be envisioned as a pyramid built for each human being from his own existential learning.

To recognize fact as separate from opinion and the works of the imagination, to understand how to locate the fact or illusion sought, and to be able to determine the factual or literary history into which this particular bit fits--the presence or absence of these mental abilities separates those who can rise from those who cannot. Language and literacy are still the basic rungs on the ladder of human achievement.

An adequate set of mental skills is the centrality of the educative process--the tools for the life-long task of learning. Librarians, using the order of their libraries, are the best qualified professionals to teach them. Our special skills in the area of materials--selection, location, control, authority, and bibliographic and human information networks--constitute our status as "best qualified professionals." If we will put these competencies to work, teaching people to think in partnership with subject specialists, the circle of education may become the perfect rounded O at last, and librarians, understood at last, will be worth their keep.

The distinction between the one professional and the multi-professional library does not seem to me to affect this question of being a teaching librarian. Why? Because in the largest and greatest of libraries--LC, Newberry, Widener and the like--only the Reference or Public Service Staff serves this function or even interacts with the patron at all. Circulation could provide some professional/patron contact, but only because of work schedules, not because of deliberate, functional purpose.

What is required, now, to add the adjective "teaching" to this chapter's title? For the profession as a whole, a hard look at our location on the short possible journey to 1984. Plot us on the knowledge process pyramid. My prescription is to stop worrying about Caesar and start worrying about God--or, to be more specific, stop concentrating on support, budget, money and what it could buy, technology and staff, and start facing the paradoxical basis of our professionalism. Is there not reason for such a reassessment when, simultaneously OPM readies to reclassify librarians into a technical series and job ads request degrees beyond the M.L.S.--M.B.A., subject master's or a Ph.D.? Webster's defines paradox as, "an assertion ... seemingly contradictory, or opposed to common sense, but that yet may be true in fact." My list is not gentle:

<u>Paradoxes hidden in the idea "Library"</u>

1. <u>Activism</u>--Practicing librarianship involves physical acts in <u>all</u> its aspects--doers--handlers--talkers--believers--selectors--catalogers--floor workers--reference librarians--teachers of library. Our bosses tend to be paper people. They do not comprehend Library, therefore our needs, our demands to close our theory-reality gaps, being Greek to them, get no's, and any unsupported personal

Thinking Like a Librarian

actualizing that we do manage, threatens their administrative ego. So--except for the rare exceptions to this situation, the more we accomplish, the more we become irritants, and strong librarians exist on this quavery tightrope.

2. Circulation--Hoarding and lenders. My assistant illuminated this in these words, "No wonder it's maddening trying to have things for library patrons when what we're here for is really to give things away!" "Neither a borrower nor a lender be," Shakespeare teaches. Yet such is our plight. We are damned by the necessity of cutting across the human grain before we begin.

3. Mentor and friend--to be a "faithful counselor" implies lineality--a hierarchical relationship based on our expertise and their desire to learn. Yet unless our patrons, students of any age, feel on comfortable, friendly and equal terms with us, they are unlikely to be open enough for our guidance to move into dialogue beyond the presenting query.

So the story unrolls from the reel. The characters remain the same. In corporate specialdom it may be that any possibility of the reference staff developing a serious commitment to teaching process has become a definite broken lance. So many powerful voices, including that of Miriam Drake, assistant director, Library Support Services, Purdue University Libraries. In her article, excerpted below, she urges not only the delivery of product but a librarian-selected and repackaged product as well.

> Many traditional librarians believe they are helping people by providing access to information, engaging in bibliographic instruction, and leaving the user to do the real work ... The process may be efficient for the library but not effective in terms of user and corporate goals and productivity.... The collection-oriented library delivers a tangible product in the form of an article or a book, but the librarian rarely knows if the client derived needed information from the documents.... The library engaging in the document delivery business provides a tangible product with little value added. The person making the conversion from documents and data to information is providing the real value, often at considerable cost.... The information management function, with its emphasis on delivery of substantive information, places responsibility for ... packaging information in the hands of the

information specialist or librarian, not the information user. (Drake, p. 229, 227)

Yes, but can the converting person afford to trust his research, corporate or personal, to anyone else? Does such a job description not put a huge burden upon the subject responsibility of librarians? Is that not the provision of an undocumented, massaged knowledge "blank check"? "Information management, by combining the gathering function with analysis, synthesis, and delivery in usable form, adds value in two ways. First, the value of library or information center increases.... Second ... productivity is increased." Yes, but, though Drake's concern for the time "When use involves behavioral, social, or economic change [and] the technological device becomes the basis for innovation" is clearly valid, is it not also an example of assuming the mastery of the machine which holds a warning likeness to the "Newspeak" of <u>1984</u>?

Status quo offends the dynamics of the universe, and growth demands money to feed upon. Libraries die--slowly. After the reprieve of Federal funds which had our name on it (until the hardware manufacturers came around) shrinkage is our lot. Genteel poverty is not a drawing card. Our penury keeps us from having both order and program. Yet program without order is myth indeed, and order without program has made Marian the Librarian a swear word.

Perhaps one factor separating the information and knowledge industries lies in the tough specifics of our role. To cast us well, the description might read: "One warm, loving human person with strong back and legs, long arms, and a level head. Equable disposition required with a strong enough ego structure never to need to be one up, or allow oneself to be put down. The weak of this world need not apply. Must be equally at ease with child and adult, the great man who visits in episode two and the custodian. A strong activist who keeps a low enough profile that his peers never feel called upon to cut him down. A humorous soul who talks and listens well but never carries tales or traffics in cruel gossip. Must type and know the alphabet. Post demands professional qualifications--right now this is being disputed."

For the individual--us--the decision points are personality, creativity, and determination. To add "teaching" could provide its own career alternative. Right now, push could supply the needed shove towards a more satisfying role--in educational librarianship.

Chapter 3
The Library in Context

The country is the real thing···to watch over··· Institutions are extraneous, they are its mere clothing, and clothing can wear out···become ragged. To be loyal to rags··· that is a loyalty of unreason···. The citizen who thinks he sees that the commonwealth's political clothes are worn out, and yet holds his peace, and does not agitate for a new suit, is disloyal; he is a traitor.

Mark Twain

Libraries have history, libraries have people, libraries have things. Libraries change their timed names but not their generic names. What is a library?

I choose to describe a library as an organized collection of the carriers of knowledge. Let us define these terms.

Organization is the most crucial idea in the term library. It is both a way of referring to an ability to locate library materials, and a way to show the interrelationships between them. The specifics of library organization are tied to and vary with specific purposes and pocketbooks.

The first Christmas after starting library school I attempted to convert my family to cataloging our Christmas cards by subject--madonnas in one place, snow scenes in another--as we strung them up for our usual display around the mantel and the living room. Needless to say, my family rebelled, but it demonstrated that I was beginning to think like a librarian--the training was beginning to take!

The term "collection" is an interesting concept. It is a keystone of library work and traditional claim to professionalism within academe. Yet, like most of the roles of the librarian, professional competence in support of materials selection is not acknowledged by either superiors, faculty, or any other group of in-house users. The collection is the stock-in-trade of the library. There is precious little recognition of the fact that only the librarian is trained in selection skills as a discrete professional competency.

The term "carriers" is a way of making the definition universal. It can include Imheptop, the Babylonian, and his clay tablets; Marian, the librarian, and her collection of Victorian novels; and Herman and his computer with electronic circuits beyond the comprehension of most people. The term "carriers" enables us to use historical perspective to

The Library in Context   43

dramatize the library's function as a knowledge storehouse.

"Knowledge," the most romantic and nebulous part of this definition, is easy to grasp; but a word about which there will be considerable argument. Knowledge is equated with Big T truth--wisdom. Is opinion, then, also knowlege, as fact is held to be? The library is the storehouse of all kinds of human learning and the foundation for tomorrow.

Why use "knowledge" rather than "information"? My adoption of this definition antedates information 1983 by 20 years. You may wish to challenge with "If it's déclassé, dump it"--forcing me to reevaluate the word choice. My response to both of us is that I opt to consider that each library carrier packages information into some higher stage of organization that merits the concept of "knowledge"--i. e., the book or serial itself holds organized and packaged information which qualifies as knowledge unless the carrier contains only raw data such as statistical tables. This aligns me with Daniel Boorstin's comment from his White House Conference speech: "Knowledge is orderly and cumulative, information is random and miscellaneous."

A particular library, then, is a group of things that have been brought together to provide specific knowledge for the use of specific people to serve a specific purpose at a specific point in time. The differences in libraries over the centuries have been great. It seems however, that, as the fabric of knowledge has accumulated and been preserved in the world's libraries over the centuries with remarkable completeness, the similarities demonstrated by defining the word library as an organized collection of the carriers of knowledge outweigh individual and type of library differences.

Another clue to library essence is found in the ways that libraries have been organized. Shelf arrangement is designed to show interrelationships among the material being handled. Alternative schemes of classification, such as chronological acquisition, where books or packages of today's multimedia can be put on the shelves in the order in which they have been received; or shelving by the type of bindings, or by size as in Folio collections, have mainly been discarded in favor of a system that shows interrelationships--comparative, descriptive or chronological--between library materials. Interrelationship is part of hierarchy. Relationship is based upon the idea of contact, of whatever is related touching somewhere, whether it be a child's relationship to a parent, a husband's to a wife. Anything on the family tree is a touching kind of thing. Sometimes this is a physical relationship--physical-spatial. Sometimes it is simply an intellectual relationship. "His ideas have touched my life!"

Librarians can be of many kinds. Some are shy technical people--excellent at the discrete non-public aspects of librarianship; others are extroverts--floor workers, reference workers, teachers--people able to pick up the challenge re-issued by today's crisis and go on to be teachers of library. Two clear areas exist--one that creates the textbook for the other to use in the service of a knowledgeable America.

To grasp the essence, consider the divisions of a large library: acquisitions, reference, reader's adviser, and technical services. The work of each one of these library divisions is a scholarly occupation. Each one has a very definite intellectual aspect. Acquisitions work, the selection and not the mechanics of purchase, involves the provision of the library's brain. It requires knowledge of the literature, of the disciplines, the bibliographic network and the professional tools of selection, and enough sense of professional authority to use them.

I was explaining the work of the ALA Reference and Subscription Books Committee to a faculty member in the English Department of Catholic University whose assistance I had sought as a subject authority reviewer. As I described the Booklist to him, he remarked, "Oh, yes, I know that journal. I thought it was intended for bookstore people. Do librarians really select books?"

I once visited an avant-garde, then-new, now-defunct, private, liberal arts college in the Southwest. The head librarian held the rank of associate professor, yet she was not permitted to select material for the collection. At lunch with some of the faculty, totally deadpan, I learned that they never read any of the library's collection of professional reviewing periodicals that were routed to them,

The Library in Context

depending only on the scholarly reviews in the journals of their own disciplines. In the main, these journals carry very few reviews, and those carried come too late for currency. Sadly, but logically, the library's shelves reflected this situation. An ability which academic scholars think they possess proves lacking beside the librarians' specific expertise, yet the scholars will not acknowledge it. Surely, our six to nine hours of MS in LS work in Book Selection plus our cumulated experience merits more than this total nonrecognition.

Teaching process or delivering product, the reference librarian is a magician who is confronted with the need to find an immediate answer to daily questions. He presides over the collection of indexes, encyclopedias, and one-volume reference books that are the backbone of any reference collection. To obtain answers, the librarian must know the limitations of each book and how, through these or the human information network beyond print, or on-line searching, to locate the answers sought. It is a scholarly pursuit. The collection itself provides the basic interrelationships for the people out there on the firing line making the connection between the library user and the material or information sought. This work is often in the field of fiction and the reader's adviser must read to achieve the connections of subject and author that are necessary for this process. The human connection between the physical aspects of a library and the intellectual aspects--between the shelves and the card catalog--is a meaningful professional occupation.

Whatever is sought exists in interrelationship with something else. Each item present has been weighed and measured and selected against something else that may not be part of the library's collections. Though all works are not physically present in any library--even LC, we librarians make our selection against the universe of the bibliographic network.

Technical services are the behind-the-scenes back-up that provides library organization, though original cataloging wanes now because of on-line networking. Do remember that the cataloger was once considered the elite of the profession. In some libraries it appears that no one else ever reads books. Even the cataloger checking Dewey numbers for insertion into an individual collection must competently sample each book to ensure that his numbers will be more than a hasty, educated guess.

Perhaps some of Lawrence Clark Powell's deep understanding of the relationship of bookmanship to librarianship stems from his stint as a cataloger at U. C. L. A. During the war years, LCP, as cataloger, unwrapped the books coming in to U. C. L. A., and I, as clerk in the Reference Department, packed the outgoing interlibrary loan books. From the serendipity of a shared place of work began our friendship and my philosophy of librarianship.

What about the whole cloth of scholarship of which libraries are the world's great repositories? I entered graduate school after a longer-than-I-care-to-put-in-print gap in my formal education. My first term paper proved a terrible chore. As I talked with fellow students, preparatory to typing it, my omission of footnotes was abruptly and horribly revealed. There was a considerable bit of footnoting for that particular paper and my notes were scribbly and vague. By the time I had reconstructed the trail required for those footnotes, I had learned quite clearly, painfully, and permanently, that scholarship is a blazed trail. These concepts can be intellectualized and taught as cognitive objectives.

In the phrase "literature search," which some fuzzy-minded souls equate with research, lives another aspect of the library as a textbook. Without the ordered chronology of library materials there would be no way for the student to learn what his forebears have already discovered--each life would then require a personal rediscovery of the wheel.

In scientific literature, there is a clear purpose for the documentation and footnoting which provides the replicable aspects of scientific research. The author of a scientific study must describe what was done, publish the data, and credit other people who have done similar things, so that the next person wishing to understand this work will have all the information required to reproduce the experiments.

The great scientific discoveries have been made by people with educated intuition. Such intuition is a personality trait, but education is the requisite foundation for all such progress in thinking. For them, it consisted of years of studying and mastering the literature in their subject before using that knowledge as a basis for their own intuitive jump into the unknown. Their special contribution has been to take this imaginative next step and transfer it into experimentation so that their presentiment, proven, could become part of the continuing record of scientific discovery.

The Library in Context

Doing authority cards for a cataloging course, we had to produce two authorities for whatever fact we were documenting. If the first two sources disagreed, you were in a gray area and a third authority had to be found. Footnotes, by giving credit to the author's source for ideas, help keep track of that elusive intellectual responsibility which the library acknowledges by "Main entry" and follows through by similar notations in bibliographies. The uninitiated believe that anything between the covers of a hard-bound book or a scholarly journal is fact. That is not only incorrect but dangerous to a society striving to be oriented toward reality. Footnotes serve as history, and so provide print beacons to truth.

Beyond serving as guideposts to sources and plagiarism, footnotes sort out facts from personal opinion. There was one grand utterance that the unfortunate Charles Van Doren contributed to a listening America: "Never argue about a fact, only about an opinion." But the majority of people have no clear idea that there is such a black-and-white difference between fact and opinion, or how to use a library to discover the difference. In whatever measure the opinions you hold do not reflect the thought processes which produced those opinions, they are untrue.

Another bead on this intellectual string is the documentation required for biography which separates it from historical fiction. An authentic biography must contain only documented fact. This stipulation severely limits the dialogue which contributes so much vitality to a historical novel.

All reading lists should validate this concept by making separate listings for fiction and nonfiction genres. The writer of a thoroughly researched historical novel, whose intuition is sound, may produce what, in truth, is a much more valid picture of the man's life, but it is not fact. It is an intuitive opinion and must be treated as such. To take any well-known historical anecdote, such as that of George Washington chopping down the cherry tree, and trace it back through its occurrence in fiction and in history would be an interesting test of the value of a library in establishing fact and separating it from opinion. The library, then, is both a place and a means of logical orderliness. In it each individual can find the means to document for himself the background for any subject he seeks to pursue, and can separate its fact from its opinion.

The historic concept "library" can be clearly described and its intellectual identity confirmed. Today, we are privileged to feel that throughout the history of mankind little has escaped this net of man's written history. Somewhere in the bibliographic network exists the clue that will bring you to the fact or document that you seek, whether it be in a monastery in Tibet, in the Bibliothèque Nationale, or in the <u>Encyclopedia Americana</u> in your own collection. Missing pieces notwithstanding, our professional predecessors have done us credit. The understory of knowledge has been safely transmitted to us as its inheritors and managers. Our task now is to prove its value to those taxpayers or corporate managers whom we want to keep paying our salaries. If the Knowledge Institutions which Boorstin equates with Library are to survive the electronic onslaught of the Information Business, we must believe in the "a priori" print network as an artifact worthy of continuing existence. A rationale for using our print libraries and their on-line access as generic textbooks in critical thinking seems one darn good weapon for the struggle.

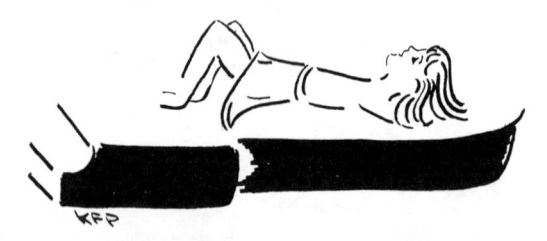

When I was a middle-aged child, a favorite mind-expanding perch of mine was the top of our baby grand piano. Lying there, I trod the ceiling and chinned myself on the stretchers of chairs, returning to the gravitational living room refreshed and newly perceptive. Recently, from the parallel perspective of the DAR Library's Beaux Arts balcony, I watched the interaction of collection and public services and reaffirmed my earlier assessment of the essence of "library." Distilled, its elixir is its intellectual order-- a sum for exceeding its component parts that creates our core curriculum in BI.

As an icon for contextual analysis, consider the library as a small independent business or concession within the institution it serves whose purpose is the provision of the materials whereby our customers may shop for and learn how to obtain the product sought--knowledge. Public libraries exist as independent institutions--their customers being their taxpayers. My personal experience in business is limited to a stretch as the feminine half of ownership of a McDonald's.

Let us begin with the store--our room, or rooms of the carriers of knowledge. The large amount of control we have over the aesthetics of the library offers an exciting challenge. We can provide a cozy place--colorful--an adjunct to the snack bar (remember books go home where the borrower may eat and drink). Let's show that we are aware of our customers' tastes and needs--even including a place for a nap! Don't get stalled by requisitions that may not leave your building for months. Use immediate resources to decorate a store that will draw business.

Look at the changed department stores. By means of the power of non-verbal communication, merchants are saying to those they want to attract--"Come, this is for you." In your library, through the responsibility you have for it, and the dominion you have over it, you can do likewise. The power is yours.

What is next? Our stock. The carriers of knowlege themselves. The chapters and verses of our knowledge textbook!

As we build our collections, it is imperative that we look at the total community resources. Believe me, McDonald's does when they survey to build a new store. In the present library climate, our only Santa Claus is us, and facing that reality now can ensure a more Christmasy present and future.

Do integrate other needs of your customers with home and the public library. These institutions form the first circle of each person's information resources--important ones--especially since the first requisite for use is availability. Let's work with first-hand reality and resist being lured into hi-tech schemes for data processed universes of knowledge.

What's next? How we organize and display our stock. To enable the customer to leave satisfied, each item must at least be findable. The supermarket wall indices and aisle signs do this for such merchants. If the stock clerk or patron can't locate the cereal, how much would go out of the store? Retrieval--one necessary function of stock organization. Look at your signage.

Library classification, though it observes the same principle of shelving like items together, goes far beyond retrieval location needs. Why? Because library research, writing a term paper, validating or locating any fact and moving from it to opinions or possibilities about it and on to value judgments about the subject, requires such material in context beyond simple similarities.

Library organization should have but one purpose in mind--to increase the ability of an outsider to use it while trying to make the customer an insider. We librarians have played the cataloging and classification game for our own sake, I am afraid, much too long. As such, they are hurdles, not handles for our patrons.

One job description reads: "Teacher of critical thinking." Our textbook is this huge clerically needful store, the library. How can we get our textbook cared for? Barnum didn't say there was a sucker born every minute for nothing, and Tom Sawyer got his fence painted. Parents, grandparents, students, and liberated librarians are available to us. They are part of humanity's massive unmet human need to be useful. What you offer is not busy work, but a chance for a meaningful service to their families and their community.

If our role is to teach someone how to think by means of our organized collection of the carriers of knowledge, and we produce some satisfied customers, they may support our work by doing the cutting, pasting, typing and filing that are necessary to create the information relationships of our textbook. Lack of clerical help is no excuse for not accepting the role of teacher.

What's next? The merchant. Who is this merchant? You. Me. Close your eyes and picture yourself. Look down. Two hands, two feet that get tired. Close your eyes again. Picture your résumé. Well, some people type better than others.

Let's look at skills. Were you ever a teacher of something? Did you enjoy teaching? Do you read at least something of what your customers read? You are reading this because you are motivated to consider the implications of being a teacher of knowledge. With this role and our store called "library" we can join the current battle for dollars between the two industries--information and knowledge--with the hope of furthering the return to a society with moorings, gained by having learned to think in a straight line.

Customers come next. They come in knowing what they want, or just looking. A good, old-fashioned salesperson knows the merchandise and, if needed, suggests a substitute or extends your purpose through suggestive selling. "Would you like some fries or hot apple pie with your big Mac on this cold day?" McDonald's counter clerks are taught to ask. Let's run our business called "library" that way--for a change. Our slogan, like Marshall Field's, 'the customer is always right. "

Who might our customers be? Parents, staff administrators, faculty, students. Parents are an influential part of the community. As taxpayers and keepers of children they are harassed. What help can we give them? We can begin with what they are about, and we can learn that by listening to them. All of the above are public library customers too. Some of them are within higher education--grades 13-Ph. D. Special library customers are just that and their special job-related needs should produce high motivation for learning to be at home in your store. Get them into the textbook called "library" and teach them about facts in context. Your merchant's goal should be books that are out and systems used to the hilt.

One explanation of the failure to integrate the library into the process of information finding and using is that subject practitioners realize or intuit that we are natural enemies. Though we do not act out our real roles as teachers of information access, all in-house experts defend a territorial view of their subject against our potential to furnish searchers with access to facts useful in challenging their opinions and value judgments. As merchant marketers what can we do to resolve this paradox of inherent conflict of interest? Let us meet their needs as persons or educators one to one! Let us adhere to the credo: "Always overestimate their native intelligence and subject competence and underestimate any skills that they may have for using our textbook called 'library,' and honor the ego strength that is required to admit to ignorance. "

Knowledge is power. What do we know? My thesis is that in our training as librarians, we were given a subject specialty like math or history. Yes, we are teachers--of the skills of cognition, which equates with primary and lifelong education. We want to teach the techniques of search and that the possession of fact is a vital requisite to successful action--the fact, opinion, value judgment pyramid. These vital facets comprise a matrix of reference points useful in visualizing the whole of knowledge in terms of the organization of our libraries.

    Everything begins with fact, upon which opinions are built. Value judgment--big T truth--depends for its thoughtful existence upon this mental progression and comparison. Past--everything came from somewhere. Present--where it is now! Future--where it may go! Everything begins with fact and our favorite subject is ourselves. Me--well--lots of facts--doors closing and opening--exemplified by my name Carolyn Dennette Clugston Leopold Michaels. Each of the cast of family characters has opinions about these facts. The resultant value judgments about divorce and re-marriage fuel powerful emotion in action. Each person, each event fits this matrix. A personal and simple current event that touches the learner is a valid BI lesson plan.

    How to get started in this role as teacher of cognitive reading and writing and thinking? Begin with the first customer and what he wants. Find out, first, where he wants to go, not colored by your opinion and value judgment of his information goal. Motivation sharpens skills. Use any query that comes to you--find its fact and try to begin there. The way to the girls' room and research toward new job skills both have a factual base.

    Don't stifle motivation by offering library lessons for rote learning, completely divorced from the rationale that is their raison d'être. If such teaching were sufficient, why are we librarians taught the "why" as well as the "how"? You answer, "Because we are the doers, not the users. These functions require different levels of comprehension. I don't have to understand banking to use a bank, or be a cartographer to use a map!"

    "All a matter of degree," I reply. The user must be brought within our purpose, our why. "Why" being so that he, the user, understands what he's bought for his share of the cost of the technical processing that transmutes book into "library." Today's omens indicate little financial enthusiasm by those sectors of society that support traditional libraries. The ideals of Carnegie, of John and Melvil Dewey--of Horatio Alger and the Open University--by thy bootstraps thou may rise--are based on free access to the knowledge that gets you to the next rung.

The Library in Context

Train your public service librarian's mind to operate in terms of the knowledge matrix and then teach those cognitive skills to each customer. But teach them because they are the way to achieve self-perceived objectives. Don't teach library skills, teach self-education skills. Carnegie built public libraries to be the universities of the poeple. If he had installed us as teachers of knowledge theory, the people would today be educated appreciators of public libraries instead of their deprecators!

Libraries hold the record of man's past. Whatever fact or knowledge need your customer brings to you is writ therein. For every "how" or "who" or "when," there is a recorded answer. Sometimes two or three. Our role is to let our customers in on these secrets by stripping away the old library image as being elitist or academic and making it the most practical first place to find out what they want to know. Be it:

How to bake a cake.	Make a quilt.
Get an abortion.	Appreciate art.
Buy anything.	Get a job.
Find great-grandfather.	Understand divorce.
Settle a factual argument.	Or do school or 9-5 work.

One response to the information explosion has been to treat education as a process in acquired generalization. Teaching librarians can fight that by showing each questioning patron the personal tools of search that will permit present and continuing education. One does not have to memorize facts, just know that they are alive and real and necessary and how to find them. The skills to construct our textbook called library and the techniques toward knowledge that its relationships are designed to provide give us our subject for public service professionalism.

Fact stood still better for those of us from earlier times. Fact was more easily apparent in a world of small schools and universities and communities. We were closer to the action.

Large schools, bigness anywhere--Madison Avenue on TV making merchandising messages a big part of our lives-- big government--being Big Brother--being self-perpetuating--

centralizing power--allowing secrecy--all have combined in
my 35 years in Washington to make the "Newspeak" of <u>1984</u>
a near reality. Consider "build down," the newest Reagan
jargon for the arms race! Jonathan Yardley begins an article "The Hyping of the Hitler Diaries," in the Washington
Post with:

> Now that the "Hitler Diaries" have been dismissed
> as the beguiling fraud that they are, perhaps we
> can turn our attention to the matter of the role of
> the press in aiding and abetting that fraud. . . .
> As definied by Stepehen M. L. Aronson in his
> new book, <u>Hype</u>, that process is "the merchandising of a product--be it an object, a person or
> an idea--in an artificially engendered atmosphere
> of hysteria, in order to create a demand for it or
> to inflate such demand as already exists." ...
> Unfortunately though, Aronson does not make anything even approaching a systematic study of the
> ways in which the press collaborates in this seedy
> manipulation of public opinion in the interest of
> "money, power, fame." ... he never gets to the
> serious issues that are raised when, in an atmosphere hysterical with hype, the press becomes
> not a reporter of news, or a commentator on it but
> a manufacturer and merchandiser of it.
> (Yardley, B1, B8)

Maybe there isn't time for the persons we could make into
informed and committed human beings to become effective.
But maybe there is!

Money--budget--things of Caesar's--you mention these.
However poor one of us is in dollars, there is still enough
"library" to support "program." You can't escape by that
route. Our any-size library business is adequate to create
a classroom in which to begin being public service librarians
who know the value of what they alone know! At any rate,
let's try. It won't cost us anything but Churchill's "Blood,
sweat, and tears." And we're paying that, anyway.

chapter 4

Our Knowledge Environment

Not chaos-like together
 crushed and bruised,
But as the world,
 harmoniously confused.
Where order in variety
 we see,
And where, tho all things differ,
 all agree.

Pope

Beyond architecture and furnishings, the non-human physicality of a library is its materials collections. The larger and greater the library, the more likely it is to have multimedia materials. The British Museum has the Rosetta Stone, the Magna Carta, and just plain print. Our Library of Congress has Stradivari violins, posters, art prints, films, records, and Braille; talking, plain, and very fancy books. Since collections began with clay tablets, scrolls, and parchment, the A-V trends that began in the sixties are really only trendy--though the electronic trend may prove the wave that engulfs.

Let us liken a personal wardrobe to the materials collections of a library in an effort to demonstrate some general principles. Library and wardrobe are both nouns and they both are collections. They both have to be selected, arranged, and coordinated toward a defined purpose. A dear friend is a well-known professional artist. In private life, she is the wife of a successful scientist with a sizable independent income. Her wardrobe is as exact as the rest of her life. She feels strongly that a working artist does not belong in the garb that would reflect the affluence of her domestic world. Her carefully chosen clothes are too bohemian for her fashionable neighborhood. Her complex wardrobe design involves a pair of emerald wedding bands she asked for as an anniversary present. When I questioned her about this abnormal-for-her acquisition she smiled and said, "Well, to tell you the truth, I do dress to blend into my world of working artists. But I'm tired of being ignored as a nonentity by neighborhood salespeople. With these rings on either side of my diamond band, clerks will know that I am enough of a somebody to be worth treating with some deference." A victorious wardrobe is not a sometime thing. A library, to be worth its keep, can't be casual or off-handed either.

In the educational library, the standard policy statement is that the library serves to provide the materials necessary to support the curriculum. The faculty, as users of the library, find such a statement of policy to their liking--if they are satisfied with the curriculum. The same situation prevails in the case of the student; if he is happy with the curriculum and finds it relevant, he should value the opportunity to use the library that mirrors it. Unfortunately, so many libraries are totally irrelevant to any of the students' self-perceived needs. Student users have gotten off the track of being goal-oriented, i.e., goals that are set for them by administration, faculty, and parents. Their problems go beyond a school-bell world.

Once we have the policy statement for our wardrobe, we are ready to make lists and go shopping. The next step requires a budget--money--plastic or "please, Daddy!" Once our financial limits are established, we can refine our generic lists with specifics--the particulars of shape and size--the colors that we like, the climate in which we live, and the amount of work we are willing to devote to keeping up such a collection of physical objects. For example, if you select a garment with much lace or pleating, its upkeep requires large cleaning bills, or the willingness to tend it yourself. If you are going to own a dark wool dress with white linen collars and cuffs, you have to be willing to sew them back on yourself, have someone else do it, or wear dirty linen. So it is with a library: if you are going to have leather-bound books, someone must rub lanolin on them regularly or time will make them very shabby. An untended Vertical File quickly becomes a shambles.

The goal of a so-called balanced collection for school libraries seems erroneous--balanced for what? If our factual materials are to support instruction by matching and surrounding specific courses, why should we tie up precious money and space in materials which do not meet this definition? On the off chance that some youngster will read it of his own free will? Perhaps, but spot checks of every school library I've visited make my answer, no. Curriculum support is surely the first priority. Such a policy would help clarify the role confusion between public and school libraries.

Another destructive theory-reality gap exists in this area of collection management. Faculty, not being trained in materials selection, are hesitant to display their ignorance, so tend to relinquish it to the librarian. Their reliance on publishers' mailings is both pitiful and infuriating. Since librarians have no need to compete in the subtle maze of disciplinary in-fighting and current curriculum theories, there should be only honest outreach on our part. Library reviews have the greatest currency though professional journals in all academic disciplines carry very important reviews and must, therefore, be read by the selector having responsibility for that subject.

In materials evaluation we are dealing with an invalid, closed system having authority on paper but not in action. Library Literature, Education Index and ERIC are replete with studies showing that teachers and educators are not given adequate formal training in the selection of materials.

An ability to evaluate specific titles as entities and also in comparison with other titles and in relation to the area under consideration as a bibliographic unit, which in turn draws upon a knowledge of all the relevant media and the critical skills, is a complex professional skill requiring training and assertiveness to perform. These proficiencies were seldom possessed even in the just-print days. Now the needed skills have multiplied enormously with the advent of the software for the nonprint technology. Formal course requirements for professionals now need to encompass film, tape, video, and software evaluation as well as traditional book selection work in literary criticism.

At the college level some of this also exists. Faculty have materials selection competence in their own disciplines--but do they use this skill to keep "their part" of the library shelves fully and currently stocked? Very often the answer must be "no." Otherwise, why would the post of collection development librarian now be appearing so frequently on the staffs of large academic libraries like George Washington here in D.C.?

In the world of "for profit" and "non-profit" membership institutions, librarians must again serve as collection managers. Expert staffers are subject specialists, but this training may not find expression by keeping their acquisition librarian supplied with constant and valid requests for purchase. Today's constant turnover rate for such career ladder climbers puts an additional burden on the library staff whose centrality and records are designed to stabilize staff mobility.

Library seen as a store staffed with subject specialists offers the assistance of analogy. Large downtown department stores that stock a universe of materialism, as do large departmentalized libraries or huge supermarkets, provide "subject specialists" to assist with individual selections.

I will long remember a frustrating experience in such a local emporium. A particular but unfamiliar kind of lamb chop was on sale. I didn't know whether it could be broiled or required braising. I rang for a butcher and posed this question. He looked at me with great annoyance and retorted with, "I don't like lamb, lady." Going into my dowager act, I sounded off on professional competence. He solved the problem for both of us by consulting a customer who happened to be within earshot, coming back and reporting that it could be broiled. Thus informed, I bought it. How often have you seen this same sort of thing happen in libraries when the librarian stands by and manages to avoid having anything to do with the informational exchange the customer seeks because he just doesn't like that kind of book. Being frightened by mystery stories is no excuse for not knowing about them.

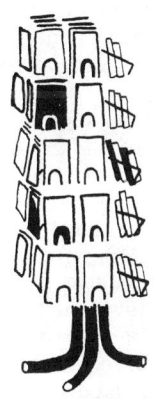

Another factor in the ecology of libraries is the dimension of the circle of feedback between producer and consumer which is operative in any specific library environment. Who actually pays the library bill? How many layers of bureaucratic insulation separate him from the librarian? How influential are the outside pressures for library as "venerated object"?

The lessons that I've learned indicate that the special library represents the tightest circle between fiscal agent and library user. Like all businesses, profit or non-profit, its pocket has a bottom without any taxpayers in its seams. More money for a library program depends solely on already satisfied customers who seek expanded resources or services.

The student, as user of the educational library, has a parent who pays the bill. But the bill payer is not the consumer. Therefore, since he is neither direct user nor the librarian's boss, he is not in the same forceful position to impose his will and demand a return for his money as is the administrator who holds the purse strings for the special librarian.

Our M. L. S. education has proved to be bullseye on target in materials evaluation and selection. Our professional reviewing media validate and inform our work. Let us not be humble but rather proudly confident team players with our faculty and corporate bosses. This puts a tangible piece of show-and-tell in our hands. Keep a coffee pot brewing in the library supported by a bottomless cookie jar and snag your key brass for selection conferences, or use lunch-hour talk time to spin this crucial part of your information web.

Next comes the matter of order. When my first husband was a meteorological cadet, the lieutenant in charge decreed that the cadets' jackets had to be buttoned and shoes tied when put away in the clothes closet. That was this lieutenant's idea of an ordered wardrobe. The war made him master and he was obeyed, but reasonable order has never returned to LBL's closet. How many librarians have generated such unfortunate backlashes by similar non-functional rules? One of the artifacts of wardrobe order, for which I have yearned, is a closet equipped with plastic shoeboxes. Using cardboard shoeboxes, I have developed a system of either memorizing the contents of unique shoeboxes or writing on them such as "old red," "new blue." Were I to become the owner of such plastic boxes, this hassle would disappear forever, leaving only memories of an occasional shower of shoes upon my head. We all have our dreams of technological rescue.

Libraries, then, like anyone who collects a wardrobe, or posters, or paperweights, must each have a strong program statement, a goal, the necessary cash to purchase the desired items and the requisite labor to keep these resources in place and in first-class condition. This last sine qua non is not given its just due by our administrative masters.

The wardrobe of the library is composed of books, periodicals, reference files, pamphlets, tapes and records, video, photographs, films, posters and art prints. Once

Our Knowledge Environment

our policy statement is written, these items can be selected and then organized. The operations that go to produce this organization--book selection and acquisition and cataloging and classification and reading shelves and shelving--can be called the housekeeping of the library. Robert Pierson in the Wilson Library Bulletin pronounces, "Housekeeping may not be the ne plus ultra of effective library practice, but it is surely its sine qua non." (Pierson, p. 952). Unfortunately, the librarian's employer--the administrator or the principal--doesn't dwell on any of this. His concern is with what he can feel or see--which is the myth--library as valued museum.

Our fiscal overlords see a library in which a librarian-type sits at a desk (damned expensive installation) and parcels out books and keeps the peace, and there is some sort of work room where other (or the same) librarian-types mess about with sink and paste, scissors, typewriters, and, now, with our computers. When I was being interviewed for my job at the American Council on Education, I remember with both sadness and humor the remark, "Mrs. Leopold, I do hope you won't be bored. I really don't think there is too much to do in the library. I'm its greatest user." This from a former university president with six lines of honorary degrees in his Who's Who bio, who, himself, never set foot in the ACE Library. Secretaries were occasionally sent with a requested title. What magnificent irony for a library, barely emerged into two rooms and a building-wide mission for all of Higher Ed at Number One, Dupont Circle, D.C.

The usual administrator seems to feel that library material requires nothing more in the way of processing than what is necessary in order to transfer the contents of a carton of cereal packages to the grocery shelf. This assumption is based on his own lack of familiarity with library actuality.

This is another one of these paradoxes that makes management of a small library such a tough assignment. The irony of this is witness to the thesis of this book: that libraries cannot come into their own until the librarian recognizes the intellectual content of the training that has made her master of the library and uses this to become the teacher of productive thinking. As Frances Henne said at the ALA Conference in Dallas, "School librarians are a sleeping giant whose strength will be recognized only when they move out on their own."

Examples of this abound: the reading expert at the Central Office of the Montgomery County, Maryland, Public Schools who said, upon coming to the Professional Library, "M-m-m. Now, that book I want was orange, and it was about half an inch thick, and it was over there." The reply to which was, 'I'm terribly sorry but since you wanted that book a year ago, we've added some new books and we've reshelved our collection. Now, could you perhaps tell me just a little bit more about it so I can find it for you?" Or the patron from Number One, Dupont Circle, who assisted me as I searched for one of his requests by contributing, "Well, now, what I can tell you is that this is a publication of the Carnegie Commission on Higher Education, and it has a cover like this, white and blue." At the DAR Library there was a wry humor in the familiar request "for that thick blue book that has my grandfather in it!"

For anyone where an accession record is still being kept, one of the tricks I learned at the National Geographic Society Library is of help. When they accession a book, they note the color of the binding, so if it happens to be missing, they automatically have a further location clue available.

The print collections--selected, ordered, received, cataloged, processed further and then shelved and reshelved-- serve the teaching librarian as her textbook--individual items carrying knowledge which are organized to reproduce an intellectual or subject order with a physical or shelf order. Beyond the broad categories that constitute the library literacy core curriculum, the details of instruction should invoke motivation by coming from those being instructed. The Michaels method for on-demand instruction urges that the aim of each reference interview be to teach process, not to deliver product, and that each BI class be based on the felt needs of each class member. Therefore, for public service purposes, in any kind of library, all that is required of a collection is that it cover adequately the subject or subjects for which that library is sought by patrons and that items sought are retrievable. If your library's shelvers (book clerks or you) are sloppy filers, the professional pyramid of order topples into a configuration of chaos.

Chapter 5
The Library Map: How to Get There from Here

Life is a copycat and can be bullied into following the master artist who bids it come to heel.

— Heywood Broun

When I wrote the original manuscript from which this present book has developed, my experience as a Bibliographic Instructor had come from many years of informal teaching while on Reference Desk duty in school and special libraries and one year of providing formal weekly instruction in "Library" for grades 7-9 at a private girls' school, Holton-Arms. Now, eleven years later, it has been broadened by four years as a researcher for the Special Publication Division of the National Geographic Society, four years as a teacher of Information Skills on the Continuing Education Faculty at Georgetown University, and four plus years of organizing the Genealogical Library of the DAR and directing the work of and serving a daily stint on their Reference/Information Desk where the mandate was to teach library process, not deliver genealogical product. Since all of this new and broadened experience continues to validate my 1972 conclusions, the focus of this book has been enlarged to apply to all information seekers.

    Of the roughly sixty adults who daily use the DAR Library, only those with library training can understand its "Introduction Sheet" without one-on-one help. They have no developed general base of skills upon which to build the specifics of that special library. They do not comprehend the dual purpose of the call number and hence have no base upon which to construct a conceptual model of the physical (shelf order) layout of the collection. They do not understand subject cataloging as separate from classification. But--and this, for me is the butt of a Dodge Ram--once this system is reduced to its basics in a process-oriented reference interview--it can be taught so that these motivated seekers can grasp and use these technical processes which transmute a book collection into a large-L Library.

    Title, as part of the package "book as organized carrier of knowledge," must carry content weight. For <u>Library Literacy Means Lifelong Learning</u> there are two major connections to be mapped: between "library" and "lifelong" and between "library" and "learning."

The Library Map

[Figure: A library-shaped diagram labeled with HOME COLLECTIONS, PUBLIC LIBRARIES, SCHOOL LIBRARIES, COLLEGE AND UNIVERSITY LIBRARIES, SPECIAL LIBRARIES, surrounded by a ring marked PRE-SCHOOL AGE, SCHOOL DAYS, COLLEGE AND GRADUATE YEARS, EMPLOYMENT PERIOD, RETIREMENT AGE — LIFELONG LEARNING]

What could the map for the first connection be--not statistically, but philosophically, not to scale but to human experience? Variables, of course, abound. Generically they encompass the resources of each individual: health--able or disabled, family, community, nation--material and spiritual. "Generic," implying a non-brand-name label, permits the omission of such as institution in place of family and the almost-beyond-measure difference in community resources between New York City and Pinedale, Wyoming.

On the early segment of the lifetime continuum, libraries number home, public, school, and college and university. Mid-course, employment, corporate and special libraries, begins at say nineteen, and, for some, ends only with death, happily or unhappily in harness. The third segment, now burgeoning, plays havoc with Social Security and private pension computations, but offers exciting opportunities for all libraries in supporting the development of new interests and skills, and helping provide information with which to solve a whole new set of human problems.

Within each of these segments there is a range. "Home" can enlarge for the large family with bookish kinfolk. The public library network varies with each jurisdiction, from bookmobile, branch, and central to the state library. School can progress from the building to the system level and then intersect on its own with the public library system.

The range of "post-career number one" or retirement years extends from hobbies (genealogy or crafts or gardening) to career retraining and home-based research (why does Fido bark at TV; or, does my micro-computer wrinkle mean a repair trip or new software?).

For some residents of a New Mexico Indian Reservation, segments, one, two, and three are the friendly monthly bookmobile. "Into town" can be more unapproachable than Mars. Someone in affluent, progressive Montgomery County, Maryland, with the maximum in inter-system cooperation, plus a five-college consortium, plus the Library of Congress, plus the best and largest group of special libraries in the United States, would find only the British Museum out of range for a lifelong library network.

All this geography is, of course, dependent on a librarian who is aware of the library network beyond the circle of her nose. A course of instruction in library skills is based upon the aware librarian's teaching the individual seeker how to get from where he is to where he wants to go. Equally important is the knowledge that you can't always get there from here.

The map of the connection between library and learning is the main business of this chapter. As each separate human being makes his own journey through time and knowledge, he makes use of the libraries that fall within his library resource map. Within each segment there exists another variable for the traveler. This is the level of his ability to think critically--the degree to which he possesses the skills needed to locate, evaluate, and otherwise process information into the knowledge needed to solve each confronting problem on the map marked "lifetime." Can fact be understood, located, evaluated, expanded into opinion, capped by value judgment and acted upon to buy this or that, or to be this or that, or to do this or that?

If you believe that "Libraries Mean Lifetime Learning," then you would agree that lifetime learning demands library literacy which requires a comprehension of each piece of "library" as part of a knowledge map. The card catalog becomes the center of that map, telling the user both the "what" of library holdings and the classification "where." Within each card catalog is listed the totality of each individual library. The card catalog is both a location tool and an information tool. Through its subject approach it answers such questions as "What material do you have on aerodynamics?"

or "What books do you have on baseball?" The author approach answers the question, "what books do you have by Somerset Maugham or Dr. Seuss?" By its title entry it tells the seeker whether a particular item sought by title is held by the library being used. Charles Cutter, himself, validates the gigantic effort required to stifle frustration and smilingly, helpfully respond to the query, "Do you have the Doe book, My Life at Home?" with "For such a specific, known item, please check our card catalog which is RIGHT THERE!

The catalog's subject approach to the library's collection is the pay dirt to the whole exercise of content classification. It is the most valuable single intellectuality in library science, undergirding almost entirely the arguments for complex organization of library materials. For this reason, the cataloger has long been considered the practicing professional elite--though the OCLC concept is changing this.

Teaching the subject approach, since its medium is words, involves all the pitfalls inherent in any language instruction. Exactitude in definition of material, transliteration from one level of speech to another, substitution of synonymous terms--and terms that are not exactly synonymous; all these semantic considerations lie just below the term "subject heading." It may be to escape these rough semantic waters that traditional library instruction always dog-paddles safely on the shining surface. Mastery of the several languages--classification, authority, and subject headings--that are cataloging notation, is a student user's first major step toward library competence.

These standard uses of the library catalog characterize it as an inventory to the holdings of a specific library. To the trained and discriminating user of the catalog, the pieces of information on the catalog card can serve a much wider use than just selection and location.

Consider the author entry. Catalog cards list the dates of the author's birth and death. This gives an automatic chronological placement for this particular person. By teaching our student to be aware of these dates, we broaden the knowledge to be gained from the catalog. For example, in doing an assignment to read the works of someone who wrote in the 1930's, if one author's dates do not fit, the seeker must pass on to another. A student with this awareness doesn't have to stop and check an additional reference tool for a second choice of author.

Recently I was working in the rare-book section of the Free Library of Philadelphia. Their superb catalog instantly told someone who was library literate that the editions of the Peter Parley books I was checking were all published posthumously. If you are concerned, as I was, with identification and monetary value of a book, this instant ability to check the date of a particular edition of a book against the author's dates is invaluable. Another time-saving use of an author's catalog dates, especially in a large library, is in locating the John J. Smith you seek from among the number of his fellows.

In its concept of main entry, the catalog notation is an avenue of considerable access for the knowledgeable person. Responsibility for authorship of material is one of the most valid library concepts to be taught today. The identity of authorship has never been more of a maze and, therefore, it seems most important that someone who will have an equal vote in a democracy needs to know the librarian's procedure for establishing main entry. Consider, for example, a government document for which the cabinet officer or bureau chief may be the one who is automatically designated the author under the entry rule for this particular institution. The individual who did the work may be nowhere listed in the publication or on the catalog card, but it is important that the person using the material, though he may still not know who the individual author is, realize that the listed author did not write the piece and may never have seen it.

Corporate authorship makes very difficult the task of determining the editorial point of view. If we cannot determine this, we may well reach the totally incorrect assumption, because something is a government document or a newspaper story or a newscast, that it is pure and unadulterated fact. At the very least, selection has been operative in the writing and has produced, a priori, an editorial point of view. I always remember the wonderfully appropriate remark a high school student made when one of our faculty members had brought English language publications from Peking into the library for his class. They were being put out in the library and my student assistants were, as directed, labelling them "propaganda." A young man looked at me, saying "And what would you put on Time magazine?"

Next on the catalog card comes the title. What are the subtleties here? I would say that they are the ability to recognize the title from the subtitle, to understand what their relation can be, why there is a subtitle, and why it is included on the catalog card. To know what a catchword "title" is, and when a work is put under a subject entry rather than a title entry. In short--to end, by illumination, the myth that all works have at least three entries--author, title, and subject.

The inclusion of the publisher's name on a catalog card offers a great deal of additional information if we can teach our student user the meaning of this information. We are well aware that the concept of main entry for a librarian concerns the assignment of the intellectual responsibility for the work. The responsibility of the publisher may be a further indication of the reliability of the work itself. A student who has been made privy to this reasoning could easily have this circle widened to include the publishing network. To check on a publisher, the trail leads from Books in Print to the Publishers' Trade List Annual, Literary Market Place, and Publishers Weekly. Using this reference network, the learner can begin to get a feeling for a publishing house as an entity and thus acquire a new dimension for judging the validity of materials.

The date of publication seems quite a simple notation but, again, it possesses evaluative qualities to those who have been taught to follow our professional reasoning.

Let us take the example of a student seeking material on the death of John F. Kennedy. President Kennedy was assassinated in November 1963. A book with an early 1964 imprint would indicate a quick write-and-publish effort. Such knowledge does not condemn the work, but simply establishes it in its proper historical context. When one considers the widely varying opinions about our role in the 1941 Japanese attack on Pearl Harbor, it is clear how crucial the publication dates of "factual" accounts are in establishing an authentic history.

Moving down the catalog card, we come next to the number of pages. Every librarian in an institution where book reports are required knows that this is one of the details on a catalog card that has not escaped the reader's attention. When summer reading lists come out, the number of pages are usually not given. The students learn very quickly to go to the card catalog and make this check before deciding which books they should assure themselves of having at hand for whatever their summer's activities are going to be. The teaching librarian can add other uses for the page notation to the student's repertoire.

The illustration note has equal value. In it lies a simple example of the relationship of the different media. If a student is seeking a book on art and the cataloging does not indicate illustrations, the book will provide for him only the verbal medium of the printed text. For a student who wants a picture of a particular individual, the portrait note is a vital guidepost in his search. The library of the National Geographic Society adds illustrative cataloging notes such as "Maps on end papers." Thus, heeded details make accessible each small part of their library resource. After my training there, I shudder when I see other librarians covering up useful maps with the like of book pockets.

Subject tracings are above price, once a patron is taught to use them. Consider the student collecting books to do a nonfiction term paper. It is of great help to be able to compare quickly the contents of one book against that of another without having to go to the shelf and find the books and check their tables of contents. That step is, of course, necessary when we get down to the fine points. For a simple general beginning, however, the knowledge that each major subject covered by the book is listed in the subject tracings arms the student with an immediate reference skill.

The classification number itself has implication for the user beyond its strictly locational function. Here is an example in the field of science. It a student is looking for something that is technology--applied rather than pure science--it is vital that he understand that the notation 600 is

The Library Map

what he wants. If the material is noted 500, it is not what he wants. A student doing a paper on fairy tales and myths would find it to be quite important to know the difference between the F for fiction category of the modern fairy tale and the 398 number for folklore and myth. If a book sounds like a biography but is cataloged under F for fiction, the trained library user knows that it is fictional at least in some aspects.

The whole chore and exercise of classification is done to sort and categorize material. For this reason, it seems to me that of all the people in the education profession who merit the sixth professional level of Hell, first rank those who either compile or permit to be compiled reading lists in which all the various categories are lumped together in one gooey mass. In such a list, the stories of Dr. Dolittle can come next to King Solomon's Ring in a section marked "Learning About Animals." If fuzzy thinking results from this, it is only a case of the law of cause and effect in operation.

Each detail of the notation on a card catalog provides reference potential for an informed user. It is a cryptography--with real clues that librarians have treated as their own personal property long enough. With the ability to read a catalog card fully, the patron not only can locate, identify and assess the library's holdings, but also make valid comparisons between items and, therefore, evaluate more cogently each individual item.

So far we have spoken only of standard cataloging for an individual print item. Mention should also be made of color-banding or similar techniques employed to guide the user through a multi-media catalog. Specifics of the notations for non-print media vary as required. The RPM note must be presented in talking about records and millimeter width in talking about films. Here again, the sum total of the information provided, both by its details and by the opportunities the catalog provides for comparison between materials, offers to the skillful user a far greater reference resource than belongs to the unskilled seeker thumbing aimlessly through the card drawers.

Book catalogs now are joined by COM (computer output microform) and on-line catalogs as time and technology have their way. The Montgomery County, Maryland Public Library divides their book catalog into author, title, and subject sections and, since the several sets placed throughout the branch I use are usually in a chaotic state, they are at least "used." The microfiche catalog exchanges the plus of little bulk for the minus of difficult readability. On-line format adds the access hurdle of a need to type and be able to follow the non-uniform, often complex, "how-to" directions in return for miraculous speed and the subject access marvel of Boolean logic. Some on-line catalogs can be accessed through "user-friendly" terminals by touching the screen. This eliminates the keyboard but is less flexible and has other limitations.

The catalog seen as an index to separate inventory items among the holdings of the library is far simpler than the concept of the periodical index as analytics to small pieces that are physical parts of larger individual pieces. In today's world where a periodical can be anything from a four-page folded sheet to a classy hard-bound item, such as Horizon, trained access to periodical literature becomes one of the most crucial skills for anyone desiring current information.

Education in the structure and complex interdependencies of the library's periodical holdings is also one of the quickest ways I know to illustrate what I believe to be an unreality--the knowledge explosion. What exists is a paper explosion brought about, among other things, by the publish-or-perish pressure and the photocopier.

Once at an NCTE Convention, while helping to staff the AASL booth, I fell into conversation with a friendly neighbor who was representing a medium-sized university press. He volunteered the fact that the commercial considerations of a prospective manuscript were minor. "Because," I urged. "Because we are subsidized by our Arts and Science College in order to provide a vehicle for publishing select departmental Ph.D. theses." Be published, or perish! This school surely protects its chosen own. And another inch of library shelving is overtaken.

When I was preparing for my M.L.S. comprehensive exams, one assignment which seemed tedious indeed, was to be familiar with every one of the national professional journals for the current month. As I listed and cross-checked, patterns and trends began to emerge. Way back then, I was dumbfounded by the duplication of both authors and ideas in those closely scrutinized periodicals. Call this situation by what you will--euphemism or epithet--it can hardly be said to represent an explosion of unique information.

The Library Map

Now that the Federal grant route--direct and indirect--has materially affected even the medical profession's need for a sizable bibliography, the same data overexposure has hit its journals. A New York physician, who has his foot in both camps--practice and academe--entertained me with chapter and verse. He recounted one small experiment that was milked for four separate articles: one as a hypothesis, one from the viewpoint of the drugs employed, one as a dramatic case history, and, of course, the conclusions. The practice of letting the junior author publish part of a study under his by-line also accounts for considerable duplication of substance.

There is often a triple publication trail that can be followed once you start playing detective. A speech is given and from the taped transcription an editor fashions a journal article. The speaker-author edits his speech and publishes that. Later the same words go into a book as an essay in an anthology. Thus the first man adds three items to his bibliography and a second man, the editor or collector of the volume of essays, adds one to his.

Another variant phrase on the theme is ERIC. A fortuitous providence deposited Maurice Tauber in my care for about half an hour when I was first professionally confronted with that entity. Out of his experience as chairman of the Advisory Committee on New Educational Media, Dr. Tauber commented, "I had never envisioned such a mushrooming indexing complex as a needed consequence of this study. Periodical indexing publications had indeed sorely needed examination toward improvement of coverage and standardization of entries, especially in the difficult area of subject entry." He told me that a well-known publisher of indices had been known to overlook an important journal if there had been a personal feud between the two publishers.

Clearly, further objectivity in this very important subject area was needed. Instead, an end run, easy way out happened and the fourteen (now 16) Clearinghouses of ERIC resulted. That publishing organization, grown to empire status is now dramatically on-line.

The old Education Index subjectivity remained and new confusion was generated by ERIC's decision to include in its index journals already covered elsewhere. Not all of the documents in RIE are available from ERIC, but disorder resulted from ERIC's listing of journal entries--none of which was available in any ERIC-related form. To remedy that a new index was begun, Current Index to Journals in Education. This lists selected, annotated journal articles while speeches, proceedings and dissertations continue to be entered in the original RIE format.

These maneuvers produced for educational researchers the fresh hurdle of coping with two discrete journal indices. Searching requires an exercise in translation between the Thesaurus of ERIC Descriptors and the Wilson list of subject headings. Education Index is the old ivy, and CIJE ERIC's the new, through which all literature searchers in education must hack. This detour into publishing history must be brief, but let it serve as an indication that a new index can have a natural parent other than the information explosion.

If we can demonstrate this pattern to ourselves, our collections can be kept manageable by our professional evaluation and selection capabilities. If we can demonstrate this to collection users, we can help produce colleges and universities where teaching, in itself, is considered an honorable and adequate profession.

How does the photocopier contribute to the paper explosion? Study the use made of a public facility in a university library. Discount the great temptation to plagiarize, inherent in such easy possession of the polished sentences of another, and ponder only the potential for legal quotations. When student assignments and faculty promotions reward length, such a goal is readily served by the instant acquisition provided by these machines. The press of a button is not visible in the scale of effort when balanced against the labor of meticulous notes. In our affluence, even a quarter a page brings too little pain of a different sort to be an effective barrier to the excesses of photocopying.

Let us consider for a moment the problems posed for a student by a teacher's class bibliography. I mentioned earlier a particular level of Hell to which I would consign anyone who puts out a bibliography lumping together fiction and nonfiction. There is another level, slightly lower, reserved for the person who makes up a bibliography and does not clearly delineate the format of material which he is listing, or for such as the editor of a major press who included--in a book on higher education--a bibliography which did not list a single publisher.

Earlier, there were only three major kinds of printed material with which to confuse the student: the book, the periodical, and the monograph. The latter of course, is

The Library Map

the one that is the hardest to locate and so most needful of clear labeling. But if a student is aware that there is such a category, he has a fighting chance of identifying it for himself.

In discussing with students the form of bibliographic entry for periodicals, it is natural to raise again the question of authorship and consequent intellectual responsibility for an article. Magazines such as the Reader's Digest and the New Yorker often use signed articles. Others, such as Time and Newsweek, generally do not, allowing corporate authorship to become quite broad. Now, when the responsibility of the television and newspaper media is being questioned on the national level, it is more important than ever to demonstrate this to readers. The interrelationship of publisher-author can be shown to go beyond the individual periodical to the larger corporate structure of which the periodical or other media are a part. By being set on a search through varying reference sources--book and human-- a seeker can assemble the network that makes for that complex corporate structure, the interlocking directorate. This corporate authorship is often the one voice to be heard on a television station, a radio station, or seen in a major news magazine.

Once bibliographic entries are complete, it becomes clear what the intellectuality of the format and arrangement of such entries really mean. One can see that there is a hierarchy in the entry itself that has meaning, the progression from specific to general, from article title to periodical name. The value in this standardization appears as they scan a formal bibliography. To give a volume number now, when less and less periodical binding is being done, seems an unnecessary roadblock since that notation is chiefly of value to the librarian binding back issues. But once again, if this is made clear to a user, the roadblock vanishes.

Many of these details of periodical organization become even more important when the form in which the ultimate material is made available is not the hard cover periodical itself, but one of the forms of micro-reproduction. Faced with a microform, the patron must be even clearer about the relationship of one issue to another than when the search for the hard-cover copies is made within a file box or bound volume. Once the relationship of periodicals to their levels of indexing has been mastered, information about specialized subject indices is in order. Let's not be deluded that such familiarity is common among even the professional elite. In my years as head of a professional library in a large school system, not more than a handful of the users of that library, ranging in educational status from a bachelor's to a Ph.D., possessed any such information. When they came seeking periodical materials, the first question asked by the staff was "Are you familiar with the Education Index?" And 98 times out of hundred, the answer was "No."

There seems no better tool than the library's reference collection with which to teach the critical use of a library. The reference collection in a school library will be fairly small and therefore a manageable instrument for teaching appraisal skills. With a relatively few books on each subject and a complete collection of all the encyclopedias for the suitable educational level, we have a clear basis for a show-and-tell on the library as an institutionalized order.

By visualizing a library with the reference collection so arranged as to permit a class to sit in the center, we create a physical structure from which to approach the totality of knowledge that is represented by the library and its classification system. Start with the general works and go on around to those on history. What a beautiful circle from which to teach.

Some authoritative current texts with which to begin your lesson planning are Frances Neel Cheney's Fundamental Reference Sources, Introduction to Reference Work by William A. Katz, and James M. Hillard's Where to Find What. If you have access to a library school library, these, plus the now out-of-print Basic Reference Sources by Louis Shores can be drawn upon without adding to the first cost of your BI program. Whether you have your own graduate school copies, or ones borrowed or bought second-hand, remember, Continuing Education means an appropriate personal office Ready Reference Shelf. The professional secrets that such writers cover under such headings as: Authority, Scope, Arrangement, and Format need to be known to all lifelong learners. As we have been taught to judge for selection, they can learn to evaluate for their personal needs.

Lessons in recognizing these categories of appraisal arm learners with basic library literacy skills. People still feel that an encyclopedia is somehow in the category of the Bible, coming to us under heavenly auspices. It follows, then, that if all of these sets of the divine word come in establishment bindings with gold letters, then the sources from which they originate are, if not identical, at least

The Library Map

equal. In teaching our course in Reference Book Selection we can familiarize the student with the work of the ALA Reference and Subscription Books Committee. Here is some solid professional ground on which to perch while pontificating on the relative merits of reference tools. Divine ancestry can be a dangerous accolade, as Louis XVI discovered. The text for this lesson--"all encyclopedias are not created equal."

In trying to make this point to a class, I would hope to be able to manage so that each student could have before him at one time a similar article from each of two or more encyclopedias. Then, as he sought to read "all about," he could perceive immediately that there are some differences in the "all aboutness," among them, of course, the variations in emphasis and level.

If one book of each type of reference were all that was needed, the contents of reference collections would demonstrate. that fact. The presence of variant sources indicates their necessity. This concept of the authority and opinion interrelationships of the collection that surrounds the student can be shown to connect with the totality of material available within the libraries of the world.

This reference network is used in exactly the same way whether the information sought is scholarly or practical. The principles and techniques are the same for writing a research paper at any grade level as for seeking personal information of a factual nature, for a job, or for parents who may not be able to read at all and are having problems with rats in their ghetto flat. One of this current crop of immigrants, seeking a jewelry store to buy a Christmas present, if he chose unwisely, might need the reference function of his public library to locate the Better Business Bureau as protection from an unscrupulous merchant, and need it more urgently than the intellectualizing college bound.

Another crucial part of the library's collections can be included under the heading of "Pamphlet and Ephemeral Material." For most librarians the term "Vertical File" is not a happy one. Not because they do not believe in it as a source of valuable information, but because it is a fantastic consumer of staff time. The administrator may feel it is "a necessity" or a "fine thing," but most have no clue about the amount of time necessary to process the slender pieces that are its fodder and brush aside the professional's request for the clerical help necessary to create a viable file from an accumulated pile of paper and a 4-drawer file cabinet.

With centralized cataloging or commercial precataloging and processing being widely used in library systems, these chores for book and A-V materials are lifted from the shoulders of the librarian. The handling of a Vertical File, however, stays right in the library workroom and the totality of its maintenance sits precisely upon her shoulders. For any administrator who may be reading these words, let me give you this hypothetical assignment. Become this librarian for a moment. Some worthy patron of the library has said to you, "In order to help you with your Vertical File, I want to give you my back issues of Life magazine. This could be a great resource--clipped, and put in the Vertical File." You are pleased and grateful. You accept. The incident is closed except for your vision of a fait accompli. That is the view from where you sit. Now hear the whole story from where the action is.

The librarian is appreciative, the donor is correct. To have much of this periodical material available in circulating folders would be of tremendous value to the patron. She smiles and says "Yes," but asks herself, "My heavens, how will I ever get all of this clipping and assigning of subject headings done?" Then, out with her scissors, felt tip pen, paper clips, and subject heading authority file. Part of this huge task is even professional. Now, boss, what would you do: take it--or refuse the gift, and the attendant work?

If such a file is not designed with imagination and kept current and weeded, a library can lose much of the impact of the day-to-day world in which we live. Because of the time demands, rare indeed is a first-class Vertical File. Yet, lacking it, our currency is clipped and a proper progression of materials materially hindered.

The ALA Glossary of Library Terms defines VF as "1. A case of drawers in which material may be filed vertically. 2. A collection of pamphlets, clippings, and similar material arranged for ready reference in a drawer, or a suitable case." Who will join me in including our patrons in our intimate jargon and saying PF, Pamphlet File, from now on?

The contents of the Pamphlet File is a Pandora's Box, but on the other hand, as Pandora herself found not, the box is there and is going to be opened. Therefore, we should process it as realistically, intelligently, and simply as possible.

Whenever I confront the combination of ephemera and

subject headings, I reach for my Information Scientist's Badge (had to make my own). A current file screams for current language. Keep last decade's terms away from today's printed ideas, but maintain clear connections. Informational language must adjust to the context in which it is used--especially when it is for public use by a broad, wide audience.

Only an intimate group has the freedom and the necessity to invent its own code. Martin Joos helps us to examine our own speech in his delightful small work, The Five Clocks:

> Intimate style tolerates nothing of the system of any other style: no slang, no background information, and so on. Any item of an intimate code that the folklore calls 'slang' is not slang but jargon--it is not ephemeral, but part of the permanent code of this group--it has to be, for intimacy does not tolerate the slang imputation that the addressee needs to be told that she is an insider. The imputations of all other styles are similarly corrosive. Accordingly, intimate codes, or jargons, are severely limited in their use of public vocabulary. Each intimate group must invent its own code. (Joos, p. 32)

Let's keep our public language straightforward--honest and open to give all possible help to our patrons. If we put irrelevant language or professional jargon on our most current materials, what have we produced? Answer--confused users who are not "library friendly " at budget time.

The classification systems--dear old Dewey or LCC-- are one primary road to the library's heartland. They little resemble any of the traveled roads familiar to childhood, though. Recently, I overheard a discussion between some MLS Students about their school library courses. As they spoke of a course in YA materials, one said of the professor, "How can she go on repeating what her book says about students in urban schools being so hot on using the card catalog? Those kids don't even enter the library. Besides, no one ever teaches you how to use any of it anyway. " Her companion commented, "Out where I lived, they made us memorize Dewey, but such Dullsville I sure forgot fast--since they never explained why it was worth learning. " "Yeah. I hear the kids here wishing that they'd known about some of this--reference tools and all--when they were undergraduates. " Another nail in the coffin marked "Instruction in Library Skills. "

Under the open library plan, as it most often operates, the librarian functions as a purveyor of materials to meet some intense immediate need for "Help." There is that annual moment of truth when, on the day that school opens, the dedicated readers besiege the librarian with cries of, "What are the three shortest books on our summer reading list?" Students who are less candid and more experienced meet a similar need by checking the number of pages given on catalog cards. Then there is that recurring moment of panic in the life of a student when the term paper is due <u>tomorrow</u>. The librarian has just enough time at this motivated moment to provide the relevent reference sources and primary books so that he can produce a generous piece of plagiarism. The final surge is provided by senior research papers when valiant librarians do eleventh-hour rescue work on the floor.

Within the education community, only educators have professional standing. Unless one can somehow be made to qualify as a teacher, no architect or nurse or cataloger can get professional status in a school system. School librarians are most uneasy ingredients in this brew. In theory (again that paradox) we are teachers and librarians, both. The credentials battle illumines this premise with the light of reality, and it's out the window. Our mythic speciality that has kept us on the professional salary schedule is instruction in library skills. Principals and librarians together give it lip service. The myth seems eternal.

In the late sixties, as head of a professional educational library in a large school system, I could document that there were perhaps two people out of each hundred using that library who were competent to unlock the resources of the organized collections that such a library offers. These teachers came bearing assignments from professors or principals--little bits and pieces of information from bibliographies, lecture notes or staff meetings. They had not heard of the Education Index, did not know the difference between a serial and a monograph, and were not familiar with the concept of subject indexing as part of the bibliographic network.

School administrators thus do not themselves comprehend the libraries they rule. This fashions the feedback to close the circle of library ignoramuses.

What of college libraries--the next rung on the ladder of formal education! Yes, of course, the need for user instruction is acknowledged and it is almost universally practiced in some guise. But before we relax, assured that those really, truly educated will be skilled in Library, let us read these words of Jon Lindgren:

> [S]tudents, faculty, and administrators embrace a myth, both actively and passively, that grievously wants exploding: that libraries are easy to use. That myth issues forth in a thousand expressions, all representing failure of the imagination. Two manifestations of the myth: the student who asserts with glib assurance that he has exhausted every route of access to resources on a topic; the faculty member who casually assumes that anything worth teaching about the library can surely be accomplished in an hour's time.
> Hence an impasse to perceiving and understanding better the proper role of the library (and librarians) in the academic setting has bulked large among library users. Not only do they not know how to use libraries effectively, they do not know that they do not know. And instruction librarians, having assaulted that impasse, retreat with the vague certainty that there remains a new educational frontier out there, and that library user instruction deserves much more attention--devotion, even--from the entire educational establishment.
> (Lindgren, p. 71, 72)

For our patrons, our libraries resemble laundry on a day when all the regular employees had left, and someone had done the labeling in disappearing ink. As the turned-on ones might phrase it--we librarians have seen our bag as so much our own that users have really copped out on us, in disbelief that our library domain has any relevance for them at all. Isn't it possible that such an often early-learned attitude is operative as the apparent current end-of-affluence forces funding choices that go against libraries?

Professional credentialing battles presently enjoined produce similar serious threats to all librarians. Federal librarians stand as first strike targets for A76 and current drafts of new OPM Standards, but the influence of these potential massacres goes beyond to each bivouac and field camp and battalion. Times are truly troubled--not a fresh thought--ever, yet some of its ingredients do seem so. The connection of this chapter--libraries and learning--blazes on all our banners. Carol Nemeyer chose "connections" as the theme for her ALA Presidency. What those of us carrying the sub-banner of "BI and Library Literacy for Lifelong Learning" strive to add is emphasis on the process which can make the connection visible reality. P. L. Travers of Mary Poppins fame speaking "literature" in these words from an address at LC, says:

> Only "connect" ... the attempt to link a passionate scepticism with the desire for meaning, to find the human key to the inhuman world about us; to connect the individual with the community, the known with the unknown; to relate the past to the present and both to the future. (Travers, p. 4)

Librarians have long performed as society's "rememberers." "Only Connect" describes the rest of our public service task and sends us out to teach the process of information connection.

Method is good in all things. Order governs the world. The Devil is the author of confusion.

Swift

chapter 6
One Librarian as a Professional

Love is the fulfilling of the Law.

                Romans : New Testament

Professional performing--one's career--a personal technical journey is individualized indeed! Some performing professions, --chiefly music and dance--demand entry at a very young level followed by a lifetime of dedicated disciplined striving. Medicine is the next most demanding of early and long efforts, followed by law and the church and academe. Teaching (K-12) and librarianship allow a more revolving-door approach. My zig-zag path has resulted in a unique yet traditional pattern of feminine life and mid-course, many-times-corrected professionalism.

Education, through to a B.A. in English (and sorority, journalism, debate team, and men); marriage, motherhood, volunteerism--the traditional steps for such as I. Then, came a life-changing loss for an only child, my mother's sudden death. As I struggled to re-group, volunteerism was dealt a wipe-out blow as I sat for one and a half hours whilst the group debated pie or cake for our spring fundraiser. "There must," I said to me, "there must be something better in life than this." My daughter was a first grader in my Episcopal parish's brand new elementary school. Lonely beyond lonely, I infiltrated to the hilt. "Yes, I'd like some coffee." "Thank you for letting me wait in the teacher's room," etc. Working women, wives, mid-somewhere too, but it soon became clear that what separated us-- kept me out of the work-kinship--was my lack of training. Be a school mother helper, yes, I could and be welcomed, but I'd done that. Now I wanted to become something else, something more. Putting myself under the microscope, what did I find? An educated non-intellectual, who, for seventeen years, had been in training to an intellectual husband from an intellectual family (now by the happenstance of three siblings as members of the National Academy of Science, considered the inheritors from the Huxleys--posing uncomfortable gene-pool queries for my children), and relished it all. My brain being demonstrably active, what were my 'druthers? A social animal, people lover--mad about decor and colors--I considered Interior Design. Yet, I was also

One Librarian 85

hopelessly bookish and, then, at the beginning of the '60's, librarians were in such demand that a M. L. S. appeared to guarantee me employment 'til eighty. Done, Catholic University's School of Library Science favorably evaluated my dusty B. A. (such a proud day) and wife/mother now undertook the third major role of student.

   Father James J. Kortendick led the school then, building the humanistic structure that Dean Elizabeth W. Stone has made into a purringly productive community of library scholars. Father advised me into a full-time first semester, and the family dynamics absorbed it, but, seeing the existence of our Christmas rest on telephone shopping and store gift wraps (free then, in that pre-GRE world), and the crisis that snow could produce, the degree slowed down to four semesters and no summer school. Family tensions didn't vanish, just slunk down to a manageable level. One agony, long remembered, concerned father's commitment to stay in town for the month just preceding Comps so I could be free for total scholarly immersion. Naturally, he was asked, then pressured, then tormented to accept a speaking engagement in Geneva. "Sorry, spouse, but you promised me first!"

   This aside is inserted for any current M. L. S. candidate who has found this book and read this far. Grouse about Comps if ventilating helps control stress. Do not, however, take yourself seriously. The learning experience that results from the concentrated professional immersion provides a robe of library competence and awareness that can be worn with pardonable pride to your first M. L. S. post and a professional platform that can be built upon all career long.

   Some of the horrors of my first job proved to be building blocks for professional sureness and strength. In graduate school my course veered toward College and University, and Special Libraries. An after-graduation reality for me was a self-imposed time limitation because I had two children, 11 and 15, who were both attending independent schools. For this reason I accepted a job in another independent school where my time schedule--daily and yearly--would match theirs.

   My in-service training consisted of professional literature, frantic telephone calls to my profs at C. U. , and fellow laborers in the vineyard. A library school colleague snorted when asked about one of my problems, "Carolyn, what you should do is go to work for a large system and find out how things are really done." In moments of panic, I agreed. The years have proven her wrong. In working through my problems I came to understand the interrelationship of the parts of a library in a way that I don't think could come to anyone who was trained in a large system. From daily experience I was forced to abstract the problem and then seek its resolution. This narrows the theory-reality gap to tissue paper thinness and brings the totality "school library" into precise focus. Anyone running a one-person library must understand the parts and how they form the whole.

Of six experiences as "boss of," four have put me into museum rooms as settings for modern library service. Maret School was the first. My responsibility—the upper school library--had formerly been the charge of a teacher of literature and drama, a delightful person who had tried valiantly to run the library and teach a rather obstreperous group of youngsters, all at the same time. When I was able to have an inside look, I was appalled. The library was a beautiful oval-shaped room in an old mansion that had been the summer residence of a President. On the floor were stacks of unprocessed new books. There were two ranges of standard library shelving. The rest, clearly designed to hold the library of an earlier individual book collector, had ornate, fixed shelving.

The enthusiastic teacher-librarian had managed to buy some books--those were the ones stored on the floor--but he had never gotten around to doing anything so ordinary as cataloging them, nor was there any inventory of the books that he had inherited from his predecessor. It was a small, but manageable, mess. The situation and I lasted together for a year and at the end of that time all the books were on the shelves and adequate supplemental shelving had been procured and the cataloging was complete. An already overburdened headmistress went over my list of titles, one by one, and rejected any that did not appeal to her. One bit of her personality surfaced when I elected to buy one of Menninger's books, A Blue Print for Teenage Living, and she crossed that off with the remark, "I am not going to have any of these damn self-help books for young people in my library." And she didn't. This red pencil through the new book list, plus a slim budget, kept the acquisitions small enough to permit housekeeping to be completed. Order now existed and even that, for troubled adolescents, can constitute program. Trying to position against oval walls the new bookcase needed to house the books piled on the floor paled into nothing in that "on the job" learning environment. Contract renewal time afforded us an acceptable parting point.

After Maret, I was for three weeks the librarian of the Cathedral Church of St. Peter and St. Paul, in Washington, D. C. I was interviewed by the business manager of the Cathedral as well as by the Warden of the College of Preachers, by whom the library was administered. The former, a gentleman of the very old school, inquired about my qualifications in terms of my general health, which led to a discussion of the importance of wearing rubbers. The building in which the library was and still is housed is a splendid Gothic structure unworkable from any technical library standpoint. In addition, the bequests establishing the Library-mandated special collections were housed in museum rooms which are absolutely inviolate and unrelated to the subject matter of a working special library in the field of religion. But I was enthralled at the idea of being on the Close to share its magic with both my children, there in Cathedral schools. I became the Librarian, was given the keys, and delighted in the clergyman who was my boss. It was a lovely affair, for all three weeks, during which time I wrote a policy statement and set up a plan for what seemed to be a reasonable way to move the library into Washington's Protestant library vacuum.

This vacuum came to my attention at graduate school when our professor of book selection, looking at the world in the traditional Catholic way and seeing Catholic, Protestant, and Jew, assigned some questions for us to look up in Catholic, Protestant, and Jewish sources. The Jewish source was difficult and the Catholic was a breeze, but oh, boy, where were those Protestants? That quest led me to the libraries of the Cathedral. The Cathedral Library sadly has not assumed this still vacant role of a great Protestant library for the city of Washington. This, my librarian's vision, I could not sell. They rather liked it the way it was-- all their own.

My fairy godmother came in the form of a telephone call from the headmistress of a girls' school to which I had applied. Their librarian, nearly 80, was retiring, and would I like to come down and discuss it further. I would, and I did, and began a very pleasant experience with a first-rate educational institution, Holton-Arms.

Though it looked good, and I was charmed by the elderly Virginia gentlewoman who had been its proprietor, the library turned out to be a whited sepulcher.

It was in order; there were no books on the floor. As far as my accumulated library experiences could see, it was functioning. But a working library means a continuous operation, something going in and something coming out, and when being on board permitted me to look more closely, I found this one stagnant and non-functional. Overhauling it took the three years we remained in our old buildings. When the school moved to a beautiful campus in exurbia, the library was in condition to enter its new home with pride.

That library was my course in the horrors of weeding a library, and I learned why so few do it. One bleak, black afternoon, when I was waist deep and wastebasket full into this weeding, the former librarian came to call. Never have I so fervently wished for the disappearing capabilities of the Cheshire Cat. She was a dear person, and deserved better than such a mountainous scene of her weaknesses. The collection had never been inventoried or weeded and there was no connection between the catalog and the books on the shelves. After the first month of school, I was fully aware of this fact and initiated action to straighten it out. Midway in straightening it out, I would pick one or two afternoons a week when the library was relatively free, and set out all the catalog drawers on our long refectory tables.

In order to discard a book from the library, one must find all the cards and pull them. The cataloging standard requiring that the main entry card indicate tracings in use in a particular library had not been followed. I had to treasure hunt for each added entry without the certainty that it would be there. Any which I overlooked remained to be pulled out later when noticed. My antics provided the escape of humor to watchers, who teased with, "Solitaire again?"

Needless to say, there was very little use of this library as a circulating collection of books. Students came to do math homework, use the encyclopedias or read magazines, but it did not function to support the intellectual thrust of the school with circulating supplementary materials. The only major use of books, beyond texts, was for the courses taught by the president of the school, who controlled the school's budget. Her History of Art Library was a terrifically expensive and complete collection for which she ordered the books and ensured that the funds came from the main library's budget. Her other course had a large collection of reserve materials in the library which, again, she ordered and for which she allocated library money.

One Librarian

With no one encouraging the students to read freely or to browse, and no orderliness for location and retrieval, the museum situation prevailed. Once the collections were in order, and a web of faculty support in place, program could be developed and meaningful use of resources could begin. The English and History department heads were, fortunately, library minded--the former, old guard, just waiting for encouragement; the other, brand-new and eager.

Library outreach was personified when I was invited to lecture on books to all the senior English sections. Term paper back-up came all year and all high school long. We managed to borrow the American Association for the Advancement of Science Traveling Science Collections and the girls could sample in books the depth and breadth of those disciplines. Foot in mouth, two left feet, mistakes--I made them all. But a gracious headmistress trusted me and my purpose was well fueled--ten steps up and five down still adds up to UP. Upon order, program was finally built.

At Holton, my experience with the intricacies of the Cutter Three Figure Number Table came into full flower. When we moved to the new school, I had an eager and proficient mother helping me. She was a meticulous person who dearly loved the Cutter Number Table and seduced me into playing with it to the ultimate, adding numbers in between so that everything filed perfectly. The Lincoln number added the s for Sandburg, and so forth. It was, oh, so beautiful. One day it hit me that such Cuttering was an awful consumer of time and that its ordered beauty prevailed only when every book was on the shelf. If every book was on the shelf at any time except when the school was closed for the summer, I was doing a lousy job of librarianship. It was at that point that my Cutter Table converted immediately to the maximum simplicity, and never again where I've been free have I used anything beyond letters of the author's name. I have always felt great confidence in this decision after I learned that the New York Public Library uses nothing else, either.

Not having held the post of librarian in a public school, my experience in recruiting student help has a loophole. Intuition insists, though, that a leader can always lure followers; a Pied Piper is never seen sans his cadre. The secret may lie in such as the Tom Sawyer fence-whitewashing story. Children and other young people, being human, like to share in a happy productive piece of work: if the taskmaster is a doer--working too and willing to be covered with dust or paste--if they can put something of themselves into the project--if they can be subcreators instead of subservient clerks.

One of the cruel cardinal sins we over-30 holders of the Mace and Seal should publicly confess is our denial to children of the real work of which they are clearly capable. What are we afraid of? "Letting them get the upper hand," "losing control," "being shown up," "losing respect"--it seems to be that our present tactics have made all these fear phrases a reality.

A 7-A section of girls could think on their feet with any visiting brain I could produce. No abstraction was beyond them. Neither was the chore of paging our new set of the *Britannica*. Given the ground rules, they paced the task and found with pride a binding error. Don't you think they weren't aware of encyclopedias--both form and content--after that?

Brains and eyes and hands and sturdy young legs climbing and bending and stopping to perch on a ladder and sample an enticing volume--surely these can be part of any school library's staff. Some reasons I've heard why public schools can't do this include the departure time of buses, competition of other clubs, laziness, low prestige of the library, and no free time in the school day. Yet this same devalued coinage, Library, is piously called the heart of the school when visitors are toured through. Here is one sickening example of status quo custom robbing our kids of the experience of moving among the stored knowledge, wisdom, humor, and company of the ages in a creative, comprehended, joyous place.

It was here at Holton that I became, for the first time, an administratively authorized teacher of "library." The head of the Middle School, Katherine Wheatly, was a very library-oriented administrator. For three years we had labored together to develop a library program to buttress her curriculum. When the exciting scope of our new school buildings became a solid reality, it seemed time to enlarge program accordingly.

After I had received the support of my immediate administrative superior and gone to the headmistress to say that Mrs. Wheatly and I were going to do this, Sally Lurton looked at me and said, "But, Mrs. Leopold, how can you talk about library for a whole year?" One practical roadblock Miss Lurton raised was, "How on earth are you going to work out a schedule for these 150 girls?" I was just enough of an actress not to let that throw me and said, "Well, Mrs. Wheatley has a plan and I think we can work it out." Her final card was, "Well, the office cannot do any rescheduling." I managed to give my best Cheshire cat smile and glided out gracefully to the door, more determined than ever to succeed.

My supporter had not given me any such plan and I was just bluffing. When I presented this dilemma to her, she answered with, "Carolyn, that's no problem. You just get each one of the girls to write down for you their individual schedule blocked out on a piece of notebook paper. Then with that data you do your scheduling." She made the announcement; each girl made out the schedule. These came in to me and within 20 minutes I had eight library programs-- eight library class sections scheduled. It was beautiful. Real problems can have real solutions.

When I returned to my office after turning in my teaching schedule, and looked at my own schedule of these library classes, I thought to myself, "Okay, now you've got the ball, what's your game?" The one thing I was sure of was that my professional education was the place to begin. Without that feeling of professionalism I would never, I am sure, have gotten to that day. This sense of professionalism can be put on like a coat. It is the feeling that you do have access to a highly specialized body of knowledge. It was my mentor at Catholic University, Father James J. Kortendick, who did this for me. He talked and talked about being a professional and, foolhardy though it may have been, I believed him.

What helped me to believe Father K was the opportunity to write my thesis on the history and current practices of the National Geographic Society Library. A dear friend of mine, Andrew H. Brown, who was then one of their senior editorial writers, was among those staffers whose judgment was trusted by the NGS Librarian, Esther Ann Manion. A careful review of completed theses indicated the value in being able to study and describe a successful library. With him as my guarantee, (and the tacit agreement that I would not publish the thesis), the closely guarded monarchical portals were opened to my professional scrutiny.

For years in any new library situation in which I found myself, I would check with the Geographic, knowing that if it were a meaningful library problem, they would have faced and solved it for their specific situation. Though my needs might be different, and I would not have either the staff or the physical requirements to be as completely adequate as they, at least I had a model--a professional and specific-instance model--against which to work.

From watching Miss Banks and Miss Manion in action, I learned also that a librarian does know how to select books. The books of the National Geographic are not selected by the staff of the Society. Yes, surely, if a staff member wants something, he requests it and it is usually in house or on order. The point is that the chief librarians selected the books. The editors supplied them with a list of projected articles and they, as professionals, gathered the books and articles necessary. It has never occurred to me to suppose that I am not competent to select books.

Yes, Miss Manion does have the additional credential of a degree in geography. But each of us has an undergraduate major and practices subject-related Continuing Education. As I watched this team move out into tangential fields, I learned the guidelines for authority in book selection. I have found them to be transferable to any subject area.

One Librarian

As Educational Curriculum Laboratory librarian I found with great glee that almost inevitably when one of our staff requested a book, the book had been "selected" and was either in the library or was on order. These are fields for which I possess no formal credentials.

In materials evaluation, as in Bibliographic Instruction, we again deal with a topic which is a prisoner of a system having authority on paper but not in action. Library Literature and Education Index are replete with studies showing that subject specialists, at any level of K-Ph.D. are not given adequate formal training in materials selection.

That library was close to perfect. There were two reasons for this. The person who set it up and had charge of it for 40 years was both a geographer and a librarian, in addition to being one of the brightest, most capable, and most deceptively possessed of a mind like a steel trap of any human being I have known. No one ever presumed to call her by her first name and yet I have never known anyone who knew her well who did not really, in the best sense of the word, love and respect Miss Esther Ann Manion. Her assistant at the time I was there was Julia Banks, a complementary personality, beautifully qualified, also confident in her possession of the abilities of a skilled librarian.

Another reason that the NGS library could be faultless was the provision of ample funds to meet the needs of the organization and, therefore, to meet the needs of the library serving that organization. Budget is a servant for them, not a master. Writing my thesis, I was privileged to see in action a special library performing all the services that could conceivably be desired for the writing of a highly specialized popular journal. These included, of course, a magnificent Vertical File cared for by a professional with an adequate staff--usually about three people. In studying this Vertical File, I learned "on the job" the principles by which such a tool should be compiled and maintained. I also saw in action the totality of one area of the bibliographic network; this, too, was valuable on-the-job training.

The present librarian of the Society was, at that time, in charge of cataloging and I learned from her how meticulously meaningful and meaningfully meticulous complete cataloging can be. Each book is noted for any features that might have particular meaning for the Society, such as maps, illustrations, or map end papers. I learned there how to put notes on the main entries for the tracings that are filed.

This exacting housekeeping creates a tight ship and affords the most complete service from whatever materials are available.

From them I also learned some of the realities of management. One must determine goals and priorities, then devise techniques for reaching them. "What" must precede "how." Take circulation as an example. For them, instant access is a must. NGS materials are lent for office not home use. Charges are as flexible as need decrees, but every item is expected to be available when needed by someone else to verify a quotation, support a caption, etc. Publishing deadlines are real. There I learned the principle of the "invisible string" that keeps each bit located--outside as well as inside the library. A system that is transferrable to all special libraries.

The siren song of the Cathedral Close came again and I went to a boys' school, St. Alban's. This change of sex in the student body required preparation, such as my daughter's admonition that top buttons of blouses must be attended to before leaving for school. But this time I was fully acquainted with the state of the library. The former "librarian," the Latin teacher, was a friend and ally. His housekeeping did leave much to be desired, but the obvious need to again transform some books and a vaguely related card catalog into a working school library did not daunt me. I have played Don Quixote many times.

A third time the scenario found the library in a beautiful room, totally unsuitable for a school library. The former librarian's philosophy had been if anybody really wanted a book, he would find it and there was no real point in worrying about making the search easy. So when the bookcases that were designed to look the part of a cultured gentleman's private library filled up, he didn't worry about it and just kept adding the new ones--tucked in any which way. If a student wanted a particular book badly enough, and it did happen to still be around, and he had enough time, he could find it.

Again, the current curriculum included no library use beyond the storehouse function. A very strong teacher who had been there forever had Reserve Books that went back 30 years and, though many titles were out of print, he had seen to it that enough copies had been bought originally so there were still plenty around. The present young head of the English Department also saw the library as a Reserve

One Librarian

Collection. He managed to talk the headmaster of the school into setting up, at the other end of the building which housed the library, a paperback bookstore and reading room. His big sign read "Don't borrow books, buy them," which, when I wasn't infuriated, struck me as a very humorous illustration in miniature of why the library wasn't doing any more business than it was. As an aside to Women's Lib, I was the sole female on a faculty of 45 men and the brain backup involved in that sign was about what I had. They loved me pouring coffee.

In order to keep the library open for the hours decreed, it was necessary to have a masculine assistant and I was fortunate enough to get a series of very bright graduate students from the neighboring university. With their help, the library was inventoried. Oddly enough, one of my toughest early skirmishes involved being able to shelve books with the normal amount of free space at the end of each shelf. How could any fiscally responsible administrator justify all those bare inches (adding to feet) of bookshelf? My stalwart male helpers were great on ladders when we inventoried the old-fashioned heights and when we shifted the new freestanding library shelves to suit my masters. One great day we put a garland on the door and declared the place an organized collection of the carriers of knowledge. Finally, media (new) entered in the form of a listening station as supplementary material for a course in Music Appreciation.

The paradox inherent in all these private-school situations operates inexorably and infallibly to sabotage development of library program. Given the "givens" extant when you arrive, the equation is surely stacked against "library." Since there had been no true library, no one really comprehends what you are there for beyond the stereotype and myth: a) Everyone has been making out o.k. without you, i.e.--nobody felt a need with your name on it; b) since the administrators were responsible for the former status quo, they are not anxiously muttering mea culpa as you enter; c) therefore, unless you are given a generous free-handed honeymoon period, you can have a fight on your hands over the simplest rock-bottom basic like six vacant inches on each bookshelf, or a library workroom. Again, I learned, often not fast enough. More skills can be needed by a school librarian than gentility ever acknowledges.

> For what is a headmaster? Is he a leader? A coordinator? Is he to be a dictator, or a constitutional monarch? There is no post of

responsibility in which a man is left so free to choose his own method. He may choose a cloistered virtue and live for the school. But the occupational hazard in this sort of life is grandiosity. He meets parents, masters, and boys. But boys lack the experience and audacity to challenge him; masters lack the energy to engage; and parents have given hostages to fortune. As for that freer audience, the governors, a self-regarding instinct will not readily allow them to question the wisdom of their own choice. A headmaster who begins by dedicating himself wholly to this closed community may end in the placid admiration of his own image. (Golding, p. 119).

In the summer of 1966 I attended the YASD pre-conference before ALA in New York, and was sitting in the front row at one of the meetings with my usual knitting. The occupant of the next chair, Richard Darling, reached over and put out his hands to wind my new ball of wool, and so became my professional future for the next three years. Curriculum Laboratory Librarian was my title and my task was to run the professional library for the public schools of Montgomery County, Maryland.

After I had come out to Rockville, at Dr. Darling's request to talk about working for the county, and the Curriculum Laboratory job had been discussed, I went over to case the place for myself. The former librarian had been a social acquaintance of mine who had retired to travel with her husband. Thus I knew I was not infringing upon her professional bailiwick when I went to survey the situation which was then being handled by two young nonprofessionals. It was quite clear that the library was not an organized collection of the carriers of knowledge at that particular moment. Things were not piled on the floors but they were more or less piled everywhere else and in looking at the catalog and in doing the things that an experienced librarian does to assess the health a particular library, I could see that this one was suffering from a lot of the ailments to which a library collection can fall heir. If I took the job, it was going to require the same amount of major technical overhaul as had every other library I had managed. But I liked the place and decided if the job were offered to me, I would certainly have enough support from a librarian of Dr. Darling's caliber to justify the plunge into a 10,000-volume morass.

The library had been originally set up by someone

who was a nonprofessional but a terrific archivist. Later, it had been turned over to a professional librarian who did many things extremely well but was not interested in the follow-through and detail that is necessary to make such an intricate orderliness alive and operable. I was fortunate to have among the people who were hired to keep the library open at night a dedicated teacher who had the time and inclination to learn about a library and go considerably beyond the call of duty. With his help as a subject specialist, we did a tremendous amount of weeding of the collection. One amusing restriction in weeding involves the number of available wastebaskets. One cannot throw out any more than the wastebaskets will hold. In this instance, the bulk that had to be dealt with was tremendous and the custodians brought us special, large trash cans. When these were full, we were through for that day. In this process, I discovered that plastic chairs, all in one piece like great scoops, make marvelous wastebaskets.

Perhaps a recipe for weeding would not be amiss here.

1. Don't begin until your patrons and their needs are clearly established.

2. Make sure there are no unmarked special collections to sabotage (I ran into that trap once).

3. Always have subject specialists helping you unless you have relevant second master's degrees.

4. Never have more than one such specialist for each special subject area in action at any time. If you do, you'll be able to use a nut cup for a wastebasket.

5. Be ruthless--of all people, we librarians know when the trash is the only place for a book or whatever. Don't pass the buck and waste time and resources of local charities with stuff you are too weak-minded to pitch. Bury your own dead.

My intuitive appraisal of the joys of working under a first-class librarian proved correct. The morning that I reported, he asked me to come first to his office where he gave me the comments on the Curriculum Lab made by the two school librarians who had filled in there in July and August. Their message, in brief: do over the library! A clear mandate and an accessible professional mentor were freedoms I'd never known before.

Working for Dr. Darling gave me my chief experience of a supervisor who is also a librarian--a rewarding environment. At last I had a boss who knew what I was talking about. This is an illustration of the problems inherent in the usual library spot on the organization chart. The library is always a special unit, whether it is a special library, a school library, or a university library. Unless you are department head in a large library, your direct-line supervisor is rarely a librarian. There is a School Library Supervisor for the school libraries, but the relationship of the central office to the school librarian is staff, not line. The Curriculum Lab was part of the Department of Educational Materials, in an equal slot on the organization chart to all other departmental units which RLD supervised.

If an administrator doesn't know how to use a library, he doesn't feel that it contains anything teachable. Therefore, he does not see the librarian's role as that of a teacher, Neither does he comprehend the terrific amount of work involved in producing this institutionalization of order--the physical nature of the interrelationship of the items within the library--nor properly weigh the fact that if they are not all accurately tagged and stored, retrieval is impossible. Both the professional competence and the need for teaching it remain unrecognized and the only thing seen is Marian, the Librarian.

For this reason, to make a library fulfill its true function, the librarian must use every wile and be the model of sweet patience to get budget, staff, and support, to say nothing of changing her boss's notion of what the library is for. These reasons ought to make it clear why we need both a philosophy and strategies.

Working in a large system brought home to me the fallacies inherent in system-wide centralized cataloging. The centralized processing for the entire county school system was done without a shelf list. The cataloging for this special professional library was no exception. Every time that LC changed Dewey numbers, the catalogers simply used the full number that appeared on the Library of Congress card. They did not maintain a shelf list for each of the individual libraries they serviced. We had many nine-digit call numbers and additional copies of a title already on the shelves came through with a new classification number. By this procedure as many as five sets of cards with five different numbers for one book came into the catalog. At first I kept these in a little box entitled "horrible examples" and later used them when teaching at the University of Maryland. But after a while the novelty wore off and I became rather pensive about the state of the catalog.

Actually, this proved a simple problem to solve, given a supervisor who could understand the technicalities. The cards were sent to us first, anyway, so I undertook the assignment of numbers myself and worked toward the simplest possible notation. One great day, the Lab was blessed with the opportunity to take charge of Dr. Maurice Tauber, of Columbia's School of Library Service, when he was down on a consulting assignment for the department. For once I hallowed every shining moment and dragged out my shelf list. Dr. Tauber stood still for this and approved! With that name to drop, I had no humility at all.

Another human necessity of the librarian, call it personality if you like, is a tremendous store of physical energy. If you wish to achieve and not matriculate out, best keep the desire to be an activist sheathed in velvet and laughter. Adequate staff, paid or volunteer, is another sine qua non. Also, you must be willing to roll up your sleeves and "do it yourself." One of the adequately humorous running battles we had with Dr. Darling was over the matter of the library housekeeping. Because the custodial staff was almost mythical, what cleaning was done the library staff did. In the beginning we managed by buying some good cleaning supplies like spray wax from the Safeway, getting payment from petty cash. Then bureaucracy caught up with us and accounting said, "No, you have to have your department head's signature." It was pointed out to us that professional librarians, etc., down the line, don't clean shelves. Paper-level people and their theory-reality gaps! If we used the stuff that was bought for the custodians, action toward cleanliness really wasn't something our time or temper would stand. The standard remark, "professionals don't do it," pays no heed to the fact that dirt is real and patrons don't want to write notes on dusty library tables or find ashtrays reminiscent of a college bar. Nor do they wish to trace library traffic patterns on unwashed floors.

The library's program depends on housekeeping. Can you imagine owning a sailboat and programming her for an entrance and win in the Annapolis Cup Race when the housekeeping department has left ropes uncoiled and sails with rips? You would be lucky if you left the dock at all. So it is with the library. The librarian's program, however ambitious or relevant it may be, can be no better than the housekeeping with which she tends the organized collection of the carriers of knowledge that are the raw materials of library program. To do the housekeeping, one has to be quite clear about the interrelationship of the various pieces that are the equipment of the house called library. God alone can help the sailor who incorrectly stows his anchor rode. In the wardrobe of a best-dressed lady, like things must be together and they must be ready--mended and pressed and polished.

My school library past comes to mind when I hear that wonderful line from the musical comedy, "I Do, I Do!" when Mary Martin sings to her husband, "There must be a better way to get a clean pair of socks than to stand in your drawers in the middle of the kitchen screaming, 'Someone has stolen my socks.'" Unfortunately, this response is standard for many a high-ranking user of the school library when he feels the need for a particular pair of intellectual socks. The note that you get from the head office is exactly that, someone standing in the middle of the kitchen and screaming. One such that was aimed at me involved delivery of the New York Times. The Sunday Times was our special pressure point, and one Monday I found the following note in my mailbox from the headmaster, who was in his office every Sunday. "Mrs. Leopold, I did not get my Times yesterday. Will you please see that this matter is taken care of for once and all!" That was the closest I've ever come to being deemed omnipotent--and by a cleric, at that!

The library of the American Council on Education was in two rites of passage when it came under my direction in 1969--1) a move to new quarters (truly from a closet) and 2) new clientele--the many organizations of Higher Education that are the tenants of Number One Dupont Circle, in Washington. The terms of the Kellogg Grant which made the Center possible required that the Council generate a "community of scholars" from the approximately 38 other higher educational organizations that make up the National Center for Higher Education. A central library was seen to be one powerful means, and so it became.

Until its dramatic appearance on center stage at NCHE, the library's history had followed the pattern of benign neglect common to many such non-profit associations. Its early appearances had been presided over by a succession of secretaries. Then came a custodian bearing the credentials of our craft, but if such could be labeled upon

One Librarian 101

graduation, his tag should have read, "Brilliant, useful archivist or cataloger if kept away from people." He had held forth during the move from garret to castle and, since no one on an administrative level cared, called the shots on new library design and equipment. His final musing to me after a period of training overlap (without stress, since he had resigned rather than assume an enlarged professional role) concerned my open door to our silent building hallway, "Yes, I can see that you probably are going to do it differently and perhaps it will be better. I really don't like people and if I could have done it just the way I wanted to, I would have cut a little hole in the middle of the door so I could shove things out to them and they could push them in to me."

The new Center Library was a very special Special Library serving a broadly centered single subject area--organizational higher education. A term classification system therefore seemed appropriate. Size and subject content and audience all came together nicely. Working closely with me were Janet Schoenfeld of ERIC, acting as subject specialist, and Sheila Gorg, librarian of the Council on Library Resources, as a third ear and eye. We began with the Thesaurus of ERIC Descriptors and culled terms pertinent for us, using it as a subject universe. ERIC, being designed for computerization used the term "descriptor" rather than subject heading and each is of equal value since there is no location requirement such as physical shelving necessitates. At the beginning of the discussion of what I termed location headings (where the book was to be shelved), the librarian knew the need, but the information scientist, trained to computer storage, didn't know what I was talking about. This complication, necessitated by physical reality--shelving--is not a part of the equally weighted computer indexing she worked with. Take recourse to a copy of Research in Education and you can still see traditional library methods in the broader context of information science. A call number--line one--is just that item's major subject heading term transposed into the language of numbers as a mechanical aid to its retrieval. Which, incidentally, makes a teachable BI example. Since then, to date, four special collections bear such a user-friendly, especially designed term-classification system.

A major mid-course correction kept me out of librarianship for six years. Just two weeks before the box of purple-clad School Libraries Worth Their Keep progeny arrived from Scarecrow, and, before all the rugs were down, my primary career fell victim to the California no-fault divorce laws. That experience of resigning my best-job-to-date to join my spouse/primary careerist's career move to U.C., Berkeley, catapulted me into Woman's Lib forever. All of these facts engendered the usual several levels of opinion and value judgment. One publishing fact is that SLWTK became my history of that family. Some human facts are that I could not bear to read it until forced to by requests to speak about it. I also regret not having published my original dedication: "to 'spouse' without which this book would have been neither necessary nor possible."

Though Thomas Wolfe carries wider authority, my "going home" did prove successful. Having already experienced the positive effects of "alternative careers" on my library professionalism, I can attest to their direct relevancy. Back in D.C., for a contract year I served as Coordinator for the ERIC Clearinghouse on Teacher Education, just down the hall from the NCHE Library at Number One Dupont Circle. My responsibilities for document evaluation and selection and work flow afforded a valuable perspective on my previous training and experience.

Now that libraries are "into" marketing, my experience as the feminine half of a new-husband's ownership of a McDonald's franchise takes on added current career value. At the time, I reveled in sitting in on the Baltimore Advertising Cooperative, attending my first "for-profit" conventions, and learning to manage staff and stock under a new set of directives. Ray Kroc, "founder" of McDonald's, leads his organization most personally and directly and is a professor most worthy of attention. One convention featured this motto: "Nothing recedes like success." Overall, the primary contribution to my library career was the realization that a patron is a patron is a customer, and to duck the full implications for librarianship of "You, you're the one we're pleasing" can guarantee a red balance sheet.

In 1974, I became a researcher for the Special Publications Division of the National Geographic Society. Filmstrip production was my first and major area of work, with exciting other assignments including two of the Books for Young Explorers: Let's Go to the Moon, which allowed me the special privilege of working with the crew of Apollo 17; and Explore a Spooky Swamp, which taught me "Okefenokee." Working in-house, 16 years later, demonstrated that my M.L.S. thesis' high opinion of their library was justified from another perspective.

Their name does open a lot of doors, including that of LC, where my bookish blood rose to nearly ecstasy level over a stack pass. Throwing over the researcher's role to roam, I explored five shelves of P. G. Wodehouse, a complete run of any favorite author I could find and savored the chance to reverently inspect such as the Heidi of my childhood and earlier and later wondrously exquisite examples of the illustrator/author/publisher's art and craft.

My Continuing Ed class spends one session at LC watching and learning Scorpio and its new on-line relatives. This past term, circumstances gave that class this privilege, but my excitement almost wasn't sufficient to kindle theirs. Why? What saved the serendipitous moment from waste was the enthusiasm with which the student from Bogatá, Colombia searched for and greeted her special section. Perhaps the broad teaching lesson is that "editions" are, by nature, timed, and their impact, like that of "courting" music, is not directly transferrable to another's chronology. After spying and announcing the find of my Windemere Edition of Heidi (black cloth binding, illustration pasted on the front cover, silver lettering), I began to read it. Before my mind became that nine-year-old me curled into a window seat in Dayton, Ohio, it caught a clever, now-trained student locating and filing publication date, and was forced to accept the boomerang qualities of successful teaching.

Using as a researcher the special NGS in-house collections, I built upon and reinforced the earlier selection training of Miss Manion and Miss Banks. Being multi-level--librarian colleague and staff patron--permitted me unusual behind-the-scenes on-the-job training in how they did it, day-by-day for four years--clipping service, adult material, and developing children's collection which supports the education materials.

There I also learned the supplemental skill of creating a non-fiction book in a personally unfamiliar subject area. This, of course, is the process followed by all lay writers, and reviewing such for School Library Journal had begun to teach me how. NGS researchers are part of this process from beginning to end. They first read to create a personal subject overview and then assemble a materials collection, select subject consultants, check each draft of text and are responsible for all textual factuality which includes the identification of relevant opinions as potential potholes in the Society's reputational road ahead--awesome and great intellectual fun! Being paid to "think," to operate at your highest level of competence comes rarely--but, oh what bliss (and panic) when it does.

The close parallel between this editorial exercise in problem solving and all critical thinking makes it a valid curriculum item for BI. In any public service position as, one on one, you assist in patron book selection, or for a class presentation, if you can generate a verbal performing arts type editor to lay out that special aspect of "book," the relationship can be surfaced and demonstrated.

For whatever quirks of fortune (or misfortune), time and tide have placed me as manager of several libraries at moments of rites of passage--a move to new quarters, new clientele, etc. For the most recent, the Genealogical Library of the DAR, it was the crusading determination of the Library's then-direct supervisor, the Librarian General, Martha A. Cooper, that led to the installation of their first professional team in recognition of clerkship's by-now dramatic 82-year failure to control that unique research collection. Their rite of passage was the final, complete retirement of a thirty-year, veteran book clerk. For a book collection numbering 70,000 volumes, un-spine-labeled, lacking any formal classification system, his departure, coupled with the DAR Continental Congress, a yearly spectacle which, for five wild days, quintuples the Library's maximum comfortable patron load of 90 and makes the needed continuous reshelving an exercise worthy of a sorcerer, provided the coup de grace. My directive "to straighten out the shelving" resulted, four years later, in a special project we called "Daughters Plus" (DAR Magazine, May 1981). This is a Retrospective Catalog Conversion which was considered landmark enough to merit showcasing as a Poster Session at ALA Philadelphia and as part of a DCLA-VLA program at Virginia Beach in 1982. This Project employed a specially created term classification based on the collection's already-in-place physical order, a team of three professional catalogers, two data input clerks, and a Chief Cataloger Project Manager, Kathryn Scott. [Its technology is a Mini Marc Computer.] Our subject specialists were the DAR Genealogical Staff.

As I write, the DAR nears the cyclical self-destruct engendered by its triennial election of officers, and the lame duck change in administrative priorities threatens the Project with a groping halt. By putting the classification system completely in the hands of the users rather than the professional staff, the determination is then made on a case by case basis without a trained eye overseeing the panorama. When

One Librarian

ignorance tampers with the system, the result is an absence of knowledge--non-knowing--a case where ignorance is not collections-management bliss. Keeping work as a trade secret mitigates against us in the sense that such lay non-knowing exists because we library professionals have never taken seriously the invisibility of our professional cloak. Sadly, "they" support the query, "But Mother, as a librarian just what do you know?" The collection is two-thirds converted and the first volume of a projected three-volume book catalog was published in October of 1982. As a senior former genealogical librarian colleague impressed upon me, without continuity there really can't be program. This chunk of administrative wisdom obviously is the culprit in many an act of collection chaotic non-sequitur and should be so noted among professional big-T truth maxims.

And, back at the National Geographic where I watched and absorbed the user rightness of a term classification system, their collection is slowly being re-cataloged--to LCC. My radar registers staff intersection of politics with substance in collision with the overweighting given by the final administrative decision makers to the expert advice of a distinguished scholar-in-residence. LCC will add a language barrier to in-house, open-stack, full-text searching while the addition of on-line search capability removes the barriers of time and pre-coordinate subject headings from out-of-house database searching.

Creating this revision of SLWTK has been a post-mid-career interlude on the technical journey of my professional performing. Beyond fact, my "only connect" turns to literary fancy:

> And only the Master shall praise us, and only the
>   Master shall blame;
> And no one shall work for money, and no one shall
>   work for fame;
> But each for the joy of the working, and each, in
>   his separate star,
> Shall draw the Thing as he sees it, for the God of
>   Things as they Are.
>   --Rudyard Kipling, The Seven Seas

>   or

> The time was when a library was very like a
>   museum, and a librarian was a mouser in musty
>   books, and visitors looked with curious eyes at

ancient tomes and manuscripts. The time is when a library is a school, and the librarian is in the highest sense a teacher, and the visitor is a reader among the books as a workman among his tools. Will any man deny to the high calling of such a librarianship the title of profession? (Melvil Dewey in Library Journal, Vol. 1, No. 1, Sept. 30, 1876)

Chapter 7
Reading ~ for Librarians

Reading is seeing by proxy.

      Herbert Spencer

Without "reading" what is a librarian? An ALA poster bears the motto "Sh-h-h-h! Don't talk. Read. You'll talk the better for it." On the poster is the outline of a human head with the brain cavity filled with informative words and phrases, obtained from reading. The unrest that this blurb stirs in my brain is "what does read mean to librarians?" What do we think happens in the process called reading? And, once we have answered these questions, what then? What are we really talking about when we declaim the merits of the happening by which, our historic stock-in-trade, print, is transformed with the aid of human eyes and brain from characters on paper or a CRT to electricity in a human mind?

I just read--period--until I married. Then, in attempting to read with my husband, I learned that educated adults attack reading very differently. My next major insight into reading differences arrived when my first child began the reading game.

Blessed with a devoted grandmother who added her stint of reading aloud to that of ours, my son's vocabulary of the spoken word was excellent. For reasons of geography, he did not meet TV until he was five. Thus equipped, his father, grandmother, and I gave him up to First Grade. By the following June he read well. But no phonics. How could he master the language and the dictionary?

Being decisive characters, we three taught him phonics during that summer between first and second grades. Voilá!--a straight shot through school to his desired goal of being a physician. He can read or talk anyone to death.

Daughter is solely a private school product. This was quite accidental. When it was her turn to go, our neighborhood kindergarten had 80 children and a brand-new teacher. To further add to the disadvantages, she would have hit the afternoon shift--the low ebb of the day for her. So we enrolled her in a brand-new Episcopal day school. Once there, we were hooked by the quality of experience that it afforded.

As it turned out, this bit of chance was pure serendipity, for she did not master reading easily, though she had had the same three adult family-team teachers. In first grade she was a question mark. By the end of second grade she'd won the book given for the student who read the most books. This lesson was that, even between equally intelligent siblings, such a basic learning difference as reading involves does exist.

While she was in the question mark phase of mastering reading, I gained further insight into the vastness of the difficulties that are possible when a child is "learning to read." The complexities of the correlation of eye and hand and brain--perceptual, motor, and cognitive skills--are numerically infinite. Thus taught, I am saddened, but not surprised, by the magnitude of the problems involved as America transfers its literacy goals to all America.

Additional learning about academic skills came while I was librarian at Holton-Arms. This involved the relationships between psychic barriers to communication and the process of academic learning. By seventh grade the clear stream of childish curiosity and friendly outreach which I'd seen in one girl since fifth grade had muddied considerably. Upon inquiry, I was told the common story, the surgery of divorce and the uncertainty of imminent maternal remarriage. Then the story developed uncommon twists--the about-to-become New Daddy had been living on the same street with his first wife and children, and all the children had been playmates for many years. As the school year unraveled, she grew more and more unreachable, and one day was taken off my library class roll.

Investigating, I learned that she had become unable to handle any academic work and was in school for only gym, art, and music. She was also under the care of a child psychiatrist.

I left Holton that June, so I did not see this girl again, but I read in the papers of the remarriage of her mother. That same winter I was at a nearby ice skating rink selecting some skates to rent when this girl and a younger sister came up to the window. When the clerk asked the elder sister to whom the equipment should be charged, she turned to her sister and asked "What is our name now?" Not to know one's name is the ultimate confusion. This lesson was that psychic disturbances can destroy academic skills.

The message of this chapter jelled at a meditative moment, "under the dryer." (A bit of Clugston family folklore--my mother's letters often began with such a "location heading.") It was multi-media, multi-print. Stretched out on the bed/desk, with a bubble dryer plugged in, my horizon was the setting sun, lighting the stained-glass star hanging in the window and transforming the far green of the trees. While I was drying and looking and composing a letter to my daughter, I glanced now and then at a children's book that was part of the print mélange. This had significance for me because the artist, Edward Koren, had been one of my daughter's professors at Brown University. This media input provoked the query, "Who is responsible for putting a story book into the hand of a child?" Journeying back as far as memory immediately permitted, educational reality replied, "Parents and teachers own the land marked 'story.'"

Before proceeding further, in the service of clarity, let me define terms. To "teach reading" or to "learn to read" concerns the ability to decode the printed symbols-- numerals and the letters of the alphabet. "Reading," once the physical skills enable mastery of the mental ones, is the use made of the learned response or decoding skills.

Language arts teachers are the professionals entrusted with the development of reading. The threshold to story is theirs. The librarian is regarded as the caretaker of the storeroom from which reading material is issued. Consider the relationship between a piece of music and the pianist playing it, and a book and the human being reading it. Libraries, be they music libraries or school libraries, store the script, and someone else, the piano teacher or the reading teacher, inculcates in the child the skill by which he can turn the script into the capability to read--notes or words. Both are preforming arts. All right then, what are we librarians saying when we tout the value of reading? Are we simply acclaiming a skill? If we are to pursue our analogy and be like Schroeder with his love of Beethoven, we would be saying, "Read, read the music, read the music." What we do say is "Read, read, use this skill. We have the script, you have the skill. We insist you use it." If you doubt this, recall National Library Week slogans.

Reading--for Librarians

Even now, I, as I write, and you, as you read, must recognize that the act we acclaim is something more than just a complex, kinesthetic performance. To justify all our emphasis, there must be something beyond the achievement of hand, eye, and brain coordination.

In <u>Webster's Collegiate Dictionary</u> we find under the word "read" these definitions: "1. To take in the sense of, as of language, by interpreting the characters by which it is expressed; to peruse. 2. To utter aloud or render something written, esp. so as to give an interpretation of its significance. a. To learn or be informed of by perusal; b. to learn, or discover the nature of, by observing closely as if in perusing a book." Webster seems to lead us to the word peruse which is defined; "1. Now rare, to go through (a series). Dealing with each unit; to inspect in detail. 2. To read carefully or critically; loosely to read." Let us go back and study <u>Webster's</u> again. "To take in the sense of, as language, by <u>interpreting</u> the characters with which it is expressed." So what we seem to be talking about when we discuss reading is a process by which something is taken into ourselves. Letters become words on a page of print and by the process called reading, become a part of the individual who does the reading.

Following this line of reasoning, one concludes that the topic "reading for librarians" really concerns the process that goes on in the mind and which resembles that poster graphic of the well-furnished mind. The physical process is an electrical, neurological complex that remains a mystery. Without words, this mystery lacks the means with which thoughts can clothe themselves and leave our brains to become characters in the human dialogue.

> Indeed, everything in her quiet world loved this girl: but very slowly there was growing in her consciousness an unrest.... A thought was born in her mind and it had no name. It was growing and could not be expressed. She had no words wherewith to meet it, to exorcise or greet this stranger who, more and more insistently and pleadingly, tapped upon her doors and begged to be spoken to, admitted and caressed and nourished. A thought is a real thing and words are only its raiment, but a thought is as shy as a virgin; unless it is fittingly apparelled we may not look on its shadowy nakedness: it will fly

from us and only return again in the darkness crying in a thin, childish voice which we may not comprehend until, with aching minds, listening and divining, we at last fashion for it those symbols which are its protection and its banner.... The standard of either language or experience was not hers; she could listen but not think, she could feel but not know, her eyes looked forward and did not see, her hands groped in the sunlight and felt nothing. (Stephens, p. 39)

Reading is one requisite means for adding raiment for our thoughts!

The Koren book crystallized the many facets beyond electricity of the process named "reading." It is a deceptively simple picture book of 25 pages entitled Don't Talk to Strange Bears. Each double spread consists of about twelve lines of verse and the sepia on white drawings. Besides serving on the Brown faculty, Professor Koren numbers among his activities doing cartoons for the New Yorker. As I read it, I kept hearing the voice of a friend of my daughter's as she described the book and commented, "Yes, there is a text, but it is minimal. The pictures are the important thing." These graphics are line drawings with the distinction common to successful cartoonists. Once taught to recognize his style, I can now leaf through an upside down New Yorker and spot a Koren.

What I want to say rests in the concept of what we, as human beings, bring to each personal performance of this mystery that librarians catalog under the word "reading." Don't Talk to Strange Bears is a series of episodes in each of which a little bear, having been sent out on a journey to the magic wood by his mother with the admonition "Don't talk to strange bears," meets someone that is strange but not a bear and attempts to communicate with him and his group. They are prehistoric animals meeting in a forest library, beavers working, or vacationing vegetables taking sun baths. These appear guileless encounters, but in the dialogue that reveals the attitude of the animals, a wealth of connotations beyond the denotations is employed that cannot help being an important part of what one is able to "read" on these charming pages. The book jacket tells us, "Children will delight in discovering and 'reading' the inspired pictures in this imaginative and antic tale." My concern is with the multi-level facets of its message.

Reading--for Librarians

Reading, for anybody, can be divided, like all Gaul, into three parts. The first is the kind of reading whose purpose is to derive a simple fact. Airports now display graphics in addition to words for all simple, vital messages such as entrance, exit, restrooms, and luggage retrieval, to obviate the language barrier. Before this, travelers had to cope with Berlitz handbooks for these very basic searches. Always simple matters these, for us, but not for the 23 million functionally illiterate adults identified by the National Commission on Excellence in Education who read in no language and memorize <u>Exit</u> and <u>Men</u> or <u>Women</u> as pictographs for minimal mobility in a message-ridden world.

A more complex example of this reading to obtain simple directives is a recipe. Jello preparation involves reading and so does quick oatmeal, although the latter assists with small sketches of cup and teaspoon and saucepan. To use a soap powder or to tint your hair, the drawbridge to such castles is reading ability. An admonition that graced my kitchen bulletin board for many years read: "If all else fails, follow directions." This, of course, can be both mythic and metaphorical, but now we are talking about the kind on the label on the back of the oatmeal box. If you can't possibly follow written directions, failure is you.

The second class of reading is a direct outgrowth of the first, but it involves the skills of internal criticism and should be called critical reading. This is the sort where you read for facts but must learn to make corrections between them and to look for some of the subtleties that enable you to be discriminating in your comprehension and acceptance of the printed word. For example, under the first kind of reading you might place a timetable. The second kind of reading would be a matter of putting one or two guidebooks and time-tables together and, from this data planning a weekend trip in unfamiliar territory.

The third kind of reading is the concern of this chapter, the type of reading where the human person doing the reading comes face to face in the totality of his being with the human person who created whatever it is that is being read.

We do the first kind of reading every day, simply as the means of surviving in a literate culture, and one of the problems with survival in this culture for so many of the people today is that they are not adequately literate and so are denied access to the simplest mechanisms of our world. In terms of human verbal exchange, this part of reading, the simple obtaining of facts, is the kind of give and take we have with a policeman of whom we ask directions.

The second kind of reading is routine for everyone who finds himself able to do it. It is the kind of reading and critical thinking that enables someone to use successfully a periodical such as Consumer Reports or compare puzzles in an I.Q. test. Such reading demands the ability to think logically and to be ordered in the pursuit of whatever facts are sought. The matter of reading critically is so important that once thought of as a complex process, it never regains any of the simplicity that it might have had earlier. Theoretically, it is taught as part of literary criticism, history or historiography, but actually, since few are aware that it exists as a technique, it is seldom consciously taught at all, by anybody.

Mortimer Adler, in his classic How to Read a Book, describes this process so magnificently that one would think it never needed to be repeated. Unfortunately, Mr. Adler is much too erudite for his message to reach any large measure of the population, but if a cross section of the so-called educated are assigned his book, its ideas do come across. I demonstrated that to my satisfaction when teaching a University of Maryland extension course in the late '60's. The reading list consisted of books I considered to be musts for anyone attempting certification as a school librarian. A course requirement was a book report on each title.

These were: the Adler book; Harold Benjamin's The Saber-Toothed Curriculum; C. S. Lewis' The Lion, The Witch, and the Wardrobe, and Four Loves; Teacher, by Sylvia Ashton-Warner; The School Librarian, by Jack Delaney; and Tolkien's Tree and Leaf. Here are some excerpts from the students' book reports on Adler's How to Read a Book. This is a book about reading in relation to life, liberty, and happiness." "Mr. Adler believes that reading is a basic tool in the living of a good life...." "The art of reading which Mr. Adler discusses applies to any kind of communication and is intimately related to the art of thinking."

Longer comments included the following:

> This book is not easy to read because of its length, the print, and the paper, but I found the time it took to read it well spent.

> Learning to read and the actual reading of great books is a means toward living a decent human life, the life of a free man and a free citizen. This instruction is part of our job as librarians. We must instill children with the desire for good reading habits and a man who can read well can also listen and talk well. These qualities are very necessary in our society.

> It is unfortunate that this book was not on my reading list 20 years ago. However, it is not too late to start trying to read properly and this book has inspired me to at least try. I have a few of the great books from the Everyman's Library stored in the attic and this is a good time to bring them out of mothballs. Since Mr. Adler makes learning to read a patriotic duty, I wonder how the country has survived these past 27 years with so few educated men.... It will take patience to read as Mr. Adler describes. I am going to find out what some of the St. John's graduates are doing today. I have one friend who is a graduate, so perhaps he knows more. All prospective librarians should read this book.

A personal example which builds on How to Read a Book grew out of an office-connected incident. Over a period of several days I carried on a discussion with a co-worker on a facet of psychology: guilt relationships and manipulative interaction. One book that speaks directly to this is The Strong and the Weak, by Paul Tournier, which my friend was then reading. In my pursuit of comprehension of guilt interactions, I had read it and, finding it clear and meaningful, had made it a part of my mind. At our next discussion over morning coffee she said, "You know, several of your comments are in Tournier's book, just the way you presented them." I replied, "Yes, but I have been taught by him." I read in her incredulity that she was interpreting my words to mean that I had actually been in a course or had had some personal relationship with Dr. Tournier. "You mean," she said, "he taught you?" And I said, "Yes. He taught me as I read his books." My words were hard for her to accept. "Oh, yes," she finally said. "You read his books and you learned from them?" And I said, "Yes, I did." What I gained from its having become a part of my consciousness, was what I could give back to her in our discussion as exact Tournier. It was so identically his that she could locate the passages in the book.

Another example of being taught in dialogue with a book is my "class" in Ouspensky. This time I was the buyer, not the pusher. The Psychology of Man's Possible Evolution was billed by the hooked one as being really very easy. Not so. It is tough reading of exactly the sort that Adler describes. I discovered that I was using, quite consciously, Adler's technique of finding out what the author is going to say then outlining it and finally going back and restating it. Conscious of each moment of the doing, it became obvious that the medium of the book, the text, exists as a fixed point of reference from which to carry out this technique of being taught by an author through his printed words.

In third level reading we offer up the totality of ourselves in a human dialogue. It is proffering of one's self to another person, albeit the person of the second part is not present in the flesh but only in printed speech. Strong and lucid words suffer little diminution over the centuries. In the human chain by which books come to us, someone had suggested to me that, being a daughter-in-law of Aldo Leopold, I would be intrigued by Sarah Orne Jewett's book, The Country of the Pointed Firs.

These connections--nature and people--produced

Reading--for Librarians

the contact between my world and hers and introduced me to this former stranger. This paperback, then 14 years old and out of print, was brought to me as that most sacred trust, a rare book. It sat for three or four days on my night table and, finally, I gave myself up to it. It was a givingness, an offering of my total attention to this person about whom I knew little but had come to meet and to hear her message. If her spirit, met in words, is something that I will accept, it will enter and become a part of me. Such a confrontation is true listening. I have come to heed her and, as she speaks, I am the silent and comprehending partner to a dialogue. After I have listened, I will be different but she will not be different. She is dead, yet she speaks. I am alive and I do listen and am changed in the hearing. Such a work of art can give one a voice long beyond the grave!

Katherine Paterson, in <u>Gates of Excellence</u>, makes this comment on the dialogue between reader and writer:

> The writer does not pass through the gates of excellence alone, but in the company of readers. Most of my readers are young, storming the gates for a good story.... But I have other readers, not all librarians or teachers ... people whose senses are as keen as any artist's, who have learned and continue to learn how to see and hear and feel, and thus truly how to read. (Paterson, p. 4)

Three levels of reading: the reading from which we attempt to extract a single perhaps isolated fact; the much more complex reading which requires that we learn to read critically for complex and interrelated facts; and the third kind of reading which brings us, as whole people, face to face with other whole people. All have one thing in common. They are building processes by which each person going through them is able to add to the furnishings of his mind. You might ask, now, what is going to be gained from a multiplicity of exposures to <u>men</u> and <u>women</u> or exit beyond an improved ability to locate such needed facilities? It might be a collection of stories to tell about the kinds of art work that often embellish these life-saving stations. As such it could become a research project for those who do a lot of nightclubbing or traveling. Some of Temple Fielding's best early humor concerned toilet paper. Each time I journey to a new land and have to cope with the search for facilities, I find that some of the clues I have acquired in earlier travels do add to my success.

In The Arts of Reading, by Ross, Berryman, and Tate, there is this interesting paragraph in the introduction:

> We assume that anyone using this book is able to read the words on a page, to know, more or less, what each word means, and in general what the page is about. This skill, uninformed by the intellectual disciplines that make up education, may be called <u>mere</u> literacy. If one acquires it, he can write <u>laundry</u> lists, follow simple printed directions, and vote. But "mere" literacy serves neither life nor civilization. This is our reading at the first level.

The introduction goes on to say,

> The merely literate man can enjoy at best only the prefabricated stories and articles of the slick magazines.... His motto is, "I get by" and so he does when the machines of society grind smoothly. But in catastrophe and crisis, he becomes bewildered. For the world is more than the moment he knows, and he has never been prepared for disaster.
>
> Like a little knowledge, a little literacy is a dangerous thing. Some awe of the printed word goes with incapacity for thinking about it. Those who can read but not read well usually believe all they read.... The curse of mere literacy is inability to criticize or discriminate, and a paralysis of the will to resist the author. (Ross, p. 2)

This "will to resist an author" is a very short definition of critical thinking and defines reading as the process whereby a mind, with nothing to operate on but the symbols of the readable matter, and with no help from outside, elevates itself by the power of its own operations. The mind passes from understanding less to understanding more. The operations which cause this to happen are the various acts which constitute the art of reading.

Adler says,

> There would appear to be several types of reading: for information, for entertainment, for understanding. ---Omitting, for the present, reading for amusement, I wish to examine here the other

two main types: reading for information and
reading to understand more ... The poorer
reader is usually able to do only the first sort
of reading: for information. The better reader
can do that, of course, and more. He can increase his understanding as well as his store
of facts ... The point is that for each individual
there exists two sorts of readable matter: on
the one hand, something which he can read ef-
fortlessly to be informed, because it communicates
nothing which he cannot immediately comprehend;
on the other, something which is above him, in
the sense of challenging him to make the effort to
understand. It may, of course, be too far above
him, forever beyond his grasp. But this he cannot tell until he tries, and he cannot try until he
develops the art of reading--the skill to make the
effort. (Adler, p. 28, 29)

For us over-literate ones, How to Read a Book is an
excellent first resource as we strive to resurrect this process from our subconscious and possibly ponder how to teach
these skills, the 1939 date notwithstanding. It outlines all the
technical problems inherent in reading for critical thinking,
as well as Adler's early warning of the collapse of the democratic process due to the failure of open access to honest information that is especially bitter medicine so close to 1984.

As we consider using the K-Ph.D. library as the
chief resource for teaching the art of critical reading and
thinking, it is reasonable to speculate how each kind of book
found in the library's collection can assume a place in such
teaching. Let us examine this, using as our guide the three
kinds of reading outlined above. In the first kind of reading,
we read to mine simple facts from a collection of words.
An example of this would be any reference book, and a very
common specific example would be word books. All of us
who write professionally have at hand a multiplicity of these
books which we mine for elemental answers. On my desk
carousel are two editions of Roget's Thesaurus. The variance between them is helpful to illustrate: 1) the difference
between the dictionary arrangement and the classified arrangement, and 2) the difference in the use of the language between
the two copyright dates, 1936 and 1962. During the 25 years
that elapsed between the publication of these two editions, the
American English language changed considerably and I find
this a useful tool for turning a phrase. For other quick
answers I have a Reader's Guide to Literary Terms, by

Beckson and Ganz; Rodale's The Synonym Finder; the Macmillan Handbook of English; and the Reinhart English pamphlet, A Glossary of Literary Terms, by M. H. Abrams. Each of us has his favorites, but all authors must depend upon titles in approximately the same categories. These are short answer desk reference tools. Ready Reference is a library description. Outside "school," such necessary print resources can be a standard dictionary, cookbooks, craft how-to's, telephone directories, and address books.

All of the nonfiction books in the general collection fall under the second category, those to be read critically to obtain complex and interrelated facts. This kind of reading creates a dialogue between print and peruser. In such an encounter, the reader judges the book as he would judge a human being with whom he was having a discussion. Where does he come from? What are his credentials to speak on this subject? What is his age and how is that important in the subject he and I are to discuss? And so forth. In such a dialogue, the book defines the subject. Next the questions must be formulated precisely. As the dialogue continues, the reader must be sure that he understands the book as it speaks. This involves not only the simple willingness to look up a word not understood, but, as Adler keeps saying, to understand the connotation beyond the denotation. The history of language written in the changing meaning of words is an important qualifier, is the 20-odd years between two editions of Roget's Thesaurus demonstrates for me. Once we understand the speech of the book and can rephrase it, we can hypothesize as to what the next argument will be. The accuracy of our "conversation" can be checked by a referral to the text. If we find ourself screaming "foul" or "lie," call for time out and bring in another participant in print or in flesh to validate one partner or the other or provide an establishing authority (remember the cataloging rule: it takes two out of three).

The uncritical love affair of person-to-person bookmanship is the bride and groom on the wedding cake of reading. Our individual reading paths often take us from a sojourn with an author in level-two dialogue, into the commitment of a step-three reading. In this, there is the same progression of questioning and testing into commitment as any two persons make on the journey from acquaintance, through friendship, to love. When I "met" C. S. Lewis and Paul Tournier, I sparred and drew in outsiders--expert and lay, before I became a Mary at their feet.

Reading--for Librarians 121

A portable printed friend can serve as a shield and buckler in a psychologically hostile environment. This retreat has saved my spiritual bacon many times. It is a protection, which like glasses, Kleenex, cologne, and aspirin, I am never without.

How can we librarians identify such kinds of books for others? The formula should include spirit and mystery or intuition if the book is nonfiction, like Lewis' <u>Four Loves</u> and the <u>Great Divorce</u>, or Tournier's <u>The Meaning of Gifts</u>. If the subject matter is provable--pure science or mathematics--there can be no lack of faith as a barrier to our deepest allegiances. If our beloved is handsome, rich, single, clear-thinking, clean living, it requires only common sense to say "yes"--no searing soul-searching.

In such a connotation librarians can confront the totality of fiction's ranks and take the personal measure of this vast printed army that will enable each of us to have a set of criteria for what we elect to purchase as companions and teachers for our patrons. Detective yarns, westerns, horse stories, romances, mysteries--they come for all ages and degrees of reading ability and furnish just such refuges.

To meet our patrons' needs for category-three reading, our libraries must overflow with a multitude of rounded human spirits in search of other such.

> Books are our commodity and it is our prime responsibility to know this commodity. We must recognize books as mortal things of cloth and paper and ink, which need our loving care if they are to survive; and ... we must recognize them also as superior beings, things of truth and dream, greater and more lasting than we their custodians are.

> To me our profession is the world's noblest. Each day we have the priceless opportunity of living with books. I urge librarians to read the books they live with, and to keep one's response to them always direct, personal, intense, and simple. Read books with body and soul, I say, and not with the brain alone, and remember these words of Yeats: "Art bids us touch and taste and hear and see the world, and shrinks from what Blake calls mathematical form, from every abstract

thing, from all that is of the brain only, from all that is not a fountain jetting from the entire hopes, memories and sensations of the body." (Powell, 1954, p. 127-128)

Reading and reader: between these two, skill and possessor, the librarian works. We have talked about several variables--all called languages: ciphers, words, pictures and music. Add to these the three kinds of reading, and our possible models increase madly. A non-reader wants a movie of a love story. A tourist seeks to discover "all about opera" for a first visit to Lincoln Center. Someone capable of category-one reading requests a cookbook. A section of class-two readers needs background material on cultural anthropology.

Librarians--the out-front Reader's Adviser kind--accept that they are supposed to know what is inside their books and also what is inside the people who come seeking guidance. What, then, are some of the specifics of this process of prescribing as we attempt to appraise the customer-reader who stands before us? Culture is one crucial molder of our life experience, and so must be a factor in our reader prescription. The person from a rural culture may use many of the same words as one from an urban culture, and we might think that as coins of the realm they are equal and exchangeable. Experience teaches us that they are not so at all. A student who is a graduate of Choate or Exeter and has spent his summer vacations traveling in Europe brings quite a different experience than one who comes from an inner-city high school and has spent his vacation either trying to work to earn money or, if he cannot get a reasonable job, somehow surviving on the city streets for a summer. Such experience not only defines ourselves, but is the matrix which determines our personal language.

Intelligence is another determining factor. My <u>Webster's</u> defines this as "The power or act of understanding; intellect or mind in operation. The power of meeting any situation, especially a novel situation, successfully by proper behavior adjustments; also, the ability to apprehend the interrelationships of presented facts in such a way as to guide action toward a desired goal." Intelligence, then, is not an absolute, a message experience grasped long before Mr. Jensen got into the act. By this definition, intelligence is distilled from age and background and levels of experience, the totality of which goes into this magical something, the human brain, and comes out as our ability to handle a situation or understand an equation or alter our behavior. The IQ of the recipient of our prescription must be ascertained quickly by a shrewd assessment of the person questioning us.

Native language is another variant for us to consider. To avoid being the ugly American, it seems especially incumbent upon educated Americans to realize the limits that we prescribe for ourselves because, almost as a nation, we have no language beyond English. Until I was able to travel outside the United States, which included time in England, I had no way of comprehending the difference between English English and American English. By its pronunciation, one learns to perceive it on the continent. In the United Kingdom you, expect, of course, to meet the variations of English English which Professor Higgins has outlined so enduringly for us in My Fair Lady, and its variants that are touched with the accents of Scotland, Ireland, and Wales. This is the Queen's English on the Queen's own soil. A visit to the continent, and you will hear a Frenchman or a Scandinavian speaking English with either an English or an American accent. Upon inquiry, you learn that they have learned their English while living with a family either in England or America. Girls of middle and upper classes are sent to live in with families as governesses in order to master a language. Such was the mechanism by which a Swedish Cinderella came to marry a Rockefeller. Geography demands that Europeans possess a second language.

The way words are used is indicative of national character. For example, the marvelous understatement of Englishmen is indicative of their whole character. Perhaps this is why so much stability and common sense have come into our world via England. Our native language portrays the set of our mind in words.

The current wave of immigrants demands continuing consideration of the relationship of language to learning. In Miami, Americans seeking certain jobs must have Spanish as a second language. My 1983 packet of hollyhock seeds has directions in Spanish and English. Fellow parishioners in suburban D.C. find themselves teaching English to, and acting as interpreters for, the Vietnamese families we are sponsoring. These are also variants of the task of the Reference Librarian.

1982 was designated as the "Year of the Handicapped."

Consideration of the physical alterations to the library to handle wheelchairs, etc. is outside the scope of this book, but of the handicaps of deafness, blindness, and degrees of mental retardation is not. Perhaps you cannot have materials in Braille, but because the hearing of the blind is especially acute audio media can help meet their information needs. A staff person trained in sign language is an important management goal, but just being aware of the patron's handicap as quickly as possible and drawing on your professional patience to handwrite simple replies can answer many information needs. The problem to be resolved is not so much one of resources, but of political will and priority. The disabled have abilities as well as disabilities, and access to the environment and to information is their right. This access is essential if they are to live full and fulfilling lives.

Let us consider the difference between seeing a whole person and a disembodied voice. When I was librarian for the American Council on Education, I talked throughout the day with a variety of people, from a variety of locales, seeking educational information. The phone calls came from San Francisco and Amherst and much in between. We got almost as many long distance calls as calls from within the city. My standard procedure was to say "ACE Library; may I help you?" After years of answering a library phone, it seems to me that this simple formula is best. If you add your name to that of the institution, you are offering an overload of facts. If they want to talk to a particular person, they will ask for the person, and if they don't, you have just intruded a fact that is irrelevant. As their words come to you, you begin to evaluate all the messages hidden in this remote contact in order to determine what it is they really want. It's fascinating to process the clues that can be picked up from the words and the sentence structures, the accent, and the intonation. One learns quickly to program the caller's intelligence and experience from these data and thus identify the personality override of the question being asked.

Let us go back to a definition of the word "read": "to learn or be informed of by perusal," "take in the sense of, as of language, by interpreting the characters with which it is expressed," "to peruse." We librarians have tended to think that "read" was something that was connected only with print and have used it not only in that limited sense, but in the simplistic sense of the first level of reading--solely as a mechanism for mining information. We have not faced in knowledge and honesty the existence of the considerable

Reading--for Librarians

learned skills to which Dr. Adler devoted How to Read a Book. This is our province; to use our training and the orderliness of the library to create this competency. One of the barriers to a real understanding of "reading for librarians" is the fact that most of us are not conscious personally of having mastered our range of reading competencies. Such mental blindness appears to have subtracted from our drive to make program paramount in our school libraries. Other entry level skills which are necessary for full proficiency in reading, which we also possess unacknowledged, are alphabetization, classification and arrangement, and hierarchy. This buried bar to library use by Susie and Sam G. Person is one cause of the failure of libraries. Picture, for a moment, yourself as a newly arrived visitor to a remote tropic island, your seaplane having been forced to stop by engine trouble. As your encapsulated familiar 20th-century world approaches a landing dock you see signs bearing messages you can't decipher, women in uniforms bristling with what you fear are multiple weapons, and wearing breathing masks surrounded by a pack of what you are sure are wild beasts. Looking down at the "beach," you see an unfamiliar substance, purple and neither solid nor liquid (like the old jokes about the Mississippi mud) but by which these beings are supported. Remembering the unsolved disappearance of Amelia Earhart, you hear the pilot say over the intercom, "My God, where are we!" Now, based on this example, what are the skills needed safely and constructively to enter a foreign land (not a foreign grave) that all accomplished travelers practice and which, once learned, slip into the reservoirs of our personal subconscious?

1. Reading--at least graphics for emergency needs.

2. Cultural information--are they our friends or will they immediately shoot to kill? What are the sexual roles, and how can we recognize a weapon?

3. Environmental information--can I breathe the "air"? Will the "ground" hold me with my feet as they are shod?

Guidebooks and maps and language are the entry-level to any autonomous trip. This is the how which enables us to get from here to there. PanAm acknowledged this in a dramatic way by advertising recorded guides to walking trips of the European capitals. Available from their offices, these are cassette tape recorders with earphones, like the familiar museum sets, which get you from here to there by direction such as "Walk two blocks, turn left for one more, look up, and there is the Eiffel Tower which was built in...." Imagine journeying at sunset into a remote quarter of Istanbul with such a guide and then having the technology fail!

Fellow seasoned library travelers, please keep the mechanics of our successful trek ever on the front roads of your mind. Novices cannot roam the world of information without the requisite skills demanded of any traveler. Newspeak of <u>1984</u> or any pre-coordinated computer printout denies searchers <u>their</u> innate human right to travel on their own through the subject of their choosing. Only librarians are the Fodors of the library map. Let's make huge posters of our bibliographic journeying abilities and be proud purveyors, not humble hoarders.

The traveler whose reading abilities won't take him beyond "entrance" and "exit" lives a barely basic life. Any pretense to being a BI professional demands our awareness that this reading, this learning, this using symbols as something from which to glean meaning, applies not only to what we call print--words on a page--but equally to the language of of ciphers, of music, of symbol, of color, of graphics, of pictures and of micro-chips. Unless we are open to the implications of this, we are in no way professionally competent to operate in today's library. When we think of the language of mathematics, we must think "Can you read a balance sheet? Can you read a formula? Can you read a fraction?" All of these mean to take in by symbols and absorb meaning. Mathematics <u>is</u> a language. It <u>is</u> read.

Music as a notation--another specific language--is another reading skill. I'll never forget my feelings the first time that one of my daughter's friends brought his musical reading to the house. As he opened his scores I looked up from my cooking, idly watching what he was doing, and he <u>was</u> reading. Dead silence, not a sound. John was reading a symphony. It was going from the printed page into his mind and he was hearing it in the same magical way that we ordinary readers can "read" a combination of letters and see a picture or meet a person. I read Shakespeare. John reads Bach. A rudimentary knowledge of the language of music enables us when reading a hymn book on Sunday to tell whether to send our voice up or down. That is reading music--Charlie Brown level.

Reading music also involves a heirarchical set of

skills. One level of expertise enables the possessor to read music for one or two instruments--organ, piano, trumpet, etc. Another level allows the reader to read/hear the full score for a symphony orchestra.

Over the centuries, people have created personal writing through many forms--stylus, brush, pen, typewriter, and now--the word processor. One recent simple form was spawned by "Sesame Street." These magnetized plastic letters and numbers came to my attention as "Communication by Icebox." One of my friends, fortunate enough to have achieved "Grandmother," used that blank metal surface as a slate for her two-year old granddaughter. Clothed in the rainbow, I read "Eleanor--Grammy." A new print medium!

Let us consider each of these different readable things. The two languages of print and numbers are quite straightforward. We are used to them. That is where we over-forties began.

From movements such as encounter and sensitivity training have come the awareness that we learn/read from fellow human beings much that is not spoken. Anyone perceptive or humanly reactive has always known that eye communication is the nearest to the bone of all human messages. There is no open intimate relationship where such eye-to-eye communication is not much in evidence. One such message that always delighted me was that which the Reverand Francis Sayre sent to his wife in her usual place in the Great Choir of the Washington Cathedral when he was its Dean. I often sat across from Mrs. Sayre and never saw him pass in procession without catching her eyes with flashing warmth. The language of this eye-to-eye--spirit-to-spirit--message speaks clearly of the depth of communication and awareness between them. Our eyes say much that can be read, and usually read correctly, by anyone who is tuned in to such reading.

Concern for other nonverbal communication--one of the popular terms now applied is body language--has also come upon the scene. One of the leading scientific minds in this field is a California psychiatrist by the name of Jurgen Ruesch. A noted book of his entitled <u>Nonverbal Communication; Notes on the Visual Perception of Human Relations</u> has this to say to this point.

> The study of the communicative behavior of man can be traced back to the advent of historical records and the discovery of archeological evidence. Not until recently, however, was the study of communication systematically undertaken, thus extending a trend initiated by early scribes, priests, humanists, and artists ... Although most people are familiar with the rules that govern verbal communication--logic, syntax, and grammar--few are aware of the principles that apply to nonverbal communication.
> This book is the result of an attempt to penetrate this more or less unexplored territory.... With the aid of still photography, we have tried to explore the informal and often spontaneous methods of communication that, when considered in verbal and, particularly, in abstract terms, tend grossly to distort actual events. Being well aware of the fact that photography introduces still another kind of distortion, we consider the present book only as a first and rough introduction to the subject of nonverbal communication. It is our hope that, with the use of nonverbal denotation devices, and with a fuller understanding of the problems of nonverbal communication, better ways may be found to approach a number of difficulties encountered in human relations, education, and mental health. (Ruesch and Kees, Foreword)

Reading--for Librarians

As we teaching librarians attempt to handle our continuous Reference Interview, the idea that is embodied in the words "mood of the moment" seems to have relevance. On the opening day of school a stranger, a new child, comes to us, and we must interpret much from few words in order to learn and encourage with every contact. Is the child giggling, is he sober, or frightened? The young child usually carries his feelings clearly written on his countenance. With age, such openness diminishes and by adolescence most countenances become closed to adults.

Living in Honolulu as a pre-professional (wife/mother), I worked as one of the volunteers who womaned the Information Desk at Queen's, the large general hospital. The desk was positioned as our Library Reference Desks--seekers had to cross considerable open space to reach us. This use of space as lead time is an old ploy. The Doge of Venice and all managers know this. Honolulu, a multi-lingual city, complicated my sizing-up process. Bearing (hesitant or authoritative), and clothing I read first, which analysis was, hopefully, corroborated by their speech. Tricky? Yes, but oh so satisfying to be able to tailor my informational response so as to soothe, guide, and cheer these edgy human beings.

With Hawaii's broad racial mixture of citizens and, therefore, of languages, it was worthwhile to learn to make such distinctions by sight alone. During the hours spent working at Queen's, this knowledge was invaluable. People come to such an Information Desk laden with the fears and unfamiliarity most poeple feel upon entering a hospital. As their guide, your need to interpret their query as quickly and correctly as possible is an even more important charge than when meeting the public as a professional librarian at a Reference Desk. My game was to see how clearly I could identify each person before they spoke. By accepting nonverbal language as a separate and valid means of communication we can establish "she reads me like a book" as one more BI competence.

A chapter on object language in <u>Nonverbal Communication</u> especially interested me and I will never again enter a strange house or restaurant or window-shop without hearing Ruesch's words. His text is accompanied by a series of photographs of domestic art--bibelots and other small personal possessions arranged as different homemakers would select and group them. The pictures bear these captions: "House as museum," "Ask permission first," "A bar like a club," "Formal informality," "Shrines and altars," and

"Wealth on parade." Similar space is devoted to commercial showcases with running commentary about restaurants: "For Bohemians," and "For neighborhood regulars," and, for show windows: "Let the label show," and "Stun the onlooker."

Every interior betrays the nonverbal skills of its inhabitants. The choice of materials, the distribution of space, the kind of objects that command attention or demand to be touched--as compared to those that intimidate or repel--have much to say about the preferred sensory modalities of their owners. Their sense of organization, the degree of freedom left to imagination, their coerciveness or esthetic rigidity, their sensitivity and fields of awareness--all are revealed in their houses. Child psychiatrists use play techniques to observe children expressing their foremost concerns through creative activities. Psychiatrists working with adults need only study the material environment with which individuals surround themselves to secure fresh insights into their relationships to objects, people, and ideas. The contrast between a meticulously kept mansion inhabited by an elderly couple and a small home filled with children, where marks of living are found everywhere, is one that needs no comment.

IDEAS OF ORDER

Through the doorway, into the hall, through the downstairs rooms, and up the stairs--this is the route of the visitor who is being "shown through" a house. At the end of the tour, and after viewing the rooms in succession, he is left with a sense of the prevailing atmosphere. The kinds of furniture, the arrangement of living space, the use of color--even to such details as bird cages or ashtrays--contribute toward the Geist created by its inhabitants, which is as characteristic of them as their names, their address, or their very fingerprints. Even when people move to a new house, the atmosphere that is based upon object arrangement and subdivision of space usually remains basically unchanged.

In the course of time, man accumulates a variety of things that threaten to clutter the home. He is faced with the problem of putting things together so that he may locate them when they are needed. The more objects accumulate, the more difficult is the maintenance of order, which in turn causes one person to leave a trail marked with debris and another to cover every trace. People have their preferred ways of storing: through piling, shelving, spreading, dumping, aligning, or through exposing or hiding. The storage of things need not, however, lead to stereotyping. Objects lend themselves to highly personal arrangement--even objects of everyday use. Thus the kinds of pots and pans, forks and ladles, and other kitchen utensils, and their placement around a stove, may perhaps indicate how the housewife feels about cooking. Similar considerations apply to the housing of such relatively uniform items as books. Since books may be used as reference works, tools of the trade, collector's items, for entertainment, or as a substitute for wallpaper, their arrangement may betray their owners as bookworms, casual readers, or merely decorators. (Ruesch and Kees, p. 135)

Such teaching moves straight toward us as keepers of the household called library.

Let us disabuse ourselves of the idea that a picture or any form of graphic art is instant communication, equal in content for all people at all times. It is a message built of symbols like a printed text. Extracting meaning (emotional or informational) from the text of a graphic involves the transmission of information or emotion to the human brain by means of symbols, as is required by printed words, and the symbols are not equally apparent or "coins of the realm" to all. All the letters or characters of alphabets of the languages that become printed texts are exact notations. When combined into words their exactness remains. Yes, over time, word meanings change, and words do sit in a matrix of connotations and denotations, but a word's immediate impact is specific. Webster's defines graphic as "of or pertaining to the arts of painting, drawing, engraving, or any other arts which pertain to the expression of ideas by means of lines, marks, or characters impressed on a surface."

Professor Gregory in The Intelligent Eye provides many examples which demonstrate that the mind sees things that in actuality do not exist. If we give ourselves up to be taught by Professor Gregory's facts and insights, we will never again use the verb "see" superficially.

The phenomenon of eye dominance is one common example of such unconsidered components of our visual mechanics. It can be demonstrated by the trick of determining your own dominant eye by making a circle of a thumb and forefinger and, holding the circle in front of you, sighting through it some object small enough to be contained within the ring of your two fingers. Then, holding hand and head motionless, close first one eye and then the other. The eye which still sees the object within the circle is your dominant eye. There is a pathology of dominance termed mixed dominance, where the lead eye does not remain consistently the same. This, undiagnosed, causes many so-called problem readers. The daughter of a friend was such a hapless victim. Always a poor reader, the problem stymied productive learning and "one of the best" schools sent her to a diagnostic reading center, whose prescriptions served only to continue classroom failure.

When she was in high school, being fitted for contact lenses, the ophthalmologist said casually to her mother, "Didn't Susie have reading problems? Children who have mixed dominance usually do." A book has its right side up to be read, a microform reader must be plugged in and working. Surely we should make equally certain that the human's equipment is functioning spatially and technically correctly, too. Researchers of perceptual-motor learning difficulties are a chorus ready for us to join.

The problems in using microfilm, microfiche, and a CRT screen should not be left out of a chapter on reading. These forms do demand a skill and a training beyond that of most people's ability to "read" words. Can you read microfilm or microfiche? Well, not handily if you suffer the visual handicaps of age or just poor eyesight or cannot concentrate while peering under a hood or into a glass darkly. Your ability to read may then be dependent upon whether you have a slipped disc or a stiff neck. To move from scanning the usual black type on a white ground to handling white letters on a black ground is a mental shift, intensified by the eyestrain inherent in the latter form. The differences in physical format between the pages, hand-turned, of a book or journal and the page arrangements on microfilm and microfiche, require learning a new conceptual arrangement, plus excellent hand-eye coordination, plus some base level of machine taming. More skills which we were not born possessing, which must be mastered on the road out of ignorance. As teaching librarians, Bibliographic Instructors, our task is to surface all the matrix of skills that each type of "reading" demands--and teach them--now.

All the world's words on "Reading for Librarians" can only fill a pool through which our minds may move. What will cling? Some spirits are impervious to alteration in environment; a filament of damp or tinge of sun are touches unfelt. Those more sensitive will acquire some drops of colored light to reflect still other images as they travel.

Within this pool, all of our human languages glide about us. The print on a restaurant menu, the script of a love letter; the map to Grandma's house and to Peary's Pole; the figures on our last bank statement, and our library's budget; a lover's gesture of refusal and the warmth of an infant rocked to sleep; the street sign to our boss's house, and the mercifully bilingual signs in Hong Kong; the Mona Lisa and our son's first drawing; our graduation picture or a snapshot from an army base in Germany. Such journeying is a sensate trip. Once our minds are blown by the drug of awareness of that reality which, seen, can never again be denied, only enlarged until our minds view every input to them as "reading." Each facet of the complexity of this multivariate skill will grow toward full consciousness. The full import of "to read," once grasped as a professional practitioner, will guarantee that this trip will never end.

If droplets from this pool cling to alter our concept of "reading" so as to make it encompass all such communications, we will be possessed of one major competency required for BI.

Then, when a fellow human being approaches the library Us with his version of the generic query, "I'd like something to read," our prescriptive response will demonstrate professional awareness of a human electric mystery. Marian can give lifelong learners an enhanced full measure, not short-change, and librarians will have joined Barbara Bush, the wife of the Vice President, on the team to defuse America's illiteracy bomb.

chapter 8
Materials as Method

*But still the heart doth need
a language,
Still doth the old instinct
bring back the old names.*
                    Coleridge

Not just "The Media," that beast that dwells in a dark, dark cave and comes out now and then to munch on Ye Traditional Values or demolish a career, and gets roundly jeered by everyone ... in the process. No, not that bogeyman. Not that, but MEDIA, which is harder to define.... "The media are everywhere...." "They are a spirit, a disembodied entity occupying no space and all space at the same time." Media are not so much part of the new environment as the new environment itself.... The biggest mistake educators make about television ... is fighting it instead of using it. Print is dying even as you read these words on this page. Some despair about this.... But these are redefining times.... Growing up in a post-literate environment, our children have received a vast store of information about the world ... without requiring the ability to read and write, a lack that would have condemned them to utter ignorance in a previous age. (Shales, p. 1, p. 15)

So writes Tom Shales in a Washington Post piece about Tony Schwartz which ends thusly, "When you step through his creaking door, you walk not into the future, but into a bedazzling, heightened present, and for a while, you may be under the lingering impression that these really are fascinating, privileged times in which to live."

In 1972 SLWTK described a school library as an Educational Media Center that listed in its color-banded card catalog the numerous carriers of knowledge termed media of education: "the book; the tape recording; the record; film, both silent and talking; filmloop; filmstrip, and filmstrip with its accompanying record; transparencies and, in the most affluent areas, videotape." And then added, "Today's teacher or educator scratches his chin and makes an individual decision as

Materials as Method

to which one of these carriers is the correct means for achieving his educational goal. The wave of technology crests. Ride or sink."

How should the topic "materials as method" be handled in this broader based edition? What has happened in the eleven years that have elapsed since <u>SLWTK</u> was published?

Reference Service, patron service, Bibliographic Instruction--these as semi-synonyms cover a lot of ground. To picture all types of persons who enter libraries and approach the human access point requires a wide angle lens and a flexible imagination. The one unifying factor is that all who come are active seekers. They arrive because they want something that they think or hope is available from a knowledge institution.

That such a want very often is for physical directions is not a cliché, but a truism. Just last week, one of the Reference Librarians at Georgetown University described how a decision to move the position of their desk stapler had restructured their weekly query report. Where am I? Where is the "it" that I seek? Birth begins this quest, with life itself the first problem to be solved. After that, except for basics of air, water, and food, paths diverge and problems vary until the other great universal, death, becomes personal.

That the biggest new "material" to become part of the Library/Information scene is the computer, is a truism also. Librarians have been talking computers since the 1950's, but 1972 ideas and 1983 reality can only be truly measured by such yardsticks as the hype of <u>Future Shock</u> or the reasoned reality of a De Gennaro. Their early use for circulation and cataloging soon added inter-library loan and acquisition, and now claims part of the reference scene as their territory as well as computer assisted Bibliographic Instruction.

So much for CLM as technical futurist! Yet, however accurate and prophetic are detailed state-of-the-art comments regarding today and computers in the reference process, the beyond-the-drawing board technology already far outruns such description. Therefore I repeat the stand that our success or failure as teachers/communicators of "Library" hinges not on technology but on the human component.

When we as professionals assume the role of teacher/ reference librarian and begin our part of the teacher-pupil dialogue or the reference interview, we must make use of some medium of instruction. The present emphasis on service to the handicapped is one current example of this. Serving on the Reference Desk at the DAR, and helping a deaf "roots" seeker to orient himself to that collection immersed me in the problems inherent in such a spontaneously written and amateurly-signed interview. Minority groups of all kinds require special media prescriptions. So do young children who may not be able to see over your desk and the elderly who have, at best, the bifocal bends.

Communicators known as the multi-media include all the sensory avenues to our minds, and when they are used in concert, reinforcing each other, they become a total larger than the sum of the parts--a media trip. The visual media available today bring the art of graphics to a larger-than-life reality and possibility. In living, moving color, plus animation and such montage distortions and juxtapositions as may seem necessary, the image awaits selection and switch-on. The oral communicators include the record and tape standbys, plus cassettes in all the particulars of a burgeoning technology.

Curriculum issues with their historical antecedents give us, I believe, a more interesting framework within which to describe the roles of the various carriers of knowledge that comprise the multimedia repertoire than would nonacademic how-do-I questions. The seeker, being taught day by day, is a current event. A teacher employs the record of the past as a starting point from which to transmit either fact or insight or awareness, to guide the learner into tomorrow's current event.

To illustrate this approach to the materials of instruction, let us picture ourselves as teachers in a chronology of schools. As an arithmetic teacher we enter a Babylonian library where the medium was the clay tablet. We would teach from sums and ciphers, and accompanying expository cuneiform text. The library helped us give antecedent material to educate our pupil--the current event in transition.

In a Phoenician school, seamanship was surely a curriculum item. The Phoenicians were great sailors and as precepts of sailing developed through experience, they were written down and stored in the library. As each new generation of sailors arose, they were sent to the library to learn from the vicarious experience extant in its records. These tablets bore words plus the hieroglyphs that we would now

Materials as Method   139

describe as graphics--line drawings of wind velocity in relation to sail.

We know that media held by early libraries were the written word and a primitive beginning graphic. The forms of these carriers of knowledge changed from the clay tablet to the papyrus roll to the vellum roll, to the first book form, which was a collection of sheets of vellum or wood, loosely tied together.

The Phoenicians, the first great sailors, carried their alphabet to the world. The Greeks and Romans further developed the alphabet they received. Change was gradual but continuous. This later teacher of arithmetic or seamanship seeking library support would have found a slowly enlarging body of knowledge on these subjects in a gradually changing format but always in the same printed medium--the written word in the alphabet of the period plus some line graphics.

With Gutenberg and the beginning of the technology of printing, the volume of library material expanded considerably. The number of libraries increased also. As a student from each of these periods of history sought the record of the past so that his education would not be purely a current event, he found a body of knowledge that enabled him to know a subject's history in order to provide a factual context for his personal learning. Each of us can locate our own time by our personal media events.

Until World War I there was nothing of any magnitude that could stand alongside the book as a different form. Books were marvelously illustrated, but the image was always an opaque graphic. The camera was developed in Europe in the middle of the 19th century and came to America soon thereafter. The work of the great Matthew Brady testifies to an established American photographic art form by the Civil War.

By then, in a library's holdings on seamanship, you would have found pictures as well as line drawings of the great ships and their related objects. The teaching of sailing aerodynamics would now be materially simplified with the help of the new graphic media. Nevertheless, the still picture was only a limited improvement in teaching this complex three-dimensional skill.

With the advent of the moving picture in the early

part of the 20th century, a major new medium arrived on the scene. By the early 1920's the talking picture became the first mechanical audio-visual medium. Regardless of what media the library holds, the original forms of the printed word and line drawings still serve quite well to teach arithmetic. However, seamanship with its dependenee on aerodynamics would find tremendous teaching value in the complex models and juxtapositions that movie film makes possible.

Today's Media Center should have a cornucopia of media for teaching and learning. There would be the items of sight, the items of sound, the items of feel, of form, of model--whatever we can imagine as useful to teach complex modern math: the abacus of the past, kits, Cuisinaire Rods, single concept film loops, transparencies, plus trade books and textbooks, and the computer--and what an "and" it is becoming. The special seeker, having mastered the historic record afforded by library organization, can carry his mathematical skill to any frontier of science chosen.

Seamanship could profitably use the entire multi-media range. The most expensive advanced technology would be of use in teaching its mechanics. On a sailboat equipped with video, its instant replay capacities could provide continuous feedback to the student struggling with tiller and sheet and movie projectors on board could make another angle of sail and boat visible to the student sailor. These media of motion and mirrored replay become valued aids in teaching this complex skill, if they don't overturn the boat.

Our task as library educators is to choose from this array of teaching aids the one which best serves the immediate teachable moment. There are two general ways of looking at these media as specific tools for precise teaching tasks. One of these generalities is related to the argument that there are two fundamental languages, two fundamental sets of symbols; one of mathematical ciphers, and one of letters and words--the language which enables man to speak and read. If the student with whom we are working cannot understand one language, then we must not use that language; we must use another. Until the young child has mastered simple Arabic numbers, there is no point in introducing Roman ones in any medium. Also, if a person cannot read, there is no point in presenting him with a page of print other than to teach him to read. A nonreader, a functional illiterate, cannot, by definition, glean anything from a page of unintelligible symbols. Those who lack reading skills must be presented with a set of symbols that they are able to comprehend.

Materials as Method

The second generalization relates to the fact, opinion, value judgment pyramid. If a learner is desirous of obtaining a simple fact, such as the birth date of an author, or the height of the Empire State Building, and can read, the simplest way to obtain that information is from a book. If we are teaching a Navajo Indian, who reads well but who has never been beyond the reservation, graphic material added to his fact of the height of the Empire State Building would materially enlarge his area of comprehension. By this means we would add to the simple facts of height expressed in number of feet the dimensional and spatial relationships of a skyscraper. A color film that would show the interrelationship of the building's height to the ground and to other buildings would be the best such graphic. If there were a film clip available of that horrible night of July 28, 1945, when an army B-25 bomber crashed into the Empire State Building, this might give a student who has lived with the forces of nature, as a reservation Indian has, a real feeling of what it is like to live in a cloud-enveloped skyscraper that was, on one tragic, stormy night, in the path of an airplane.

Perhaps a person who seeks factual assistance is a rural illiterate adult who comes for job counseling. He inquires about a job in a factory that is housed in a high-rise building. It would be a tremendous help for the library's employment guidance collection to have a short film clip of the inside and outside of a skyscraper to give the person an idea of how it would feel to be working in something that is taller by far than his village church spire, in contrast to what he has previously experienced, living close to the earth.

To the question, "What was it like to be a child in ancient Greece?" asked by a fifth-grade student who reads extremely well, what shall our media response be? Living in any particular place, at any particular time, is clearly a multimedia experience for anyone with normal sensory perception. Give the student some of Olivia Coolidge's excellent books on Greek life. Here are fictional characters which afford an imaginative depth that the recorded facts alone cannot supply--opinions and value judgments. A map of the ancient Greek world will furnish the geographic base for studying travel and natural barriers. Excellent art books like the National Geographic's Everyday Life in Ancient Times offer accurate recreations of domestic scenes and help fill out the canvas. Recorded music played on actual historic instruments is available to add the dimension of valid sound to help authenticate a new experience. A factually accurate, technicolor sound film made from a Coolidge book would provide one ultimate vicarious experiential answer to such a query.

If the seeker were a semi-reader, the visual and the oral media would be the main knowledge carriers. The whole idea of matching the medium to the capabilities of the questioner as well as to the information sought produces a complex challenge for floor work. We must hear the person behind the query in order not to be as irrevelant as was the mother whose young son came home and asked, "Where did I come from?" After she had explained in great detail about the birth of a baby, the boy said, "Yes, but Joe said he came from Chicago."

To explore further, let us analyze this reference query: "I am doing a term paper that will be a study of John F. Kennedy, and I want to have a way of checking his speeches against the charisma of his personality so as to have some idea of his intellectual soundness and its relationship to the Kennedy myth." This seeker appears to read very well. Therefore we can draw from the complete range of print and nonprint. We should tell him that JFK's Senatorial speeches are printed in the <u>Congressional Record</u> which provides a complete text. Once the learner finds a manageable area to isolate to sharpen his point, we can help him locate some old film clips of JFK delivering a speech for which the complete text can be located. He can judge the effect of the words alone and then be able to add to the verbal impact the dimension of this magnetic personality in action. This exercise then becomes a multimedia report.

A Peanuts-reading second-grader, curious at Hallowe'en, asks, "What is the Great Pumpkin?" We might offer some stories about giants and help him look up their history in the encyclopedias of folklore and mythology. If we could pull out of our multimedia bag a film that would show in moving graphics the interrelationships of size and power which is part of what Schultz is talking about, we would have provided for that youngster much that a library could offer to help him ponder the reality of Great Pumpkins. More than a collection of facts, a giant spirit is an idea from the collective racial unconscious--an opinionated value judgment!

A humorous vignette that demonstrates some of the problems of our multimedia world involved an incident with

Materials as Method 143

high school students who were designing scenery. They had a large map of the Land of Oz laid out on the hall floor. It was an accurate map, except for the colors. I inquired "What about the colors? Have you got them right?" As if I were a particular breed of adult insanity, he said, "What colors and what's right?" And I said, "Well, the Munchkin country is purple, and the Quadling country is red. Haven't you read the book?" And he looked at me and he said, "No. I saw it on television and it was in black and white," and continued producing his own Oz reality.

Another way of considering multimedia learning is to take an elemental idea such as water and examine what is involved in teaching it to differing people with varying levels of literacy skills. The most dramatic learning example I have seen is in the play Miracle Worker, when Helen Keller's teacher, Anne Sullivan, finally makes the connection between word and idea in Helen's mind. Standing at the pump, the teacher pours the water into one of Helen's hands while she taps out the sign for water in the palm of her other hand. Miss Sullivan was using two media: the language of the deaf and the rushing water itself. Once Helen had grasped this concept of the connection between something tapped in her palm and some substance she could feel, the foundation was available on which to build words and relate them to thoughts. We can make a visual presentation to a person who cannot read but at the same time that the visual presentation is made, another medium must be employed to embed the symbols of cognition in the person's consciousness for relationship and recall. This need for communication symbols must be one of the central concerns of media use.

From their earliest infancy, most human beings have an experience of water. For the Rio de Janeiro slum dweller, one experience of water is what a mother can carry 500 feet up the slope from the public tap at the bottom of the hill on which his shack is perched. People in rural western America, where water is in short supply, could also relate to it as a limited, precious object. For the rest of America, tap water is one of the public utilities: water for utilitarian purposes, drinking, cooking, and bathing. We pay for it as part of our rent or with a manageable fee.

It is not difficult to lead a person who has experienced water as a living substance into the world of water as a fact to be studied about. If these are readers, a book seems the correct carrier. Print can adequately communicate that water has many properties which, the reader having experienced water held in a bowl or a stream, can be taught as facts. Water through heat can be turned into steam. Water freezes. Water when it freezes becomes larger rather than smaller. The complex idea which is held in the word "lake" would not exist at all were it not for the simple fact of the freezing properties of water. If water froze from the bottom up, a lake could not exist, since it would never thaw and no marine life could survive at its bottom depths. Once aware of water, such facts can be taught to readers by the linear medium or to non-readers by the spoken word and diagrams.

The facts about fresh and salt water could be presented by a simple realia demonstration of two glasses of tap water. Have the student add salt to one and drink from both. The New York resident could be expected to comprehend that tides move up the Hudson River to tidewater and, coming from the ocean, are salt water. Understanding of the entity salt water vs. fresh can develop this way. At best, it comes when you can lie on the prow of a small boat and experience the special qualities of salt water as spray coming to your face and contrast this with memories of fresh water face splashings at the washbasin at home. Next to such direct reality, a colored moving picture can afford anyone the greatest measure of meaning.

A Manhattanite seeing the Hudson River can understand the idea of river as a floating, murky, entity on which boats float and into which garbage is thrown and over which bridges cross. To teach about the pristine river that the Dutch settlers found, to anyone who had never experienced a large mass of clean water, would require a moving visual for such an environmental history lesson. A colored motion picture could communicate this, or the tactile reality of a pool or fountain where we might say, 'This is clean, fresh water (rising above minor pollution like chlorine) that the river was like when the early settlers came. "

To teach water safety measures to anyone going to camp for the first time could be a difficult assignment. A person who has not even been in a bathtub big enough for him to slip and find his nose under water would have a hard time comprehending the meaning of drowning. This feeling requires experience that water is an all-encompassing, all-pervading fluid and will enter any doorway that is open for it--canals or irrigation ditches or noses. The awareness of water as a larger substance from which elementally we come, having spent the first nine months of our unborn existence in the embryonic fluid of our mother's womb, is difficult to present in any other way but by immersion.

A very complex idea of water is a glacial stream which has exactly the same properties of flow as any other stream. With all these factual and either vicarious or direct experiences of water to be built upon, it is quite possible to hear, "Now, there is a glacial stream," and be able to respond, "Yes, of course," and then describe it in detail. I speak as one who was taught for over 32 years by an in-house engineer-meteorologist-geologist-hydrologist-ecologist. But for the person who has only the experience of water in the glass or the coffeepot, to thus understand and visualize requires our best bag of media helpers.

Beyond the factual capabilities of the library's collections lie vast sensual servants able to provide librarians with the materials to hasten the development of mental awareness and insight in the learners whom they serve. Awareness can be defined as the existential ability to exercise total sensory perception in each moment of human beingness--to see, to hear, and to transmute these sense data into our own moment of reality. The sensory options afforded to the library by nonprint media add vastly to the library's abilities to provide meaningful vicarious awareness. To use a book as a path to vicarious experience, one must have the ability to read. Imagination takes over from the ideas that the book offers to the human mind to create the pictures that feed our visual awareness. It may be, when more neurological facts are in, that reading burns some kinds of input into the brain more deeply than any other medium because of the significant imagination requirement. Mental pictures can be described as the furniture of the mind. They are continuously built.

When I was seven and going to California for the first time, I'd just read Heidi and the image of the Alp-grandfather's house on a mountain top was very bothersome to me. Was the mountain pointed? If so, the house would teeter on the top. If the mountain was to accommodate the flat bottom of the house, it must be flat itself--which did not sound very top-ish to me.

If I had asked an experienced adult, I might have been given these additional verbal images--the house nestles on the mound of the mountain, or it rests on a foundation built into the side of the mountain; but I just boarded the train and pondered. My California uncle was puzzled by the urgency of my request to "go to the mountains where the houses are."

As the road wound up the Hollywood Hills, I saw the reality of how houses and mountains live together and how this climaxes in "the house on the top"--the one at this top was owned by Rudolph Valentino. Once seen with the eye, the house on the top of the mountain became a comprehensible spatial interrelationship. From this experience it was easy to go back to words again and continue to build this mental furniture. But without the seeing, the visual experience, it is vastly harder to develop that still neurological mystery-- the well-furnished mind.

With media to add the visual dimension of space in physical relationships--what the house on the top of the mountain is--we can offer to someone reading Heidi a film or a filmstrip to illustrate this new geography until it is grasped. If we want to expand from this to the idea of what it would be like to look down upon the Alp-Grandfather's house, we could use a film loop of a bird in flight with a recorded poetic description, or a film of Swiss or California mountains taken from an airplane. This way dimensions in space become quickly comprehensible. To transmit the spatial awareness of the meeting line between architecture and nature to a city person, one could describe how it is to lie underneath a Christmas tree or roost above a tree in a cloud, or inhabit a tree house, and then call upon the media to help you. As a teaching/learning medium the method of the computer is highly structured. Though the for-profit speaker at the LIRT Program, ALA, 1982 amazed many by her negative response to a question from the audience, computer access is chiefly through keyboard typing. Hype can say "touch," but from manual to electric to electronic, a key requires typing skill. Program language is rigidly precise. Miss a dot or misspell a word and you will read such as "syntax error." During one rather grim, late-afternoon class practice session I was asked to "logoff and restructure your request" after repeated replies of its euphemism for "you dunce!" On a monitor or CRT, the dot matrix causes reading problems for even the bifocal level of visual handicap. The line limitation of 40 characters on the monitor and 80 on the terminal printer produces some startling word breaks such as whic-h and goin-g. As a medium of instruction and information access, the computer is rewarding and demanding.

The new technologies are valuable aids if those who select, purchase, and process--who recommend and dispense them--ask themselves the right questions. The questions were there, even for the Babylonian teacher of sums or the

Phoenician teacher of prospective sailing captains. The number of questions and answers is what is different, and this is in direct proportion to the wide range of learning abilities and disabilities in each new heterogeneous reader we advise or knowledge-seeker we must show how-to. The case by case model we must answer is multi-faceted indeed. Twenty-five years ago--and today--the necessary problem-solving facts vary in number and complexity as do those needed to create a one-thonged sandal vary in relation to those for a tight fitting, thigh-high boot. But any ill-fitting information is painful.

Right now I worry that our library shelves resemble a shoe store in a Hobbit district whose stock was selected for Icelandic giants. Our wares are great and potentially saleable--but suitability and fit must be demonstrated first.

Today's library customer is a new breed. Yes, of course, those readers that go with Marian the Librarian still belly up to the check-out desk. Humanistic you and I are here to validate their existance. In our schools are students whose chief curriculum is TV. Their long attention span is captured by the visual high excitement of video games. Their poor verbal skills don't fuel enough of an attention span to comfortably master the detailed, static black and white web that is the print route to knowledge.

Formal learners who go beyond the grades to a college or university possess a reasonable level of verbal skills and some motivation to use them. These who comprise the current base of the pyramid called academe are the chief customers for true library reference skills. For their Bachelor's to Doctor's study they need and must master at least some part of the blazed scholarly trail. Not publish or perish, but term paper and thesis, or else!

For all others, "information" needs are seen to demand other materials and methods. The problems of daily living require people-to-people skills--the telephone network, current data barely older than last month's magazine or yesterday's paper. Annuals or periodicals--Encyclopedia of Associations, Government Organization Manual, Literary Marketplace, Consumer Reports--do offer check points on a job hunt or other specific practical problem-solving search to those who enter library doors. But--and this is a huge but-- my current experience with the beyond-school anybody says that the materials they seek may be well suited to TV screen format. Without library literacy they seek not knowledge but

but information, not to master facts but to access a database--bibliographic or full text!

Our BI task is to demonstrate how the process symbolized by the fact-opinion-value judgment pyramid turns data through information to knowledge and how that process is necessary to ensure that the problem achieves a valid resolution. Once the knowledge access process is internalized, library literacy can be understood as applying to all problem-solving needs--scholarly and day-to-day pragmatic.

A paradox operating here lies in the relationship between the naive lay connotation of database access as a simple, unstructured query and the denotive reality, which is that on-line searching demands absolute user compliance with a rigidly structured path. To those of us in D.C., acquaintance with the Scorpio and related in-house databases at LC demonstrates the high hurdles to such searching in spite of all the very user-friendly on-line and print tutorials. Getting there from here is light years faster for those who make it, but at least equally demanding of the skills of critical thinking. Information high-tech does not in any way eliminate the need for library literacy.

The motivated queries of our customers/patrons/students/seekers are as varied as is the technology now at our disposal. They are as different, and as clearly identifiable. But I don't believe that valid knowledge needs change in proportion to the high and higher tech being produced to serve the information market. Materials are always and only a method. Media comes high tech and low tech, and even though a beautiful woman, gowned in rustling taffeta, trailing a perfumed wake, uttering seductive syllables, is a low tech multi-media male dream, it may not be the material for every guy's method.

Chapter 9
Our Ears as Channels of Information

It takes two to speak the truth
One to speak, another to hear.
                              Thoreau

Before beginning to discuss the two main media categories, let me scotch an assumption that, to me, is fraudulent enough to be ridiculous. This postulate says that any human being, educated enough to qualify as a professional librarian, once exposed to in-service training in handling media, becomes immediately able to master these contemporary collections of bolts, nuts, screws, wires, chips, and telephone connections.

All professions have their blind spots, jargon and accepted mythology. Educators, however, have played these unusually close to the chest. The primary fact that there are two kinds of intelligence, verbal and non-verbal, would seem to me, as something of a maverick, to be the first thing that educators would point out to parents. Actually it is as hidden as a woman's age. Were this assumption to be brought out into the open, even in the educational community itself, it would make the balky bronco of technology much easier for some of us to manage.

If I may be permitted the personal example of a shaky non-verbal I.Q., once, long ago, I determined to learn to use a tape recorder in order to bring home our office machine and listen to a tape of a workshop speech.

I was duly checked out by our master in-service educator. At the end of the day I carted the tape recorder home and sat down to open it. The tape recorder had, unfortunately, been open when my lesson began. I pushed and I pulled, to no avail. The fact that I had thought I was on top of the interior mechanism was of no value. Back to the office, back to the expert. "Push the lock," he informed me, "then if it doesn't open, whack her one." So, duly taught, I accomplished the trick. I whacked her one and she opened. With the shell open and the pearl before me, I was ready. I plugged in the microphone, made sure that the tape was successfully threaded, and then got the electric cord and inched my way across the floor to the wall outlet. I looked at the outlet and I looked at the plug. The wall outlet had two holes and the recorder cord had three prongs. By the time I had been told that if I had just been bright, I could have located a domestic appliance with a three-pronged outlet and carried the tape recorder out to the washing machine, I'd lost interest in the project, and moved on to another role where one only gave advice and didn't have to actually do anything about the media oneself. Having, I hope, made this point, a discussion on the media of sound can commence.

The tape recorder is one of the simpler and more tractable pieces of hardware. Let us define the tape as a recording of the human voice and not as a recording of music alone. Let us consider first the merits of a professional tape as comprising a part of the educational library.

In one of his books, Bishop Fulton Sheen made this point about the steps involved in getting to know another human being. First we hear about a person, good old John Smith, a fine fellow, a great doctor, a great fisherman--whatever, and then we go to a party at which this man is to be a guest. Across the room we may catch a glimpse of good old John Smith deep in conversation with a comrade and a mutual friend says, "Ah, this is the moment for you to meet him." So, the two of you walk across the room and come within sound of John Smith's voice. Then you move closer and the voice is addressed to you, "Yes, I am happy to know you," and he will put out his hand and touch yours. Hearing about, seeing, hearing, and then touching are a series of progressively more revealing personal communications. This is complete social communication. You have known about him, you have heard his voice, and you have seen and touched his person.

Today, in our slap-on-the-back, cocktail-party kind of world, we don't often think of some of the old taboos and magic that concern the possession of another person's name. The fact that these things form an important part of religion and legend should make us pause and consider our familiarity in treating a fellow human being to instant first-name status. This idea seems relevant to a consideration of the medium of disembodied verbiage. The totality of the physical human person is a much more complete communicator than the person's voice alone.

Reputation precedes a person and can be obtained from mutual friends or biographical reference sources, but each of us uses that factual background only as a base on which to build our own personal opinion. Dress, cut of hair, openness of countenance, firmness of handshake--all fill in our estimate of who this human being actually is. But a depersonalized human with just a voice and a reputation--not even the amount of body of the Cheshire cat-- is thin representation indeed.

Most informative speakers average 100 words per minute, while the average listener's thought speed is about 400 words per minute. Compare these figures to those for an average reading speed--300 words per minute--and for a maximum reading speed--900 words per minute. Quite a difference. But if John Smith and you are working on actually the same problem, and if it is vital that you get his most recent thought as quickly as possible, it may be worth your time to spend this additional percentage of it in order to hear his taped words recently delivered rather than wait until this speech is available in print.

In a large system where high-priced consultants are brought in often, it would seem that a tape library would be of considerable worth. The merit, I think, depends on two factors: the quality of the speaker, and adequate, complete, and quick cataloging. This means the raw tape can be listened to at once by a capable professional in the specialty of the speaker, who can edit it and ensure a concise copy. This person could do the annotating so that the tape isn't an unknown lecture by good old whomever, as is so often the case.

With the tape quickly at hand, someone who feels that a speech was of major impact can then recommend it to his colleague. The colleague, going to the library, can hear the new good word before this particular version disappears. into the general intellectual grab bag that is present in any large institutional system.

It would seem reasonable that such tapes should be kept for no more than one year or two at the most. If the consultant is of any stature, his words get into print first as a speech, then as an article, and then as a section of a book. As an example, let me offer this publishing history. Some words of Luna Leopold's were first a speech presented before a meeting held by the Northeastern States Resources Council, in January of 1958. This speech was subsequently printed three different times: in the National Parks Magazine of

April-June under the title of "Gacho and the Flower Bed"; in Forest Notes of Spring 1958; and in the Geological Survey Circular 414-A of 1960 under its speech title of "Conservation and Protection." When you consider the relative rate of absorption between listening to the spoken word and reading, we might best spend our time whenever possible upon the written words rather than upon disembodied speech.

The suggestion was once made to me that libraries of professional tapes, available on a subscription basis with the necessary hardware, be made available in the professional library in cassette form. The plan was that our teachers driving in their cars could listen to the wisdom of good old whomever. I did--and still would--declare that this would be more than dangerous to the life and limb of the teacher trying to unravel educationese in traffic. We do listen to the radio, true, but not to follow a reasoned argument as attentively as we would expect to after the fuss and bother of procuring the tape and hardware for our front-seat theatre. To me the suggestion seemed an ultimate technological folly.

What of the students for whom the dial-access tape bank is designed? The premise is that the student, having missed a class, is eager to hear the lecture and so make up the work missed. If he has such motivation, merely pushing the right combination of digits will bring to his ear the teacher's classroom presentation.

The justification for this is based on a fallacy: that the disembodied voice of the ordinary teacher is adequate to hold the interest of even the student motivated enough to search out the tape. Experience in the educational world should have taught us that the average teacher, live in the classroom, can, at best, be tolerated by his students. When the same level of mediocre performance is put on the depersonalized plane of any canned medium, it is usually below the level that will sustain pupil interest.

Other drawbacks appear when the pupil uses the tape to hear a formal presentation. For the verbal student, whose ability to read is up to grade, we have the same drawback that we had with adults. By using his ears, rather than his eyes, he is increasing immeasurably the amount of time necessary in which to absorb information. He also is using a technology where it is more difficult to play back a word or a phrase to put pieces of an argument together than it is with the medium of the book.

When the presentation on tape is of dramatic impact, such as the "You Are There" living-history series, the situation is quite different. Churchill and Roosevelt were masters in the dramatic immediacy of the situation. These recorded words of World War II still bring tears to my eyes. This, of course, may only be because I lived through those years and know those voices. It may be that even this incorporeal theatre has little impact upon a person who is not re-creating experience or who has little background to build upon.

Tape as a medium for pupil production presents quite a different picture. Work with something creative generates feelings of self-confidence that vastly increase one's own awareness. Preparing tape to accompany film strips, taping background noise for a program, recording a class presentation--all of this is actual experience, and provides learning experiences far beyond pushing a button to activate a teacher-prepared tape. However, to me, the spoken tape as an important means for transmitting information to the person who reads well still remains seriously open to question. As a means of getting to know a person, the medium of tape, like radio, is very thin soup. Ample knowledge about the speaker, including his education and accomplishments, furnishes the next thickening agent. Only sight and sound, preferably in the flesh, put real bones in the media brew.

For a non-verbal person the value is obviously much greater. For a person who has yet to learn to read or is unable to read at a useful level, the spoken word and the graphic are open channels for information. However, this non-verbal person--unable to read--is very often, for the very reasons that make him unable to read, one who has the maximum need to feel the impact of a total human personality, not the disembodied voice alone, in a learning situation. It is the one suffering psychic unhappiness who has most need for any positive human relationships. The person who needs most of all to know "I'm okay" often comes to us in the guise of a reading problem. Such feelings of okayness develop through interpersonal relations. This seeker with low academic motivation may enjoy fiddling with the technology, if he doesn't wreck it first, but that is a far cry from getting enough content from the software to justify the technology.

Video tape has a larger interactive human impact than the purely oral tape. But, surely, there is adequate research data to indicate that television in any form does not develop language or motivation. This latter concept was given words and professional substance for me when Lovisa Tatnall, then a senior staff psychiatrist at Washington's Children's Hospital, said "No child has ever tried to please a television set."

The education of society's functional illiterate, however, does offer valid opportunities for tape. These people can have very high motivation. Their need is to absorb the factual matter requisite for either employment advancement or a general ability to handle the complexities of society. These disenfranchised Americans use what written words they have mastered as an international traveler uses the picture language of international airports and highways and water faucets. They memorize EXIT as a pictograph.

Ponder for a moment how your relative social position would change if you couldn't even read the words, let alone the connotation of "if all else fails--follow directions!"

In selecting materials for such a person, we must consider the type of voice and level of language as well as the method of presentation. The child from an illiterate home who uses "I ain't" to a teacher who doesn't, recognizes such as communication. One can sympathize with the hardheaded teacher. To her "I ain't" isn't language. A librarian friend who moved to Washington's racially and economically mixed Capitol Hill neighborhood has been learning a new language as she tries to work with two black brothers from her block. Not only are there new words to define, but familiar words, unfamiliarly pronounced, are a language barrier, too, because children who can't read can't be asked to spell such words for her.

A sensitive human speaker can tailor his language to his visible audience. We all have such ranges of verbal expression, but does the canned teacher need to prepare a tape in every speech variant that could be required by any classroom in America? This will necessitate an infinity of editions. Cultural differences are expressed in language level and inflection, and the ghetto already has too solid a Berlin wall. The tape must ensure that the listener will be comfortable with the vocal carrier if we are to hope for profit from the information presented.

For the blind, ears and fingers are the channels of communication. Some blind students have difficulty with Braille. So, for them, and for those with degrees and kinds of visual impairments such as dyslexia, taped books become a crucial path to knowledge. Henry Mitchell in one of his "Any Day" Washington Post columns describes the activities at Recording for the Blind, Incorporated, a volunteer outfit in D.C. Many technical books are not available in Braille and only someone knowledgeable in the subject of the book that has been requested can give the correct inflections, phrasing and pronunciation needed to create a substance intelligible to the listener. Such taping is a two-person team effort--one reading and other monitoring--which may produce ten pages an hour. Mitchell comments:

> It wouldn't be so bad if all the blind students wanted "Don Quixote" or "The Frogs," or "archy and mehitabel." If that's what they wanted, you could spend your hours reading to them on tape, confident that you were holding the torch of majesty, as it were, and passing it to dark kingdoms. But it is hard to be noble when you're reading for them about gastroenterology, old age pension schemes, phonetic alphabets.... This work, clearly, shows the bonds of community in America, which still keep us a society of humans, not a herd of beasts. (Mitchell, p. 1, p. 3)

Records have been a medium of instruction since Edison applied for a patent for a "phonograph or speaking machine" in 1877. In the 1920's and 1930's, the public schools had a limited number of phonographs in use for purposes of instruction, but not until the fifties were phonograph records widely adopted. In the elementary school, the principal use was for music appreciation. In the secondary school it was for literature, social studies and physical education. Magnetic tape recorders were introduced in the late forties and furnished the first practical recording technology for classroom use, offering the benefits of immediate playback and a reusable tape. With the advent of radio, recorded and live music could be transmitted directly into the classroom. The earliest broadcast talks were in Los Angeles, California in 1923, on the geography and history of that state.

The spoken word on records, used to provide supplemental aural experience, multiplies teaching possibilities. The correct pronunciation of old and middle English would add authenticity to the study of etymology, yet few teachers are able to produce such language themselves. Such a disembodied vocal ancestor would be a valid learning supplement.

For any vocal presentation which the teacher herself is unable to produce, the tape or record furnishes a vital assist to the teaching situation. Sounds like the river for <u>Little Toot</u>, or the clop of horses' hooves for "The Highwayman," or the lawn mower, airplane, and elevated train for a lesson in noise pollution add an important dimension of authenticity to the classroom.

The language laboratory with its tape banks helped change America's modern language instruction. Once the teaching emphasis moved to the spoken language, the properties of the tape for reinforcement through imitation and feedback became a valuable instructional material. The hardware of dial access, when it works, is only an expensive simplification of the tape recorder. Now our cultural anguish bemoans the roller-coaster decline in any K-college foreign language learning. Surrounded by the current wave of immigrants, America again demonstrates the inability of technology to solve a problem that people don't view as a problem.

For the pre-school child, records are a source of much satisfaction and learning. The content usually is music or literature, not a presentation of factual information. A fondness for melody and poetry seems to be part of the equipment with which everyone enters the world. My own daughter at two would sit on the studio couch absorbing her favorite record and banging her head in rhythm against the bolsters. The rhythms of poetry charm a child as does the song and story combination. There are myriad ways to use these to please. The dramatic vocal presenation is invaluable for a teacher who has difficulty telling her own stories or wants another kind of voice to pull her learners into the circle of the story. In individualized instruction the canned story clearly comes into its own. For the able early reader the written word alone is an adequate ticket to the world of literature.

For the functional illiterate the picture is completely changed. Literature of the imagination is a structuring of man's experience toward meaning and insight, and, for spiritual growth, these people must have access to a medium that can provide these growth experiences without the intermediary of print.

Because of the circle of communication between artist and audience by which the tale is continuously cut to fit, storytelling is the best vehicle for stories--regardless of the age of the audience. In the person of the storyteller the listener has access to informative media beyond the verbal. Think about a Will Rogers, W. C. Fields or Mark Twain and visualize, if you've ever seen them impersonated, how much the pictorial carryover adds to print as you read the words of any one of them. Human personality can sustain material that would never survive in print. The mechanical medium carrying an artist's vocal performance is a poor, but sometimes necessary, second best to a live storyteller. For all inadequate readers with high motivation, the mechanized oral presentation is a successful instructional material.

The dramatic presentation in recorded form is a godsend for the shut-in, for the blind, and, I've discovered, for the seamstress and housewife. Most of the housewife's time is used in what could be called scut work, leaving the mind available for better input than radio routinely affords. So, for these special needs of women I recommend procuring recordings of great theatre, poetry and stories, and enriching the mind while sewing a fine seam, or dusting, or cooking. That surely is a form of liberation.

The immediacy of production, and the instant reply capabilities of tape, make it comparable to the Polaroid Land camera. We find important satisfaction in executing our own tapes. Personal happenings can be reproduced this way.

Sensitivity training is a specialized happening. What did happen is an important thing to be demonstrated at such a session. John "heard" it this way but Jane "heard" it that way. Where is fact? Perhaps few of us feel competent to undertake such a demonstration but it is a viable potential of tape. Instant replay of an unaltered tape brings a core of proof to anyone willing to face himself, and by insight alter his view of subjective reality.

Tape as a tool allows us to raise and discuss the questions that should be asked about the taped excerpts used in radio and TV. Chief Justice Burger once hit the headlines by refusing to have his public speeches taped, forcefully enumerating the misuses of such tapes.

In a small way, the tape recorder can demonstrate the qualities necessary for an accurate recording of a current event. "This is what happens." Take, for example, the reporting of violence in America. America is an aggressive, violent nation. Violence surfaces from quarrels. Well, what is a quarrel? If part of the class were assigned to demonstrate this as director and technical crew, they could hide a microphone in the classroom, and, selecting a provocation and provocateur, a minor or major quarrel could be sparked, recorded, then stopped before it reached proportions beyond the project's scope. Handled so that the participants would not feel naked and cheated in front of the class, the quarrel could be instantly played back to the group. Where there already is compassion in the classroom there is no better means for people to begin to hear themselves and to develop Reik's "third ear" with which to walk in another's moccasins.

The tape could be the ultimate "show and tell." If there were enough tape recorders to permit overnight loans from the Media Center, the classroom speech or special recitation could be taped and taken home by the pupil. "Look, Mom and Dad, this is what I did and, now listen, and you can hear me." This tape can come back and be erased and go on to John's or Jane's speech, to serve as an immediate solid token to connect home and school in a pleasurable context. On the tape could be the teacher's introduction and the class' applause as a wonderful way of the learner's being able to share with family that so necessary, "Look, I'm in class, I'm there, the teacher is with me and I'm okay."

Noises of the world outside the classroom could be taped for a curriculum unit on noise pollution or local color. Noise is an immediate pollutant, which fortunately does not accumulate in the atmosphere and persist. Once, sitting on a Wyoming dude ranch porch, I noted these various sources of sound. Across from my cabin was the barn, where the sound of sawing was made by a handsaw like the one Geppetto might have used for Pinocchio. At intervals in the noise of sawing, from the position of three o'clock, came the squirt of a lawn sprinkler. From about 9 o'clock came the sounds of the ranch house, about 300 feet away--the screen door and the icebox door being closed. A very small noise from under the plank porch was made by a ground squirrel scurrying out at ground level, shut out by the thud of the passing cowhand's horse, and overall there was the sound of birds. Part of the environment called "ranch" is its unique sound track. A tape of that moment could add a meaningful dimension of place to a literature or social studies class on western America.

Recording the noises of home and classroom offers varied possibilities in such a study of environmental noise. If a tape recorder can be taken home, the learner has the advantage of using his own technological know-how to record what he hears and what Mother/mate hears, and what each of you hears the other doing that is annoying. Again, insight and awareness, as well as information, can come from the immediate feedback of this medium.

Technology enables a person to walk the sidewalk, wearing an earphone radio--a Walkman. What more complete way to be cut off and dehumanized than to be surrounded with a personal piped-in atmosphere in the midst of a crowd! Electronic music also creates an atmosphere that can serve to separate people, and generations. As someone remarked after a rock party before my daughter's wedding, "Yes, the music was great, if you wanted to come and not have to talk."

"If the love fits, put it on" paraphrased could be this BI banner: "If the query comes at you, the answer will fit." A winter of Jazzercise has taught me that music rightness motivates muscles. Confronted with a not-my-kind-of-musical beat, there is a non-fit which creates a block to motion that instantly changes to an inner energy when "Hello Dolly" sounds.

Because of our ever more complex, fascinating, and accessible gadgetry, the danger today seems to be that the medium of canned music will become such a pervasive part of the human environment that it will cease to have any meaning at all. Consider the supermarkets where blandly structured over-30 dance and show tunes never intrude upon the shopper's mind but provide a womb of happiness in which to go on forever choosing--and spending.

Two places into which recorded music has managed to ooze, that most upset me, are elevators and the private booths banks provide for solitary commune with one's safe deposit box. Somehow, when I'm alone in the elevator, out comes the urge to act out my impulse, and I reject the recorded music that seldom matches my own dance step. The safe deposit box was the ultimate in the privacy of a Midas-and-his-gold-mood, until some progressive banker insinuated music to match his interiors and robbed me of my right to broody silence--or to my own hum.

Before further invitation to music to enter the learning

environment, let us carefully examine our goals. Traditionally, live music, supplemented with records, has been used as a performing art in music-appreciation courses, in assemblies and opening-day exercises. Areas for meaningful expansion seem to be where music is an integral part of the subject or atmosphere one is trying to present. Let's consider some curriculum roles for music.

Music, by adding one more facet to the emotional climate of a country, can be an important part of instruction in the social sciences, particularly in the elementary grades where the emphasis is on teaching "how it is" by using a detailed cultural basis for geography. For an example, take the concept of national pride.

In many large cities there is a group called the St. Andrews Society, people of Scottish descent who band together to continue some customs of their ancestral land, such as the annual kirking of the tartan. To Scotsmen, plaid is a "length" of their tartan, a fabric of the design that the world calls a plaid, which they wear over their shoulders pinned with a great brooch of silver and cairngorn stone. These tartans, each representing a clan, are carried into Washington Cathedral, to the accompaniment of a marching band of bagpipe and drum. All the men who participate wear the full Scottish highland costume of black pumps with silver buckles, tartan hose, kilt, ruffled blouse, and velvet waistcoat; the plaid worn over their shoulders and their tartan bonnet top it off. To the uninitiated American, this whole scene--visual and audio-- is quite foreign. Modern attire notwithstanding, a grown man in a short skirt is still a jarring note. Jarring is a minor, minor, minor word for the effect that a full Scottish marching band with drum and bagpipe brings to novice ears, especially indoors. At the time I was present at this ceremony, I was among the initiated. I had been to Scotland and fallen in love with the music, pageantry, and vitality of the Scots. Once you surrender to the bagpipe in its native element, your thralldom includes all Scotland as well.

As I stood in the front pew of the Cathedral's Great Choir with the organ and the choir of men and boys that joined the marching band to create a mighty tumult, all of this intense sound and sight suddenly rendered the idea, "pride," incarnate before me. Certainly, Scotland has managed through the years to lose most of her battles, but the fearsome pride of every man there before me was still the dominant chord. In the old country, too, there still exists a race of men who are kind and concerned for the traveler, yet still possess their own souls, in contrast to the denizens of many countries who boot-lick eagerly for the tourist dollar.

What seems to lie beneath much of the world's unrest today is the quality of pride; its presence in some, its absence in others. Self-respect is an individual affair, but in a class on social science we could be discussing pride as a national characteristic--a racial quality. The pride of origin of underdeveloped countries was built on cultural attributes that are not valuable currency today, and as a result, their race is punished. For the black American, pride is a most important present need and many who support Afro-study programs do so for this reason. A minting of the currency of racial pride is needed to produce a jingle for the pocket. As the music of the Scots helped me flesh-in the identity "pride," music can serve the needs of learning as we all study to understand cultures beyond our own.

Music as a national sound is now an easily available teaching partner. If a discriminating ear can be built, it will help relate music to its own place and time. About once a year I used to go to Central City in the mountains above Denver to attend the old Teller Opera House and hear opera presented by the Metropolitan Opera Company. This is a re-enactment of late-19th- and early-20th-century history when opera was performed there for the Central City mining aristocracy. Before each show a company of young people from Denver square dance in a loft across from the Teller House. The dancing is announced by ushers from the opera striding down the steep main street singing western songs and ringing the hand bells that will later announce the beginning of the opera.

To any sensitive ear, there is distinct dichotomy between the music that goes on inside and the western music that goes on outside. This can tell us a great deal about what life was in the period that is recreated in Central City. The indigenous music was of the historic west. Enough of a pseudo-aristocracy existed to justify the importation of that European nobility-opera. Bromfield's novel, <u>Colorado</u>, speaks to this point with wit and warm understanding, as does the musical comedy, <u>The Unsinkable Molly Brown</u>.

The teacher's need to depend upon audio help as a

tool depends on two variables: the complexity of the particular audio experience needed at a particular moment, and the innate abilities of the teacher. To project my musical talent into the role of kindergarten teacher makes audio support mandatory for any music that classroom purpose would decree.

I was privileged to audit a course in music appreciation taught in a boys' prep school where I was librarian. The teacher was just out of college, had never taught this subject on this level before, and was dealing with very highpowered 17 and 18 year olds from his seniority of age 21. The classroom had full audio equipment including a piano which, second to the organ, is his special instrument. As I watched, these boys developed a musical ear, plus an appreciation of the historic development of musical form itself. I can visualize a very complex programmed instruction developed from his lesson plans which would afford a feedback similar to that provided by these live musical capabilities. He used records, piano, singing, and speaking to teach and answer questions. With considerable book learning, I could have the abilities to teach this programmed course--provided one of the students handled the technology. The presumption in this hypothetical classroom is that the student body contains that kind of mind which is willing to be limited to those questions allowed for by the programmed instruction, not demanding a hearing for its personal response to the canned media of instruction. Judge for yourself whether such a learning box is right for bright minds!

During my exposure to Gabriel D. Offiesh's course in Educational Technology at Catholic University, I discovered that all real learning is programmed. Until hardware hit the classroom, human dialogue provided the means whereby learning was programmed. If I don't savvy your point, I can raise my hand. Even a lecture by Adler has its question period.

The higher the IQ, the less likely are the questions to be those that the program has anticipated. To teach music appreciation without instruments and the ability to use them is severely to limit creative learning. Unless the live or canned program can demonstrate instantly the tonal quality and musical notation under discussion, only those illustrations and questions programmed for the nonexistent average mind can be answered, no matter what the opportunities of the teachable moment. To illustrate, an ear for musical spaces was taught by this ability of the teacher's to have a continuing musical dialogue between the students and the piano. When using the phonograph for symphony or opera, and a question was raised about the relationship of one instrument or melody to another, this performing artist could pick out first one and then the other on the piano, thus supplying the clarification needed to reinforce correct learning. The logical conclusion seems to be that unless the teacher possesses an adequate range of skills in the subject being taught--including a performing skill where necessary--the availability of audio support is only a definite second best.

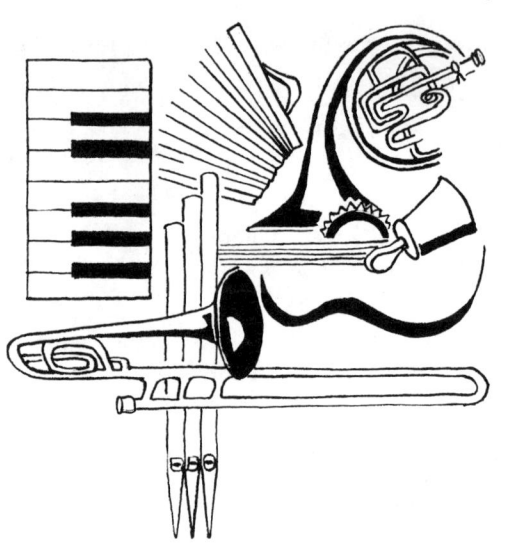

A type of modern music that lends itself naturally to a mixture of live and recorded forms is chance music. In this musical form, akin to improvisations, part of each composition comes from accidents of instrumentation that are not written into the score but just "happen." Such a piece was performed in our school chapel at an early morning communion on All Saints' Day. The idea stuck in my mind, after exposure to the concepts of chance and probability as developed in the course on hydrologic research I used to share.

On the cathedral close there are two peals of bells, a full peal in the cathedral tower and a small one in the school chapel. On a misty morning, after chance music had entered my life, I was walking along close to the Cathedral on my way to the chapel services that began every day. The fog was romantic and I was playing at a Wuthering Heights mood. The cathedral carillon was loud and insistent through the fog and, at a particular point as I walked from one church toward the other, I could still hear the cathedral carillon and yet begin to pick up the chapel bells. It was exciting hearing the notes of the bells overlap as I walked out of the sound of one and into the sound of the other. As I discussed my experience with the teacher-musician later in the day, he said, "That, Carolyn, is chance music."

This is a simple concept and of relevance to children who are always interested in games of chance. In a class in mathematics or natural science, this natural bent of childhood can be expanded by chance music. It is something the children can create themselves by using a simple hand bell. With a tape recorder present, they can record it and then play it back again. To the first simple rhythms can be added the overlay of a second rhythm. If two tapes were available, the first rhythm and melody could be repeated on a second tape and then, against this, a fresh level of chance music could be created. Playing back these two tapes in rapid succession would provide a deeply personal experience of the reality of chance.

These are some personal examples of the places where canned audio support is a real teaching tool and others where it is not. Again--and always--the teaching-learning recipe is not simple.

1) In a class in music appreciation, recorded music is better than no music at all, but without a teacher's own musical capabilities there can be no spontaneous teaching.

2) The better the programmed A-V support the broader is the range of learning built in.

3) The plodding middle-of-anything student is more apt to be fitted by canned program instruction.

4) Both extremes, the gifted and the deprived, demand a real live performing teacher. Therefore, all the fancy technology money can provide still will not teach those who need it most: our best, who offer the world its genius; and the needy, who threaten to engulf society.

The technological assist that tape and record systems

afford is great and, with the simple one-machine unit, inexpensive and easy to use. They are almost idiot-proof.

In a humorous (but serious) vein, let me put forth the idea that Mother or any single parent is the most complete multimedia package yet known. Discounting the obvious factors of the prenatal completeness of mother as an environment, let us consider the postnatal condition "mother" as a multimedia package.

"Mother," one way or another, is food; is security; is a sheltering bed. Mother is transportation. Mother is communication. Mother is an artistic environment. All these properties come from the ubiquitous multimedia parent.

For our purposes, let us take two of the specific human faculties, complex speech and music, and look at Mother as the chief medium for their development. Flat statements are always dead, usually before they are uttered, but I am going to make another one. Speech develops only as a human interaction which, if it does not develop at the agreed-upon proper chronological stage, will never reach the height of ability of which the individual human would be capable had his development taken place at the proper time. A mother or a mother-substitute is that proper time and place.

> If more young mothers (and fathers, too) were aware of their role in transmitting language to their children, of how "a vivid word sense in the nursery" may be acquired, and of the high adventure for both children and parents as they go "from nature and life to words, from words to life and nature again," they would become agents in improving the quality of language and of thinking and be invaluable participants in "Project English" ... many young mothers ... who are deeply concerned about their children's physical and emotional well-being and future education, ... are often not aware of how sensitive small children are to the sound of language, how quickly they absorb on-the-wing what a parent knows and enjoys, how quickly they appropriate what is authentic and use it in their own contexts, the value of so-called nonsense, and how much children crave the nourishment of stories and poems, pictures and songs, shared with their parents at home. (Norris, p. 145)

These words bring memories of my daughter. I delighted in her infant speech as I chatted with her through all the carryings on that mother and infant share. It had a quality different from my son's baby noises. I liked to read as I gave her her bottle and this annoyed her. She wanted my full concentration. I kept trying to solve this by getting small and smaller books and holding them farther and farther from her, which met with some success in escaping her vision. When this scene was graced with some new reading glasses with purple, uptilted Pierrot-kind of frames, she took one look at them and burst out laughing, making quite clear her amusement at me and my taste. Her father, who disliked the specs also, was audibly proud of his offspring's "obvious aesthetic prowess"--which ensuing years have validated.

Human interaction is possible on this level where the emotional content is real but the verbalizing is of the nonsense syllable type. While waiting my turn at a counter I was fascinated as I watched closely the interaction between an engaging upper middle class British father and his small son. The patterns of the baby's speech followed those of his father precisely and though the toddler demonstrated no ability to use meaningful words, he understood perfectly the actions indicated by his father's words.

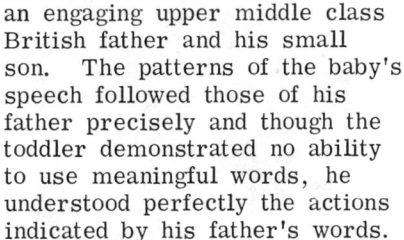

Another example of such language patterning development involved a 14-month old strawberry blond, a Renoir recreation, who is the first child of highly cultivated, humorously insightful southern parents. On the balcony of the apartment upstairs sat two Italian-Americans who were intimates of Jennifer's parents and their 3-month old baby daughter, Jennifer's buddy. Standing, with her daddy, outside the picture window from which I watched, Jennifer produced a loud string of "Italian" directed upward toward her friends on the balcony. No words, but clearly a Mediterranean speech pattern. She would laugh, listen, and then chatter back with a perfect Italian speech pattern. But she always "spoke southern" to her parents and me--a circle of language input and output in human dialogue.

In the field of music, I took particular joy in the multimedia supremacy of mother during my years as the parent of small children. Previously all my musical ability had been rated zero, zero, zero, and great pains had been taken by all to make quite clear that, as William Glasser remarked to a group: "You are a failure. I will tell you you are a failure and I will tell you to tell other people who are failures like you that you are all failures together." Subtitled, "Please, Carolyn, don't sing during sorority rushing and, since we know you better, do ask Patsy not to sing either. But pul--eeze don't be obvious!"

Once my children reached the age of musical discretion, they realized I was a tonal failure and it required the acceptance of their 20's for them to be willing to permit me to sing along with them in church. As multimedia mother I was encouraged by a pediatrician who, noting my humming in his office, said to me, "Mrs. Leopold, if you like to sing, your SOLE opportunity to appear as a Lily Pons is to your children," and he was right. The deduction from that, since my children have gone on to be interested and proficient in music, is that it is not the quality of the maternal hum but the joyous awareness that the mother herself feels in what is going on that is the crucial ingredient.

Poetry and music are much akin and, as John Ciardi once said, all children are born with the love of poetry, and school simply manages to take it out of most of them. Notwithstanding my limited ability, I could translate a parent/child experience into terrible poetry, yet produce in the shared experience very palpable joy.

The educator is also a multimedia package. Looked at in one way, he functions as a means of remedying part of the failure of the inadequate multimedia package "mother." When a child comes to meet the multimedia-package kindergarten teacher, he comes prepared, however it has been for him, by his home to meet a new set of experiences. A kindergarten teacher must have demonstrable artistic ability-- enough musical ability to play simple melodies on the piano for dancing and musical games, and her singing must be better than mine. Kindergarten-age children might still be satisfied with my vocal ability, but no self-respecting taxpaying parent would ever be.

It seems to require more lack of inhibition than expertise to be a theatre in the round for the young. An enthusiastic, spontaneous, mature, human being can be a relatively complete media package. Such a teacher can read poetry, tell stories, play chopsticks, provide a simple dance and create costumes, sound effects, and lighting. Once I experienced the poem Evangeline ground into the consciousness of a fifth grade class by words, words, words--aided only by some pale sketches decorating the blackboard. Surely, Evangeline could have been dramatized by the use of sounds. Indian moccasins worn by one student while another clumped around in a heavy pair of walking shoes would supply an awareness of the difference between walking as an Indian and as a white man. A record of river music and a tepee jerry-rigged in one corner of the room to give the child an idea of the silence within, and the hole in the tepee through which to imagine the sky and the sound of birds and warriors' chanting, are simple extensions of a human teacher.

What of the beyond-school lifelong learner--the truly handicapped and the chronologically handicapped! The ears of the blind and the sight-impaired are primary intake channels. Whether the sound is human, or live, or canned, beyond the touch of a hand, a curve of sculpture, a familiar domestic pathway, or Braille, listen they must. As our population of elders increases, they constitute a major market for librarians concerned with lifelong learning. Visitors to Senior Centers, public libraries, special leisure-related collections, and denizens of retirement homes include many people whose ears are still good but whose eyes have dimmed. A mixed medium like TV does not always carry enough verbal component to support the whole import of the production. Tape, record, and radio, being single medium, are sufficient in themselves to bring content to the visually impaired. More than that, they resemble books in that they are less media-hype, Madison Avenue, and art-by-committee.

"Let the ear despise nothing, nor yet believe anything forthwith," Phaedrus offers for our musing. Sophocles can add, "Ears are eyes to the blind." Now it is up to us!

Chapter 10
Reading Pictures

We see things not as they are,
but as we are.

H.M.Tomlinson

As teaching librarians, what should be our concerns about the media of sight? What considerations differentiate us from a movie critic or a psychologist or a filmmaker or a neurologist? We are not taste influencers, nor research scientists, nor clinicians, nor moneymakers. Our educational responsibility defines our task, which is to understand the essence of the visual media. To be good shepherds for patrons entrusted to our care demands that our expertise as materials selectors and prescribers cover each form of instructional media.

Knowledge of destination is the first step in a journey. Then comes selection of alternative routes of transport. The visual media provide a variety of routes to educational goals. Like all forms of narrative, pictures can be both fact and fancy, opinion and poetry, logic or emotion--"The Blue Boy" or a mug shot of a Mafioso! An illustration can do anything that a sentence can. Each visual form has its own criteria with which teaching librarians must be familiar to reach a teaching-learning objective.

A hard look at some relevant verbs may help locate guideposts for the trip toward media competency. Are we talking about carriers of information that we can see? We see print. Is it then seen or read? Is that seeing separate from reading? If not, do we then read pictorial graphics?

My dictionary, a 1975 Webster's Collegiate informs: "See--to perceive by the eye; to look at, examine or scrutinize; to discern; understand." Remember the party memory game played with a tray of objects? Each pair of eyes sees the same articles. Each mind recalls differently.

See--to perceive, to discern, to understand. A description of a process by which the light rays and physical objects composing our environment affect the nerve cells of the human eye which, in turn, using electrochemical processes, affect the human brain in such a way that the content

Reading Pictures

of the brain is altered and something is there that was not there before. I see. What is this "to see?"

Once I saw Mount Kilimanjaro--the African mountain made famous by Hemingway. The <u>Snows of Kilimanjaro</u> was my bedtime reading the night before we were to go there. My dictionary defines the class of physical object we call mountain thus: "Any part of a land mass which projects conspicuously above its surroundings. "

Kili indeed qualifies. It is conspicuous by virtue of its breadth of base as well as by being a lone peak--a real snow-capped sore thumb. During several hours we drove within sight of Kili. The angle changed. The light changed. The cloud cover changed. I saw Kili. I saw its proud, eternally white crown and I saw its broad, elephantine base "projecting above its surroundings. " But--I never saw its mid-section. That remained shrouded in clouds. What did I see then? I knew from experience that what I saw and what I accepted unseen, as through a glass darkly, was a solid land mass projected upward into a mountain. But, except for my previous experience of mountains, is this not like the ladies of the Siamese court who thought that Anna must have a shape to match her voluminous hoop skirts and not legs like theirs until, amused, she permitted inspection?

What I saw--the physical process--is inextricably bound up with the garniture of the brain. It seems dead wrong to approach the use of the visual media of instruction as if all viewers were equal because all who are not visually handicapped can "see. " Do we really believe that visuals are not like words? That there is no problem of entry level or vocabulary? That all viewers are created equal?

"What skills are needed if people are to be able to learn from pictures of many kinds? Can we grade these skills in order of difficulty? Can we teach them?" Among those are left and right--"as it looks at me or as I look at the picture?" Another such special convention that we teach is when we refer to "in front" and "behind" in a picture.

Anyone able to read this book has many such skills buried in his subconscious mind. These abilities were, for us the fortunate, fed into our brain storage at the earliest age that the mechanism was ready to accept them. Each one, then, was there, available to be built upon by the next piece.

Perception, which <u>Webster's Collegiate</u> defines as

"awareness of objects; consciousness ... what is known of an object by seeing it or hearing it," is a very complex, learned ability. Professor Gregory devotes a book to the knowns and unknowns of human perception and hypothesizes much that must be the brain's role in this process.

"Read--to take in the sense of, as of language, by interpreting the characters with which it is expressed, to learn or be informed of by perusal, to learn or discover the nature of by observing closely, to attribute (a meaning) to what is read."

So advised, the answer is yes, a picture is read. I take it in, ... by interpreting the [symbols] with which it is expressed. I do also see print. I use it to discern and understand.

Such ideas are a reversal of the common use of these terms. Seeing print or picture is the surface use. The meaning implicit in "to read" is to transmit to the electrochemistry of the brain the import of the communications source. By defining reading as absorption by interpretation of symbols, we imply a search for the intent of the message carried.

Facts derive from a message carried in some format-- some tangible or visible collection of atoms in which to embody the symbols from which we learn. A word is a symbol. The letters that form the word "hat" are neither a skullcap nor a mortarboard nor a dowager's cumulus of feathers. A picture is a symbol, too. It is also an icon, being in the shape of what it represents.

In his book, The Intelligent Eye, Professor Richard L. Gregory offers this insight.

> In this book I propose to consider the inner "logic" of perception. The main argument is that perception is a kind of problem-solving. Pictures are regarded as a remarkable invention, requiring special perceptual skills for seeing them, leading to abstract symbols and ultimately to written language.... Pictures have a double reality. Drawings, paintings and photographs are objects in their own right--patterns on a flat sheet--and at the same time entirely different objects to the eye. We see both a pattern of marks on paper,

with shading, brushstrokes or photographic "grain," and at the same time we see that these compose a face, a house or a ship on a stormy sea. Pictures are unique among objects; for they are seen both as themselves and as some other thing, entirely different from the paper or canvas of the picture. Pictures are paradoxes. No <u>object</u> can be in two places at the same time; no object can lie in both two- and three-dimensional space. Yet pictures are both visibly flat and three-dimensional. They are a certain size, yet also the size of a fact or a house or a ship. Pictures are impossible. No eyes before man's were confronted by pictures. Previously, all objects <u>in themselves</u> were important or could be safely ignored. But pictures, though trivial in themselves, mere patterns of marks, are important in showing <u>absent</u> things.... Pictures, and other symbols, allow responses to be directed to situations quite different from the present; and may give perceptions perhaps not even possible for the world of objects.... Perhaps man's ability to respond to absent imaginary situations in pictures represents an essential step towards the development of abstract thought. Pictures are perhaps the first step away from immediate reality, and without this reality cannot be deeply understood. (Gregory, p. 31-33)

Professor Hugh M. Culbertson reports on research done for his Ph.D. thesis at the Department of Communication at Michigan State University in this article from <u>Journalism Quarterly.</u>

The basic nature and impact of pictures have become popular topics in the communications literature. Researchers have shown that pictorial and graphic presentation can add attention-getting power, enjoyment, and comprehension, and that it can influence connative meaning ...
Theorists often call attention to the resemblance between pictorial symbol and its referent. Such resemblance has been called iconicity ...
The idea that pictures have stronger impact than words suggested that increasing the iconicity of a message part should lead readers to "weight"

that part more heavily in interpreting the total message.

Here are some specific roadsigns:

> College students, having relatively high verbal ability, may have little need for graphic aids to understanding. At the same time, their school experience and ability may help them become more sensitive to subtle clues such as pictorial embellishments. ... It would seem that a shared attribute must be salient to a reader before it will greatly influence his interpretation ... [the] extent of psychologically relevant object-symbol resemblance depends partly on the reader--on whether shared attributes are salient to him. [It was] found that different people may simply see different things while decoding a mass communication message ... a certain amount of incompleteness--of leaving things to the imagaination--may have attention-getting power.... Interpretation of many pictures and graphs requires reasoning from subordinate to superordinate classes, and perhaps the reverse. (Culbertson, p. 300-301)

Reading pictures, we are being told, is a skill like reading words. Only a moment's reflection, then, should make clear to us that educators' simplistic approach to pictures as materials of instruction is almost criminally head-in-the-sand. Visualize the masses of books on the teaching of reading in our Curriculum Libraries and in the thousands of reading workshops that dominate each summer's program of in-service training. What is there on learning to read pictures? Books of art appreciation for elementary school children do exist to prepare the young for touring art museums. What do we know about reading pictures? Precious little that we are conscious of.

Some will argue that perhaps drawings and paintings do possess characteristics that require entry level skills for their mastery, but "seeing" a photograph is like looking out of our normal windows, our eyes. Don't believe such talk. Photographs are pictorial representation, too, and we should not assume an ability to grasp the content of their message. Ignorance of the skills of visual perception creates this fallacy which, being hidden, is doubly destructive.

> The comprehension of pictures depends on learned skills: we have not analyzed these skills, nor have we techniques for teaching them. As a result, much of our "visual education" is needlessly inefficient. (French, p. 6)

So speaks Arthur French in an article in the periodical Visual Education. His conclusions came from personal experience in the Demonstration School of Makerere University, Uganda. Full teaching use of the immediate school environment was an important part of his curriculum strategy, and, to that end, special photographs were taken. The students had spent time in supervised study of these surroundings, so they were familiar with the school neighborhood. Surprisingly, in using the photographs they demonstrated real difficulty in distinguishing flat land from hilly, open water from swamps, and cultivated land from fallow bush.

Black and white photographs were chosen for the first tests. Dr. French drafted multiple-choice questions about the agricultural scenes selected and tried them out on Makerere University students to check the validity of the test questions, not to test the perception of these more experienced African students.

> I was so surpised by the results that I changed my plans completely. Out of 70 questions we only agreed completely on 7. The students were confused by perspective and made odd judgments about slope, position and size. They were confused by light and shade and reflections. They were unsure of the language used in the description of pictures. A young African woman who had had 12 years of school and 3 years in the Art School came up and asked: "What do you mean when you speak of the left and the right of a picture? Do you mean the left and right of the picture as it looks at me, or do you mean the left and right of me as I look at the picture?" A good question! Do we realize, do we teach our own children, that this is a special convention? When we refer to "in front" and "behind" in a picture we are using the other convention. Presumably our own children pick up these conventions

through a multitude of instances, if indeed they pick them up at all.

I followed up this experience by choosing a number of pictures from Pictorial Education and from travel magazines ... that is, pictures which my students, all training for secondary school teaching, might be expected to use in their work. In addition to the expected difficulties, I found that they were much influenced by intellectual prejudices about the subject of the picture. A landscape of Scandinavia was often interpreted in terms of snow and ice (though it was a summer picture with deciduous trees in leaf) presumably because they knew that Scandinavia is a region in the extreme north of Europe, stretching up to within the Arctic Circle. Social history was a conspicuous weakness: many clues which we should use from our experience of our buildings, or from our knowledge of paintings, or in other ways, are not available to them, and they were not even sure of the difference between colour photographs and realistic paintings, even when the paintings were several centuries old. (French, p. 6)

Little is known about the relative effects of presenting the same material in different media. In T. J. Scanlon's experiments, groups of viewers were shown the same events recorded by color TV and black-and-white TV, and asked to record later their reactions. The results showed that viewers of the scenes in color saw different things and generally were more absorbed in the event. But they did not see as great a variety of material and paid less attention to the spoken commentary than viewers who saw the black-and-white scene. (Scanlon, p. 366).

We do not even know what are the results of using different media, yet we act as if it were patent that more complex technologies are better teaching aids. Educated man's vast subconscious storehouse of learning skills must be acknowledged to include those of reading pictures.

Tomie de Paola, under the media microscope as the 1983 winner of the Catholic Library Association's Regina Medal, given for excellence in children's work, supports Professor French. De Paola urges us to discourage passive viewing in young children by forcing them to read the pictures in order to comprehend what is taking place in the

Reading Pictures   179

world of page-by-page art. He is another authority who
feels that people lack the ability to read pictures and thus
operate as visual illiterates.

John Holt, commenting on the use of visuals in the
television series "Sesame Street," describes an incident involving spelling and the letters OVEL.

> The adult began to say, in that typical teacher
> condescending-explaining, how-could-you-be-so-
> stupid voice, "But Big Bird, you've put the L
> after the word, and you should have put it be-
> fore it." She said this several times, as if it
> were self-evident that "before" meant "on the
> left side" and "after" meant "on the right side,"
> and as if all she needed to do to make this clear
> was to say it often enough. In fact, there is
> nothing self-evident or natural or reasonable
> about it at all. We just do it that way. But
> nothing makes school more mysterious, mean-
> ingless, baffling, and terrifying to a child than
> constantly hearing adults tell him things as if
> they were simple, self-evident, natural, and
> logical, when in fact they are quite the reverse--
> arbitrary, contradictory, obscure, and often
> absurd, flying directly in the face of a child's
> common sense. (Holt, p. 74)

Again, the paradox of the assumed-to-be-known, and therefore untaught, being, in fact, a vital missing skill.

> The fact is that most fourth- to seventh-
> graders don't read as well or as much today as
> their counterparts did in past decades. They
> are, however, exposed to more visual media
> than ever before in the form of film, television,
> video games, computer graphics, and advertising
> art. The picture book is the perfect bridge be-
> tween print and graphics for these children, es-
> pecially in light of the fact that their artistic edu-
> cation is just as neglected as their literary edu-
> cation. They have little background to help them
> evaluate the very media to which they are most
> exposed. It is obvious that a well-designed and
> -illustrated picture book could not only serve the
> purpose of cultivating their artistic awareness
> but also give them practice and comfort in han-
> dling a book and reading it.

The trick, then, is to overcome the format barrier for older children picking up a "young-looking" book--if the barrier exists. (Hearne, p. 1280)

This helpful "philsophy plus strategies" comes from the Co-editor of Children's Books for Booklist. Would not this insight also be applicable to those of any chronological age who "don't read as well or as much today" for whatever reason?

Our first destination in proficiency in the visual media is the awareness that pictures are a unique language. Training in the conventions of reading iconography seems a prerequisite to their employment as materials of instruction. Pictures and words are two languages, between which the trained mind translates.

My comprehension of this grew through the following experience. The layout editor of the ACE publications division and I were discussing the design of a flow chart of educational reference materials as an access route to information in Higher Education. This piece was to be a poster. The problem was to ensure that the editor understood the text in order to prepare copy for a preliminary printing. Midway in our dialogue, she said abruptly, "Do you think that I don't like it, or I'm not listening to you? My vacant stare means that I am visualizing the ideas you present as pictures of the lay-out for this piece. That's the way I work."

Picking up a manuscript from her desk, she continued, "This will be a brochure for the Office of Research. When the scientists brought it in, I asked if it would lend itself to pictures. They said no. But when I read it, pictures just leaped out at me--athlete, bookworm, younger brother!"

As we pondered the concept at issue, I exclaimed, "Of course, these research psychologists speak two languages--words and ciphers. Their translation is between them. When they write 'athlete' they see a figure on a graph. You see a youth in a baseball uniform." As media managers, our profession is to be trainers in image and symbol exchange--in the languages of our human brains.

Another avenue to understanding the relative communicative capabilities of narrative and pictures lies in the different amount of space required by photographs as compared

Reading Pictures 181

to text in a combined medium. To cite the National Geographic Magazine as an example, about three times as much space is allotted to tell a story by photographs as by text. In addition, pictures chosen for publication must qualify as illustrations, portraying their subject in an important, informed and significant manner. The ratio of three to one serves to illustrate the obvious point that pictures demand more display space than do words.

What is not so obvious is the breadth of range of narrative versus emotional factors in the elements of a photograph. Lighting for effect is one such constituent. In the early days of color photography, the Geographic's picture editor chose to print mainly pictures that were shot between 10 a. m. and 2 p. m. when the lighting was straight and flat, giving maximum clarity to all details. Now few such shots are used. Another factor in the reality versus emotion quotient of pictures is composition. Once the camera was technically capable of becoming an accurate reporter of straight facts, photographers turned to the creation of art prints.

Photographs, then, can be taken to present fact or opinion or literature. Just as in a newspaper, words are worked into straight reporting or an editorial or a story, the pictures that accompany text are created from the world's store of things to serve the same very different purposes. A picture is a poem, or a love story, or "Duck Soup!"

Pictures used as texts for formal instruction pose content reading problems which are as complex as those of a printed text and less understood. Yet problem readers are the issue that has turned the educational community to pictures as their current savior. I have cited three different scholar-educators' comments on the complexities of reading pictures to act as the peak of the iceberg to reinforce for librarians the uncertainty that pictorial language poses for its readers. There are no conclusive answers, but many warnings. Let us not accept and disperse visuals, as if they were sexless, colorless stretch socks. If we do, the creation of a new myth, to block learning, will, in part, become our sin.

Concentration on the factual is the keystone to a critical approach to the world's web. First, determine the fact sought. Next, place it in its contemporary context, and then place it fully by determining its history. What is the fact?

Where does it fit in? Where did it come from? Where might it be going? A space shot, a maxi hemline, love beads, a river, a baby.

It has been my experience that all critical touchstones are slipperier in the mass media than in a singly authored work. Hidden or multiple or corporate authorship, and publication by a conglomerate rather than a discrete known house, play large roles in weaving these fancy webs. The words of print are static and while trying to follow a thread, one can pick up a reliable authority and ultimately isolate the issues and authenticate or nullify the facts presented. The sweeping generalization can be clarified with the library's help when print fixes it for the reader. Our critical faculties have at least a fighting chance when the medium is print.

Take the same superficial exposition. Shorten it to allow for the time factor of the spoken word. Add an elusive visual fade in and out and a musical sound track that is chosen for its power to influence our subconscious minds, and all but the strongest, best trained, fighting Irish intellect will waver and succumb.

Once in 1967, I used films in a classroom. The purpose was dual: to make a class of teachers studying to be librarians aware of the capabilities of the A-V media, singly and as they reinforce each other in combination, and to make more tolerable the endurance test of a three-hour--4:30 p.m. to 7:30 p.m.--class session. Furthermore, I'd been smiled into it by my boss who, when I requested permission to moonlight, responded, "Yes, I'll give my consent--provided you push the multimedia approach."

Our Educational Materials Center had a terrific film collection and since I had not make advance booking, I previewed available films and stayed a week ahead of my course outline. At the peak of this, there was a brief spell of success when I actually was able to set up and run the projector myself. Some of these "approved educational films" proved to be so full of errors and misleading generalizations that I could use them to puncture some of the prevailing A-V mystique and teach critical evaluation of films. One gem I'll always remember portrayed Gutenberg "inventing type" and taking stock of his closetful of Bibles.

When the EMC moved next to the library, I caught many moments of film (handy, having the office fridge in an informal movie theater). I never ceased to be horrified by the violence done to fact by film scripts. Through the osmosis of a long marriage to a dedicated scientist who taught for any available audience, I know my basics of geology and meteorology and ecology. What shades and ghosts and distortions of truth filmmakers devise for their products! Oddly enough, the cartoon graphic, which is a most effective device to portray such subjects as geologic history, seems to be especially susceptible to script embroiderers and distortion of actual scientific history. The medium transmutes the message.

Pauline Kael adds an acute arrow to this target in one of her New Yorker columns,

> Television is blurring the distinction [between ads and editorials] for all of us; we don't know what we're reacting to anymore, and, beyond that, it's becoming just about impossible to sort out the con from the truth because a successful con makes its lies come true.
>
> A lot of the "film-generation" talk is, of course, business-inspired--an attempt to create a new youth market to replace the older audience lost to television--and, via the schools, the businessmen are making it true. The textbook The Motion Picture and the Teaching of English, financed by a grant from Teaching Film Custodians (an affiliate of the Motion Picture Association of America) to the National Council of Teachers of English, heralded the push into the schools, and teachers who want to be hip have taken up movies as what's happening. Publishers have rushed to prepare

books to take advantage of the new film courses, and conglomerates have bought up the 16-mm. film-distribution companies in expectation of educational funds being poured into film rentals. Everywhere in the media, one has begun to hear of the wonderful new "visual literacy" possessed by the young--how, without effort, they have acquired a magical new kind of education from television. Teachers who couldn't get their students to do any work and couldn't think of anything else to do with them have begun to see the virtue of bombarding them with images, and so across the country the schools are acquiring the hardware of "visual literacy...."

While students don't go to many movies (they read even less, and perhaps that's why they've been named the film generation), the few movies each year that they do care about they seem to take more personally than earlier generations of students did. It's the jackpot of turning out one of those few that the new moviemakers aim for. The movies that are popularly considered the best movies at any given time may or may not be good movies--they may be important bad movies--but they touch a nerve, express a mood that is just coming to popular consciousness, or present heroes who connect in new ways. They not only reflect what is going on in the country but, sometimes by expressing it and sometimes by distorting it, affect it, too--such movies as "The Wild One," "Rebel Without a Cause," "Blackboard Jungle," "On the Waterfront," "Morgan!," "Bonnie and Clyde," "The Graduate," "Midnight Cowboy," "Easy Rider," the new "Joe," and probably the new "Five Easy Pieces." Movies like these enter the national bloodstream, and, at the moment, the few big movies seem to do so faster than ever before, and more directly--maybe because that "best-educated" generation in history is so nakedly vulnerable to whatever stirs it emotionally. This susceptibility, rather than "visual literacy," is the distinctive trait of the "film generation"; the young go back to reexperience the movies they identify with, entering into them with a psychodrama involvement. (Kael, p. 74, 80)

Some problems in the use of photographs as a

Reading Pictures 185

language have been discussed to offer a flag of caution as we work with this relatively unproven language of instruction. Another side of the visual carriers for us to debate is their specific abilities within the media of sight. Among these are their ability to show motion, and either their opaqueness or their transparency. To sort out the uses of these qualities and thus analyze them as teaching tools, let us turn to the subject of water.

The colored plates abundantly available in such national magazines as Holiday and the National Geographic are superb examples of this art form. There must be some such artifact handy. Pick it up, select a picture of water and pay it close attention. Then visualize the projection of a colored slide of this print. The slide demonstrates an ability to pull us into the picture by a depth of field and intensity of color beyond that possessed by the opaque photograph. Can we then accept that for any unmoving experience of water--like a pool, or a canal--a color slide is an adequate visualization?

To teach about moving water, a moving graphic is indicated except when we have only the nonelectric multimedia human to rely upon to provide such a demonstration of the quality of motion, or when the electricity is off, or the projector broken. Under such constraints one could try to present the idea of running water to a class of city dwellers by calling their attention first to a classmate standing still and then to someone briskly running around the room, and then quickly make the thought transfer to a glass bowl of still water on a desk which could at once be poured into a second bowl. Back and forth--running person, running water-- still person, still water.

A New Yorker has probably seen the Hudson River but if we are talking about the runningness of a river, our illustration must go beyond the stately lower Hudson. In one of the early Disney nature films, there was a sequence on the Grand Canyon that magnificently portrayed a storm in the canyon; the water falling down the canyon slopes, hitting its sides and moving with a force that, in partnership with the cutting edge of the river itself, has carved this gorge over so many centuries. The rivulets from the storm sweep down into the river in ever-changing patterns of moving water. The river itself, at high flow and swollen by the storm, is a tremendous coffee-colored swirling mass. These pictures were of such turbulence that they produced nausea in several watchers. The intense rhythms of Ferde Grofé's "Grand Canyon

Suite," which accompanied the film, did much to reinforce and heighten the visuals. A similar pictorial effect was obtained on a family Colorado float trip when the movie camera was dropped at a moment of crisis in a rapid and flopped around by itself on the raft. To produce the vicarious experience of swiftly moving water, a colored, moving graphic is the medium of major teaching power whether the learner be highly verbally literate or illiterate.

From an image of dramatic movement, let's turn to something quiet--embroidery. This fine art has been passed down through the centuries from mother to daughter and is an important part of our current craft revival. Embroidery is a design on a piece of fabric executed in thread. A colored, opaque graphic or a transparency on the overhead projector or via a filmstrip can show patterns clearly, examples both historic and contemporary. Caught without electric power or lacking multimedia helpers, a teacher can use a piece of paper and a colored pencil, or a piece of cloth and a magic marker to illustrate the idea of pattern. After she has created her own design, out comes an embroidery needle and some floss and the stitch itself must be presented. A still black and white diagram can illustrate different stitches adequately enough for the highly multidimensional pupil. In a small group, the teacher can demonstrate the cross stitch one by one and so, herself, individualize instruction. In a classroom with closed circuit television, one teacher could do such a demonstration once and reach a large lecture hall of students.

For the person who needs help in mastering certain stitch techniques, a single concept film loop could individualize instruction to teach an ancient craft with the aid of meaningful modern media. In both these examples, pictures, still and moving, can measurably extend the capabilities of a human instructor.

Next in the progression of efficient and expensive media of instruction would come the colored movie. I can imagine a film in which a learner could watch embroidery growing before her eyes with a cartoon technique that employed slow motion and speed-up and overlay to demonstrate a complex design.

I spent ten days one winter within the precincts of Canterbury Cathedral visiting two of my children while my then son-in-law was their visiting organist. One evening my daughter and I sat in the frigid dark of the cathedral's great choir, enthralled still figures listening to him practice for a recital. The year was 1970, the 800th anniversary of Becket's martyrdom. It was harder to resist his ghostly presence than to submit to the spells that dwell in the stones which form that part of the apse called Becket's Crown. On the dimly-lit medieval frontal of the High Altar I could see in brilliant embroidery, outlined by couching in golden thread, a procession of the pilgrims coming to visit Becket's shrine which had stood there for 400 years until Henry VIII despoiled it--400 years ago. Imagine what a movie maker could weave on film, using this legendary embroidered frontal to whet the fingers of those in Needlework I.

From Canterbury, where legend and history overlap to create mystery, let us return to current reality. These ideas about the visual media as extensions of teaching skills beyond those possessed by a multimedia human will, I hope, serve to heighten the precision of library use of multimedia. As man's first book served a specific purpose, so must each succeeding carrier of knowledge serve an equally exact end. All five senses exist to channel sensation to our brain. These electric avenues that are our nerves are not interchangeable. The software of teaching and learning is a multivariate prescription which, to be effective, must be fitted by precise sensate avenue to the cognitive or affective objective sought. The software of vision are powerful weapons to storm our minds. But, as in all encounters, the stronger the blast, the sharper the rapier, the more precise must be its deployment.

This is especially important when several media are used to intensify an experience. I prepared one such multimedia trip for the climax of a course for which the students, working in small groups, had created similar materials packages as their term papers. My subject was rivers, the Colorado and the Amazon. Under the stolen format of The Incompetent Wizard, the show opened with a tape of a strong masculine voice reading from John Wesley Powell's log of his exploration of the Colorado; this was joined by the music of the Moldau and an overhead transparency of the same Powell text. The presentation continued with the addition of color slides of the Colorado, and climaxed with the simultaneous projection of two films: one a friend had made when he ran the river, and one of a river scientist (or fluvial geomophologist) describing river mechanics. This was followed by a short film the EMC crew and I had made from some special library footage and clips from films damaged beyond repair, which specifically illustrated the points of multimedia reinforcement. The mid-portion was a question and answer period between the class and a panel of experts which included the then librarian of the Geological Survey, William Heers, a senior editor of the National Geographic Society, Andrew H. Brown and Richard Darling; and the finale was a Geological Survey film on the Amazon for which Ed Pluhowski of the Survey was discussion leader. Our conclusions were that we were, indeed, all INCOMPETENT WIZARDS before the observable but not understood reinforcing power of the media.

Content and purpose are the major determinants for media prescritpions. Form, however, should also be considered as we select or recommend a carrier of knowledge. A simple illustration is a comparison between the film strip and the slide collection--each having merit.

One of the justifications for the use of a film strip rather than slides lies in ease of operation. It is a lot simpler to take a film strip and thread it into a projector and turn it through than to organize individual slides into a carousel. Sequence as a concept is also involved. Individual slides, in order to present a sequential narrative, must themselves possess a sequential nature. We all have sat uncomfortably trapped by the amateur slide presentation of a friend just returned from Europe, where he seemed to have spent less time seeing than in taking pictures. Individual slides require a story line and quality control to be really effective transmitters of visual intelligence. The amateur is often an inept technician and a beastly bore to boot.

These hurdles to the use of individual, personal slides as a teaching tool notwithstanding, an important principle of authenticity does operate that should not be overlooked. Anyone who has taught writing learns early in the game that the quality of writing produced by an individual rises measurably when the subject is something the writer understands and wants to talk about. The quality of the vicarious visual experience that passes from presenter to audience also seems to exist in larger measure when an individual is showing his own slides. The views projected are personal and such genuineness is not lost on the viewer. The photographer has more to give because the picture seen by him has thus become a part of his mind. The particular images were captured because the sight held special meaning.

Only once I watched this particular phenomenon operate

Reading Pictures

with adults in a formal information setting. This was at a meeting of the Maryland Library Association in Baltimore when an A-V authority was speaking. His first pictures were commercially prepared and the audience exuded the restlessness that comes with the same old horse trotted out again by a speaker who isn't turned on by it either. Then, he switched to some slides that were his own from a European holiday and the moment became fresh and vital for those on both sides of the rostrum. The medium, then, was not mass or corporate, but person to person.

Personal visuals do carry the major impact just as do personal writings. Our family film of a float trip on the San Juan out-communicates, to us, any Disney. Movies of a daughter's honeymoon hold that first love alive forever. Families overlook flaws in their own--flesh or film. But an outsider looks critically, as he should, and professional standards must be met in transparencies, charts, et al. The logic is inescapable. Librarians who employ their own visuals to teach must be trained in the complex techniques of software production. Not all of us are born equal in these graphic and small-muscle abilities--but if I can learn to print spine labels well, anyone can. Furthermore, we as librarian-keepers of materials are free to demand professional standards for any work, stored in and used in and from the library.

Since I speak from zero academic credentials in psychology, I feel free to disagree with any pro--especially when my appraisal of an expert leads me to the conclusion that his conclusions are also just guesses (though educated ones). One such pronouncement I don't believe (and I use that word advisedly) is that of Marshall McLuhan's on TV as a cool medium as opposed to film as a hot medium. I'll stand squarely on my intuitive hind legs and argue that film is film--audio tape or movie film, and a moving graphic is a moving graphic however manufactured or transmitted to us, be it a flick run on TV or a TV tape cassette handled as film. Until there are some new data that we librarians can comprehend that demonstrate otherwise, I urge my colleagues to consider as identical twins these two visual forms.

As we librarians dispense our media prescriptions, remember that we are dealing in a media-matrix into which are embedded symbol-language equivalents. Don't administer a potion that the patient can't handle. An infant can't gargle or swallow a pill. A 14-year old with the verbal ability of an 8-year old can't handle a word prescription beyond his abilities. A blind man must have braille or recorded speech. A disadvantaged person does not have the metaphorical symbols to comprehend middle-class images--be they visual or verbal.

It would seem obvious that programming such skills into our media prescriptions is vital to our success as masters of multimedia collections. If we remain strangers to the depths of our own abilities, how can we develop enough mediaability to justify the professional licenses we now have to prescribe so widely and--I'm afraid--wildly?

Let us learn routinely to ask ourselves those questions which might enable us to uncover the fantastically complex set of skills with which we manage our personal media consumption and thus, furnish our minds.

Now, television, the CRT and video game screens absorb the major share of the time almost anyone spends watching visual media. TV has been around for roughly 30 years, computer screens for about 15, and video games for 10. Considered for its graphic impact alone, TV's use of very sophisticated techniques enables it to make a mockery (or a dodo bird) of reality. Fade in and out, freeze frame and studio mounting enable producers to create image after image that exists only in a video world--never in a natural one. Gravity and countless other physical realities vanish in such displays. Slow motion and instant replay all make us gods over time and nature. Where are we? "This is so and so at the White House." And we D.C. denizens, witness to these floodlite playlets, can only groan at the projections of inside power they are staged to imply.

Early television was content to be just entertainment. Now it purports to offer truth in the form of documentaries and news programs. You are there with "Eyewitness News." But if newspapers only afford clues to such truth, how far from factual and conceptual accuracy is a few seconds of selected film footage or one person's concept of an issue cloaked in documentary footage! Where the camera is pointed, what shots are selected, etc., make our library book selection hassles look like routine administration.

To us, missing facts and context raise instant queries. The linear skills of classification--categories, sequence, analogies, and logic--are part of our subconscious mental baggage.

Even the <u>National Geographic</u> in its TV specials evades

Reading Pictures

the full, factual implications of some of their visuals. For example, St. Brendan's boat--tiny replica of an ancient sailing craft, was portrayed as being all alone crossing the Atlantic. All alone--first you accept that implication--and then the double take--but who was taking these pictures? We were not told.

When we become critical of sketchy locale attributions and identifications, these swift and slippery video texts rarely make a passing mark on our test of factuality in media of information. Generalizations, errors of omission, the stereotype as truth--Mister Magoo an object of derision for the visually impaired; an object or person blown to bits in one scene and back together in the next--the commercials where feelings are up for sale--sex, power, beauty, not perfume, or a car, or a shampoo--such examples abound! Materialism as icons--the outward and visible signs of an inward and invisible commercial culture fill the screen.

This, of course, is not accidental. Which brings us to the concept of manipulation. The word is defined by my desk Webster's (New Collegiate, 1976) as "to treat with the hands--or manage skillfully"; to control by artful, unfair, or insidious means, esp. to one's own advantage; ... to change by artful or unfair means to serve one's purpose."

The next step is to examine manipulation as it operates in both the print and TV media--books and the tube! Books are created, staged, designed, of course, and someone (our concept of main entry--who carries the chief intellectual responsibilty) did this to present a perspective--slanted, structured. A book is no more random organization than is a TV program. Both can be defined as having been created by manipulation.

When we start to apply our selection and reference techniques and criteria to assessing factuality, authority, and provenance to these two media, the night and day difference appears. Author, publisher, date, publishing history, footnotes, bibliographies--the blazed trail of scholarship from and with which we librarians create our cataloging and our reference (database) networks exist palpably in the artifacts of print. You can check my Webster's reference and my quotes. What authority I, as personal author, own can also be a locatable fact. Beyond Scarecrow's reputation are entries in professional directories and reviews and references by other writers. You then have facts upon which to build your own opinion of my opinions. And--and--all this stands still. Each sentence can be re-read to decide what is really meant. A solid checkable structure of linear thought is the information base that print builds. For video there is only the authority of the rare, known figures and the screen credits as they roll by. Where did they say they were? What was that dollar amount? What is the source of, authority for, etc? Clearly not a media product to be judged by the same standards.

So, to return to manipulation. Yes, both books and TV are created and controlled, but in the former we can tell better who is in charge and thus, perhaps, be better evaluators of the scenario. Edwin M. Yoder, Jr., in a Washington Post column of post mid-term elections 1982 comments: "elections of, by and for television in which it is the triumph of the 'media consultants' to get us to view the finer processes of a vibrant democracy through their eyes.... Living-room elections conceived in electronics and dedicated to the proposition that all voters are created manipulable."

The seemingly infinite ways to combine the moving visual and a written or spoken message have been judged such a powerful persuader that the apparent impossibility of banning cigarette commercials is now law. Can I assume--or hope--that this fact is enough of a clincher to make librarians at least consider the distortion available to--and in use by--much TV and many movies? Commercials can be useful to us to help equip peoplekind with the skills of critical thinking. Talking back to TV is an educational game the whole family, or class, can play with structured cognitive objectives.

Informational TV is an art form, a controlled report, but, unlike print, the reality implicit in its pictorial form gives it the force of undoctored reality. Unless we as media experts face this truth we cannot manage video media honestly.

Any misuse of the capabilities of these media should in no way damn them as teaching resources. Especially if it helps us to see them for the power they are. We are less than vigilant professionals, however, if we fail to keep potential distortions and manipulations of thought on our checklist as we preview and select from the visual carriers of knowledge.

These are negative attributes that are not inherent

Reading Pictures

in the media themselves. They are there by virtue of either the slipshod state of producers' standards or the deliberate misuse of the great audience impact by devices that violate the high standards we must demand of anything to which we give house room.

As carriers of factual matter, visual media must be used either to do a specific something better than print can, or to supplement print, or to substitute for print when the seeker cannot adequately handle print. Once these criteria have been satisfied, then a specific title of visual software must be purchased or prepared to achieve the exact learning objectives sought. Just as the physician first diagnoses the bodily ill, and then chooses one drug or one therapy to handle the solution of the physical need he has identified, so must the librarian as mentor in critical thinking, or selector and prescriber, accept professional responsibility for the match between patrons' abilities to handle media learning goals and the therapy or media prescribed.

Selectivity is the magic method of all art. The graphic artist wields craft to put in or take out the extraneous until the vision sought emerges clear and unfettered by the unnecessary--stripped to essential symbols. The power of vision enabled by craft produces a work of art whose message is louder and more compelling than any reality. In this lies its powerful ability to reach and alter the spirit so touched.

In addition to meeting the standards for selection of printed materials, visual media must meet further criteria related to their special nature.

A checklist of concerns expressed in this chapter might be entered in our media manual thus:

1. Why a visual?

2. Which kind of visual--and why?

3. A visual for cognitive objectives must pass strict tests for:
    a. Factualness of content--both verbal and graphic;
    b. Separation of fact from opinion and labeling of each;
    c. Ability to identify author or producer of intellectual content of work;
    d. Artistic quality of the graphics used--is it

suitable for the message carried?
- e. Correctness of the level of the graphic--i.e., Is the subject matter handled with a sensitivity related to its power or does it show more than a watcher may be able to handle?
- f. Accuracy of the descriptive material--i.e., historic or geographic details--proper bird or flower or terrain or ruffle or hairdo.
- g. Is the verbal track or script absolutely accurate? Are facts and opinions clearly labeled and all the grey areas lying between so indicated also?

4. Visuals for affective objectives must pass additional tests for qualification as a work of art.
- a. Does form fit content?
- b. Does it show artistic unity?

5. Does the work demand more of the viewer than his abilities would justify in:
- a. Perceptual skills of vision.
- b. Perceptual skills of listening.
- c. Emotional capabilities--individual anxiety levels or specific problems of family or peer relationships.
- d. Entry level experiences or capabilities such as vocabulary or aesthetic discriminations.
- e. Technological skills--can the hardware be mastered by the learner for whom the medium is intended if individualized or independent study is to be utilized?

Make these professional regards part of the transaction each time you select something for the library's collection or help a faculty member select materials for a course or match an eye and brain to something with which to enrich mind or spirit. As you teach critical thinking through use of library materials, keep the picture of all the variables of the individual work and the individual patron in your mind and heart and try never to settle for less than a terrific resource, and a comfortable fit.

Wright Morris, distinguished American novelist, who is now achieving recognition for his books combining photographs and words, lectured at the Corcoran Gallery of Art this spring. The following words offered there are my nomination for thoughts upon which "to go forth and be":

Photography has grammar and syntax. Behind each framed, walled image lies overlooked details. The artist focuses his camera to create arrested moments in the life of objects. The picture establishes an authority of time and place. Its existence postpones the finality of parting--a loved one does not "vanish into thin air"--and so a photograph can end the act of death. I began as a writer, verbally making pictures in my novels. Picture books distract. Lookers couldn't read and readers don't want to look. If we want to possess something, it must end as words. A picture can have no communicable self.

Chapter 11

Entry-Level Library Skills

Come hither, then, good little boy,
And learn your alphabet,
And then a pair of boots and spurs
Like Papa's you shall get.

— Mother Goose

Once possessed of the desire to use your present power and resources to further library literacy for your unique clientele, the next step is to prepare your skeleton curriculum. By allowing professionalism to rest upon mystery--such as the source of a DDC number or what is meant by port. or OV., we have practiced backwards logic. Turning the rationale behind the technical processing that is done to create a resource for patrons into a trade secret has neither made friends nor created a knowledgeable constituency. They when needed to support our work, are, by frontwards and direct logic, "library unfriendly."

The "library" curriculum has two levels: entry-level skills that form the "in-place" base, and those that are termed "library." A return to our own childhood's days of learning may help us determine how to make these concepts of level one explicit to all "entry-level" patrons--the very young or anyone who is still at this level of learning. This gives any public service librarian a large "class" to teach. Learning how to help others learn means learning how you learn--or learned. The toddler practices independent study; so also does any freely self-directed learner. This seems one flagged area for directing ourselves to E. W. S's "Challenge of Lifetime Learning" as it applies to a being a professor of BI.

While keeping the librarian-educator's mantle tight around us and using many of the skills that such training demands, let us step beyond and into a strange role. This new identity implies a willingness to divest ourselves of most of these skills that enable us to sit in the spot of librarian or teacher/librarian-in-training; roles that the world considers educated. Thus to put off a complex set of skills that has taken most of our lives to acquire means forcing these competencies into the forefront of our conscious minds. Such skills become so buried that they surface only when we attempt to teach them to others. Have you ever taught someone to park a car, or to read a road map, or use a library?

Entry-Level Library Skills

The mastery of reading has been discussed from the viewpoint of an adult vainly trying to recall learning to read. The abilities requisite to library use include a considerable number of specific skills that go far beyond those of reading. They fall within the hierarchy of the linear medium as McLuhan outlined it in his messages.

In the order called library, the qualities of the linear medium determine. The need to comprehend and manipulate the two basic sets of linear symbols--the alphabet and Arabic numerals--comes first. Reading follows next. The linear concept of hierarchy is of a higher order of abstraction than those just named, but innately part of the same whole, nonetheless. Only one skill, interrelationship, can have a multi-spatial application beyond that of the up and down of hierarchical relationships. These specific abilities all make their contribution to the reality of the library as the institutionalization of ordered learning and could be described as the entry level for library use.

Let us make an expanded listing of these and then, looking at the list, determine what each can communicate about the place of such in the pre-BI curriculum. These skills are the knowledge of the alphabet and Arabic numbers, the ability to understand the idea of a classification system and a dictionary arrangement, the ability to comprehend what is meant by a subject discipline and the interrelationship inherent in the idea "interdisciplinary," and the ability to comprehend the idea of hierarchy that is part of the idea of classification.

A. Knowledge of the alphabet;

B. A knowledge of Arabic numbers;

C. Knowledge of alphabetization;

D. The cognition of the concept of classification;

E. The idea of and the ability to use--entry--access;

F. The idea of a dictionary arrangement;

G. The concept of a subject discipline--i.e., math or chemistry;

H. What is meant by the term "interdisciplinary";

I. The idea of hierarchy as a sine qua non undergirding any classification system.

For other than young children, skills one and two should not need to be overtly taught, but, rather, can be elicited as concepts from the student's own experience.

These skills have been listed in the order of their difficulty. In looking at them, we can see that something more is appearing than just a progressively difficult obstacle course. The something more is the ability to discriminate and the ability to generalize, two basic cognitive attributes.

The exact timetable of the appearance of these cognitive skills is not absolute. One child psychiatrist puts it at age seven, and stresses the need to nurture and teach these skills through concreteness. Since all that seems to be certain in this permanent-floating crap game called learning is uncertainty, perhaps these seven "Golden Rules" of Edward Lee Thorndike will adequately serve as directives:

1. Consider the situation the pupil faces.
2. Consider the response you wish to connect with it.
3. Form the bond; do not expect it to come by a miracle.
4. Other things being equal, form no bond that will have to be broken.
5. Other things being equal, do not form two or three bonds when one will serve.
6. Other things being equal, form bonds in the way that they are required later to act.
7. Favor, therefore, the situations which life itself will offer, and the responses which life itself will demand. (Joncich, p. 88)

Surely instruction in alphabet and numbers comes first among these skills librarians use as an entry level base. After that, painstakingly one-to-one wherever possible, each human must be nurtured into whatever needed generalizations and discriminations are attainable for him that day. There is quite a bit of difference in the ability to understand classification as opposed to learning merely to recognize the symbols and order that are involved in the alphabet or the simple numbering system; still, it is something that one could envision being taught in its simplest form at the kindergarten level. If these basic skills and their library applications were to be taught in kindergarten,

Entry-Level Library Skills

we could imagine a first-grader, when his reading skills develop, finding it quite easy to use the library. Even at the beginning of first grade, when he is in possession of only alphabetical and numbering skills, not reading, he could learn how books are arranged on a shelf. How to locate a science book under an abridged Dewey arrangement and use 555 to find books on the earth seems a reasonable goal of such instruction.

This is one of the advantages of a terse system such as that afforded by the very basic abridged Dewey. Because of the simplicity of its numbering system, a very young child could find mastery of it possible. Of course, he would not be able to use the catalog until his reading skills were at least middle first grade. Nevertheless, a child who, at the end of kindergarten or the beginning of first grade, could accomplish the feat of locating a book on a desired subject, would be well begun on his path to lifetime learning. By using the letter F for fiction or E for easy, he could find a book that he liked the looks of, to take home for a parent or an older sibling to read. Sent on a library odyssey by the teacher to choose a book for story hour, he should successfully bring booty back. Such simple library skills can come before he has the ability to read, and can make this young learner feel so much at home that library non compos mentis would never be one of his stumbling blocks. The same level of technical ability should provide even greater gratification for the older, disadvantaged seeker after library literacy.

The alphabet and beginning simple whole numbers are taught routinely in the kindergarten; yet at a dinner party, a distinguished scientist told the incredible story of an elderly scholarly acquaintance who had never mastered the alphabet.

This man possesses maximum reading skill, but has never mastered the alphabet. This is ironic and difficult to believe, but is in the same category as that of a minor sub-dean of Harvard who recently wrote an official request for information to a national organization that was answered, "Have you considered looking in Widener Library?"

For a late 20th century person, a major time wrench is needed to make us think of the existence of a civilized world before the use of such a simple principle as that of alphabetization. Lloyd W. Daly states that the principle involved in the use of an alphabet was well known to the Greeks, as a consequence of knowing the sequential Phoenician alphabet. Yet he says that it took five centuries before Callemachus of the Alexandria library recorded for posterity evidence of its use.

Knowledge of the alphabet and simple Arabic numbers can be the skill of a 2-1/2-year-old. I saw a demonstration by a young mother who had lettered cards and, using the "pick a card, any card" approach, had her son recognizing and sounding p--op, c--op, etc. He could also count to ten on his own. Though such precocity is rare, we teaching librarians probably can count on those two basic skills being available as a platform for our lessons. Dear heaven, I hope so!

Alphabetization is more complex. Strategies for teaching concepts A-E to young children illustrate or diagram the how-to for all learners with limited verbal and conceptual skills. Content and body language should, of course, reflect the appropriate age and interest level.

The concept of alphabetization lends itself to games such as a form of solitaire played with large, single-letter cards. Each learner could make his own name tag and take turns alphabetizing classmates round a circle. Nonsense rhymes and songs naturally flow from such attempts to manipulate and structure the alphabet. The exercise of making a family telephone directory would also demonstrate this in a personal form. The "Sesame Street" magnetized plastic letters and related metal board are intriguing and should help eager fingers devise their own games to learn alphabetization.

"Classification" Webster's defines as "systematic arrangement in classes; systematic arrangement of animals

Entry-Level Library Skills 203

and plants in groups or categories based on some definite scheme, now usually that of natural relationships."

Instruction in classification could begin with some of the props and games mentioned earlier. "Let's put all the A's together--all the 2's together, all the 3's together." Use that classic catch-all of humankind--pants pockets. Ask for a volunteer to turn his out and then a second. Get the class to name and then match classes of objects so produced. Some of the "Fish" type games of my childhood are still around to enliven library lessons in classification. One set on trees I still remember because the leaf shapes so delighted my young senses.

With my adult ed classes, one strategy is to assign the task of listing categories or areas of their domestic belongings that they feel are classified. All ages use things where this principle can be tangibly realized. "Home" offers good teaching relevancy as does any other area with detailed physical parts--bank, grocery store, or toy store. Adult collections--jewelry (which was most appropriate for educating DAR Members about library classification), or buttons, menus, or matches, if they interest the learner, will serve to make the point.

Entry--getting there from here! One example is transport such as subway entrance points, or thruway off/on ramps. A discussion of trying to use the phone book to find a friend's address when all that is known is first name and phone number is usually successful teaching. The concept involves understanding that the piece of information--what one wants to know--has a handle and that finding the item sought is contingent upon knowledge of the handle. "You can't get there from here" is humorous and accurate.

Dictionary arrangement is the simplest form of access to those who are alpha-skilled. Having at hand a clutch of tomes so arranged, put one in each student's hand long enough for him to realize, "Yes, it is alpha!" Then send the books around the group 'til everyone has examined each one and come to realize how widespread are the reference books so arranged.

Next in our list of mental equipment for library use is the notion of a subject discipline. This intellectuality underlies cataloging and classification and they are hard to use well without such basic training. The school curricula have been no help here, as they have tended to lose the historic academic disciplines by the adoption of broad, umbrella terms. Two such that come instantly to mind are Social Science and Earth Science. New disciplines such as the applied technologies of aerospace and computers require course realignments and new editions of Dewey. If this practice is to wear the positive garments of interdisciplinary blending, doesn't it stand to reason that some feeling for the integers is vital to the equation? The seamstress has better luck with the finished garment if she does not make it of two fabrics which require totally different cleaning techniques.

The young can learn "subject" as one definitive other name for "all about. " The grammatical concept of the subject of a sentence carries the lesson. Doll, ball, bicycle-- all are subjects, which ultimately become subject headings. Once academic subjects are understood as discrete, another underlying concept of library skills is in place for us to build library upon.

Interdisciplinary is tougher. Between and among the academic subjects is needed for a thorough mastery of print subject entry and vital for Boolean logic on-line searching: Perhaps real toy building blocks are the best way to help the young visualize these ideas. One can paint and letter blocks to represent the disciplines and build with them an interdisciplinary structure such as Earth Science, or Liberal Arts, or the Humanities. By this device, graphics and the power of names join us as teaching aids.

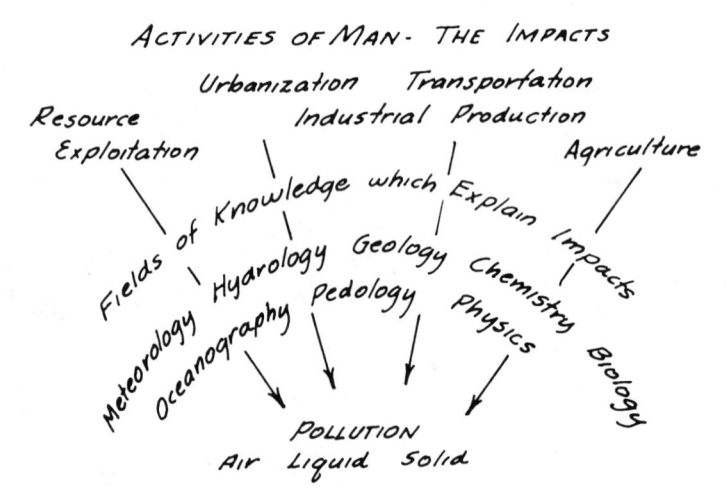

ACTIVITIES OF MAN - THE IMPACTS

Urbanization   Transportation

Resource   Industrial Production
Exploitation   Agriculture

Fields of Knowledge which Explain Impacts

Meteorology Hydrology Geology Chemistry Biology
Oceanography Pedology Physics

POLLUTION
Air   Liquid   Solid

If it won't take, except for the exceptionally exceptional, relax. It can wait til verbal skills can be built. Using the analogies of interplanetary and interpersonal as take-off points, we can transmit the overlap and in-betweenness of interdisciplinary programs. The historical method can come to our aid. "Earth Science" has developed from man's new insights into the interrelatedness of the physical world. Ecology is the latest example of this way of thinking. Systems analysis and computer capabilities have provided the technical capabilities for cybernetics.

Hierarchy, in the sense that is relevant to library skills, Webster's defines as "a series of objects, or items divided or classified in ranks or orders, as in natural science or logic; a hierarchical arrangement." The other common meaning involves: "a body of rulers ... disposed organically in ranks and orders, each subordinate to the one above it." The possessor of polished library skills must have this precept as part of his entry level knowledge.

Dewey cannot be comprehended without an understanding of hierarchical arrangement. Beyond the first ten large general classes, everything is in ranks or orders. Consider the import of such a skill when a catalog is classified, as it is in most library systems designed on the British model. This is no small part of the civilized world, as I learned on a round-the-world trip. The classed catalog is used in Canada and the rest of the British Commonwealth, and in Japan and Israel. Hierarchical arrangement is also intrinsic to comprehension of academic disciplines and their interrelationships.

Hierarchy as a concept involves size and position. For the young or anyone not easily able to grasp an abstraction, those bright nests of boxes or carved wooden eggs-within-eggs prove useful demonstration objects.

With a child you can use such as the story of Goldilocks and the Three Bears and the wonderful repetition of Mama Bear, Papa Bear, and Baby Bear. This is a hierarchy based upon relationships within the family which even the youngest can comprehend. High school students studying the family might learn about hierarchy from a discussion of the nuclear versus the expanded family unit. The Roman Catholic church, the military, the school system, where curriculum-related, can be shaped to our purpose. One brand-new course which would seem a perfect vehicle for teaching about hierarchy is "Student Rights and Responsibilities."

The Library lessons of level two to be discussed in Chapter 12, "Library" as a textbook for climbing the knowledge pyramid, are:

1. Alphabetization
2. Dictionary arrangement.
3. Book as both a knowledge package and an artifact.
4. Cataloging and classification.
5. Subject entry.
6. The reference collection as a unit and specific reference fields in depth.
7. History of Libraries and their carriers.

Two other areas to be interwoven throughout wherever appropriate are computers and on-line searching and critical thinking--the former because it is "today" and if you don't display it as a constant icon, your credibility with the learners of "now" will suffer; and, the latter because it is the electric brain wave counterpart of the process you are teaching with your textbook called "library" and your jungle-gym of learning, the knowledge pyramid--the skill that puts it all together and makes us truly human. "Ye shall know the truth, and the truth will make you free."

Put the total impact of your will behind the belief that your library is the best non-human resource to teach the skills of cognitive and affective learning and that your role is to make every professional decision serve that belief. Your professional training gave you a gift that you can now give back to children, their teachers, and their parents.

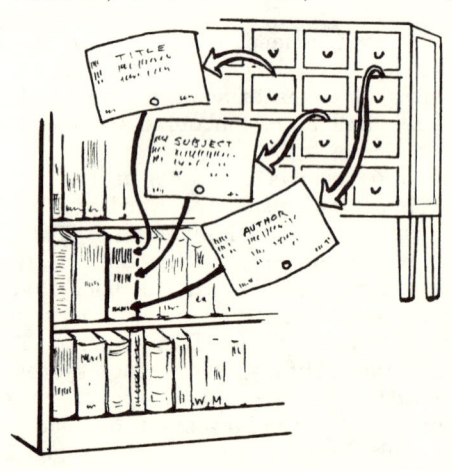

Chapter 12

Library as a texbook for Climbing the Knowledge Pyramid

Error of opinion may be tolerated where reason is left free to combat it.

— Thomas Jefferson

Teaching is a most special and difficult form of communication. One of its traps is hierarchy--respect and order and yet open dialogue without undue fear of humiliation or failure on the part of either level--sage or seeker. Another is temperament. The cliché "teachers are born, not made" exists because it is a paradoxical truism. This book, among millions of its fellows, offers counsel toward making ourselves teachers, yet, our personalities overwhelm, for teaching success or failure, any classroom script. Communication is a process consisting of these several steps:

1. Ideation--just what is your goal? Get a date, encourage a child, increase your budget?
2. Encoding--transfer into a physical form from a mental one--put into media a symbolic equivalent of an idea. What symbols? Words, candy, a hug.
3. Transmission--write a letter, make a phone call, speak out.
4. Transmission received.
5. Decoded--into a facsimile of the sender's message.

Does this book deal with communication? Devoutly do I hope so. Those of us who believe in the power of the printed book to encode a human thesis must believe equally in its transmission power. A strong ideation, clearly encoded, on ph neutral paper, offers a most satisfying variant of eternal life. For those of us without grandchildren, this is a powerful prod to our pen. Why include this list? As a symbolic way to demonstrate the traps of communication. The audience for this book is at least reasonably successful at this technique--possession of our at least M. L. S. higher ed credentials validates this assumption. Why is communication Continuing Ed needed? Because confrontation with the perhaps long buried mechanics of a crucial skill warns us anew that to teach implies a hellishly difficult human commitment.

"Library" as a Textbook 209

I would draw the parallel with my experience in teaching a son to drive. To teach parking required me to surface the long buried steps of that complex process.

When you assume the role of BI, all the pitfalls that lie between message en-coding and de-coding hide in your words. Teaching dialogue means language with its many potential barriers to understanding. Shaw said that the Americans and the English are separated by a common language. Other division points that can cloud or wipe out reception are ambiguity, varied meaning possible in paraphrasing, imprecision of metaphors, etc. Accurate communication demands precise language, if words are our symbolic code. In Hawaii I served as one of the Volunteers who peopled the Information Desk at Queen's Hospital. Behind a desk, able to use the long vista to assess the approaching questioner, I would smile while evaluating all the clues to nationality, education, etc. in order to know how best to encode my response. Service to students of Lifelong BI requires an equally conscious symbol prescription. Watch your words as you move from one age, income, national, and educational level to another. What is a red flag word--Viet Nam, Hitler, handgun, Chairman--to one is SOP to another. We cannot send messages--only symbols, and the impact of these carriers depends on our personal dictionaries. Our brains do not interface. Intimate verbal exchange implies transmission on a single frequency--one psychological language. Interpersonal sensitivity to the art and science of communication is a crucial element for us who must individualize instruction and truly meet the student decoder.

Teaching the collection of skills that answers to such various names as library skills, information skills, library literacy and study skills demands much of its practicioners. These demands are of two kinds--subject and personal. Study skills belong, traditionally to the purview of the classroom teacher. Critical thinking and information appraisal are two of these. When information skills mean how to use the card catalog and what is Dewey or LCC, the academic librarian becomes the one responsible. Beyond and outside of "school" (K-Ph. D.), such teaching falls to a public service librarian--to the persons peopling the Reference Desk or Children's Room.

Teachers are supposed to be extroverts or, at least, not to hate humankind. That is also one requisite personal qualification for Reference Librarians, and even then, these front deskers are being felled by what is being called "Librarian Burn Out" to describe the oftentimes overwhelming stress placed on public service librarians striving with curtailed budgets to survive the current emphasis on libraries as community centers.

For most subject-related classroom teaching, curriculum guides and textbooks structure the subject. The M. L. S. courses that created us librarians are similarly mapped. If our job as teachers of library was to replicate such, no improvisation would be required, and, if supervised exposure to a good layman's how-to text would produce confident library literates, the job would not demand an unusually strong ego. But--and this is a but to put out front--nowhere in education is it more vital to relate timing and explanations to the queries of learners than in library teaching. The bare bones of Library Orientation and a lecture on term paper preparation don't stick to create a cumulative competence because they offer generalities, laid on top of the listener's preoccupation with personal specific goals. There is no textbook that can provide you with the analogy or anecdote that will drive home the rationale for each individual's unique information lack. If we are still arguing with the overwhelming evidence of the crucial need for learner relevance in teaching reading and writing set down by such as Dan Fader of Hooked on Books, for shame. Who wants to learn to read, unless they want to possess the knowledge held in the strange squiggles? Who, indeed, wants to internalize a lesson on the card catalog unless it directly serves such a personal, immediate need to know? In all of education, nowhere is individualized instruction more crucial than in BI. Therefore, to accomplish this, its practitioners must be comfortable thinking on their feet.

In the K-Ph. D. context, faculty can be lured into the library curriculum to add relevancy for the student. Beyond this, the only unifying and central theme is the student's specific need which propels him to the Reference Desk or into a Continuing Education course in "Information Skills."

If the Reference Librarian keeps to the traditional role and delivers product, one more chance to teach process has been lost. To add the component of process to the Reference Interview forces the librarian on duty to produce on demand a technique for making the process connect in the

"Library" as a Textbook 211

mind of the student. That, clearly, is a harder act to perform for a stream of questioners minute into hour than offering product, the answer sought. A button proclaiming "Dear Lord, give me patience--right now," positioned to cheer the librarian on duty at the DAR Reference Desk, addressed this professional trauma.

Yes, indeed, one of the reasons why all the efforts toward library literacy have come to almost naught, is because effective teaching demands one whale of a lot from practitioners. Those of you who have read thus far realize that, justified or not, my ego qualifies. The rest of this chapter consists of the best on-the-job help I can contrive to furnish those whose personality urges them on. Since, by now, my teaching spans 26 years and ages 6 to infirmity and includes the Continuing Education student and users of special libraries in four different subject areas, there is breadth to the hopefully inspirational examples that follow.

To discuss lessons in library skills using the nomenclature of education might sound like this: If there are cognitive goals, affective goals, and educational goals, the librarian's work includes them all. The educational goals would be to teach the pupil the organization of the library--both specifics of the materials and the philosophic overtones which determine collection organization and, on this base, to teach access to materials in whatever media is needed throughout the library network.

Affective goals are really the long-range and overriding reason for the validity of this whole exercise. If affective goal means a change in behavior, then we want to produce the change in behavior from the present baffled, embarrassed, put-down, or totally turned-off library avoider to a person who can enter, feel at home in, understand library organization and use it for lifetime information needs. This is a behavior change that must precede the second desired change in performance which is competency in critical thinking. Using the library as a textbook, our aim is to generate the ability to read and think critically. The student's behavior thereafter would be affected by possession of these abilities.

A motto for our minds and our walls is "no busy work." Within academe (K-Ph.D.) tie lessons to the curriculum as it comes to us from faculty and students. Beyond or in the cracks of "school" our teaching hope lies in the motivation behind the presenting query. All queries represent patron problems. Our job is to demonstrate the problem-solving abilities of our library.

Specific skills to be taught, beginning, of course, yesterday on the first day of kindergarten:

1. Alphabetization--a catch-up wherever needed.
2. Dictionary arrangement.
3. Cataloging and classification.
4. Book as both a knowledge package, and artifact.
5. Subject entry, including hierarchy and subject disciplines.
6. The import of the Reference Collection as the place to begin to use the library as a means to critically think through an information problem.

1. Alphabetization:

If we think of the places where the alphabet is a must in library access, we see a catalog card. In addition to the first direct alphabetizing, there are further complexities--exceptions and refinements that must be surfaced by us practitioners and then organized to teach in response to a patron/pupil's query.

To teach the alphabet as a library skill, one must go beyond the simple a, b, c, of the 26 letters. The student must learn that the second letter follows in the same alphabetical principle as the first in letter by letter filing. It is a second level entry skill to realize that on a catalog card you use the alphabetical principle for the top line and again for the second line of the card. These, of course, are degrees of difficulty to be mastered. As each one demonstrates the ability to master the simpler concepts, then the more complex ramifications of this principle can be presented.
No one can use the catalog regardless of how well he can read, unless alphabetization is mastered.

Another example of the library's use of alphabetization lies in the second line of the call number, the book number. Without alphabetical skill and an understanding of this principle, the user wouldn't have a prayer of finding Galsworthy between F and H, thus losing the help of one of the mnemonic devices in library classification.

"Library" as a Textbook   213

2. Dictionary Arrangement:

   The idea inherent in our term, dictionary arrangement, is another primary stone in the library arch. The Bookman's Glossary defines this as "One in which all entries (e. g., subject, title, author) are arranged in a single alphabetical sequence (as opposed to a classified catalog)." (In checking to put this page reference on my manuscript, I realized that this time such an oversight would not be serious because Bookman's Glossary is itself a dictionary arrangement.) There is always the interwoven yet obscure presence of the needs for alphabetic skill in Library IQ. Anyone lacking entry level alpha cognition cannot even crack the contents of a pocket dictionary.

   A dictionary arrangement is the most common because it is easiest to use. Why is it the easiest for beginners to use? Because the only mental key that you need to possess to unlock it is the mastery of the alphabet. With other kinds of arrangements, such as subject or classified, the system employs complexities far beyond the alphabet. The order that is involved in such a reference book or catalog demands further skills of a competent user.

   To graduate in catalog IQ, the patron must grasp the idea of the catalog filing rules; i.e., "We file by the top line of the catalog card." This seems best demonstrated by the exercise of learning to make one's own set of catalog cards. Have the learner bring in a favorite book to catalog. If anyone has an author-relative or friend, encourage him to bring in such a book. Again, we learn most from what is dearest to us.

   Experience makes me an advocate of the divided catalog. The greatest patron hang-ups, once over the Library IQ threshold, are in the confusion between title and subject entries. After the catalog is divided, the patron has no barriers to the access he seeks: author and title (definite already-identified items sought), or subject--I want material on _____.

   Author entry seems to be a great hurdle even to most adults. This is especially critical where so much material is organizational in origin and format. If something is an American Council on Education publication, what is its author? The Library of Congress cards have not been the consistent intellectual support that one would hope. This was demonstrated for me, as we began to develop the Council archives with our chief of publications, Robert Quick, as expert. After 25 years of ACE experience, he knew the story of each publication and, many times, what LC cited as author, as having the intellectual responsibility, was not the correct attribution at all. Whatever the LC in-house reasons are, time and time again they ignore a responsible publisher's identification of a personal author in favor of a corporate one, with all the attendant confusion and lack of simple factuality.

3. Book:

As the print unit with which the print network is built, "book" demands a top billing in a BI Curriculum for lifelong learning. It serves two main teaching goals--to demonstrate that it is the source of the data on a catalog card or an on-line citation or any other bibliographic description, and to demonstrate that its unique structure organizes and affords varying degrees of access to the information it packages. That any reference work worth its salt answers all its own organizational questions is a basic red-flag point in this curriculum and, even fiction, when it has become a Jane Eyre, offers such structure in its critical and editorial essays. During my adult ed course at Georgetown University I devote an entire two-hour class to this topic. There are two umbrella points. The first is that the intellect that created each non-fiction book thereby produced a discrete organized unit of information. Between two covers each part makes its special contribution to the whole data package. After the class break, the lesson goes on with each student selecting a book from the cart-full lent to my within-the-walls classroom by the supportive Reference Staff of Lauinger Library, and actually studying "books" as incarnate information.

The second point is that library organization, with classification as structure or design, builds on each such information package, to create a physicality whereby information linkage is actually made visible. Try using the laundry analogy. The model drawer of male socks--can we say Prince Charles'--makes visible the concept of "sock" as an integral component of wardrobe where, the larger the collection, the more detailed selection is possible. Refer back to "library" and, by actually walking your students through, demonstrate your points by pulling out specific books and explaining how each unit relates to

"Library" as a Textbook 215

those within its classification designation and related numbers.

The paradox of an almost religious reverence for the physical form "book," combined with the equally widespread ignorance of its structure, gives the BI instructor the considerable advantage of being able to provide add-on knowledge about a familiar household icon. The checklist of the parts of a book that are worth curriculum space might read like this:

    a. Book jacket, cover, and end papers--details, such as maps, art, and blurbs, all have meaning for readers.
    b. Title page--don't overlook the amplification provided by the subtitle.
    c. Verso of title page--vital data on publishing history of this book.
    d. Illustrations--ask what is their purpose?
    e. Preface--difference between it and the following section.
    f. Introduction.
    g. Table of contents--subject headings for this book.
    h. Body of the text.
    i. Footnotes--the scholarly trail.
    j. Bibliographies--do they lead the reader further into the subject or merely provide full citations for work quoted or noted?
    k. Index--the detailed analytics of this book.

The understanding of these segments and how they can work for us is one of the specific library skills. The body of a book is the one part that does seem to be more or less universally understood. The relationship of the chapters to the table of contents is an understanding possessed by most people who find themselves doing library work. The subtleties of the index and its use are skills quite rarely possessed by any but librarians, or trained researchers.

Let us consider specific library classroom approaches to the mastery of these eleven skills and concepts. Any such lesson for persons of any age or cultural or educational level should be taught first from a personal book of the student's. This permits you to individualize instruction by drawing your points from the examples before you. It is, of course, necessary to have selected and brought in to class, as back-up, examples of each item you wish to illustrate. These book lessons are bi-level--physical artifact which is the creation of the book-maker/publisher's art and information package. These two levels combine to say that the book still remains as the sole comprehensive and proven method of self-instruction--portable, energy-efficient, demanding only an able reader and some form of illumination.

    a. Book Jacket, Cover, and Endpapers: these lessons fall chiefly under artifact and serve to begin to focus the student's thinking about book design. Search the books brought in for good examples to illustrate type (size and style), page layout, and the effect which the kinds of binding and sewing have on how the book opens, endures, and feels in the hand. There are, however, information points to be made as well. These include the blurb on the jacket--whether the book's design accurately reflects its message or is deliberately misleading in order to promote sales, etc.

    b. Title Page: Bi-level also. Everyone relates to title and personal author, but explanations about the information component of a subtitle, corporate author, and publisher's imprint are usually news to those not professional book people.

    c. Verso of title page: Publishing history, the genealogy of a work, offers another information source that is an almost totally new resource for readers. Sadly, some major publishers are no longer going to provide this factuality. Verso, title and half titles are useful pegs upon which to hang publishing facts of value to students.

    To illustrate publishing history, ask, "Is the book new? What is the extent of the revision if it is based on a previous publication?" This is vital when using the telephone book, especially if a family is of the kind that collects old telephone books or isn't too careful about the cuurency of a reference source. It is important to realize that one must seek the most current edition or face some humorous or tragic consequences. Once the student grasps these points, they are transferable to any directory that he seeks to use, be it school, office, community, or national.

    d. Illustrations: artifact lesson plus information components such as these; Do they purport to be fact (photographs especially), yet are used to transmit a heavy emotionalism? Dialogue drawn from in-hand examples of faked photographs (stuffed animals, incorrect clothing, etc.), outdoor

"Library" as a Textbook 217

lighting that raised questions of accuracy, etc. can help to educate toward photographic literacy.

    e. Preface: I always bring my Bowker's Bookman's Glossary to class and share its definitions as class discussion raises needful points. This reinforces the concept of Desk Reference and trains class thought toward the concept of authority.

    f. Introduction: Interactive points with preface.

    g. Table of Contents: This lesson helps learners comprehend as a concept our librarian's use of subject headings. Be sure to introduce a discussion of degrees of classification between Table of Contents, Index, and Card Catalog.

    h. Body of the Text: Draw from as many specifics of the books brought to class as is necessary to present and reinforce the fact that each non-fiction book text block is organized information--the building block unit upon which all the larger networking of libraries is constructed. Be sure to communicate with as many examples as you can seize upon the fact, opinion, and usually value judgment content relationship which some one (thinker/writer/editor/compiler) or some group has organized from a related subject area to serve specific communication goals.

    i. Footnotes: Points to be made relate to and reinforce the concept of scholarship as a blazed trail. Turabian and the like are "must" Desk References for you to bring in to support your authority. Find examples of complete and incomplete citations. Discuss access from citation to text. Plagiarism is one obvious component of library skill lessons and this is a curriculum peg as golden as any.

    j. Bibliographies: Continue the dialogue about access to full text from a citation and refer to the relationships of networking, ILL and on-line searching. Use these as a springboard for individualizing instruction on the work's progression from fact to opinion to value judgment--i. e., does the bibliography give both sides? Does it span the subject's full history? Does it become philosophy?

    k. Index: Relate this lesson to the points about Subject Headings made when you talked about the Table of Contents. Next, stress the degree of closeness of classification between these two parts of a book and tie that into the card catalog with as many examples as you can elicit from your students. Be a "detail person" and explain the difference between an every-name index and a broader subject one and point out small index clues such as the bulk of information being noted by a configuration such as 89-102 or a type variant to indicate a picture.

Librarians have much to learn from the noted teacher and author, Sylvia Ashton-Warner as she urges teachers to elicit from the child his own interests--his own words and subjects. This is a complete switch from the poured-in outside world of Dick and Jane. In her books, Spinster and Teacher, both the "why" and the "how" of this method are clearly spelled out. Using Mrs. Warner's device of writing each child's own daily words on pieces of cardboard and patiently watching these build into sentences (not formal grammar) and then stories, we can teach our charges to make books in all their physical reality. Old magazines, paper, scissors, cardboard, paste, pen, colored paints and pencils will yield covers, and title pages, tables of contents, stories, and indices. These parts of that organized "carrier" must become part of every student's mental library literacy equipment if there is to be a sturdy foundation in place to support the knowledge pyramid.

Book making and book production is a fertile field for teaching. Some lively discussions have been in this area. Since bookbinding was a family hobby, with my daughter being the practitioner and myself the comprehender and appreciator, I have specific past-master's training to share. One trick that proves quite dramatic requires as a prop a worn-out or deceased book. If you can't find this kind of book in your own library, it can be bought for pennies at a thrift shop. The important thing is to have a stock of them on hand for the time when you are ready to discuss bookmaking. As Father Capon, in The Feast of the Lamb, discusses peeling an onion as a symbolic way to discover its integrity, I peel a book for the student. Call it a bibliophilic striptease, but it is effective.

If you can bring to class, from your institutional or personal library, truly special physical specimens of the genus book you can widen your student's understanding and appreciation of the origins of the world's reverence for the physical book.

Exposure to the editor of a "fact" book offers an

"Library" as a Textbook

intriguing and successful lesson in critical thinking. The process by which an editorial team, strange to a subject field, can become familiar enough with it to organize the knowledge package "book" affords a palpable show-and-tell in print information processing. This process is my information pyramid. Working in publishing has both schooled me in how this is done and given me direct access to appropriate teaching treasures. Joseph Goodwin, a former colleague at the Geographic, now an editor for Smithsonian Exposition Books can be cajoled to class. He describes isolated facts and opinions as "play pretties" that are put on his desk by writers and researchers and which he must arrange into the information pyramid he has chosen to present. Without the factual base, it is not responsible expository writing. Without the capstone of value judgment, there is nothing of a writer's or editor's special insights. Opinions are a requisite step on the ascent.

His "show" includes a current work "in process" and the beauty just off the press. Since these volumes are profusely illustrated with both photographs and charts, students also have a "book as multi-media lesson." In addition, because these books are widely available, students easily relate to the instruction and usually overflow with "whys?" and "hows?" Editorial guests can be recruited from technical and scientific editors in government agencies, journalists (for one terrific class session I was able to demonstrate in most human form the differences between book and newspaper editorial constraints), consultants, and your own faculty. Since these professionals tend to enjoy their work and also need to expand the pool of discriminating potential customers for their efforts, they have many good reasons for joining our BI team.

The entity "books" provides other BI lessons. The routine act of overseeing a book charge-out can be used by an alert BI librarian to add one more cubit of book power to a student's Library IQ. And, lest because of my Passion for Books I be accused of media blindness, let me state that response to such criticism helps us to see the relative accessibility and convenience of books and media software-hardware. Only such as a President can command a movie theatre to curl up with, all the YA filmmakers notwithstanding. The tinkers among us will rightly purr over cogs and glorious meshing gears and electronic circuitry. Today, even though each child armed with a school movie camera may be equated with Lincoln and his copy book, there do exist differences in performance and availability and cost which we overlook to our profession's peril.

The history of the carriers themselves is also a necessary part of our curriculum in library skills. The past that is prologue lives in these carriers--be they the Rosetta Stone, the Koran, or a roll of Egyptian papyrus from the temple library of Edfu. A modern such object is added each split second. Each spawning has its own story. We owned a rocking chair which came from an accretion of dusty furniture in the cellars of Conant Hall which Harvard disposed of to graduate students for a pittance. My children, who enjoyed countless lap hours therein, particularly relished my original "history" of that chair, from its present owner, back through the life of Conant Hall. Half-told, half-sung to the accompaniment of the hero's distinctive creaking, it was a comforting way for young children to capture the present that lives between the unfamiliar past and the unknown future. Keen explains this need of humanness to be nurtured by the unity of history through story:

> each people had its own cycle of stories which located the individual within the tribe, the tribe within the cosmos, and the cosmos within the overworld. (Keen, p. 85)

Contemporary man has become lost. He cannot light the ritual fire or recall the proper prayer and may be nearing the end of his ability to see his own life as part of any story. By using our training in the "once upon a time" of the physical objects of the records of history in relevant teachable moments, we can help our students combat the alienation of rootlessness.

Whether religious or agnostic, we should be able to see the value of knowing about the story behind the Talmud, the Bible and the Koran. "No, John, the tablets on which the Lord wrote the Ten Commandments are not in the British Museum. But there are things called the Dead Sea Scrolls, written before the birth of Christ, which are in their own special museum in Jerusalem." To teach such lessons in the history of books, one might need to call upon an expert beyond grade school faculty. I did once. My scholar was Mrs. Marian Kelloran of the Virginia Theological Seminary who held 30 thirteen-year-olds cross-legged on Persian carpets as spellbound as did Walter Farley of Black Stallion fame. I followed Mrs. Kelloran's visit with an exercise

"Library" as a Textbook

sheet containing four versions of the Thirteenth Chapter of First Corinthians--the familiar faith, hope, and charity passage. By drawing from the students the basic expository statements, and then helping them identify the literary devices used to add the chronological to the literary dimension, we can build the skills necessary to evaluate any carrier of information or wisdom or imagination as just that--and assist in puncturing the myth of book as a product of some heavenly Tome-of-the-Month-Club.

The power in books, symbolic and actual, has driven men like Hitler to put them to the torch. The cry of revolutionaries now is not to the torch, but to the moving van (industry in--librarians out); to defrock us as wizards, this time, the newest answer is electronic technology. To avoid the put-down of transference from ostriches to dodos, let's modernize that ancient symbolic lamp of knowledge and set it merrily blazing to advertise our "teaching with books and libraries."

Now seems a proper moment to consider again Marchant's words about the professional uptightness produced by faculty members' imagined need to stay always one-up on their students and forever overflow with right answers to any student query. Their fear of the "Yes, Virginia, I am afraid to say, 'I don't know'" syndrome is very real. Our role as sorcerers of the book is to start a chain of questions, and to provide the materials where answers--and more questions--can be found. The picture of any librarian behind a desk transferring knowledge from her head to students via the lecture and note-taking method negates the concept "library." Our badge prepares us to educate by enabling students to acquire the skills necessary to collect, process and evaluate information. That schools really do the reverse accounts for the absence of any meaningful proportion of lifelong learners among the American people after a more than fair trial of the broadest-based, most expensive bill for public education in all of human history.

Myth and fairy tale in the variant editions provide another useful teaching resource for teaching the History of the Carriers of Knowledge. On cue from the English department, plan a lesson tracing one title such as <u>Pride and Prejudice</u> or the <u>Wizard of Oz</u> through several editions to the media variants--the T.V. scripts and the great movies. We can ask, "How are these printed versions different from each other and from the pictorial productions?" When classroom dialogue has sorted out salient points demanding answers, turn the students loose in the library to collect, process and evaluate the "whys" to be found in such ready-references as May Hill Arbuthnot's Children and Books, Constantine Georgiou's Children and Their Literature, and Contemporary Criticism.

The variants of literary style and form emerge from such comparisons as visible as Mt. Kilimanjaro. Surrounded by variant and historic editions of "Snow White," we can ask this question:

> What language do we have that is not obsolete? There is such a language, one forgotten and out of style, but one we are rediscovering. In his brilliant book, The Forgotten Language, Erich Fromm tells us that the only language that cuts across all barriers of time and place and space and culture is the language of dream, fairy tale, fantasy, myth. I would include also the free and disciplined reaches of imaginative language, the use of metaphor and simile, of poetry and parable. Only by being particular are we able to make the abstract concrete, to see order in chaos. But is this language true? ... A professor of philosophy at one of the great universities told his students, "You shall know the truth, and the truth shall make you free." He also told them that he could not remember the source of the quotation, but no matter, it was terribly important.
> But just to try to know the truth ourselves is not enough: we must also communicate it.
> (L'Engle, p. 662-663)

These words from The Horn Book belong to a distinguished scholar story teller. The ability to identify such universal and eternal language is the cognitive objective for this lesson. The comparative texts themselves, clearly marked as to age, author (or adapter or editor), illustrator, etc., offer the materials from which each learner can program his own instruction in understanding ancestry and placement of literary language. Again, we need to have available source materials to answer the "whys" that each student will generate.

4. Classification:

What is the relationship between the call number function of classification--word transformed into numbers, a change in the form of an idea to facilitate a physical address for locating each volume--and the subject identification function? In American libraries, the call number serves as the book's address--the invisible string connecting the catalog card to the physical book described. If the shelf arrangement were sequential (1-infinity), the connection notation would reflect that simple numbering system as would library shelf order. Access to anything physical, person, place, or thing, demands a location notation. Drunk or sober, prince or peasant, you can't get there if the location of "there" is an unknown. This is use number one--for the patron to be able to "call" for the wanted book.

Use number two is the subject information function of the call number. Numeric sequential arrangement notation informs the patron of library growth as would chronological notation. What we librarians call classification adds the information increment of subject identification to the retrieval component. Knowledge of a class notation informs the catalog searcher if the book being considered for use is a hit or not. Otherwise, all the class number accomplishes is the provision to the patron of an address with which he can then search through open stacks for his prize. Sadly, though, the subject description function of shelf classification is largely news to our patrons. Richard Joseph Hyman puts this in context in his excellent book, Shelf Access in Libraries. According to him, Dewey was primarily loyal to the classified catalog and the DDC was designed to be used in that way. Collection organization for content identification and retrieval by its users he describes as "bibliographical" organization; arrangement in catalogs and indices is "bibliothecal" or physical organization. His first chapter is an account of the history of shelf access which he feels "culminates in American libraries with the contradictory policy of shelf classification as divorced from a classified catalog for which the classification scheme was originally created." (Hyman, p. 2)

When collections are small, human memory can provide adequate access to their contents. Any serious book collector knows this from firsthand experience. Books with like-subject content are placed together to facilitate use. (Unless, as with my uncle, that use is pure decor.) The early catalogs served as stimuli to and then substitution for the librarian's memory. After reading Cutter on this point, I found it to be a valid BI reply to a patron's hopeful query; "Do you have the History of Whatever?" The catalog functions to answer these three questions: "Do you have it?" "Where is it?" and "What is it mainly about?" Having it or not, except for all the exceptions, is absolute, yes or no. Locations can be "relative"--in relation to others of its kind or "fixed"--near a door or window, or as patrons wistfully or fiercely announce, "It was right here!" Items one and two are obvious. Item three is not. Yet it is our costly but routine inclusion of the subject relevancy component that transmutes shelves of books into "library" and thus into a textbook in information process and problem solving.

In many parts of the world the classified catalog is the norm. Travel to New Zealand and Israel, two countries widely spaced geographically whose libraries are influenced by British methods, made real for me this third part of their already divided catalog. The words that accompany the classification number are on the top line of the catalog card and the cards are arranged in class order (these are Dewey) like a shelf list. This gives the patron access to the item by its main class number. The classified catalog equates with shelflist so the resource does exist in all professionally managed libraries. (I write this with feeling and personal knowledge since the DAR Library did not have a shelflist until the advent of the first professional team began one in 1978.)

Teaching the concepts inherent in classification has proven a rewarding experience and one that has lent itself to innumerable tactics growing out of the students themselves. There are two main principles: that of like things being together, and that of the hierarchical notation to show a progression within the classification. Usually it is a progression from simple to complex, but whatever it is, it has to be demonstrable and inherent.

The most important principle in teaching is to teach the "why." If, as practicing librarians, we can't find any organic reason for the why, I seriously recommend abandoning the practice in the library to which we are responsible. Why is always easier with a gifted group to whom why is second nature, but if the learning atmosphere is open, somehow the teacher's "whys" don't seem to fall on totally unresponsive ears. Teaching the notation system that we call classification must also show why. Start with the idea or order--there must be an order to merit its name. Run through the various possibilities. This will give substance to the concept of a library classification system. To show how the notation grows and becomes a three-line call number, one might say, "You live at 2905 King Street. When you are on your way home in a car pool and the driver asks "Where do you live?" you say, 'I live in the subdivision called Green Hill.' At that, the driver will head toward Green Hill. Next, 'Where now?' 'I live on King Street.' All right, that's pretty close, and you probably could walk home, but then, on the other hand, exactly where do you live? 'I live at 2905,'" and then you can be delivered to your door. The arrangement of books is like that. Your main classification number would be the subdivision in which you live. The decimal notation is the street, and your unique house number is the book number-- the third line of the call number." That a three-line number shows something specific beyond the normal two-line call number is easy to dramatize with some such example of locational hierarchy from the learner's own experience.

A STORY ABOUT THE DEWEY DECIMAL SYSTEM OF CLASSIFICATION

BY THE LOS ANGELES COUNTY PUBLIC LIBRARY

The story of the numbers used for nonfiction books

Some years ago Mr. Melvil Dewey devised a system of classifying books which is used in many libraries. He chose certain main subjects and numbers, so that all nonfiction books on the same subject would be together on the shelf. He chose these subjects by imagining himself to be a prehistoric or primitive man. He asked himself questions he thought such a man would have asked.

100 Who am I?
PHILOSOPHY AND PSYCHOLOGY
(Man thinks about himself)

200 Who made me?
RELIGION
(Man thinks about God)

300 Who is the man in the next cave?
SOCIAL SCIENCES
(Man thinks about other people)

400 How can I make that man understand me?
PHILOLOGY (Language)

500 How can I understand nature and the world about me?
SCIENCE

600 How can I use what I know about nature?
APPLIED SCIENCE AND USEFUL ARTS

700 How can I enjoy my leisure time?
FINE ARTS AND RECREATION

800 How can I give to my children a record of man's heroic deeds?
LITERATURE

900 How can I leave a record for men of the future?
HISTORY GEOGRAPHY BIOGRAPHY

000 GENERAL WORKS

In explaining Dewey, teach the breakdown in whatever detail your library employs. The minimum breakdown is the easiest for the student to grasp. One powerful argument for this is that the simplest notation is all you can hope to keep shelved with any kind of precision. One useful DDC teaching tool is the following whimsical piece created by the Los Angeles County Public Library. By providing the help of "story" it manages to elicit recognition and a glimmer of identification in learners of all ages. It begins with this rhyme:

>Numbers, numbers in a row
>On so many library books you know.
>Why, you ask, should this be so?
>
>Why are some books in the 500's about the sea?
>And some in the 600's on how to make tea?
>Why? Oh why? Oh why? You'll see.
>
>Why in the 900's is the history of Cathay?
>And in the 700's--football and how to play?
>What is the reason for this, you say?
>
>To this puzzle of numbers there is a key.
>So, if you'll turn the page, you will see
>How these classes of numbers came to be.
>
>   Mayo Short

There seems ample justification for learners at any age or stage to commit Dewey's ten classes to memory. Armed with this mnemonic support, a user possesses a meaningful map of the majority of libraries. However, the Dewey Decimal System is taught, there is, in my experience, ample justification for anyone who intends to become an educated person to commit these ten classes to memory. By learning this classification system, one immediately possesses the key to the arrangement of the stacks in most of open-stack libraries. My greatest benefits from the skill came in graduate school where competition was predictably keen. Catholic University Library then was still largely under Dewey. One of the best edges that I devised, having mastered the stacks, was to get to them on a dead run the moment a class was over, locate the book just assigned, and complete the assignment before the professor realized that the book should have been put on Reserve.

"Library" as a Textbook 229

As the high school student goes on to the university level and is confronted, as he will usually be today, with the complexities of the LCC system, a good bit more desire will be required to master that system. On the other hand, one educated to Dewey has the foundation classification skills to master the LCC system if he wishes to have this short-cut to the stacks on a continuing basis. No mnemonic features are claimed for LCC, but there are a few. An example of one such lies in the second letter of the A Schedule. AM stands for music, AN for newspaper, I for indices and Y for yearbooks. The T schedule is Technology. Mastery of the principles of classification is all the grounding possible upon which to develop seasoned LCC stack alacrity.

No, satisfied recipients of Reference Desk Product Delivery aren't grabbing our collars and demanding their right to be taught how to do it for themselves. But--if they knew the import for them of the total bill for all the hidden costs of their lack of library literacy, they would do so.

Of all the subject disciplines, the one where classification is most indigenous is in the natural sciences--biology, particularly. Some of my most vivid and desperate freshman memories of college concern studying for my freshman biology final. There were what seemed like whole books of taxonomy to be memorized. These genera are long gone from my mind, but the cognition of hierarchy was burned deep.

Part of the intellectuality of the academic disciplines is historic and this is an idea important to relate to cataloging and classification. Make this part of the mental equipment for each of your "library" students with the help of your needed subject experts--the departmental chairpersons.

History of science, for example, has fascinated me as a teaching husband unrolled it for me over 32 years. Everything material we use--every natural process that we are subject to--falls somewhere in the history of science and technology. In teaching, present the logical division exemplified by DDC. Pure science is what the natural world is and does, the laws by which it governs itself. It is the word of nature, whoever wrote that word, as man is discovering it. Applied science is what man has done on his own with those laws as he learns them. In the human body, pure science exists as the autonomic nervous system which controls all the physiologic processes of breathing, heart beat, digestion, and the like. Petroleum and oil geology are pure science. The plastic industry which uses these as a base is applied science. Meteorology is pure science--the laws of weather and climate. Weather forecasting and artificial rainmaking are applied science--technology.

Myths are the place to start a young person on this trail of scientific history. With these stories, primitive man sought to comfort his fears by finding explanations for the natural world around him. As Rollo May explains so succinctly in <u>Love and Will</u>, man seeks to diffuse fears by naming them. The family doctor who comes and names the illness does just this. Or, as a character in <u>Mr. Sammier's Planet</u> says:

> "All men by nature desire to know." That's the first sentence of Aristotle's <u>Metaphysics</u>. I never got much farther, but I figured that the rest must be out of date anyway. However, if they desire to know, it makes them depressed if they can't name the bushes on their own property. They feel like phonies. The bushes belong. They themselves don't. And I'm convinced that knowing the names of things braces people up. I've gone to shrinkers for years, and have they cured me of anything? They have not. They have put labels on my troubles, though, which sound like knowledge. It's a great comfort, and worth the money. You say, 'I'm manic.' Or you say, 'I'm a reactive-depressive.' You say about a social problem, 'It's colonialism.' Then the dullest brain has internal fireworks, and the sparks drive you out of your skull. It's divine. You think you're a new man. Well, the way to wealth and power is to latch on to this. When you set up a new enterprise, you redescribe the phenomena and create a feeling that we're getting somewhere. If people want things named or renamed, you can make dough by becoming a taxonomist. Yes, I definitely intend to try out this idea.... (Bellow, p. 103)

One useful exercise is to have each person write out the complete citation for a personal book brought to class for

"Library" as a Textbook   231

this purpose. Then, relating each piece of information to
one of the book shelving arrangements one can see what the
connections are.

For example, if the library arranged its books
chronologically by date of publication, the date of his
citation would be the first key to locating the volume so
sought. If the arrangement were alphabetical by author,
this piece of information becomes the crucial access
code, and so forth. Thus, one realizes the need for
and the value of a complete citation. Some day, then,
people so trained can develop into top managers who won't
lose time in obtaining needed materials because they send
a secretary to their special library with a citation that
makes an old pro weep.

For young or information-unsophisticated students,
analogy and simile can produce such useful examples as
a visit to a department store. Imagine the difficulties
in purchasing a specific item in a department store if
there were no classification in that store's arrangement.
Such emporia are sorted out first by some general overall classification, as clothing or kitchenware, and then
within that broad grouping there is a fine classification
to differentiate party dresses or work clothes, or electric percolators. In Phoenix, Arizona, a friend and
I were shopping in J. C. Penney's, trying to find some
geological work pants. Going to the classification section
of the right age (middle-aged), we looked where the genera
"pants" were stocked. We queried the salesman--there
was absolutely nothing. Finally, in desperation, I asked,
"But don't you have any of the kind of clothes that are
what Penney's used to be all about?" And this very dap-
per Englishman, a bit of an anachronism in the wild, wild
West, looked up disdainfully and said, "The work clothes
department is downstairs, madam." Whereupon, we went
downstairs and there, in the proper classification, were
exactly the kind of pants sought.

The grocery store provides another lesson in library classification for the young or the unsophisticated.
All of us visit such stores occasionally. One thing all
families have to buy is food. Ask, "If you are looking
for your favorite kind of cookie, do you find it hidden in
among the cans of coffee, or do you find it beside the
milk cartons? When you find them, how are they arranged?" The answer is probably going to be that the
cookies are just sort of all there together. You indicate

understanding of the togetherness of cookies and suggest remembering to look on the next trip to the store for some other additional arrangement. You and I know that sometimes they are arranged by sub-classification--Pepperidge Farm in one place, the voluptuous ones that are really candy bars clustered, the graham crackers chastely alone together. Other stores shelve by manufacturer. Whatever grouping is reported to the class, the student has learned about shelf order. "Why does the store do it this way?" is your next query. And, remembering shopping errands, the learner understands that there is an advantage in having like things together from which to select--whether socks or snacks! There are homely familiar library lessons in the index to the grocery store--the big alphabetically arranged board placed on the wall in supermarkets. Draw the obvious parallel. Books have indices. Libraries have indices (catalogs) that are directions to books. Book indices lead us to ideas or facts. The index to the grocery store leads you to "sugar," "flour"--things for sale there. (A subject-heading lesson can be piggy-backed here--spices, condiments or what will get you mustard?) Send them away asking, "When you come back to class, be ready to report what you have seen like these signs." This should at least increase their perception of signage. Relate this to a curriculum assignment where there is some mathematics of grocery stores or sociology of grocery stores, and you have a unified lesson plan--educational utopia!

For example, consider the query of someone who comes to us to learn about caring for a pet goldfish. The catalog is checked to see if there is a suitable book in the library. Goldfish not being among the subject headings, we have exhausted that first tool. Where, then, is the seeker likely to find material on goldfish? Let us for this discussion rule out any encyclopedia or periodical article to find the information. What is the next maneuver? We need to move up to the larger catalog topic in order to locate such a book. Larger than goldfish would be tropical fish. The subject heading "Tropical Fish" proves unlisted also. Next we try a still larger heading, "Pets." Perhaps under this subject heading there is a book. Explain then, how to look first in the table of contents and then in the index to find material on "Goldfish." If one were looking for some particular aspect of the care of goldfish, this would probably be too small to be listed in any table of contents and the only recourse would be to the index. This ability to use both the table of contents and the index of a book as an

"Library" as a Textbook 233

expansion of the analytic network of a library is something that does not seem to be in any measurable way taught as part of the educative process.

Such ubiquitous examples of the principle of classification produces productive lessons for the information-illiterate, regardless of chronological age. Conceptual skills are abstraction skills which must be mentally surfaced or created in the learner from already held, non-threatening concrete specifics. Classification is one such conceptual building block crucial to a curriculum in library skills for critical thinking. One assignment given to my Continuing Ed class is to survey their home precincts for examples they recognize of domestic classification such as are found in a closet or a kitchen.

For my appearances on the white-glove DAR luncheon circuit or the in-house routine 15-minute lectures on the DAR Library given to any requesting group, I found that the concept of domestic laundry is a universal and thus useful example to help relate the principles of library classification to these genealogical researchers. My monologue described the categories of dirty laundry, clean laundry, and, beyond the unit of clean, that of clean socks and still closer classification, husband's clean socks, and closer yet, socks paired and sorted by color and yarn so that black silk dress socks are readily visible when a black tie affair suddenly produces a domestic crisis. Another adult example is a collection of personal photographic slides. Ask how they arrange their slides. In a lump in a box--my slides, or arranged by year taken, or by subject, Johnnie at all ages, etc. If your teaching takes, it will be reinforced every time they touch a sock or a slide.

Since our chief justification for subject classification lies in its provision for comparison within a given subject area, this seems the time to teach all its ramifications. We need more than one book on each subject because:

1. There is more than one reader.
2. There is more than one point of view on a subject, each worth having.
3. There is more than one level of difficulty or purpose in vocabulary--as well as more than one ethnic or social group represented in our library and its institution.
4. There is always a newer book being written on

each subject yet many older titles merit keeping--
ideas have history.

Therefore libraries feel it is worth the great trouble,
time, and expense needed to determine the subject content
of each piece of material cataloged. Classification is neither
an extrasensory trip nor a secret Chinese code, but the intellectual map to a library's resources.

5. <u>Subject Headings</u>:

Subject access cannot be fully understood divorced
from the subject description function of shelf classification.
That one must know the address of a sought physicality is
easily taught and eagerly grasped if the BI is offering a clue
during a personal treasure hunt. That only one address is
possible raises no instructional roadblocks. Then--oh then--
comes the swing concept--that non-fiction usually treats more
than one subject--that a broad subject such as the environment contains smaller ones, like pollution (water, air), economics (national, international), etc., and the catalog indexes
or makes visible this multi-faceted subject information.

One address--one major topic, but other minor topics
are highlighted for the seeker by another physicality--a note
to that effect--a subject heading--a card headed, "Pollution--
water." Learn to search the catalog for your main class
number if you know one title or author in that subject field.
Then search the shelves for all of its fellows (that are in
when you look). That is one way to search in an open stack
collection. The other way is to use the catalog to find the
most specific item you seek by means of the word or words
that the subject cataloger has used to describe it. As a DAR
Reference Librarian that was sentence three of my spiel to a
new patron. In genealogy, where facts sought are geographical or familial, "the specific item you seek" added "person
or place."

Early library literacy concepts need reinforcing at this
juncture--alpha by top (subject) line and dictionary (with all
those classed exceptions) arranged. Genealogy is a simple
discipline for form of word entry. Personal and geograhpical
name changes are learned early in roots research.

Instruction in the principle of subject entry should
logically follow classification. The precepts implicit in the
classed catalog provide a valid foundation but how can we

"Library" as a Textbook

implant this in a learner's mind? Taking advantage of the high motivation inherent in anything personal, let's start with the query, "If you wanted to find something about you in the card catalog, where would you look?" Teaching from the rule of progression from specific to general, the response to your question would move quickly from the precise "Ole Olson" to Swedish Americans, or engineers' (work), farming (family hobby or antecedent), etc. Our own preparation must include checking out all these avenues of entry and obtaining suitable hand-outs to provide maximum visual reinforcement for discussion.

Hierarchy--animal--pet--goldfish--is one principle used in the establishment of a subject heading table. The crucial, basic concept is that of an idea's being subsumed under a word--some single word or group of words.

Beginning these semantic exercises in entry linguistics as early as possible should be the first great objective. With practice, such word juggling will become a habit of mind. After all, don't we librarians have such a habit worn into our neuro tracks? Any classroom assignment or personal pursuit that involves library materials beyond a catalog search by author or title can be used to teach entry skills.

The crux of the pitfalls in the deceptively simple phrase, subject heading access, lies in the fact that each book or article sought is entered by one individual human cataloger alone at a desk, following a list and a set of rules, not as a machine is programmed in rigid paths, but as a separate computer of cognition, guided by its own rules and interpretations of the published rules. Ranganathan, among others, has tilted in vain at this windmill of the dichotomy practiced between subject headings and the subject component of classification.

The insights of Sylvia Ashton-Warner can help us apply the principle of words drawn from our children as the subject building blocks of our inner-city school library catalogs. For these young people, the middle-class English of Sears and LCC Subject Headings can be a foreign language. If they must seek their entry to information through such an impediment, the least we natives of the catalog can do is to recognize the existence of this problem as the first step in solving it.

Non-librarian people have had to learn to equate class number with a subject word--the item's major subject identification. Now we ask them to undertake new learning--to select their word (not transformed into numbers) for "what the library has on--------" (subject entry), and thus begin the potential translation exercise from their word to the catalog's word (or words). No wonder library literacy makes a visible leap when patron learners actually see (hold in their hands to browse through) the DDC or LCC schedules from which standard headings are chosen.

All of us library literates have had our job-related turns on this jungle gym. Once, at ACE, the Library was asked to locate material on the reorganization of a liberal arts unit of a university, for a major university which was about to begin such an effort. We went through "cluster college, liberal arts, curriculum, innovation, and organizational structure," and came up empty-handed. When we found the right term, it was "institutional self-study."

Inherent in this principle of subject access are such hidden traps as:

1. Levels of language--colloquial vs. formal language.

2. Currency of language--look back through some old editions of <u>Sears</u>.

3. Entry mechanics: word-by-word, letter-by-letter (user screaming "What are you talking about?"); prefix--used as entry, or not? "As if" or "as is."

4. Relation of title as subject entry to separate subject entry.

5. Word as overarching symbol is tough to begin with.

6. For a clincher, not at the bottom of the list, language needs of the rest of the world as library user: subject headings for the black, for the immigrant, ghetto denizen--in fact, for anyone whose native tongue is not establishment middle- /upper-class American.

Let's refer to the laundry example. The subject of socks has these numbers in Dewey: hosiery, production of 338.4768732; social customs, costume and personal appearances--outer garments, 391.41; home clothing and construction--

"Library" as a Textbook   237

646. 42. , add 01 for men's, 04 for women's, and 06 for child's; manufacture--687. 32.   Not one of these really fits.   But, households use words--hose, socks, anklets, etc.   Ordinary domesticity attempts simplicity of access for its unique holdings. In 1958, when I provided the professional direction for the overhaul of my St. John's Norwood Parish Library, my ongoing experience at the National Geographic Society led me to devise a theological word classification system with the help of the rector, the Reverend William F. Creighton, later the Episcopal Bishop of Washington, as subject specialist. Twenty-six years later, that simple, intellectually accurate term classification is considered one reason for the Library's continuing usefulness to the parish.

An advantage of term classification is that when a user goes to the card catalog and chooses a book from the regular collection he has in hand a word used by the library for the subject he seeks. With that book or periodical he can move to the related class designation in Reference to find referral points in reference tools to help him assess and mine from the other titles. In this way, we can show how the informational and appraisal functions of the library are not separable functions. Each piece of information must be appraised before it can be acted upon and the technique for its use transferred from a scholarly assignment such as a term paper to a private investigational subject such as how to buy a Christmas present.

Consider the yellow pages, the classified section of the telephone book as a ubiquitous informational and appraisal reference source. Gaining information from it requires an understanding of the subject heading principle, and many of these books provide a subject listing in the beginning of the volume. A person who is sophisticated enough to seek that index first has gotten the entry term before fingers wander all over the telephone book.

The phone company is now classifying the white pages, turning some of them blue and creating a trap for the unlibrary skilled. This print database depends upon a pressure-sensitive "Take a Look Inside" label to warn of its major organizational change.

Now that the hold of "Ma Bell" is shifting, informed sources predict more variation in all phone operations, including the arrangement of local telephone books.   Potential lessening of our worldwide A-plus standards is a worry.

The January, 1983 Northern Virginia volume of the Washington Metropolitan area set has major errors. The Alexandria School numbers are in the white "Business-Professional-Organizational" pages, not in the blue "Government" section and the number for Alexandria School that made it to the blue "Easy Reference List" gets you the Arlington Schools. C. & P. Telephone says, "Oh, dear!" This telephone information is, of course, also on-line, but these library lessons are written for print medium--the one that stands still for close examination.

To teach phone book information appraisal, beyond the simple request for a number, tailor your examples to your students' needs and interests. Street locations and advertising graphics are two resources the phone book provides for such lessons. The search for the best vendor for a purchase, jewelry, typewriter, etc., offers a useful teachable problem. Two facets of this search are location and graphics. Location, thoughtfully considered, is a guide to nearness to home or public transportation and to the price class of the store's neighborhood. Informed use of advertisers' display of graphics can also be a mini-curriculum. Tiffany's famed windows expand the lesson beyond the phone book and the newspaper to books and articles, and they make the point inescapably. Jurgen Ruesch's Nonverbal Communication; Notes on the Visual Perception of Human Relations can give us whatever on-the-job training we need to teach these lessons in visual information processing.

The DAR Library provided continuous reinforcement of patron need to be furnished with every reasonable aid toward access. Main entry, defined as that person or body having the intellectual responsibility for the work, is a discrete, easily mastered, helpful handle for searching. Genealogy, as a subject, is overfull of author traps because its publications (monograph, serial and reference) have been and still are largely the work of amateurs. Family histories tend to be either vanity press or author-published. The DAR itself did not copyright its own publications until recently because of non-professional naïveté.

Government documents are usually cited as the number one example of these problems of main entry. Indeed, they have them all--compounded by the press' application of a popular title for any piece that really catches public attention. My point is not that a simple solution can be found for the quirks of publishers, though surely standardization and

"Library" as a Textbook   239

simplicity should be a visible by-product of on-line searching.
The lifelong learning remedy lies in the training of library
users in the concepts involved, so that, forewarned and fore-
armed, they will a) get a decent citation, and then b) know
what else in the catalog to look under to find the volume
sought.

"Filing title" is another facet of main entry cataloging
traps. Just why, when a patron requests "the new book by
Aldrich on Governance," and this same book carries Thomas
Z. Aldrich as editor, LC gives it a title entry, escapes whatever sanity I am possessed of at such a moment. True pro
that I am, however I give the spiel--"the cataloger at LC
has access to information not obvious to us." As I think--
cataloging from source--what is going on?

Once these ideas become part of our pupil-patron's
library know-how, the dictionary catalog can assume its
rightful role as the simplest approach to entry. Imagine
what you and I would endure as we read and write and study,
if the basic principles of access were as baffling to us as
they are for almost everyone else.

Periodical indexes challenge our ability to actualize
for teaching transmission the relationship between the item
indexed and the bibliographic entry. The relationship between
a periodical, a periodical abstract, a periodical index, and
a periodical directory can confound anyone. The periodical
is simply its own physical self, from which the abstracts,
indices, and directories are derived. There is a relationship between the physical periodical itself and the index to
it and the description of it in the directory. At the media
level, of course, amplify this by the relationship of microforms to print.

One classroom example in such BI that taught to the
point of full comprehension centered around the events of
President Kennedy's assassination. At that time I was
teaching a terrific A section of seventh grade girls, but
even for them, the idea of a periodical index was proving
elusive. There was an additional dimension in this shat-
tering incident for us because the fathers of many of these
girls were high government officials, connected in one way
or another with the backstage drama that accompanied the
change of command in Washington. Relevancy was present
for sure. I had the girls save the magazine issues on the
assassination to which they had access at home. The ones

in the library were held as we awaited the Readers' Guide that would cover the assassination. When it did arrive, the individual issues of the periodicals were brought to class from home and the library. By looking from the individual issues to the periodical index, the relationship of one to another was clearly imprinted upon their minds. Since this was a vivid happening that each one of us had experienced deeply, it also afforded a clear indication of the various periodical biases. There were cases when, because of their fathers' positions, these young people knew firsthand what had really happened. This was an unusual opportunity to teach periodical criticism, one that is not commonly available. The high drama of tragedy offered an intense learning situation.

Today, electronic publishing has moved beyond just nibbling at the entity of periodical literature. The New York Times is on-line in full text. Bibliographic data bases expand to fall over each other. The enclave of scholarly journals is under study as a gourmet platter to be redesigned and consumed by the new commerce. So far, no luck. Tenured Academia, having surmounted all the information media since just post-cave, combines the strengths of the turtle, the elephant, and the lion. Remember, though, that we are teaching print skills, and allude to non-print only enough to dispel any notion that you are defunct.

At the risk of seeming to pontificate over an obvious truism, one very real problem in teaching "library" is that the doing demands both a library and a library classroom to which large numbers of the library's books can be brought via book truck. Books are heavy; books are costly. Only for a graduate library school could one dream of a classroom in the center of a model reference collection with its own "teaching" catalog. To flesh out the conceptual basis of "library" demands access to its flesh and blood--books and card catalogs and in 1984--computer terminals.

One personal book per student can usually be generated. I do this for the lessons on the parts of a book and cataloging because learning to describe a friend makes a more lasting lesson. For the rest, the teaching librarian must have access to a collection from which advance selections can be made and brought to the class site on wheels, not backs and arms. These teaching tools must be able to be borrowed in generous number because, otherwise, there is no prayer of being able to match the query to the answer or illustration.

Not only must you have all that is obvious: books in abundance, the A (or any one), volume from all of the general encyclopedias, masses of related reference tools and even--(ideally) enough catalog drawers to provide one for each several learners--but there is worse to come. To teach--to show--the how and why of classification and subject cataloging, you must have the schedules themselves in their buckram flesh. Yes, of course, pages are xeroxed to provide a unified teaching example. This, however, especially for older students and adult learners is not adequate to enable them to comprehend adequately the rubrics under which catalogers work in their "back rooms."

Maximum learning comes when a searcher can page through a volume of Dewey or LCC subject headings and find an area of personal interest and combine subject knowledge with library know-how. Our fellow professionals may respond to requests to "share" their tools with heightened anxiety levels. No, it is not washing private linen in public or revealing the gang password, but it is letting "them" in behind the scenes. Never have I been refused, though I more than sensed some raised hackles. Fortunately, my adult ed course at Georgetown is at night and lending to my BI effort did not interfere with the catalogers' work day. You should, though, be prepared for your own qualms at being a reference/teaching librarian enlightening others by means of these perhaps by now unfamiliar to you editions of tools of your technical service fellow librarians. As you learn your students' areas of subject interest, try to give them a schedule volume that will intensify their learning by providing the incentive of familiarity.

6. Reference Collection:

If "library" is the textbook for BI, and BI is taught as the textbook for critical thinking, the Reference Center (catalog plus Reference Collection) is the primary curriculum. So far, this chapter has dealt with concepts that can be stuffed into the catalog as a generic totebag and labeled "Finding Aid" tutelage. Now must come the tricks for teaching Reference--not the traditional Library School Reference Course which covers book by book as tools of the librarian's trade, but lessons that emerge from student requests that teach about the Reference Collection as the incarnation of fact.

Reference implies a first place to look--for facts. Its books are not meant to be read (though my Aunt Cora read her dictionary) but to be mined for discrete items of fact. A reference book can be defined as one designed by arrangement or treatment of the subject content to be consulted for information specifics.

Now your BI curriculum means doing for the concept "fact" what was done earlier for classification--surface it as a concept. Define it, and extract every homely example possible from your physical surroundings and the experiences of your pupils as they will offer them to you as a precious trust. Fact has physical levels--as "teacher" point to the desk top and recite the progression from sub-atomic to, "Is it wood or plastic?" and then comment, "Yet Scientists tell us that there is more nothing than something in the atom, so perhaps the fact is that what I am leaning on is nothing at all." Topographic levels affect fact. Discuss how the building in which you all are would look from an orbiting space ship, a high-altitude jet airliner, a small plane, a balloon, and a nearby much taller building--then add, "Yet the building itself, as an architectural fact, was just the same all along."

For the sight-impaired, glasses, no glasses, or a different level of correction between pairs creates another varying set of physical facts. At parties now, if I wish to see details such as the jewelry of a fellow guest, I must look through, not over, my half-glasses as I do in just conversing. Otherwise, my visual fact disagrees with what I know must be reality.

Chronological age affects facts. Carbon-fourteen dating produces facts but they lack exactitude in relation to dating available for space missions or presidential assassination attempts. Once the concept of the "fact" within the fact within the fact is established, the class will reward your blood, sweat, and anxiety with feedback ranging from literary to last night's family argument.

Object size affects fact. While researching mountain heights for an NGS filmstrip, I learned that authoritative answers to such could vary within several feet. The relative value of such statistical facts also varies in direct correlation to the size of the factual object. A dentist measures dimensions in microns. A mountain climber does not have to plan for a few feet out of many thousands unless they are unique.

We librarians, however, subscribe to the reality of fact and to its residence in our libraries. Authority for the factuality of our Reference Collections is a keystone of intellectual freedom along with the right to free access to all sides of an opinion or all subjects.

The crux of the Reference Interview is determining just what fact is sought. In genealogy, this means diplomatically silencing twenty minutes of family history with the sometimes oft-repeated positive comment, "And just what can I do to help you?" A dialogue to establish the subject of the wanted fact can provide substance for instruction in process.

Reference Collection as a concept progresses from the general, 000, through the ten major subject classes (if Dewey). The general encyclopedias, being general, have broad subject coverage which varies somewhat from set to set based on grade level and editorial perspective. Suggesting that individual information appraisal should begin with checking a familiar section of the work encourages this as a lifelong information habit. A former Continuing Ed student is now completing her M. L. S. at Catholic University of America and working in the Library School Library. Yesterday, while appraising "New Books" before borrowing, I commented to her, "This bibliography has gaps. A primary item is missing, and the new edition is out." Her reply was, "Yes, that's what you taught us, to check first an area about which we know something." Well, at least that idea stuck once!

The BI progression then moves along to the other classes of knowledge for a broader or deeper treatment of the desired factual area. Try to elicit current controversial topics as interest-linked springboards for a discussion of identification of opinions as they appear, salted through the expository text. The use of a personal area of interest and expertise is vital to a speedy turning on of the light of, "Oh yes, I see how that works. " Almost everyone is interested in something and our Reference Collections offer almost everything.

For all but the very young or very poor readers, exposure to our professional guides to such reference books as Winchell, Sheehy, Frances Cheney's Fundamental Reference Sources, or Christine Wynar's Guide to Reference Books for School Media Centers can produce instant fascination. The principle of personal interest works, handicapped only by the unavailability of enough copies to go around even a small class. A dedicated BI (I use that in truncation--Instruct-- so it can be retrieved as Instructor or Instruction as meaning requires) could build a teaching collection of out-of-date guides by circularizing colleagues, frequenting charity book sales, or getting in on a Gifts and Exchange Program such as that at LC.

During the Montgomery County, Maryland teacher's strike of 1968, we Central Office Administrative and Supervisory folk were asked to go out into the schools and class-sit. My assignment was high school--math and music. When my then college age daughter grasped the full import of the gross competency non-match which this represented her non-faith in bureaucracy sank even lower. Math and music skills I don't have. Should I then, also, react dramatically--flee, faint? Then--but think, I have academic skills. My subject is information. And that's what I taught. Lesson plan? After introducing myself, I began the dialogue by talking about the strike as an information item. How did I learn about it and know to come to their classroom? How did they learn about it and thus accept me? Our information sources were the Superintendent of Schools, the radio, TV and their mothers. Then we talked about evaluating all these as valid information reference points.

These students participated--thought--both of us "on our feet. " Through time, serendipity has not granted me proof or non-proof of any learning that may have occurred within the minds of the young people, but I learned--that I

"Library" as a Textbook

do know. I learned that, if the subject is you, motivation exists, and that if the specifics are meaningful to pupils, these techniques can evoke for them information as a generalization and concept.

The relationship of the life span of an individual to that of the rest of the world makes a valid use of the concept "library" as a teachable entity. The details of such an exercise must vary with the age of your teaching library; whether it is younger or older than the majority of the students. To dramatize the library's age, one could use runs of serial publications such as Current Biography, Readers' Guide to Periodicals, or Book Review Digest. The dates of these runs dramatize temporal history. If they are available, encyclopedias covering the time period of the library's life help make history visible to the young. A retrospective collection in a subject field, dating from the library's beginnings, is another useful resource for such lessons.

For example, ask each student to write the date of his birth and some ideas about how he feels the world has changed since he entered it. To make valid curriculum use of this exercise, it must be clearly subject-related. One curriculum need that we might be filling in this way is the history of inventions. Pick a 10-year-old to show what technology intersects his time line and how that, in turn, relates to the library's age. On December 11, 1972, Apollo 17 landed on the moon, thus closing the lunar mission. That was the year that our student was born. At the age of ten he intersects with the beginnings of the Space Shuttle. The library, age 20 plus, holds both reference and circulating material dealing with this student's world of space technology.

This concept can be broadened with; "In Mrs. Smith's class you are studying the history of the great inventions of transportation technology at the same time as we are trying to understand libraries and what the age of the materials in them can mean to you." Then with blackboard graphics or a transparency create a time chart of the history of inventions of transport. Go back to the evolution of the horse and its use as a vehicle for man. Then the wheel was invented, and the horse could be used as a force for pulling loads. The first bicycle in New York City appeared from England in 1819. The first passenger train was operated in England in 1825. Then came aerial trams, cable cars, trolley cars; the advent of the motor car, somewhere around 1916; the airplane at

Kittyhawk, 1903; and then the manned rocket which arrived in 1961. Have the class mathematician make an average of their birth dates and, displaying these data visually, comment, "The average of the class is this date. Where does that intersect a transport time line?" You are now off on a very useful graphic lesson that may have some philosophical and practical value for a wide variety of people.

7. <u>History of libraries and their carriers:</u>

Neither libraries as institutions nor their carriers were born yesterday. The physicality of both, being diverse yet ubiquitous, offers "library" lessons that are unlimited, at hand, relevant to each learner, and prepared for by our M. L. S. The history of each step of the knowledge pyramid can be exemplified in this way.

One approach is to make a time chart for the advent of libraries. Man's earliest information storage and retrieval system was spoken language. By its use, all knowledge could be passed on from one generation to another. When man realized that spoken words could be represented by visible symbols, he invented his second means for the preservation and transmission of knowledge, writing. The medium of writing has been in use for this purpose for 5,000 years.

The writing system of the Sumerians is the oldest system known; we have records of theirs that date from 3,100 B.C. The Egyptians added to this, developing an alphabet of

"Library" as a Textbook   247

24 consonants which they combined with pictographs. The next credit line belongs to the Phoenicians who are responsible for the alphabet as we know it. In one language or another the manuscript carried information until the 15th century when movable type was developed. The automatic presses of the 19th century were the next great breakthrough, and so on through to the present. On the graph of the development of writing, and of books and libraries, we can superimpose an overlay of the development of manned vehicles for transport.

In this exercise, we can draw on the library as a unit. If the institution is old--100 years--the library will make a meaningful entry on the time chart. If it is new, discuss the idea of a retrospective collection--that you just don't start a library with only the books that were published in that year. The matter of books and how long they are in print can be touched upon here. This might be a good time to mention whatever special historic collection your library holds--probably the complete file of your in-house newspaper, yearbooks, etc.

The lesson serves three purposes: 1) It helps the student relate to the overall picture of the subject being studied. 2) It helps him understand something of the time span of the written word so that when he is looking for library material, he knows how to be guided in his search by the age of the library; 3) It calls to his attention the existence of books which can help to discern the totality of the world at any given time. At the elementary level some helpful books are Genevieve Foster's George Washington's World, The World of Captain John Smith, etc. For all readers (of print), Who Was Who; a dictionary of contemporaries, is a profitable resource for such learning.

For older students and adults this can be an opportunity to introduce the Books of the Western World, a series edited by Robert Hutchins and Mortimer Adler. These volumes trace the history of 50 different great ideas from their written beginning to the present. The 50 ideas themselves and the factors involved in their selection fascinate me. The fact that the development of any idea can be so clearly traceable is an indication of the meaning of scholarship and its implications as a blazed trail. These books are organized by chronological arrangement of the work of the writers chosen. Indexing by an individual idea brings you down to page and line to locate the reference to the idea being traced. From such documentation of the progress of ideas throughout cultural history comes contemporary man's ability to build the future on the past.

Once in my BI teaching experience I had the chance to present this series of books at a teachable moment. A teacher was doing a term paper on an idea they trace. In combination with An Encyclopedia of American Facts she had resources for a paper. Working with Continuing Education students, these volumes are also useful to dramatize the history of ideas. You must, of course, have chosen them carefully and put marking slips in relevant sections to be able to match your guess as to the students' spontaneous query if there is to be real learning.

Networking as a concept fits under this topic. Physical inter-library loan and on-line searching within your city, state, and region strike responsive chords in those learners on the "carrier" or data trail. We, as a civilization, got here from somewhere known, and are heading somewhere unknown. Though our progress does resemble a race car outdriving its headlights, learners, and perhaps society itself, can be materially aided by the guideposts we are able to provide by our instruction in climbing the knowledge pyramid.

The subject of political discretion and sagacity does not, perhaps, properly come within my purview, but as a bookman, I offer a few recommendations for linear wisdom. This bibliography includes Berne's Games People Play, Shostram's Man the Manipulator, May's Love and Will, The Peter Principle, Townsend's Up the Organization, and Parkinson's The Law of Delay. These books won't aid in determining program, but mastery of their principles will help in obtaining the needed time and access.

When I began to teach library skills I had no intellectual rationale. It was simply an old-fashioned seat of the pants venture. I knew that I possessed special knowledge and skills, and that mastery of a good part of this was required for getting the most out of a library. Teaching in an academically oriented school for the college-bound, there seemed no question that these young people needed to know in some measure what I knew. After six years of working in schools and watching people almost totally unable to use the library--faculty and students alike--I had concluded that initiated library users in any majority were a myth.

The most important ingredient for political success is

"Library" as a Textbook

the belief that one has something to give and the ability to transmit that intellectual faith to other persons. Such a person was a scholar, a disciplinarian, an English teacher, and academic head of our Middle School. All this somehow produced in her an intuition that there was something in "library" to teach. I never had to spell out specifics. The most important concrete clue I can offer is that what teachers and principals want is some of their teaching problems solved. And, for most of them, one of the perennially pressing problems that they think of as being library related, without comprehending how or why, is plagiarism.

For the beginning writer of term papers the question is not "what is plagiarism?" but "what can I put in my term paper that is not plagiarism?" It is easy to understand that what you have stolen--e.g., words from a book--is not yours. What is difficult for the unlearned scholar to comprehend is what of his own can provide the substance of his term paper.

Since all facts must be stolen, that is, plagiarized and thus not acceptable, or borrowed and thus must be acknowledged as the property of another, and erudite opinions are obviously not original either, the student must be taught what products of his mind do fall between these forbidden stools.

To assist our students in this search for a personal intellectual input into documented expository writing, let us clarify for them these three relevant terms:

1. Literature search: Ascertaining the relevant studies made in the past on the subject of concern.

2. Research: Basing work on the information derived from a literature search, the student moves on into what had not been known before.

3. Term paper: A documented work in which the choice and organization of material is the author's contribution.

It should be clear from these definitions that it is in the development of the term paper thesis and its defense that the student's own thoughts lie. By showing him the negative image, what is not his in the library-based paper, we can produce for him the positive semblance. To return to the figure from Chapter Two of the human brain as computer, it could be said that the accepting, rejecting, discriminating, synthesizing abilities of the brain are the writer's contribution to a term paper. The input, especially for the young, is choice and organization based upon the rediscovered trail of scholarship which, by its continuing library existence, prevents each new generation's need for a fresh rediscovery of the wheel. The computer print-out from the student's brain (the term paper) is a well-reasoned statement of an idea proved, or disproved, by the personal synthesis of the documentation selected. With our libraries as materials of instruction, and such a presentation of the concept "library-based paper" as lesson-plan, librarians as tutors should be able to eliminate the sin of plagiarism by innocence. An apt work of art like the Washington Irving essay, "The Art of Book-Making," which appears in Eleanor Parker's collection, <u>I Was Just Thinking</u>, can be a powerful ally to logic when included in such teaching.

John Lubans, my introduction to a place at the Library Instruction Round Table of ALA, offers this analysis of the library component of a written exercise in thinking competency:

<u>Reading</u>: a student should be able to use features of books and other reference materials.

<u>Writing</u>: One should be able to gather information from primary and secondary sources.

<u>Reasoning</u>: a student should be able to draw reasonable conclusions from information found in various sources.

Nine Steps for completing an assignment:

What do I need to do?
(formulate and analyze need)

Where could I go?
(identify and appraise likely sources)

How do I get to the information?
(trace and locate individual resources)

Which resources shall I use?
(examine, select and reject individual resources)

How shall I use the resources?
(interrogate resources)

"Library" as a Textbook

>What should I make record of?
>(record and store information)
>Have I got the information I need?
>(Interpret, analyze, synthesize, evaluate)
>How should I present it?
>(present, communicate)
>What have I achieved?
>(evaluate)
>
>(RQ, Spring 1982)

A good reference lesson for non-"school" learners must connect to their motivation in coming to you. Logic tells us that each person saw some personal information-related need that he felt unable to meet alone. I begin my Continuing Education Course by requesting written answers to these three questions: "Please define information." Then; "Please define library." And, lastly, "What were your goals in signing up for this course?" This one gets my foot in the mental door of the quiet ones and enables me to relate teaching examples to their self-perceived, but unspoken individual information needs. The appropriate reference area for these lifelong learners has proven to be almost exclusively beyond the academic subject-oriented bibliographic network. This strikes me as validating two very sobering points: that a community referral service belongs with "library," and that only truly fresh marketing efforts can serve to generate patron-excitement in our library knowledge industry.

Perhaps there is one such trick in the grandparent-grandchild link. Whoever is the best reader/most library excited could be our focus. There is a Grandparent Day provided by the greeting card, florist, "general fifty" lobby group. Let's capture it for some new public and school library literacy programs as a humanly dramatic example of the lifelong learning continuum.

One beneficial idea to implant is that each reference book worth its salt explains itself. Yes, Virginia, I do mean that it will/should have explanatory text as part of its front matter (remember, we taught that concept under "book") that tells you how to use its special conventions of abbreviation, arrangement, etc. Personal experience has demonstrated that this is difficult to do and easy to explain. The DAR Library Catalog; Family Histories and Genealogies which Kathryn Scott and I produced, including authorship of the front matter, reinforced other bookmaking learning resulting from service on the ALA Reference and Subscription Books Review Committee. Public service library duty has demonstrated that the patron at the moment of high motivation, baffled by "that strange set of numbers or letters" is eminently reachable and teachable by a kindly "this is where you learn what it means and.... "

John Dewey, as quoted and commented upon in a feature in the Spring 1982 issue of Learning Today, offers one spotlight on the repeated failure of traditional, formalized BI. His educational theories that relate to "Books and Libraries as Teaching Tools" center on these related concepts: that one mark of an educated person is the ability to produce relevant and discerning judgments; that problem solving demands the mental work of confronting ideological obstacles while exercising the discipline of order in identifying the problem (a state of doubt) and then locating material with which to remove the doubt and produce a mental solution; and that learning occurs only when a person meets a problem that he chooses to solve.

To internalize and act upon a philosophy (why), "how" becomes requisite. To implement the philosophy of LLMLL requires an always-packed tote bag of tricks. As help in achieving this, add some of the good "how-to" books to your personal desk reference collections. Search them out and use them as textbooks for you, but not as workbooks for your student patrons. If workbooks in library literacy worked, they would have and Dewey would be wrong and we would not be a nation of library illiterates.

No stand-up comedian can ever have enough generic jokes to tailor to the audience of the moment. Neither can an interactive lecturer/teacher ever have enough examples, techniques, and tricks to re-cut to fit each now. Thinking on your feet feels better with a full thought tank! Humanistic, intuitive "just being around" research forms the basis for my BI philosophy, plus strategies.

Specialized ears perceive the information quandary, the human story of personal helplessness that the soap opera's crisis non-management dramatizes. "Miss Manners" and Ann Landers handle this on one level. Judith Martin does follow the information pyramid--to her, etiquette is fact and thus able to support opinion and value judgment. As social animals, all that is permitted to us is to listen to the human dilemmas, since they are presented as conversation, not as action items. As public service information professionals,

"Library" as a Textbook 253

our responsibility is to take advantage of what Lubans has characterized as our "windfall" chance to profit by education's current black hole and "forge a partnership" with learners and teachers by offering materials and analyses for the solution of every quandary brought within our range and marketing like mad to increase our chances for such contacts.

Chapter 13

Determining Library IQ

For every evil under the sun,
There is a remedy, or there is none.
If there be one, try and find it;
If there be none, never mind it.
          Mother Goose

No matter how we all chorus agreement that libraries possess a quintessence beyond their ordered shelves, and that our mission is to transmit this to our patrons, our first step of commitment demands a second step of action. In the interim between the present and the millenium, what are we going to do about the problem? Acknowledgement is the beginning of the solution. Knowledge is power.

If "school" (K-Ph.D.) cured library illiteracy, most adults would be information-able. If "school" faculty would join our ranks, we could, together, eradicate this plague of civilization in an individual's school years. The current efforts of the College Board to re-demonstrate the relationship between academic competencies and study skills puts a current dress on an old, old stalemate. Pious platitudes collide with the ancient stone wall of teacher and faculty unwillingness to allow learners' minds to range freely in academic pastures at the crossing where education in critical thinking based on library skills intersects with an individual teacher's unique view of his subject. This is a place where basic human anxieties regarding professional academic competence are confronted by a threat so strong as to force denial of its objective reality. How many teachers, at any level, have you known who encouraged student challenge to their special patch of academic turf?

Are you now saying, if BI is really an impossible goal, why keep breaking lances on real windmills? No, indeed, my thrust is to devise a sortie that may maximize our chances of helping faculty gather the courage to join us. The harsh economic realities that darken the days of schools and colleges as well as libraries could pit the fear of unemployment against that of subject ignorance and make library instruction the lesser evil. It at least can be said to have more historic sanction and thus afford more mental security than many other spectres of threatened educational change.

In 1984, where such already devised and printed tests

of library skills are hard to avoid, a reader may well ask, why waste a book chapter on a discussion of developing your own in-house testing program? My answer is, again, if what others have either actually done or talk about doing or devise tests for doing were going to produce any measurable improvement in library literacy, such would have occurred. Therefore, my belief in the power of the requisite self-study by both library staff members and faculty and the cross-fertilization resulting from such a mutual effort seem to justify these few pages of "how to."

What you are going to propose is that a series of tests be devised that will be so handled from inception to presentation of test results as to provide an unequivocal statistical base upon which to structure your library program. To ensure this result, your administrators and faculty must be so tightly tied into every twist of the net that only death can free them from acceptance of its results as guidelines for action.

To warrant this effort, its validity must be secure. One crucial facet is that it be demonstrable at the entry level of all persons entering the school or system. For any academic institution, this is your incoming class level. For a trade association or any organization employing a cadre of researchers, a similar competency pre-test should be of value.

For this project to be successful, it is crucial that there be nothing in its design or presentation that can assign responsibility to anyone within your school or organizational family for any negative result your survey may produce. With cooperation an invisible library test can be built into the first assignments students or staff are given in the early days of their new school or work situation. It will lose a good deal of its validity if those being tested discover that it is their library skills that are being measured.

My experience indicates there is no particular variance in the groups I've watched demonstrate their capacity for informed library use. The threshold to such use is the ability to use the library catalog or at least realize that there is one. Patrons either show competence or are totally at sea. There seems to be no middle ground. In all likelihood there will be more high IQ's in library competence in the sections of gifted children or Ivy League freshmen or trained subject researchers.

You are certainly going to find a higher proficiency among those who read well than among those who read badly. What is wanted is testing as objective as possible, yet that hides its true test purpose from the students. Any such testing must possess the support of the faculty and/or administration before it is administered so that the results will have clout.

Once the goals and general proposals of the library staff have been defined in writing and accepted, the specifics must be waiting in the wings of your brain. One vital specific is a valid statistical design. Fitting the whole together, it must be so constructed that the results will indicate that five percent will have an A-level competence, 20 percent a B-level competence, and so forth. Pass-fail gives inadequate data from which to design a program to build library awareness and adequacy.

The components of Library IQ look like this:

1. Ability to use the card catalog, including:
   a. Author and title.
   b. Subject headings.
2. Ability to make the transition from card to shelf which involves comprehension of the classification number and the relation between the class number and book number.
3. Ability to determine authority.
4. Ability to use the catalog in conjunction with reference books in order to locate required bibliographies beyond that of card catalog.

5. Ability to use the library collection to provide a multiplicity of views of a subject, or a controversial biographee.
   6. Ability in the whole field of periodicals:
      a. To use a general periodical index as a current bibliography;
      b. To demonstrate understanding of the relationship between the periodical indices listing and the article itself.

In "school" such mass testing might best be handled by involving the heads of the department of English [Language Arts] and Social Sciences. In higher education, academic departments are the logical working units of subject specialists.

Within the organizations served by special libraries, those responsible for the work of staff researchers are the logical people to act with you in a test design. The work of lobbyists for trade assocations, paralegals in law firms, researchers in all manner of publishing houses and curators in historical societies relates to their library literacy. The costly magic of on-line bibliographic searching as a part of reference capabilities adds just another technological dimension to a searcher's need for library skills. As library budgets shrink, to free library staff time by improving research staff skills seems a helpful managerial move.

Sell your plan to each department head on an individual basis. The next move for the library staff and the non-library converts would be to approach the academic head or the organizational chief and gain that level of support for the project. Unless, of course, such is already yours. In which joyous case, you do your Up the Organization down. You must have rapport with those who direct your users before they will trust you enough to support such a scheme. Once this is green light--go--, meet again with the department heads, academic or corporate research together this time, to pick out the special points that would become the responsibility of each individual department. It is worth the time to work this out in a group, since some of the skills of Library IQ are much more easily adaptable to a history class than they would be to one in English, and vice versa. When these steps have been completed, it would become the responsibility of the subject staffs to make up these tests. This accomplished, the next step would be for the quizzes to come to the library staff for substantiation as valid entry level tests from the standpoint of the library skills involved. They would then go back to the individual departments with whatever additions or corrections the library staff had made. At this point, the tests would be ready to be administered.

Another facet which must be organized in advance is a means whereby there will be some watch committee of faculty and administration in the library to observe behavior so that this visual check can be added to the verbal. Optimistically, the sight of faculty reading or preparing their lessons in your library is not so strange that it would immediately arouse the suspicions of the students. One thing going for such a spy-in is that the pupils, being new to the school, might not be hopelessly surprised to see the school principal or the head of the English department in the library.

Such an exercise in witness would yield a broadly based look at whatever behavior is involved in library use. Is your A-level group going to assist other weaker students? If so, you want to know it. The only way such data can be obtained is by having a watch group on deck with you as the exercises are carried out.

As you evolve test exercises in Library IQ, it may be possible to extract one more advantage from them. Most of those who express themselves publicly agree that teachers, principals, and managers are not themselves knowledgeable library users. It follows then that anything that can be done to help them see this clearly yet privately will be of value as you strive to develop a widely supported teaching program in library skills. One soft-sell procedure would be to take the above outline of desired skills and, appending to it the tests that have been made up by the different departments, give these to every member as an optional self-study. Quizzes like this are sure-fire people bait. All of us are drawn to tests that we take alone and mark ourselves. I remember with ironic humor one in which our family came off smashingly well--a test for membership in the Jet Set. What put us in the exclusive bracket was the query, "Do you have an air-conditioned wine cellar?" We arrived because our wine rack happens to be in an air-conditioned basement! A self-test is a honey that draws a great many of us bees.

Let us now consider some ways of framing questions to determine our first entry level--the user's ability at the card catalog. The standard, simple, tried-and-true method is to let the student make a list of three books by

Determining Library IQ

a particular author that the library holds. In an English assignment one could do this without being caught. A subtler ploy that would avoid having the catalog thumbed to death in one area or producing a mass answer, would be to ask "what books by your favorite author are in the library's collection?" However you do this, you will determine whether they are aware of such an author listing and their capacity to use it to produce a bibliography.

To determine ability to use the title part of the catalog without being caught at giving a library exercise may be a little more complicated. One could prepare a list of titles and ask to have them put in order by publication date. Perhaps a subtler way to do this would be in a history course where one could say "Here is a list of ten titles. Please tell me what these books are about."

The subject area of the catalog is easier to test without being unmasked, because surely there will be a need for students and researchers to devise their own course or project reading lists. This device usually proves productive in showing whether the patron considers the card catalog as something from which to answer this question.

One way to test a patron's ability to use the reference collection to check authority is to ask for a list of books by an author who was alive at a certain period in history and not give the author's name, but require that they read a book by or about a man who was alive during, say, the years 1795 to 1850. In order to do that, it is helpful to make available a book such as Who Was When, or a chronologically arranged historic reference such as Langer's Encyclopedia of World History.

Another exercise that will test this skill uses a question such as, "Find some authority who has chosen and listed well-known books in the field of American colonial history, and write a brief report on two of these books." In order to do this, one has to know where to find such a list and how to relate that list to what is in the library. There should be people in the library watching behavior to determine whether the librarian on Reference Duty is used as a source for needed help.

The test for an ability to extract a diverse or balanced view of a controversy or controversial biographee can be combined with the test of skill in library periodical techniques. One assignment that was big in my days at Catholic University was a list of questions on polemics of the moment, in reply to which we were to produce answers from the three points of view, Protestant, Catholic, and Jewish. Currency automatically sends one to magazines and thus periodical Library IQ can be tested. Such an assignment goes beyond the construction of a bibliography and tests the ability to make the connection between the index citation and the journal itself-- whether hard copy or microform, or on-line searching.

It is crucial to the success of such tests that they be given in such a way that performance can be monitored. This may sound difficult, but it is only a matter of having the test ready at some proper beginning with directions that do not provide strong clues that it is a library test. It may be that more would be lost than gained by trying to disguise the fact that library IQ is being tested. Perhaps students and searchers do not even realize that there is such a capability. Such considerations are what make mandatory the stationing of non-librarian members of the testing project in the library so that the asking and answering of such queries can become as much a part of your test data as are the resultant papers. If you do not have witnesses in the library, you are going to lose validity of data.

To extend the value of this testing, a logical next step might be to prepare a course-by-course chart of the total instructional program and then attempt to determine what level of library IQ is required for successful work in each. Such a map would be a real help to the library staff in their teaching.

Our ability to sponsor successfully such a testing program should help us build credence as subject specialists. It will also ensure a valid foundation for our library curriculum.

There is a story about a young mother with an able three-year-old who was being tested for pre-school. The little girl could dress herself and was bright and apt. The school required an intelligence test. When the mother was brought in to talk with the psychologist who had done the testing, she was informed that the child was dull and recalcitrant. When they got down to cases, it developed that part of the psychologist's testing had involved two long strips of cloth--one with buttons and one with buttonholes. The little girl had been asked to button it. The child looked at the adult and said, "But it doesn't button anything," and refused to do the buttoning. Any in vacuo test in library skills is just as inappropriate and senseless as buttons without reality.

Chapter 14
Our Public Responsibility for Education Toward Humaneness

> The soul is not where it lives but where it loves.
>
> — H.G. Bohn

By inventing language, the human race invented story.... In story, the dividing line is not necessarily between fact and fiction.... Some fiction claims to be true. We call it history. Some truth claims to be fiction. We call it literature. Both are aspects of story, nonetheless. In the broad sense of the word, story ranges from the Book of Job to the report of a street accident.... Storytellers, in realism or fantasy, create illusions not clinical studies.... The test of illusion is how thoroughly it convinces us of its reality ... how deeply it moves us to new feelings and new insights. Such illusions may be the truest things we know. 'Art,' says Picasso, 'is a lie that lets us see the truth.' As a conscious work of art, story tries--as all art does--to make sense of a world not especially noted for making much sense at all.

So speaks the noted storyteller, Lloyd Alexander (p. 3-4).

All our lives long we need human interaction and the raw materials from which to fashion the value judgments that undergird our personal sense of order. What could/ should connect librarians and education toward humaneness? By extending school to include college and university and then adding all adults under the institution of lifelong learning, this argument goes on for collection managers and public service practictioners, cradle to grave. Quite a bit of emotion--anger and horror--may ensue simply from the consideration of such a subject in a book on teaching library skills.

In the elementary school the consistent use of works of fiction as the raw materials of reading instruction and the ubiquitous book report require that fiction be a major part of the library's holdings. Literature in large doses is definitely tied into the elementary curriculum. In a secondary school,

Education Toward Humaneness

literature holdings can be, and often are limited to books that are read in literature courses. During my years in the school library world, I found that school librarians separate into two far-apart camps--those who believe that recreational (fun and games and re-creation) reading has a place in the school library, and those who do not.

By mandate of job description, a school librarian employs the generic book and library to serve and supplement the curriculum. Those who do not see an involvement in non-curricula, non-fact (non-Language Arts) materials as their role, deny the affective goals of personal development. They serve only factual man. Unless Huck Finn and Meg, Mary Poppins and Robinson Crusoe, and the inhabitants of Pyrdain and Anastasia Perpetua Krupnik, and E. T. are there, along with the girl in the next chair and the boy next door, the library holds nothing with which to nurture a student's intra-, inter-, personal growth.

Arguments have been made for defining the role of the school librarian as cognitive curriculum expert and teacher of critical thinking, i. e. critical reading. The library itself, the raw materials for such an exercise, is the textbook for this teaching. When we move into the affective domain the librarian gets full mileage from her role as a non-grade-giving school-based adult. As co-journeyer on the path toward human fulfillment, the librarian is in a beautifully free position from which to interact with the developing personhood of the child or adolescent. If this role is played successfully for young people (as in President Reagan's case), though we librarians would prefer to hold a larger societal role, we at least are seen as being good for something.

The rationale for a strong school library fiction collection divides into two age levels and two arguments. The age levels are childhood--now kindergarten to sixth grade, I suppose, and lowering rapidly; and adolescence--seventh until they leave for the halls of ivy or some other kind of halfway house. The first argument concerns the necessity for the vicarious, structured interpersonal contact that the art of the story can provide. The second speaks specifically to the need for a reservoir of values and the responsibility of the librarian to supply learning resources toward this goal.

The pitch for a strong fiction collection in an elementary school library is based on Gesell, Piaget, and Erik

Erickson's <u>Childhood and Society</u>. In my experience, the loving librarian, being a free-non-grade-connected adult, has a unique chance to reach the quick of a child's being. Outlined, it might go thus:

1. Children develop through identifiable stages.
2. A school librarian has the opportunity to truly know students.
3. Children develop only through interpersonal relationships.
4. Great fiction provides larger-than-life interpersonal contact.
5. Childhood is the time of greatest development and openness.

Therefore, a major charge of an elementary school library should be to provide a fiction collection and staff able to meet these growth needs of its students.

For the adolescent years, Robert Carlsen's <u>Books and the Teenage Reader, a Guide for Teachers, Librarians, and Parents</u> provides my authority. He writes,

> At the beginning of adolescence, most individuals do not act consistently. On Monday the teen-ager may believe in the Boy Scout oath and on Tuesday believe in the antithetical code of his gang. By the end of adolescence, however, each individual must come to terms with his beliefs ... (p. 14)

> The satisfaction one seeks from reading changes as one moves toward maturity. First there is that stage when a reader discovers the joy of losing himself completely in his reading; he wants the book to last forever. Reading becomes an escape from daily life so absorbing that he forgets he is reading at all. He is actually so involved with the characters in the book that he comes back to reality with a sense of shock. Until a reader has had this kind of experience with books he will not move on to the deeper satisfactions of literature. Ordinarily this type of unconscious delight in reading will occur in late childhood. (Carlsen, p. 31)

What should be our responsibility for the education toward humaneness of the 12-Ph.D. and the out-of-any formal school lifelong learner? One role model for happiness requires the ability to discover and master increasingly complex actions and to be able to improve the appropriate related skills. Children seem to do this naturally. Adults, often constrained by their surroundings, struggle to realize their potential--to see the forest for the trees. The illusions of childhood, followed by the disillusion of the "real world," can, sadly, culminate in indifference and nihilism.

To overcome environmental limitations by breaking through and out requires a means to new horizons, new people, new dreams. The world of fiction provides this and is far more to be trusted than the world of drugs and alcohol sought towards the same end. Just as new technical skills demand the help of relevant technical manuals, new people skills demand the help of new people and new human worlds.

What should our librarian's/learning director's role be toward this need of the adult population? First, what are the types of libraries that serve the whole as opposed to the workplace adult? They are college and university, public, and special libraries. Colleges and universities, being teaching/learning institutions, fall under the same humanistic mandate as does K-12 education. Literature is part of the curriculum and the book collection should mirror its specifics. In academe, as in all education, the accepted selection procedure has faculty selecting for their own subject area. Likewise, as in all education, form seldom follows function, and, in actuality, adequate selection depends on the library's Acquisitions Department. Professors pay attention to textbook selection and to the contents of their Reserve Shelf. These areas define their specific plot of disciplinary turf and successful territoriality rests upon keeping it fenced and weeded. The provision of adjacent and supplementary or conflicting intellectual ground devolves upon the librarian as selector.

Since one of academe's chief societal roles is to preserve culture--here and there and now and then--currency carries limited weight in both buying and weeding. Shakespeare and Socrates are thus secure, being "demanded" at many levels. What is not charter-mandated by society or faculty or administration is an interest in the existence of a collection for the affective curriculum--inter- intra-personal development. If those within academe are to have access to the literature of escape and companionship, Acquisitions and Reference must provide and market this special print product. The public library owes everyone under its historic mandate to be the university of the people. Fiction--literature--

story--such books fill an important percentage of public library shelves. At present, the major collection-building issue is "demand" versus "mother may know best," with the Baltimore County Library System acting as a chief spokesperson for "giving'em what they want." Two, now and for tomorrow, specialized voices offer these comments:

> [I]f this [demand] theory is carried to its extreme, the library might house a collection of literary trash.... Perhaps the philosophy of the library should be to nurture the cultural needs of its patrons ... to eliminate the possibility that the library could degenerate into a purveyor of inferior literature. (Cabeceiras, p. 201)

> [T]he agency will not serve as the community's bookstore, the free paperback rack; that is the function of a congeries of commercial outlets. (Martin, p. 21)

Moderates have history on their side. The pendulum's swing is a timed fact. Today's emphasis on marketing as a way to save our library bacon supports the "demanders"-- no customer means no store. The one world, global villager, happy with the steady homogenizing of America, also supports the "on demanders." If we're all reading one book, when we're not not all watching "Dallas" or "Masterpiece Theatre," we are manipulable--unified.

If, as Toffler posits in The Third Wave, America is de-massifying, then more variety in our literary diet, more skeins on our literary loom are in order. If, as many of us hope, we are to continue the battle against sexism, racism, and materialism begun in the sixties and work toward a truly open America, selection standards beyond popular pressures must operate by making a major criterion of what serves the goals of personal integrity and dignity and human cultural differences.

Future readers need to find literary role models and print companions from all literary epochs not just from the people hotly in print today.

This excerpt from a book review by John Malcolm Brinnin in the Washington Post reinforces these generalities:

Education Toward Humaneness

I first read [Elizabeth Spencer's] The Voice at the Back Door when it appeared in 1956. In the decade or so to follow, the years of marchings and murders and, for onlookers at a distance, the years of bewildered shame, the steadying voice at my own back door was Elizabeth Spencer's. No other voice so clearly reminded me of a way of life obscured by outrage and oversimplified by headlines. No other work of literature or any exercise in polemics made me better understand that the term "civil rights movement" was but a paltry designation for a vast shift in awareness that had already occurred and awaited only the sacrifices of martyrs, black and white, to cause it to be written into law. It seemed to me that, like other realists before her, Elizabeth Spencer had written of the life she knew with the kind of bare documentary exactitude which time lifts into metaphor--as though, from the mythological murk of Faulkner territory, she had emerged holding up a crisp photograph negative on which black is visible only in relation to white, and vice versa. (Brinnin, p. 10)

If the public library elects to trash our varied collective past, it is then beyond the reach of most people. If public library acquisitions librarians do not elect to do more than react to best-seller lists, OPM and the texpaying patron, will, more than ever, have reason to question their need for an M. L. S. degree and professional pay scales. Special libraries do not really enter into this discussion. Non-profit and corporate managers correctly see their libraries and information centers as single-focus collections. Whether it be Ma Bell, the American Bankers' Association or the DAR, their staff's craving for the literature of education toward humaneness lies outside their library's bottom line. Such a valid constraint need not keep special librarians from taking the lead toward the provision of an in-house fiction lending library which can be either membership or a bring-one-borrow-one arrangement. Busy career ladder-climbers especially appreciate being able to find a print companion or an other-worldly escape as they rush toward car pool or subway.

This is the bare bones of my thesis. Its argument, I suppose, helps only the convinced minority who may find someone else's printed prose useful in personal administrative skirmishes. For those who now breathe righteous indignation at my invasion of the work of the public library children's room, or at the proposed waste of lesson time, or the intrusion into the lives of adults, let me spin a larger, subtler web and begin by a consideration of how to serve the non-bread needs of humankind.

What about this whole man, the one the Bible speaks to in the quotation, "Man does not live by bread alone, but by every word that proceedeth from the mouth of the Lord." Man, as Nietzsche said, is a valuing animal. The individual person stands in two dimensions, as an individual and, being that individual, as part of the totality of man himself which we usually designate by the word "human." Whatever human is, it is something outside the individual man, to be guessed at and read about. To design his own life, each man must be aware of the multitude of other human lives. By the daily making of his own unique value judgments, man writes his own life.

> Seat thyself among the moons of Saturn, and take high abstracted man along; and he seems a wonder, a grandeur, and a woe. But from the same point, take mankind en masse, and for the most part, they seem a mob of unnecessary duplicates, both contemporary and hereditary. But most humble though he was, and far from furnishing an example of the high, humane abstraction, the Pequod's carpenter was no duplicate; hence, he now comes in person and on this stage. (Melville, p. 301)

Life and literature, Melville tells us, are built from such individual lives.

As librarians, we who have ourselves profited from the ways in which the literature of emotion can expand the range of human encounter with the vicarious encounter of print, value "free reading" very highly. It would seem to follow, then, that in our "floor" work we would elect to push "story" as a proven medium for helping our patrons in their efforts to become not "high, humane abstraction[s]" but discrete humane persons.

The formula that's just been devised states:

> Totality of all humanness = sum of individual humanness

Education Toward Humaneness

Individual human = a function of available human models.

Logic, then, would seem to say that the highest goal of education may be to deal with this paradoxical nature of man and assist him to find those values from which to fashion a personhood. The process must include affective as well as cognitive skills. To accomplish such growth during a lifetime of development, individuals must be taught how to recognize, interpret, compare and use values.

What is a value? Where are their origins? What is their history? What is the relationship of values, each to the other? How do I translate mine into action?

In the capacious purse of philosophy are three classifications of truth that might be useful as a reference point as we ponder the role of the librarian in establishing an inner-directed hierarchy of values. There is propositional truth. There is existential truth. There is subjective truth. Truth in my family, especially after my son began to think like a philosopher (the result of an innate tendency to argue and an undergraduate philosophy major), has been thought of as being of two simplistic kinds--big T truth and small t truth. Small t truth is rational, provable, demonstrable, intellectual truth. Big T truth is the truth of belief, that combination of ideas to which any person at any time subscribes, which through this subscription or belief, defines his own humanness. Small t truth is the proposition that 2 and 2 make 4. Big T truth is the proposition that all men are created equal. It is what Tolkien is describing when he writes:

> Fantasy can ... be explained as a sudden glimpse of the underlying reality or truth ... an answer to that question, ... 'Is it true?' (Tolkien, p. 71)

The same point, approached another way, lies in these words of Carolyn Horovitz's:

> Part of the problem that adults have in determining what is or is not appropriate in fiction for children comes from an inability to appreciate the child's capacity to absorb and enjoy a great variety of experiences as long as they are controlled ... It almost seems that children are driven to fiction; their lives seem to need this extension, not

> into the reality of adults, but into a kind of fantastic exploration which is even more believable ... The truth, in fiction, as in children's play, is hidden deep, like an iceberg. Something that "really happened," presented with only a veneer of fictitious treatment, may be totally unbelievable. The assumption that reality equals truth is well used by television advertisers who expect that a woman whose hair is up in curlers or who speaks with a nasal twang is going to look so real to viewers that they will believe what she says about her particular detergent. (Horovitz, p. 396-99)

There is no argument about small t truth and libraries, only about big T.

Propositional truth, as the philosophers use it, would be our small t truth; anything that can be demonstrated by rational means. Propositional truth is of long and honorable use in the world of philosophy and can be defined as the statement of hypothesis followed by the proof of this propositional hypothesis. Hard science, of course, is one of the greatest practioners of propositional truth.

Truth as subjectivity is an idea of Kierkegaard's. His philosophy describes it as being the subject of truth. Truth is for him almost an environment or climate, and the individual person who holds such ideas he describes as "to be in truth." Another phrase of his, "inwardness in believing," is a lovely metaphor for librarians who connive that youth shall devour their bookstock. In this process, the substance gobbled becomes oneself, so that the belief that has come from the book world outside becomes part of the very substance of the person partaking. Kierkegaard's thesis is that reality is the existence of this created self. This is big T truth.

The third kind we might consider is existential truth; a philosophy that gained its greatest strength under the French philosopher Jean Paul Sartre. Existential easily becomes existence, to be in existence, the existence of which becomes again the self in becoming. The idea has much similarity to the former one of self in our subjective definition. We constantly define and redefine ourselves on the basis of our daily experience. This, also, is a figure for taking into the self something on the periphery of the self which again changes the self. The librarian thus is a constant practitioner of the existential situation of her patrons.

Of these three categories of philosophy, the first, propositional truth, is the province of the critical thinking that we've been discussing as the librarians' role in the educative process. This is the substance of the mind at work in the natural and scientific and technical worlds.

Education is the constant, and hopefully consistent, building of fact upon fact, contact upon contact, until the human mind has at its disposal in adulthood more connections than any computer has so far been programmed to handle. Out of these myriad factual connections comes what we call our judgmental ability. Here is a simple example. A sleeping adult is awakened by a noise. In his mind are stored the clues to what that noise might possibly be. The mind performs as a computer, scanning, sorting out the irrelevant ones and coming up with the most likely one that stored experience offers. Based on this, he makes the further judgment (criminal or cat?) as to whether to arise and search or roll over and seek sleep again.

The other two kinds of truth, truth as subjectivity and existential truth, are those from which human values emerge. What is a fact is not a value. A series of facts can be ranked as a matter of priority or selected to be put down on an examination. Two and two is not a value, nor is that fact that it is raining. What we call fact has many gradations and is often not black and white. These are very simplistic statements, but, in order to propose an argument, one has to assume that there is a clear division between the world of fact and the world of value.

Today, value has returned to the theatre of education. The idea that we, as librarians, should provide source material from which human values can grow may now escape a charge of heresy. The educational commune is slowly rediscovering another wheel of Truth. These two kinds of truth which relate to the state of man's being and the health of his values are more important parts of life's curriculum than any discipline of hard fact.

A concern with reading to develop humaneness which a minority of librarians even consider to be part of their purview, is a most vital function as we work in education. Historically, the public library has been thought to be the place to get one's share of fun and games outside reading. Yet the percentage of children who have a regular acquaintance with the public library is very small. Sometimes this is due to economic factors, sometimes to geographical factors. Let me give an example of a sociological factor from my experience.

A fifth grade teacher insisted on having one book touching on Christmas as the December book report for each one of her students. This, as you can imagine, presented logistical problems for me, the librarian. In self-defense I was trying to suggest to one student that, since she wanted a special book which we did not have, she try her own neighborhood public library. Feeling that I had made my point, I looked up and found that the teacher was signaling me to sign-off. Later, when the teacher and I sat down in conference on the matter, she said, "Oh, Carolyn, I'm sorry I didn't warn you. Susie's mother is an alcoholic and she has no way to get to the public library." Three cars and two horses at home, but she had, being only 11 years old and a prisoner of motorized suburbia, no way to get to the public library.

As children's librarians, we must not only read children's books professionally--to ascertain their contents preparatory to acting as their successful vendors to our clientele--but because we find them speaking meaningfully to us. To quote again from Tolkien in <u>Tree and Leaf</u>,

> Actually, the association of children and fairy-stories is an accident of our domestic history. Fairy-stories have in the modern lettered world been relegated to the "nursery," as shabby or old-fashioned furniture is relegated to the play-room, primarily because the adults do not want it, and do not mind if it is misused.... Children as a class--except in a common lack of experience they are not one--neither like fairy-stories more, nor understand them better than adults do; and no more than they like many other things.... But in fact only some children, and some adults, have any special taste for them; and when they have it, it is not exclusive, nor even necessarily dominant.... It is certainly one that does not decrease but increases with age, if it is innate. (Tolkien, p. 34-35)

Any adult who could not pleasurably read <u>Wind in the Willows</u> on the day he reads these words should, in my judgment, best depart the education field forever. Unless there lurks a child within there exists nothing for the growing humaneness of the seeker to grasp. At one point, I was doing a lot of mental gymnastics trying to evade a firm administrative dictum forbidding any student to "read in the library. " Study, yes, but to read a book, absolutely a waste of time. I stalled the issue with, "Well, now in order to choose a book you sometimes have to read a paragraph or two, don't you?" With that proviso, I managed to get enough of a foot in the door to begin to develop floor work with some students. As the program gradually grew, I took great joy in the sight of a young girl perched up on top of one of our old-fashioned wooden ladders, lost in a book, making a new friend. Finally, there was enough positive feedback from parents to save reading in the library.

Of course, to believe (and I use the word wittingly) that teaching of interactive reading is a vital part of our job is something that comes with experience. Once acquired, it is a faith that we wear against all comers. Once you do elect to become an ardent practitioner of this art, you must become the kind of librarian whose favorite object is "book. " Not the telephone book to boost up a small child at a table, or a row of shelved books, or a catalog that lists books, or an automated book, but a read book.

Father Bernard Theall, the Benedictine treasure who taught me Book Selection at Catholic University stoutly maintained that he never had less than five books on his night table. 'To allow for my moods and fend off boredom, five choices is a minimum. I am a complex man!"

Know it or no--each of us also possesses such otherworld needs. My 90-year-old mother-in-law, for whom I am now the primary purveyor of large print books, wants romances. Believe me, Silhouette Books, et al, are missing a large Gray Panther market that Reader's Digest isn't satisfying.

Because we talked earlier of a library as the institutionalization of order, it is needful now to discuss how literature in the sense of story fits into this ordered universe. Any one of the definitions or descriptions of man which indicate his dual nature, mind and heart, doing and being, is a sound justification for dealing with individual humanness as a most vital part of a library program. Our human judgment is a composite of all the big T truths which lie beyond the reach of the facts constituting the ordinary. If we considered "library" to be the whole of the stored memory of man without a large provision for the teaching of values, we would be doing a whopping disservice to our users. The central thesis of Admiral Hyman Rickover as he warned us that we are being run over with technology, is that man, if he does not have values by which to know what he wants to do and thus to be, will find his ends determined by technology.

Creative literature can be separated into two parts: straight literature, wherein the value lies in the larger-than-life presentation of individual people and individual cultures; and fantasy, folklore, myth, and fairy tales, where the purpose is to build the symbolic means with which to interpret both the history of the race and the history of the individual members of that race. Myth, from a Greek word meaning story, was the original means for describing man's efforts to understand the world around him. Beginning science was a myth as man strove to explain thunder and the power of the ocean. Can you imagine the problems involved in trying to explain the flight of a moon rocket if you could not use the technical language and scientific laws that are at our command today? This is how man must have felt when he first tried to interpret a volcano or describe what had happened when, upon striking dry wood together, flames appeared.

Mythology is a treasure house of man's self-interpretation--a historically accurate pattern that gives direction and meaning to experience.

> The world was not fragmented. An idea did not suddenly grow, like Topsy, all alone and separate. For them, all things had antecedents, and long family trees. They saw nothing shameful or silly in myths and fairy stories nor did they shovel them out of sight in some cupboard marked only for Children.... And do you think they are true?.... What is true? As far as I am concerned it doesn't matter tuppence if the incidents in the myths never happened. That does not make them any less true, for, indeed, in one way or another, they're happening all the time. You only have to open a newspaper to find them crowding into it. Life continually reenacts them. (Travers, p. 15)

The great truths of interpersonal relationships can be found in myths and legends. For example, having experienced any of the relationships portrayed in Medea, can you experience the play and think it was written because there was no

Education Toward Humaneness

other plot line handy? An eternal truth is there. To shift 2,000 years, LeGuin's <u>Wizard of Earthsea</u> taught me why possession of a man's name gives you power over him.

Myths are stories of the relationship of man to his gods. They developed as explanations of observable facts, which were felt to be controlled by remote forces outside man's control--the gods. The beings of the myths do not relate intimately with man as do the creatures of the folk tales.

The great epic legends were, like the myths, national in character. Greek, Norse, Anglo-Saxon, African--all represent man in his development as man. Again, the individual developing as part of a group. Hero legends, like Beowulf and Arthur, enlarge upon the fact of a known person.

In the beginning there was no distinction made between folk literature for adults and for children. The whole tribe together sat around the camp fire, as families or groups still do under similar camping circumstances today.

Tolkien, in the dust jacket blurb for <u>Tree and Leaf</u>, describes his purpose in writing the essay "On Fairy Tales" as an attempt to rescue the fairy story from the academic theorists on the one hand and the sentimentalists on the other. The essay comments:

> If adults are to read fairy stories as a natural branch of literature--neither playing at being children, nor pretending to be choosing for children, nor being boys who would not grow up--what are the values and functions of this kind? ... First of all, if written with art, the prime value of fairy stories will simply be that value which, as literature, they share with other literary forms. But fairy-stories offer also, in a peculiar degree or mode, these things: Fantasy, Recovery, Escape, Consolation, all things of which children have, as a rule less need than older people. (Tolkien, p. 45-46)

To approach this matter of imagination from another angle, let us consider some of the ideas in the book <u>Parents and Children Learn Together</u>, by Katharine Whiteside Taylor. From her observations of children whose parents and teachers encourage their creative fantasies, she has come to realize how keenly children see and feel their imaginary images and companions. (My son's was Little Green Pickle, a bird. One day the mother of his bosom buddy, normally no bird watcher, rang up and announced in hushed tones, "Little Green Pickle is sitting in our tree.") The inference for educators is that we must continue to provide a rich fare of fairy tales at home and at nursery school. She continues by saying that children, as each relives the history of the human race in the stages of his individual development, react strongly to the symbolic meaning of these tales. Without conscious awareness of their purport, the children's psyches are nourished by fairy tale and myth. Surely, Jung's concept of the collective unconscious no longer requires defense. The relation of fairy tales to both the individual and the collective unconscious, and the obligation of all teaching librarians to provide the books to nurture creative growth, need to be stated, defended and fought for.

Another discernment of the interaction between imagination and metaphor belongs to Arthur Koestler. In Insight and Outlook he asserts that the artist's way of handling facts as a stimulus to imagination and the scientist's use of imagination to handle facts spring from a common base which he calls "biosociation"--the simultaneous correlation of an impression to two otherwise independent operational areas. Nonsense rhymes and all illusory literature may be profitable experiences in biosociation which prepare the learner for future discoveries.

The distinguished American philosopher Paul Weiss. in his book The Making of Men, makes a very strong case for the value of the story in education;

> To sense what existence is in essence one needs the guidance of art.... The story brings the child and teacher to the heart of the mystery of existence.... From the story the child readily learns something of the careers open to hope and fear; it there gets to know the weights and the rewards of bravery, industry, and patience....
>
> ... A story is not a report. [It] serves as an epitomization of the entire scheme of things, which must be mastered if the child is to be able to maintain itself against brute reality, ... to freely be. (Weiss, p. 13-14)

Weiss believes that the story teaches by showing that there are verities of the steady aspect of existence which, though obscured by the details of daily life, are there to be turned to in success and in misfortune. The story delimits personal experience as a child among children, still keeping the finalities in focus, though never clearly. The darkness of the dimly perceived is ominous and inviting, wondrous and dismaying. "Awareness of finalities is achieved mainly through a telling and retelling of stories." (Weiss, p. 15)

To a Dancing God, by the sociologist Sam Keen, offers other perceptive thoughts on the place of the story in the humanizing process.

> The centrality of storytelling in the formation of the identity and culture of preliterate man is well established, although it remains somewhat embarrassing to modern man. Since the enlightenment and the emergence of less dramatic but more scientific modes of thought, Western man has found comfort in telling himself that he has come of age and passed beyond the primitive darkness of myth into the full light of reason.... The march to the sun has begun! (Keen, p. 87)

What a vanished comfort! Our vaunted reason isn't even an adequate governor, let alone a compass for our technologically plundered planet.

Dr. Keen continues,

> In telling stories, traditional man was affirming the unity of reality. The individual, the tribe, nature and the cosmos fit together in concentric circles of integated meaning all of the parts which were necessary to form a coherent and artistic whole ...
>
> Another article of faith hidden in the act of storytelling is the confidence that the scale of Being is such that a human being can grasp the meaning of the whole.... Man is a microcosm; thus, in telling his stories, he may have confidence that his warm, concrete, dramatic images are not unrelated to the forces that make for the unity of the macrocosm. While his images and stories may reduce the proportions of reality to a scale that is manageable by the human spirit, their distortion serves the cause of truth [big T]. Traditional man had every confidence that his symbols,

myths, and stories were the most appropriate means to grasp reality and were not merely illusions projected out of his isolated, subjective brain. (Keen, p. 97-98)

A child knows when "once upon a time" was. It was the time when the lion lay down with the lamb, and Noah filled the Ark. The quality of imagination, exemplified technologically in man's being able to set foot upon the moon, comes to us mainly through creative imaginative literature. Rare is the adult who believes--in man or God--who has not become a comfortable denizen of the world of faerie--early or late. If there is not an unknown next step that can be made known, there can be no feeling that such a step is possible, therefore no contemplation of it, therefore no realization of it. As the line from "South Pacific" goes, "If you haven't got a dream, how can you make a dream come true?"

Another facet of imagination is belief. One dictionary defines it as "Trust, confidence, ... the acceptance of a thing as true." For the word "believe" we read "I believe you"; "to have faith in the existence or efficacy of." and ... "to believe in God"; "do you believe in ghosts?" One place to go from this foundation is such an act as St. Augustine's leap of faith.

Belief in fairies has proven a good way of testing human beings. So far this test has produced a pretty valid correlation. The person who responds to the question "Do you believe in fairy tales?" with a flat, clear, unequivocal "no" is erased from my list of fully human beings. My personal survey has shown that the man who does not believe in fairies doesn't believe in love, and can't believe in God. Much has been written to demonstrate the reality of love. Many wives, when asked "How do you know if your husband loves you?" respond by offering the fact that he gave them a mink coat for Christmas, or a new vacuum cleaner, or flowers. "I know he loves me because he is a good man. He brings his pay check home and he doesn't beat me." End of "Dear Abby." Confusion of the purely material with the corporal as a visible sign of the invisible quality called love can come most easily to one who is not in touch with his imagination. Joan Anglund, in her A Friend Is Someone Who Likes You, provides comprehensible witness for this theorem. For its leap of faith to the belief in love, the art of loving depends upon the individual human's ability to believe in anything

Some avid social scientist may someday devise a

reliable check-list for determining the presence or absence of love in any human relationship. Some avid theologian may find a way to make concrete the proof of the existence of God. I don't think so, for I believe that if God becomes a surety, faith turns into nothing more than paying the premium on the insurance policy and awaiting your check when you suffer the final loss. Likewise, love, not being a business transaction, depends upon the leap of belief for its existence.

Symbolic language can be traced, item by item, back through the centuries to the early, aural myths of our culture. From Greek and African and Judeo-Christian traditions come today's traditions and symbols. The person who is cut off from these antecedents is left rootless and without a dictionary to the symbolic language of his immediate world. It is very difficult to know where you are if you haven't a clue as to where you came from.

Since the myths were begun by our ancestors at a primitive stage of their cultural development, they belong to the world of the young. To wait until adolescence or adulthood, or for the culturally deprived, forever, for this mental furniture to become part of one is to cripple emotional growth unnecessarily. Jung's hypothesis of the collective unconscious explains how myths, by what Pamela Travers called their "only connect," relate each individual to this reservoir. The language of access to it is the symbolic vocabulary of myth and fantasy, legend, fairy and folk tale.

The ancestry and verity of these tales needs no further documentation. The science of folklore is a recognized academic discipline. Every incident can be both traced back to its historic origin and shown to be present at some period in almost all parts of the cultural world. In the recent past when anything not factual was considered out of fashion, man was left to pilot himself by his rationality--his possession of facts and his ability to act upon them. Such cyclical professional blindness deprives us of a very vital part of our soul's fodder.

During the Season of Advent when the house is filled with pre-Christmas trappings, my mind hears the stories of Christmas. Those stories, whether one conceives of them as divine revelation or cultural legends, are excellent reference points for this discussion of the need for story in the lifelong learning process. The Christmas season turns on an axis of giving--the gift of God to humankind in the divine infant. We repeat that awesome gift as each human celebrant gives to his own human circle. All the handiwork of love, the gifts which will be returned, the cards of cheer that relate a year's crop of death and divorce--these are messages of giving--our best, or our worst.

If values could be made visible by any factual statement, the great Truths of the world would not be presented most powerfully in works of literature. The idea of giving can be stated simply in a few sentences: "It is that we give of ourselves. Each gift represents a choice--of our good or bad angel. Acknowledge the integrity of the recipient of the gift and honestly match the one to the other." All of this when couched in prose seems either obvious or fatuous. In neither case does it bear repeating, yet the true gift, correctly conceived and bestowed, is one of the rarest fruits of a human relationship. Since the GNP demands from us regular offerings of love, give we must. The recipe for these great human insights waits for those who seek it in the complex simplicities, the top-of-the-fence Truths that are the warp of the great web of people-lore and fantasy.

Let us begin with the Bible. The parables of the Bible seem to hold those truths that are perhaps not self-evident, but are eternal. As each hearer grasps their insights for himself, these are transmitted from generation to generation without the problems of dated language inherent in an expository statement. Ponder this as you hear the Bible in sacred or secular context. Is it not chiefly by parable that Christ taught?

To look at this strange business of the teaching of

Education Toward Humaneness

values in another way, any adult knows in the depths of his heart that it is the uniqueness of his life style, not the facts and advice given that will shape character. This human witness transmitted will enable the other to comprehend the mentor, and react to him in continuing judgment. The cliché, "Don't do as I do, but do as I say" speaks to the heart of this matter, as does, "What you are is so loud, I can't hear what you say."

There is, I think, quite a bit of between-the-lines information available in the subtle difference between two genres of writing--the supernatural and science fiction. The distinction between these two bodies of literature is valuable to us as professional bookpeople because it helps to illustrate commonly hidden thought patterns. Today, science fiction is considered by some of its pundits as pointing the way to future reality, since so much of what is now our present technology was first recorded in science fiction. Let us dig and see what such literary excavation may reveal.

As is often the case, the terms themselves offer clues to a deeper significance. The term "supernatural" is composed of the prefix meaning "above, in addition to," and the noun "natural." Some of the Webster's Collegiate's definitions of natural that seem relevant are "of, or by birth, innate, inborn; in accordance with the nature of its kind, normal species as parental love, pertaining to, in accordance with, or determined by nature; in or found in its native state, not artificial, synthetic, processed, or acquired by external means." "Supernatural" is defined as "of or proceeding from an order of existence beyond nature or the visible and observable universe, ascribed to agencies above or beyond nature, miraculous."

So an acceptable definition of "supernatural" literature might be that kind of writing which goes beyond the inherent in man and the natural world to whatever outer being or forces control nature's "super" existence. It is a story in which the writer seeks to illuminate the essence of nature or of man and move above that to whatever the writer feels is the invisible next level of command. Since supernatural writing seeks to describe the ultimate, it is a prescription for a man seeking his own clue to what, if any, part of his innate development lies beyond the observable natural world. The Greek word khyfis, literally growth, from which our conception of nature is derived, originally meant much the same as mana, namely the occult force that makes things grow and develop.

The miracles in the Bible are supernatural parables. The writings of Edgar Allan Poe are perhaps the most famous American supernatural fiction. Such stories attempt to distill the essence from the two concepts man and nature, by the creativity of the writer's selectivity and insight. Since man created neither himself nor nature, such a distillation is a process of divining. These two worlds cannot be divided, though technology and hard science tend to attempt this in a schizophrenic blindness. Nature is something created, not replicable by man. The natural human reproductive process is still hanging on, though the test tube babies of Brave New World have now begun.

Webster's Collegiate defines science as "a branch of study concerned with observation and classification of facts, especially with the establishment of verifiable general laws, accumulated knowledge systematized and formulated with reference to the discovery of general truths, especially such knowledge when it relates to the physical world; also called the natural sciences." Another definition of Webster's that is germane to this discussion is that for fictitious literature, specifically novels: "that which forms, invents, or feigns." The genre of writing called science fiction is then a fashioning or inventing within the confines of the laws of the natural world which we call science.

This eerie description of an online information search, from Robert Silverberg's Nightwings, is an example of such scientific validity from our own profession of library science:

> After the conclusion of the early period of orientations, I was given trivial tasks. Chiefly I was asked to do things that in an earlier time would have been performed wholly by machine: for example, to monitor the feed lines that oozed nutrients into the brain-boxes of the memory tanks. For several hours each day I walked through the narrow corridor of the inspection panels, searching for clogged lines. It had been so devised that when a line became blocked, a stress pattern was created the length of the clear tubing that contained it, and beams of a special polarized light illuminated that pattern for benefit of the inspector. I did my humble task, now and again finding a blockage, and I did other little jobs as befitted my status of apprenticeship.
>
> However, I also had the opportunity to pursue my

own investigations into the events of my planet's past.

Sometimes one does not learn the value of things until they are lost. For a lifetime I served as a Watcher, striving to give early warning of a promised invasion of Earth, while caring little who might wish to invade us, or why. For a lifetime I realized dimly that Earth had known grander days than those of the Third Cycle into which I had been born, and yet I sought no knowledge of what those days had been like and of the reasons for our present diminished condition. Only when the starships of the invaders blossomed in the sky did I feel a sudden hunger to know of that lost past. Now, as the most elderly of apprentices, I, Tomis of the Rememberers, rummaged through the archives of vanished time.

Any citizen has the right to go to a public thinking cap and requisition an information from the Rememberers on any given subject. Nothing is concealed. But the Rememberers volunteer no aid; you must know how to ask, which means you must know what to ask. Item by item you must seek your facts. It is useful for those who must know, say, the long-term patterns of climate in Agupt, or the symptoms of the crystallization disease, or the limitations in the charter of one of the guilds; but it is no help at all to the man who wishes knowledge of the larger questions. One would need to requisition a thousand informations merely to make a beginning. The expense would be great; few would bother.

As an apprentice Rememberer I had full access to all data. More important, I had access to the indexes. The Indexers are a guild subsidiary to the Rememberers, a donkey-guild of drudges who record and classify that which they often do not understand; the end product of their toil serves the greater guild, but the indexes are not open to all. Without them one scarcely is able to cope with the problems of research.

I will not summarize the stages by which I came by my knowledge--the hours spent shuffling through interwoven corridors, the rebuffs, the bewilderments, the throbbing of the brain. As a foolish novice I was at the mercy of pranksters, and many a fellow apprentice, even a guild member or two, led me astray for the sheer wicked joy of it. But I learned which routes to follow, how to set up sequences of questions, how to follow a path of references higher and higher until the truth bursts dazzlingly upon one. With persistence rather than with great intellect I wrung from the files of the Rememberers a coherent tale of the downfall of man. (Silverberg, p. 93-94)

A person, regardless of his literary qualifications, who attempts to work in sci-fi must have a thorough grounding in whatever science he uses as the base for his invention. Otherwise, the writing lacks the framework of authenticity. Star examples are the stories of Jules Verne which defined a tradition that has come down to us in the works of Clarke, Heinlein and others.

A point of demarcation between the two kinds of fiction lies in the fact that the supernatural is a divination from a non-man-made base into an even less knowable level of the ultimate infinity, whereas science fiction is technologically oriented and predicts goals toward which man's technological ability can carry him if he so chooses. With technology's present advanced state, most competent authors' inventions are plausible enough for any research unit with sufficient money and imagination to tackle as a serious project. By now, so much of the world of science fiction has become fact. The imagination of Jules Verne remained fiction for 70 years, Clarke's 2001; A Space Odyssey, with a copyright date of 1968, bids fair to become reality in half that time.

This establishes a circle of conditioning that is worth a hard look from book people. Fiction is acknowledged to wield a powerful influence with far greater access to the ability to control our actions than a similar collection of facts might possess. Science fiction is a philosophical guidepost to our time and temper. If technology is to be our slave and not our master, let us be aware of this additional factor of conditioning as we select science fiction and discuss it with our patrons.

Library materials seem, then, to be divisible into three classes: fact, opinion, and emotion. The class labeled emotion is treated in the discipline that some call literature, and Paul Weiss calls stories. Friedman, in his book entitled To Deny Our Nothingness, states that

Literature is the real homeland of the image of man, for it retains the concrete uniqueness of individual men. At the same time, it allows us a relationship with these men sufficiently close for them to speak to us as bearers of the human. Yet in its very particularity literature defies the easy generalizing and universalizing that holds good in other branches of human culture and, unlike other fields, forces us to remember the varieties of man and the varieties of culture. Literature is art, not life, yet art that remains more closely bound to life than most forms of art and certainly than most forms of knowledge about man.... It is the dialogue between author and character that produces the image of man; this image is never a direct expression of the author's views, but a genuine product of this dialogue. (Friedman, p. 27)

The genus man is then a combination of the lives and personalities of individual men. A value can be considered a disembodied quality, but it is difficult to internalize when detached from an individual human life. By logical sequence, then, it follows that to understand values and, by comprehension and identification, move on to a personal absorption of values, each growing human needs to know as many other people as possible.

The literature of emotion can assist us in this search in many ways. Some are practical, others selective. By including the people of fiction among our potential acquaintances, we vastly enlarge our range of humanity. A person in a small town needs this vicariousness more than a person in a large city. Consider for a moment the factor of empathetic experience as a purveyor of growth experience. Then calculate the quantity and quality of vicarious experience that has come into your life through reading in comparison with that which has entered through the tales of our fellow human beings. No wonder that the hero of the Music Man cut such a swath in River City, or that the banishment of storytelling, elderly kinfolk has so impoverished the young.

Waiving the statistical method in favor of field-tested intuition, I would like to state and then discuss the proposition that the human post-childhood male is far less interested and involved in interpersonal relationships and internal concerns than the female because he reads almost no fiction and is thusly deprived of that wealth of vicarious experience.

Approaching the idea another way: no single lifetime is adequate for the magnitude of people contacts required to develop good people skills.

Parenthood is one good case. Only those who work with each stage of childhood from newborn on could conceivably have enough understanding of childhood to be able to generate any objective context into which to bring and rear personal offspring. An only child has no direct experience of any degree of siblingness. One from a large family has no way to project the feelings of an only child--and so forth. You say "What about Dr. Spock and such?" My reply is that this is a prescription for how to externally care for, not how to walk in another's moccasins.

Men, in general, stand outside other individual human spirits and do not avidly seek entry. Their style is manipulative management unreached by empathy. My field testing has taken the form of querying each male whose conversation indicates a high degree of humaneness. My most recent subject was a Norwegian book publisher, serving on a panel celebrating Childrens Book Week 1982 at the Library of Congress. His warm literate prose was clue one, but the clincher was his last poetic paragraph in which he spoke of the "lost language of childhood"--a time when a personal fifteen minutes is forever and Sleeping Beauty's 100-year sleep is perfectly reasonable." Yes, indeed, he did read a lot of fiction.

Experts tell us (and I believe them) that human beings develop only in relationship to others of our kind. All loners-- the autistic, those infants withered by denial of adequate human presence, the Hinckleys--dramatize this. Great literary portraits, like great painted portraits, attract readers and never lose their lure because the creative selectivity of the artist has delineated a distinct and unforgettable person--an icon. The so sharply drawn people of print meet our lives fully because the insightful skill of a great author has hewn a fellow creature whose clearly defined portrait repels or attracts us: Pippi Longstocking, Toad, the Nome King of Oz, Madame Bovary, Jane Eyre, Scarlett O'Hara, Heathcliff for starters. Because the selectivity that is art has drawn them distinctly, they possess reality beyond the real.

The principle of art by selection is most easily recognized in the field of graphics. After a first visit to the American West, a painter, sharing with me some completed canvases of places I know well, remarked "This painting shows

Education Toward Humaneness

the way it feels to me. The West for me is great space--a great blank openness. My canvas portrays this by having the simplest geographical outline and really nothing else but color on it. All other things are struck out. The particulars of house and fence confuse that huge scale which is the essence of the quality I find in the western country. Its vastness is my message from New Mexico. The details of house and tree often incorporated in such scenes can rob the landscape of its integrity by seeming to enrich with a clutter of homely detail."

We can translate this principle of artistic selectivity into the field of literature. It then becomes clear that the artist, in building his character from words, has given us something that will make certain emotions and values more clearly visible than does the reality of the natural condition of the human landscape.

Robert Butman, a professor of English and Drama at Haverford and Bryn Mawr, led a book discussion group to which I belonged, using plays, poetry and novels to lead us skillfully beyond ourselves into emotional insights and growth. He believed that a work of art is the best vehicle for accomplishing this because it affords a discrete situation with clearly delineated characters to form a framework for grasping the human scene. In such clarity, spelled out in symbols--in this instance words--resides the means whereby several people can discuss a human situation in terms commonly accessible to all.

The person created by literature provides another boon --the opportunity to know him intimately in a way that we are actually permitted to know very few individuals, even in the course of a long and warmly gregarious lifetime. One can comfortably come this close to many fellow creatures if he can turn them off with a snap of the covers.

Since our personal lives can show constant change, an especially valuable feature of the hero in literature is in the ability to select one that is right for any particular time. This exactitude can be accomplished much more easily by pulling a book from a shelf, especially with the help of a friendly librarian, than by going out into the circle of real people. A piece of literature that qualifies as a work of art is designed to make a point and to cross-connect individual lives in meaningful interaction. It is a clever matchmaker.

The limits of time itself can be conquered by the

the experience of historical or science fiction. Distance too disappears when our novel lets us experience another land--another culture. Before traveling afar, I read relevant fiction because I have found that this vicarious living is a preparation that lingers to accompany me in a way that straight history or a travel guide will not. Thus by these vicarious knowings the reader of fiction comes to be comfortable (or "un" as the case may be) with as broad a spectrum of fellow creatures as she chooses.

The handle-like intellectual utility of a work of art as a means to provide tangible parameters for learning about our own and others' humanness also has its pitfalls. The literature of emotion serves to assist education toward humanity--but it is hardly the vehicle for instruction in grammar. Among the examples of such ghastly misuse of art, let me share one. In ninth grade my daughter was required to unravel the sentence structure of a verse from the Odyssey. Rather like using a rare old Persian carpet as a mud scraper for boots. It destroys the former and doesn't help the latter.

All right, you may be saying, so affective literature--the story--is a requisite for the production of a mature human person. But why should the librarian assume the mantle of story provider for the child, adolescent, young/old adult? Why not the parent? Why not the English teacher? Why not the adult with personal acquiring?

For the child, just one reason. The only one who is trained in children's literature and has all children exposed to her influence is the school librarian. Parents in some degree exist for most children, though there are real orphans and others who might as well be. Legions of English teachers exist whose personal snobbery and attitudinal constitution make them side step "kiddy-lit" like an ill-smelling puddle. No one should fault the zeal and devotion of the denizens of our public library children's rooms, but they do not have access to the universe of the young. Furthermore, talk of turning public library children's work over to the schools has already reached a noticeable stage. The contest for tax dollars makes such propositions inevitable.

For most basic learning, early childhood provides the most productive time for absorption of a skill or perspective. Which truism only serves to reinforce the crucial role of school librarians in the development of the human being into an information-able and people-successful adult person. For all those beyond grade 12, pragmatism requires suggestions for designing Continuing Education lessons in humaneness. Discussing "Popular vs. Good" in current fiction Jonathan Yardley of the Washington Post writes: "It goes without saying that there are distinctions between books that seek to entertain and books that seek to illuminate." If you agree, then what! My solution pushes all book professionals, those of us whose credentialed status forces us to stand with the good, the pure, and the beautiful, to enlarge that stance to include getting off the fence and onto the side of "books that illuminate." Our recent selection pondering or pandering has not produced professional prosperity.

The voice of Lillian Gerhardt, one of the most powerful credentialed liberals, speaking through her contribution to the 1980 festschrift for Betty Fast, Excellence in School Media Programs, urges current practitioners toward a responsible use of their purchasing power. Airing her regrets at not having spoken out earlier on the "irrationalities and anti-intellectualism" practiced by revaluation of children's collections guided only by sexist and racist criteria, she goes on to request collection selection on the basis of "literary excellence" and the impact of selections on the development of readers.

How can we overpower OPM and claim professional competence beyond technical skills if our acquisitions and selection policies ignore what our M. L. S. courses taught us about literary quality? For some of us holding degrees from Catholic University, the ghost of Father Bernard Theall keeps us from going soft. The charisma of that opinionated Benedictine survives now even beyond reinforcement of his personal presence. Some will call it simplistic or reactionary to establish guidelines for using books where authors have employed their skills to point our way to the stars and to provide us with positive companions, fictional friends, and support groups as guides to our personal needs. The distinguished American poet Witter Bynner supports this position with:

>   Words, if words are wise, go on and on
>   To make a longer note of unison
>   With man and man than living persons make
>   With one another for whatever sake.
>   (Bynner, p. xiii)

Don Quixote himself never rode totally alone! Are we less than he in our hope of generating support for professional value judgments--emotion in action!

If you in your work will endorse this precept, then school, college, and university students and faculty and tax-paying public library users can benefit from time spent in a printed, fictional world that can counteract the mindless pap and violence of TV and the pandered titillating escapism of romantic paperbacks.

Chapter 15
The Science of Who-Me? Folklore and Festival

He who flies from his own family has far to travel.

Petronius

Beyond and outside academe, K-professor, or when constrained by a faculty of un-believers, a BI public services librarian cannot look to the academic curriculum to provide subject content for a class. What then? Are there subjects that will intersect and interest all ages and levels of society, that will permit individualized instruction without boring the rest of the group, yet have the high motivation of "something in it for me?" Yes, because everyone is interested in self, and has, at least occasionally, the need to touch base with physical reality. My choices are "Roots" and maps, "The Science of Whereabouts" that is Chapter Sixteen.

When SLWTK was written, my certainty included only folklore, people-lore, as I had experienced it extra-curricularly through a project of the Folklore Committee of the Department of English of the University of Arizona at Tucson, the "Folklore and Cultural Awareness Project," directed by Byrd Howell Granger. In the past eleven years work experiences have increased and widened my surety.

As an educational publications researcher for National Geographic I studied "Food for the World" and confronted the cultural anthropology that underlies food customs such as that in which the bride and groom feed each other wedding cake signifying the establishment of a new and separate family unit. This intellectual eye-opening also showed me the food customs of my new tribe, the Michaels. Four-plus years in a genealogical special library taught me the obvious. In addition, very shortly after I came to the DAR, Judith Reid of the Genealogical Reference Staff of LC crossed my path and, together, for three lovely years we "did" the Genealogy, Local History, and Folklore Interest Group of the District of Columbia Library Association. These programs proved my intuitive hypotheis that the three related subject areas constitute a wondrous context within which each differing human seeker could enlarge his sense of personal place--a pedigree back to royalty, a genuine great-grandfather, or an ethnicity of village or nation.

The Science of Who

Folklore has a bad name with some genealogists and the general world of those who disbelieve in anything they can't see, touch, or smell which, unfortunately, includes love and God as well as "faerie." To capture the attention of these two camps, the Interest Group employed the stick of "but that isn't what we mean," and the carrot of listening to such as Byrd Granger and Arthur Kurzweil, editor of Toledot, who actually do practice licensed audience wizardry.

My Webster's establishes that folklore is "traditional customs, tales, or sayings preserved orally among people." "Folk" is defined as "the great proportion of the members of a people that determines the group character and that tends to preserve its characteristic form of civilization and its customs, arts and crafts, legends, traditions, and superstitions from generation to generation." Webster and I agree. That is what folklore, properly understood, adds to genealogy and local history to round the circle of social man, leaving no one without a findable context and history.

The Cultural Awareness Project began in the summer of 1969 when 15 Arizona teachers became members of a group which embarked on a new program; the study of folklore with a view toward using it in classroom teaching either as a way to humanize subject disciplines or as a unit by itself.

A brief newsletter report attracted my interest and the initial exchange of correspondence culminated in my joining their expanded 1971 workshop. In a two-day exposure to this academic encounter group, I saw adults change before my eyes and the armor of separation and division we all wear dissolve toward a true Joseph's coat of many ethnic colors. Through the rain of diversity the flowers of unity can grow. Out of "what" comes "who."

The teachers came from junior high schools with enrollments representing a wide ethnic base, including native Americans from the Navajo, White River, Apache, and Papago Reservations; Spanish-speaking Americans and black Americans from nearby urban areas; and the whites of middle-class America. Their credentials were in a variety of subject areas and their teaching experience varied from nothing to many years. The project sought to unify human beings in an age of cultural fragmentation and dissolution of tradition by stimulating awareness that the essential likeness of all people lies in their lore--the things they do, make, believe, and say. These human acts become visible to us in folk custom and folk art, costume, drama, music, architecture, legends, holidays, and games. This teaching centered around the rites of passage--ceremonies attendant upon birth, puberty, marriage, and death.

To join them, hear a teacher give her reaction to learning about these customs. At the conclusion of the lecture on the dignity of death and the wherefores of feasting and drinking at wakes ("The Devil hates a cheerful spirit"): she had this to say:

> Last year a child came to me, close to tears, and said he was ashamed because his parents had come home drunk the night before from a funeral, and I, in my ignorance, said, "That's all right. When you grow up, you won't be like that." Because I did not know enough, I took away from him something precious. I should have said, "But of course they did! People in many lands do that, because one should be cheerful in the presence of those who are gone." (Granger, p. 18)

These teachers' comments are transcriptions from tape. Here is the experience of a teacher in a school district in northwest Tucson where the students were primarily Anglos with a few blacks, Chinese, and Mexican Americans. The grade level was 7th grade average and 48 students were involved. The teacher speaks:

> I wanted to give them the opportunity to talk about something which was kind of taboo because of fear. I wanted to get rid of that fear. I hoped they would come to the conclusion that customs and beliefs are universal in time and space.
>
> One of their projects was to study death customs, and as part of this project, they interviewed a mortician. They wanted him to bring a body into the classroom in a coffin, but I was afraid it would turn into a comic routine and take away some of the seriousness. They agreed and instead sat around in a gab session as though one of them was graduating from college and wanted to know what kind of career he might have as a mortician, and he was interviewing a mortician and then talking it over with his friends--customs, rights, and so on.

From the same class:

> I had one Chinese girl, a very shy little girl who never spoke. Well, when we were studying marriage customs, I stopped beside her desk and said to her, "I know you must have some beautiful custom. Why don't you ask at home and then tell us all about it?" Well, she did, and the next day in class that child began to talk and now we can't keep her still. She is still a little shy ... but she likes herself better, that I know. (Granger, p. 15)

Now let us listen to a mathematics teacher on the Papago Indian Reservation with an 8th grade class:

> I was in a tough situation because I teach math in the first place and so I had to carry math along with folklore ... then those silly kids who were so shy started dramatizing the stories I was telling them and they wouldn't quit ... from then on I went on in how fire was brought to earth--you know, how Prometheus brought it and how the roadrunner brought fire to the Papagos. They dearly loved that ... we are still collecting stories, and when we had an open-house, I couldn't get rid of the parents. (Granger, p. 21)

A language arts teacher whose students were Mexican-Americans and Anglos says,

> We talked about rites of passage. We are all born, grow up, marry, and eventually die. We see all this in our own families ... I had to do it the only way I could. That was, I'd say, "Let's talk it over." Talk about customs in various cultures ... and superstitions ... They were fascinated by the supernatural and would tell me stories they brought from home ... It is hard for me to really assemble what kind of learning took place. I will say one thing. My children are the ultimate in school haters. They are totally defeated psychologically--totally defeated when it comes to a classroom. While they were in class, with folklore, school took on a miraculous change and these kids were fascinated with what was going on in class.... Somewhere

they have been pushed around, they become defensive ...

... Their defenses are so vital that they are not going to let you get through ... but having folklore we had a medium in which we met and talked and they began to build a kind of respect for themselves. The only effort they could usually make was one they were ashamed of, but in this medium they could behave correctly because it was free. (Granger, p. 23)

A teacher of social science from upper middle class Anglo Scottsdale (a suburb of Phoenix) speaks:

Teacher interest was very high. Communication with parents was undoubtedly strengthened. One student "complained" that at the dinner table she said she had to turn in proverbs the next day and they were still at the table at 10 o'clock by which time they had a list of about fifty proverbs. One instance stands out very strongly as an illustration of increasing self-esteem. We don't usually have much of a problem there, but in this one case, I had a boy from an Italian family. He brought in a gold chain with an anchor and a heart on it. It took him a long time to get around to bringing it in. He first mentioned it when the class was talking about the evil eye ... but it was three weeks before the boy brought it in. Then he was proud of having it and the other kids were sure interested. They wanted one like it. (Granger, p. 26)

Here are some comments from a music teacher who says that this has been her most valuable teaching tactic:

This [people-lore] makes it possible for these young people to explore their own background, to identify themselves with the past, to see themselves in the present and what they have to give to the future. It cuts through all the webs of wordy, redundant, educational jargon and gets to the heart of these people in a way that they can understand. These people, the White Mountain Apache tribe, are doing considerable research to preserve what they can of their history, heritage, and culture before it is lost. They are going through a great transitional period. Many of the old customs have been left behind and if these wonderful old legends and dances are not recorded, they will be lost to the future generation. This institute could not have come at a more opportune time for our school. (Granger, p. 70)

Speaking about a classroom witchcraft unit, a teacher says:

Folklore is one of the most interesting, pleasant, and immediately applicable methods I have ever used to teach English. Since students of this age do not respond positively to large doses of reading or lectures, I presented the material in films, filmstrips, recordings, and bulletin boards.... These 7th graders did the bulletin boards extremely well. One board entitled "Folklore in the News" aided the students in making scrap books which were turned in at the end of the unit for a large part of the grade. Such items as the Loch Ness monster, reports of witchcraft being practiced in the United States, unexplained fires in Arkansas, and spooks in the smith shop, are a few of the subjects covered. The society columns presented sources for introducing customs and beliefs about weddings and even christening parties in which firecrackers played a ritual part. Questions came from the students naturally and allowed me to tell the class about many interesting beliefs which had passed into custom ... collecting family, city, or State folklore was another way my students added to their knowledge. Real folklore is passed on in oral tradition; my students, possibly for the first time listen to the stories of their parents and grandparents with interest. Some of them were brought to school on tape, others recounted in class the way life used to be in the "olden days." We enjoyed many interesting customs, stories and jokes, as well as ways to cure diseases by herbs, by wearing a copper bracelet, or by carrying a buckeye. This was the way to do homework without a textbook and every answer was correct. (Granger, p. 33)

Are you getting a feeling for how lore can give us an always appropriate, high learner motivation, high librarian extemporaneousness subject for library literacy?

Following the introduction of folklore and the method of collecting it, I presented the subject of witchcraft as seen through literature. I read a short article on the Salem Witchcraft Trials to my classes and their questions enabled me to present an informal lecture on the ways, habits, and signs of a witch.... The pieces of literature I used were not authentic folklore since they were created by Poe, Hawthorne, and Frost. However, all three were writers who were accurate in recording folklore and who used the symbolism which is so often found in stories of the supernatural, darkness, and evil.... The stories by Poe were "The Tell-Tale Heart" and "The Black Cat," "Young Goodman Brown," by Nathaniel Hawthorne, and the "The Witch of Coos," by Robert Frost. The stories were presented to the class from records and they took notes in picture form. The student kept his picture notes with the name of the story and author. After all four stories had been heard and discussed, they noted how many symbols reappeared in a story. The evil-eye, the black cat, penknife, candle, number 7, hangman's noose, skeleton, skull, moon, etc. appeared regularly in their notes. The next assignment was to make a collage using either hand-drawn symbols, those found in magazines or a combination of the two. These assignments were fun and were hung in the back of the room making one massive collage which created a strange and colorful effect in the classroom. The last activity in the unit was the retelling of each one's favorite tale in front of the class. I had been conducting the unit as much as possible in the oral tradition of folklore. My students were attuned to listening to the tales of their classmates. The tales from which they might select the one that they would tell had been selected from more than 30 volumes of folklore.... Besides the experience of telling a tale in front of the class and seeing how stories change or are modified by the teller, they heard many of the same plots over and over. The time or place changed, not the basic plot.... Depending only on their ears to catch voice inflections and their eyes to see the facial expression and gestures of the story teller, my class experienced and enjoyed tales in the true tradition.... I believe this unit narrowed the generation gap between students and their parents and grandparents. I do know that many skills such as listening, library usage, and public speaking were sharpened.... The unit proved that learning can be fun and that it need not come from a textbook. (Granger, p. 35)

Creative teaching can use multimedia as an open recipe for non-textbook learning. What you have heard these teachers describe anecdotally turns into a straightforward teaching aid in this description of one Project, "Southwestern Customs and Lore as Examples of Universals." Dr. Granger describes it this way:

It can be a unifying theme for an entire school year and, more than any other study, involved relatives of students and older people of the community in collecting and providing informative material.... It increases the student's esteem for others as well as for his immediate and distant ancestors, himself and his place in a tradition. Like a book of poems or recipes, the unit may be put aside and picked up again without a break in continuity. Variance of a "local" proverb illustrates the theme of universality and serves as an introduction.

America - "An egg today is better than a hen tomorrow."
Arabic - "A thousand cranes in the air are not worth one sparrow in the fist."
Babylon - "A cucumber now is better than pumpkin in the future."
English - "Better a bird in hand than three in the wood. Better a sparrow in the hand than a pigeon on the roof. One bird in the net is better than a hundred flying."
Italian - "A finch in the hand is better than a thrush far off."
Latin - "One bird in the snare is worth more than eight flying."
Swedish - "Better one bird in the cage than seven in the bush."

Students and their kin seem excited about collecting materials when they realize that folklore societies all over the world value and are anxious to preserve their knowledge before it is lost. A collected item should be prefaced with the following information: Date collected, collector, informant's name, informant's background (where he was born, his occupation, etc.), place where item was collected, where did the informant learn about the item, when did the informant learn about the item. I have had greatest success in collecting information about calendar customs, special recipes, superstitions, home remedies, proverbs, edible desert plants and their preparation, and local legends. Students are generally amazed to learn that almost every item has a counterpart in all corners of the world. Even superficial, individualized search on their part verifies this. Here are a few suggestions for student projects and reports. (Granger, p. 37)

Dr. Granger's list follows:

PROJECTS:
1. Scrapbooks of newspaper clippings on any of these: Jokes, Riddles, Epitaphs, Proverbs, Game Yells, Limericks, Superstitions, Home Remedies, Home Beauty Secrets.
2. Recipe booklets containing descriptions and recipes for special foods for special occasions.
3. Instructions for making items of folk art.

4. A series of sketches of symbols with accompanying explanations of their significance. For example, sun symbols, trees of life, birds, flowers, birthstones, signs of the Zodiac, Christian symbols, Pennsylvania Dutch symbols, symbols for numbers.

REPORTS:
1. Fortune telling.
2. Magic potion.
3. Amulets.
4. The Devil's disguises.
5. Hexing.
6. Omens.
7. Rites of passage--Special Customs--Birth, Confirmation, First Communion, Quinceanero, Wedding, Bar Mitzvah, Initiation, Puberty, Death.
8. Mandas and results.
9. Holiday customs.
10. Making natural dyes.
11. Edible desert plants.
12. Uses of desert plants.
13. Unusual local foods.
14. Local religious holidays.
15. Witchcraft.
16. Folk medicine versus quackery.
17. Successful hunting techniques.
18. Successful fishing techniques.
19. Curandero.
20. Folk dance.
21. Folk art.
22. One type of folk song.
23. Voodoo.
24. Little people.
25. Ghosts.
26. Haunted houses.
27. Werewolves.
28. "How to" report, e. g. , How to make soap, how to dry fruit.
29. Lost mines.
30. Buried treasure.
31. Local legends, supernatural, or comic.
32. Local legendary sites.
33. Local folk heroes.
34. First hand retelling of accounts of Pancho Villa's activities, perhaps from a grandfather or neighbor.
(Granger, p. 39, 40)

Why does this subject, people-lore, seem such a natural for the teaching of library skills throughout all age groups and across the whole curriculum? For one reason, because this group of teachers tried it and found that it would do just that. For another, because it seems clear that every type of library material and library skill can be a part of lesson plans such as these. For another, because the many languages we "read" are part of such teaching; the language of numbers, of symbols, body language, pictures, and music. All the facets of "reading" that comprise the media-mix fit into this approach to library use. And lastly, because, since there "is no wrong answer" in the oral tradition, and since we, as humans, own personal lore ready to offer, folklore is a content area each of us should feel comfortable in approaching. Not that such is not an excellent "for instance" to support Dr. Stone's words on continuing professional education. It is. The helpful "but" being that beyond the definitional basics it is truly a democratic subject. Another plus is that, since we are all part of human contexts beyond the professional, folklore can serve our personal lives as well as our work lives.

Stressing freedom from the strait-jacket of textbook teaching, the reading lists for these people-lore units cite reference books in all the disciplines, fiction and nonfiction from the general circulating collection, as well as periodicals and pamphlets. Pictures are also fully utilized. These pupils read the art of history from the cave paintings of Altamira to the sand paintings of the Navajos and sophisticated op art. Aural skills were involved, the verbal tradition stressed, and the students were brought back to the customs of their ancestors as they learned through listening, using their ears to note, compare, and discriminate. Nonverbal communication through object language is also spoken when such a treasured artifact as a gold anchor and heart locket appears.

As I listened it seemed that perhaps sex education would be spared much of the trauma it is now undergoing were it, too, to be taught as a rite of passage under the discipline of people-lore. The rites of puberty however they are celebrated, from those in Coming of Age in Samoa to the American version of Bar Mitzvah, indicate clearly, if we but listen, that sex itself is a rite of passage from childhood to maturity--at least to physical maturity. Taught as Dr. Granger's Institute is advocating, people-lore is seen encapsulated in the framework of ethnic traditions and cultures. Sexual maturation can become much more manageable when held in this matrix of personal culture, which then broadens to relate personal ethnic traditions to the humanism of the whole world. Under this anthropological umbrella, sex comes into its rightful place as a public observance within the context of the rites of passage. This is not to say that individual sex is not private, but rather that, as it unites an individual to his ethnic group in the fabric of custom, it can serve to relate our youth to their own society and to the values that it represents rather than turning them out to be alone in a strange country. The exercise of firmly embedding sex education in its cultural fabric saves one, anyone, from the fallacy of thinking that any cultural practice, sex or any other rite or custom, can be properly used out of context. If one wants to indulge in cannibalism, practice it among the cannibals. Likewise, anyone wanting to come of age in Samoa had better make the geographic trip.

A revealing sidelight comes from my stint as librarian in an all-male high school. I bought several sex books--in 1964 one offered nothing as specific as the "how-to-do-it" books common today--only to discover that they weren't on the shelf very often, neither were they ever checked out. Presenting this to some of the teachers with whom such analysis was comfortable, I learned that, indeed, the boys were carrying these books around and bringing them up for discussion in class. But they would not, at least with a woman as librarian, even though the charge system was self-service, subject themselves to the public knowledge that they felt the need to have access to such a book. The children's author Lois Lowrey added a humorous footnote to this at a recent lecture for the Resident Associate's Program of the Smithsonian. Her comment was "Boys know that you don't have to look a book in the eye and it isn't going to tell you that you have egg on your face." In a girls' school the reverse is true. Whatever they want from the shelves they feel perfectly free to borrow openly.

My faith in the efficacy of Dr. Granger's project comes from the fact that in the words of these teachers one hears four things over and over again. First, that student attitudes are changing and with these changes in feeling come improved skill levels. Second, that teacher attitudes are changing enough to merit the hope that adult consciousness itself is being transformed. Third, that a full range of media resources is being advantageously used to suit both the course content and the students' learning capability. And fourth, surely of great import, is that the generation gap is being closed. When a sense of cultural history, family or tribal, comes to the present generation, they automatically look up to, instead of down at, the older generation because they become the custodian of traditions suddenly of worth to the young participants. These stories flesh out a process whereby students accept themselves through acknowledging their heritage and sharing it as parents and grandpartents bring their treasures and lore to class to participate in the world of their young people. Is this not a meaningful subset of "Love Thy Neighbor as Thyself?"

The Project also demonstrated that people-lore can be interwoven with every subject by tying the academic discipline to the student's own world through the liveliness of folklore and myth. A small episode that has remained long in my mind occurred on a long cross-town bus ride. I was listening to two high school students from a parochial school discussing their physics class. These adolescents obviously were being taught a very traditional academic discipline in a classically orthodox way that had absolutely no meaning for, or point of contact with, their daily lives. The thought that overwhelmed me as I listened was "My heavens, no one teaches them that physics is an actual part of the life of every human being--jugglers, jacks, 'what goes up must come down." We are presenting an academic discipline as if its relevance existed only within the context of textbook and report card.

Now Emeritus, devoting full time to her writing, Dr. Granger's Project update follows:

> To assess the impact of the "People and Their Lore" project is somewhat akin to trying to count innumerable ripples and their overlapping backwash created when a large boulder plunges into a broad, deep, and hitherto placid pool. To tally them is, quite simply, impossible. One notices a particular wave because of its size or a bit of irregularity which smooths out, or looks at a series of smaller but steady ripples reaching the periphery. The analogy applies to a "wave impact" in Alaska where students in the program made rapid progress up the administrative ladder and applied its principles broadly with excellent effect among Eskimos, Indians, and others in schools of the Bureau of Indian Affairs. The project made a moderate wave in Montana when just over one hundred teachers and administrators took a special summer course, with several Native Americans participating. The project was aimed to lessen misunderstandings and to increase respect within ethnic groups, and it did so measurably. Among other "ripples" are advanced studies in cross-cultural awareness which led to higher degrees and to special programs under the aegis of those who earned doctorates. To my knowledge, there was no failure. Their greatest hindrance is the lack of lore resources in school libraries.
>
> For me, the accolade came inadvertently in 1980 while a guest in Florida. I was watching a TV program on the subject of graduation. The

TV crew had traveled to a school in Coral Gables
notable for its LACK of racial tension. A Black
girl graduate was asked how she would account for
that fact. She looked a little surprised and said,
"Why, man, what's the big deal? We all respect
each other here." That's all it takes. And I
knew why they felt that way.

(Granger, personal communication)

Under the capacious umbrella of cultural anthropology, folklore and genealogy can walk appropriately together--guaranteeing perspective. Hereditary societies, properly, do not stress such a comradeship. For their purposes, a pedigree is a relevant branch on an approved tree (or passage on the correct boat)--not the tree's seasonal and fascinating fruit and flower. Yet, on St. Patrick's Day, in the local Irish pub, "Danny Boy" and re-embellishings of the tales of the Patron Saint are proper, and no one inspects for pedigree charts. If acting Irish makes you feel good, you can. A pedigree gets you such things as a coat of arms or an inheritance or a peck of trouble or a society membership. Personal ethnicity gets you tales to tell and songs to sing and a colorful inhabited land for belonging.

As a context for instruction in lifelong learning, "The Science of Who" works. The major rubric, "What's in it for me?" is axiomatic. Everyone has "it" and, since it begins with themselves, has some comfort within "it." Material resources range from the personal to the highly organized, international institutional. The self discovery and healing inherent in such telling and sharing and researching follows the natural folk process which grounds and connects us all-- the oneness of the whole of Man in the Family of Man!

[American] folklore is the adobe house of New
Mexico, the sod shanty of the Kansas and Nebraska
frontier, the log-and-clay cabins of Virginia, the
strung-together barns and houses of New England.
It is the rhymes and games of children ... and a
tongue twister from Massachusetts.... Folklore
is the hand-whittled lobster buoy of Maine and the
branding iron of Wyoming, the hay lifts of Utah,
and the rail fences of Kentucky. It is the bawdy
story in the smoking room of a Pullman and the
jargon of a crapshooter.... It is a juke joint
jumping with improvised steps.... It is the
speech of Alabama and the Bronx, and the regional
niceties of our land. (Emrich, p. 4)

Cultural awareness supplies a powerful tool with which our country can productively welcome the current wave of immigrants. Would that it were possible for the non-other-than-English illiterates that most educated Americans are to do a Berlitz blitz and eliminate the language barrier! By surfacing the concept of personal, cultural lore--Preppie, Polish, Irish, Jewish, German, Latino, Indian, WASP, or whoever--we can, however, possess the next best means for creating an immediate Pentecostal communion. We can all meet at the bridge of food customs (once we realize we have them). Being religious, I can bring my Episcopal faith and customs to meet their Buddhist ones. Clothing provides another universal for demonstrating our simultaneous dissimilar similarity. For us professional communicating rememberers, this seems an appropriate opportunity.

Folklore's close tie with community festivals is another plus for its use as an "always at the ready" topic for classes in "library." The continuity of the calendar then becomes a relevant text for program. Many contemporary theologians are stressing man's need to return to true celebration and festival. Because cultural awareness deals with things historic and traditional rather than simplistic and general, its use can tie a "library" curriculum to the specialness of each seeker. For personal professional Continuing Ed, try <u>Feast of Fools</u> by Harvey Cox.

These special days identify and dramatize the uniqueness of each cultural group. Find the broadest appropriate framework so that minor religious and secular holidays can gain equal time with the more dominant celebrations. In this way, the minor festival of Rogation or Harvest Sunday, which I was privileged to share once in a rural parish in England, can add its seasonal relationship of a very ancient land-related lore to the more commonplace Norman Rockwell Thanksgiving, and All Saint's Day can add its historic connections to those of Hallowe'en. In early November of an election year, that ceremony appears on our calendar and, though not a rite of passage except for the politician, it too has a long cultural history.

Cultural awareness deals with the Christian Christmas story in a fashion that links rather than separates. Bookish references to historical fact, such as the festival's date being set to relate positively to the Roman feast of Saturnalia, contribute an objective context in which all have a place. The Greek Eastertime mirrors another calendar.

Since festivals relate to all age levels, they are useful for outreach to anyone beyond "school" as well as to anyone within. Weddings involve the bride, her mother, her grandmother, and sisters as bridesmaids or flower girls plus all the age-spanning male roles. There is no more gigantic exercise in problem solving than a wedding. Divorce currently occupies center stage as a problem-generating non-calendar-related rite of passage. Fiction for all ages offers that type of bookish supportive assist which such as Reading Ladders for Human Relations organize for us. The 398-page bibliography of the 6th (1981) edition offers the help of "story" to those who wish to promote improved human relations for pre- through high-school people. Ladder IV," appreciating Different Cultures," reflects the Blackfeet/Cherokee heritage of Jamake Highwater and ends with this guidance:

> Today we are learning that people are not the same, and that we cannot evaluate all experience the same way. We are also learning that everybody doesn't have to be the same in order to be equal. It is no longer realistic for dominant cultures to send out missionaries to convert everyone to their idea of the "truth." Today we are beginning to look into the ideas of groups outside the dominant culture, and we are finding different kinds of "truth" that make the world we live in far bigger than we ever dreamed it could be--for the greatest distance between people is not geographical space, but culture. (Highwater, p. 14)

By surfacing and learning and teaching our non-media culture, we can make a professional contribution to humanizing our 1984.

Chapter 16
The Science of Whereabouts ~ The Lore & Use of Maps

The use of travelling is to regulate imagination by reality and, instead of thinking how things may be, to see them as they are.

— Samuel Johnson

As "teachers of library" we need subject areas that are ours without possession of "beyond M. L. S." credits. This enables us to perform competently, comfortably, and irreverently. Our "off the cuff" subjects must cross all disciplines and be valuable and comprehensible to any audience. As students or lifelong learners their need is for useful content in which everyone can recognize something of immediate interest.

To adhere to the rule of no-busy-work in our BI presentations requires of us some mind-stretching homework. To possess a ready fund of cross-grade age-level examples with which to support faculty, or be able to ad-lib dialogue to teach process at the Reference Desk or interest a group at a Senior Citizens Center requires a supply of standby concepts and related library materials firmly in mind.

One can think of learning as the absorption of information into a continuously organized pattern. Each of these words has significance. Information implies not merely facts but ideas. Organized implies that these facts and ideas are related to one another in some meaningful pattern. Absorption implies that the organized information is presented in some way which is sufficiently meaningful to the life of the learner that he can retain it.

To teach is to provide fodder for the learning process. Therefore, the tools of teaching must have to some extent the characteristics described above. One of the most basic of such tools, frequently overlooked, is the map. The map, by its very nature, has the characteristics required to transfer "information into knowledge," our most special subject specialty. It contains facts, organized both spatially and in categories, and if chosen appropriately, can be related to the concerns of any individual or group.

Maps meet all these requirements. The game of hopscotch, the route from home to school, to the ice cream store or a prom date's house, a sketch of the room a female wants to redecorate, a graphic presentation of the plot of a novel, a plan for a vegetable garden, Columbus' route to the New World, the route for a field trip, the strip on the wall where a dad keeps a record of all the children's heights, and the AAA trip map that helps escape the freeway on a summer getaway--all these are maps.

> The nature of cartography can best be explained by the simile of the ant on a rug. The ant walking on the rug will notice the various colors and textures, but they will have no meaning for him. Let us imagine that some of the ants want to find out what these patterns mean. They assign parties to measure the whole rug and every patch on it; other groups will collect these measurements and will devise methods to draw them on such a small scale that the pattern of the whole rug with all its patches will be visible at a glance. They will be thrilled to see a beautiful design revealed which they did not know before. Immediately some of the wisest ants will propose various theories for the possible use and ultimate meaning of this pattern.
>
> The ants' task is relatively easy, compared with that of man. The ant is a million times larger in proportion to the rug than a man is in comparison with the earth. The richest oriental rug is much simpler than the carpet of the earth.
>
> First the surveyors measure the land. Cartographers collect the measurements and render them on such small scale that the earth's wonderful pattern shows at a glance. The geographer analyzes this pattern, studies man's relation to it, and theorizes about its ultimate meaning. About this, we hope, he does better than the ant, who probably has only a vague idea, if any, of the existence of man, the creator of the rug.
> (Raisz, p. 1)

This difference between two- and three-dimensional perception is a crucial separating factor that can free or box-in creatures. A two dimensional creature would continuously follow the path of a circle drawn on a piece of paper as if it were an eternal, endless road. Without our third dimension of height, there is no way for him to visualize his path as a closed circle.

In my other life I had access to the wondrous third dimension of small plane flight. Aloft, our vision contains a wider and fuller sweep, and records and digests more detail in a moment than in long studying on the ground. What a fabulously instructive experience to drive through some unfamiliar, open Western country and then, from a plane, suddenly see both bed and breakfast, river and mountain simultaneously. "Oh--look--that's the way it is--I mean--look at that horseshoe bend we floated ... so that's the way Rainbow Bridge really is!" Mind-blowing omniscience from which the perspective men call God suddenly seems more possible.

My heart aches for all the poor, mind-closing teaching in America's past when I am confronted by the commercial air traveler's mass indifference to the map about to take shape beneath the wings. On a clear day, a flight from Phoenix to San Francisco at 55,000 feet allows one to encompass a whole state in one glance.

Geography is not the only map flying affords. Many a modern abstract painting suddenly appears beneath the wings to tease the imagination. Clouds and fog, characters in many a work of art offer to the air traveler an eyeball-to-eyeball intimacy with movement that is mesmerizing.

Terrain seen from a plane is a map as we usually think of one--a representation which, because of scale, is different from the landscape as viewed by a person standing close to it. Picture a tree as seen from a point on the ground next to its trunk, and then from a perch in its branches, then by a bird just a few feet above it, then by a camera carried in a kite, then by a low-flying light plane, then by a jet-liner descending to land. There is a watercolor I see often which is such an artist's map of a pine tree as known by a nestling bird. All this involves is scale, which is anything the map maker chooses to use as a measure. Your dirty footprint on a white carpet seems a large measure, but try to measure the Sahara with your foot and the scale becomes minute. Scale is so important in maps that it is a key to their classification.

Atlas maps afford a general view of the earth's surface, of the shapes of continents, boundaries of countries, maps of mountain ranges, and important cities. <u>Topographic maps</u> increase the scale to show forests, creeks, ponds, trails--data useful for aerial or military purposes or for country trekking. Next in scale is the cadastral map or plan which shows property or estate divisions like houses and barns that assessors and fire wardens need to know.

Consider the possibilities in a map as a teaching tool for a grammar school student. Geography has tended to become an anathema to students, not because it is devoid of interest but because it is too often not related to their world. Rather than the economic geography of the Congo, assume we ask the student to draw a map of his neighborhood including both his home and school and the things in that locale that interest him. He might produce a map somewhat like the one illustrated below.

Just to draw such a map requires that we separate out objects of interest from all others, which is a form of organization. Then symbols must be selected to depict these categories; a school is shown in one symbol or picture, which is different from that used for a house. Spatial relations are expressed. To visualize space is a highly necessary orientation skill which we do instinctively but might do better if we

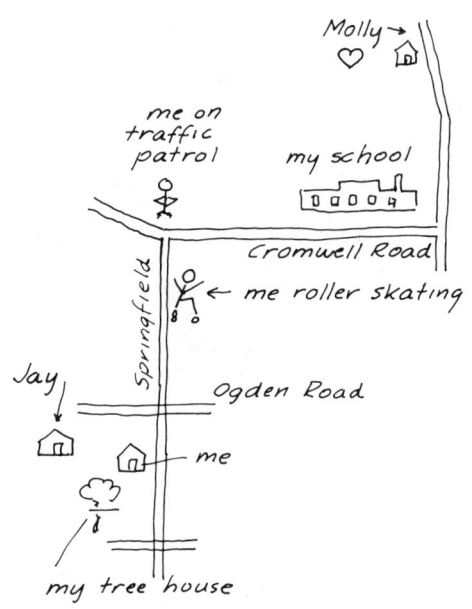

realized that it is both necessary and a skill. How many wives there are who complain, "My husband gets so mad at me when we take the wrong road, but I can't read a map that well."

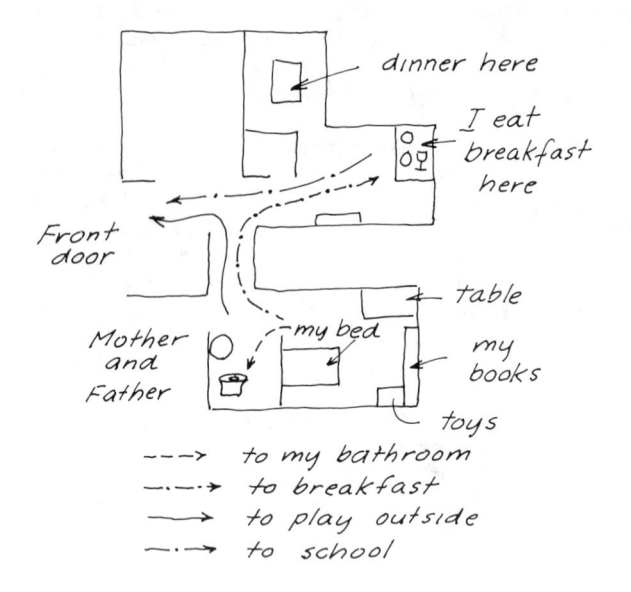

[Hand-drawn map of a house with labels: "dinner here", "I eat breakfast here", "Front door", "table", "Mother and Father", "my bed", "my books", "toys"]

- - - → to my bathroom
—·—·→ to breakfast
⎯⎯→ to play outside
—·—→ to school

    Now assume that the student is assigned the task of making a map of his house designating commonly traversed access routes. Perhaps this would result in a map like the one just above.

    One of the first things to emerge from this map is the fact that for a given purpose not all known information need be used, and selection is not only possible but expected. The child will no doubt be much more clear and specific on those objects, routes or relationships important to him than on others equally concrete but not important to the matter at hand. Note also that however incomplete, the second map conveys a good idea of the house depicted and implies much which is not specifically detailed, even about the family routine.

    This is a characteristic of maps and mapping; much of past history as well as present character of a locale is implied by the spatial relations depicted. Even more is often read into place names, a matter of sufficient interest to have engendered many books such as Place Names in Arizona, by Byrd Granger, and Names on the Face of America, by George Stewart. Market Street and Fisherman's Wharf in San Francisco, Water Street and Bishop's Lodge Road in Santa Fe, or Lover's Lane in any town tell stories of their own.

In the second example a particular map characteristic is illustrated--routes. Routes of travel are especially important in our lives, more important than cardinal directions. For example, the radial patterns of streets in my city, Washington, D.C., make the exact bearings relative to north hard to estimate, especially since the radial pattern is not perfect, symmetrical, or consistent. As a result of this, plus my personal lack of a directional sense, I would be hard put to say what is the directional bearing for Massachusetts Ave., which I travel each day. But the route and the spatial relations of landmarks I know better than the palm of my hand. So it is with many people.

These routes, with their attendant landmarks and spatial relations, are of great importance to us, and can best be described by using a form of map. To teach someone how routes can be differentiated, symbolized, and interrelated, is to assist him in the specific visualization of a technique which, though he would learn it gradually by experience, can be immensely useful if made more specific and real to him.

A map lesson useful to almost all people concerns the highway or road map. One distinct joy of time recently flown was the availability of these useful advertising pieces free, from most gas stations. As a data base this tool is unsurpassed. Except for the provision of eyeglasses, all sighted drivers and their navigators have, in such folded paper an information package usable in any lighted spot, desert or city, driveway or cabin. Now, more effort and some money and/or ingenuity is needed to secure highway data. These treasures are still so ubiquitous that rarely does one look at them carefully as an example of cartography. Usually we are too busy finding out what is the number of the highway going from Rockville to Frederick. But taking a closer look, several things of significance are revealed. These can serve as the basis for relevant library lessons.

First is the system of classification used. Symbols differentiate towns and cities of various sizes, roads and highways of different size and importance, rivers and streams of differing magnitude, and even the maintenance responsibility, which may be federal, state, county or city.

Begin by asking for an explanation of the symbols found on the road network. In all likelihood someone will not look immediately for the box depicting the list of symbols, but will try to categorize the various examples seen on the road network itself. We then teach process in how to use a "reference book" by pointing out the significance of the key or legend.

A typical road map will have the roads broken down into nine categories. Less frequently, the number will be eleven. A student can learn something about classification schemes by inspecting these categories.

How many ways are there to judge distances on a road map? First there is the map scale, usually expressed not only by a graphic scale but by an additional explanation, "one inch equals about 9 miles." Then there are point-to-point distances written in black on road segments, and distances between starred locations. Some maps offer the help of a linear table showing mileage between locations, devoid of any form of spatial relationship.

Under the description, "additional data," may be 15 or so symbols differentiating public campgrounds, forest headquarters, airports, county seats, tracts, and the like. One can ask the student how many categories can be distinguished on a good road map by symbol alone, without using different colors. Usually it is not more than four.

Now inquire the source of the basic information from which the road map was compiled. Despite a common misconception, the basic maps are not prepared by National Geographic or Exxon but by the U.S. Government. The principal network of exactly determined locations is surveyed by the Coast and Geodetic Survey. These locations are used by the principal map-making agency, the U.S. Geological Survey, which actually creates the maps from ground surveys and aerial photographs. The published government maps are not copyrighted and thus special compilations or redrafted versions are made by commercial firms from the government maps incorporating data found in the federal census and other statistical summaries.

The learner might then be led by steps to such marvelous compilations as the National Atlas of the United States, compiled and printed by the U.S. Geological Survey. This compendium contains maps of soils, climate, vegetation, commerce, commodities, population, economic facts--to name only a few.

Topography and its depiction is a little known but highly useful type of information presented on some maps. In the

The Science of Whereabouts 321

United States, the land elevation at any point is shown by contours, or lines of equal elevation above sea level, on the quadrangle sheets of the U.S. Geological Survey. These amazingly accurate maps are sold for about 50 cents at various public and commercial outlets and depict, at a scale of 1:24,000 (about 2 inches to the mile) on sheets of 20 x 28 inches, a large part of the country. Special maps of principal cities are also available at the same scale. These maps can be obtained at a reasonable cost by writing to one of the two addresses listed in the bibliography.

The contour lines or lines of equal elevation are drawn by a technician looking at a pair of aerial photographs in stereoscopic relation, and tracing the path of a little white ball which he keeps moving along the projected photograph always in apparent contact with the land surface which he sees in three dimensions through the instrument.

As we consider maps, library classes, and people, here are some of the less common sorts of maps of which we can train ourselves to be aware:

    1. Mental maps--our bedroom at night; directions to a stranger; impressions of distance, turns and objects.
    2. Star maps--authority to the young of my day to leave the dance floor and explore the sky.
    3. Weather--from the newspaper and television into clouds and a vision of the earth's atmosphere.
    4. Timetables--planes, trains, buses, and subways--linear and chronological measures together.
    5. Graphs--a chart of homely domestic chores of home or elementary schoolroom, or illustrations for science or economics projects.
    6. Vegetation--where are the azaleas in your yard? How many oak trees as hazards on a golf course?
    7. Geology--dig a flower bed. How far down is the clay you must replace with good soil? What is the striped or wavy pattern you see as you drive through a highway roadcut?
    8. Rainfall--a trip is planned--what about wardrobe? Consult the rainfall charts in World Book. You are planting a vegetable garden. What does the seed packet temperature and rainfall chart tell you about your locale?
    9. Blueprints--a house is being planned. Learn to read its map and you have a most useful--and rare--special skill.
    10. Stream channels--sketch the patterns rain makes when it falls on bare earth.

Each such map has its own special language. In addition to scale, all maps have direction or orientation in space, and signs for natural features like shorelines and vegetation, and special symbols for man-made objects like pipe-lines and bridges. In reading nature as a map, one must learn to observe the clues of light and shadow at midday, the constellations in the night sky, water marks at ebb tide, and underwater relief when studying a lake.

To support such instruction we can draw on atlases, loose maps, specialized periodicals such as Holiday and the National Geographic, and all the illustrations and text of materials on travel, botany, zoology, art history, anthropology, geography, and history. The stalwart library globe is a vital teaching tool for visualizing this spaceship, Earth. Maps printed as gores are available from which a globe can be created.

Moving into the A-V media there are many library projects:

1. A film or photography class can map the route to someplace.
2. A collage map is a natural art project.
3. Art history suggests a map of some facet of Sir Kenneth Clark's Civilization.
4. Language study begs for maps.
5. The language of mathematics is really a map in itself--fractions and geometry, abacus and sets.
6. Psychology suggests maps in interpersonal relations like the one on page 323 which shows units of social encounter in transaction--people interacting on some personality level.
7. In home economics learning, a dress pattern is a map and so is an interior decorator's scheme for a room's floor plan.
8. A geography lesson could be taped directions to walk between home and school or public library or Senior Citizens Center.

Map history offers valuable perspective and context for understanding the current scene. These excerpts from the Preface of Animals and Maps by Wilma George furnish an example of such resources:

> Mapmaking must have begun in the very remote ages of man's past. The first maps were probably simple route maps, for members of so-called primitive communities in the present day

The Science of Whereabouts

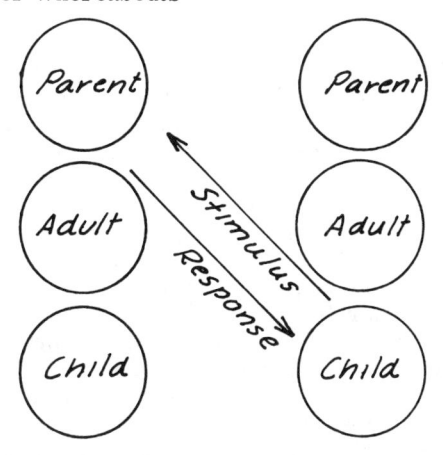

```
   ( Parent )              ( Parent )
              ↖ Stimulus
   ( Adult  )    ⤢         ( Adult  )
              Response ↘
   ( Child  )              ( Child  )
```

are found to possess an innate skill in drawing rough sketches of a limited area to show directions, distances, and relationships between places. This type of mapmaking predates the development of a written language. From such simple sketches, no more perhaps than a trace in the sand or cuts in the bark of a tree, more elaborate route maps came to be made. Features along the route would be represented in perspective, as landmarks to guide the traveller, and so a route map became a regional map, showing local topography. The most famous of all early road maps is the Peutinger Table, a map of the military roads of the Roman Empire, drawn about AD 280 probably from a survey made for the Emperor Augustus in the first century AD. Completed ca. AD 500, it is now known in a copy of AD 1265. This map depicts, on a strip twenty-two feet long and one foot wide, the whole of the world as it was known to the Romans. On it are prominently marked roads, cities, towns and villages, watering places and temples. Natural features such as rivers, lakes, mountains and forests are indicated; and in the three great cities, Rome, Constantinople and Antioch sit three rulers, believed to represent the sons of Constantine, enthroned as symbols of a tripartite empire.

Another type of mapmaking was devised for purposes of delimiting property or territory. Traditionally, the invention of geometry and the development of the allied craft of land-surveying are said to have taken place in ancient Egypt, where the yearly flooding of the Nile obliterated land-marks and encouraged cadastral survey as a record of land-ownership. The only surviving example, other than plans of buildings and gardens, is a map of the Nubian gold-mines, drawn on a papyrus roll in about 1300 BC, and now preserved in Turin. It marks in red the gold-bearing basin east of Coptos, and shows in addition the main road, the temple of Ammon, and some houses. A similar form of cadastral survey developed in ancient Babylon, where plans of properties and towns were inscribed on clay tablets, a number of which survive, the earliest dating from 2000 BC.... Such maps were made as an expression of man's very basic instinct for territorial possession. The European estate plans of the seventeenth and eighteenth centuries, embellished with rich iconographic detail to flatter a landowner's pride of possession, and the great Renaissance maps of a sovereign's domains, may be regarded as descendants of the simple property surveys typical of ancient Egypt and Babylon.

These two classes of maps, the route map and the property survey, were made for practical purposes. When local plans or estates were enlarged into regional maps, and itineraries were fitted together to form a survey of a whole empire, these two types of mapmaking began to converge upon a third type, the mapping of the world. In this evolution there was no orderly sequence, no simple progression from local to regional mapping, and from regional mapping to the world survey. Philosophers, not geometers nor land measurers, were the first to make maps of the world, constructed partly from personal experience and observation and partly from information available at secondhand. In their speculations on the nature of the earth and of the universe, it was natural that they should turn to some form of graphic portrayal. The earliest map of the world is a Babylonian tablet of 500 BC showing the world as a flat circular disc, surrounded by the earthly ocean and the seven islands of Babylonian cosmography. The earth itself is shown as no more than the kingdom of Babylon, schematically portrayed.

The Science of Whereabouts

The history of mapmaking shows progress and change both in man's ideas about, and knowledge of, the physical environment, and side by side it displays changing techniques for depicting the environment. The maps which have survived from many ages and lands show certain common elements in the language of expression. The drawing of features in profile, the bird's eye view and the perspective drawing are natural devices to use.

In the sixteenth century cartography was developing in two opposite directions, becoming more ornamental and also more exact. The exploration of new lands invited pictorial detail to convey a vivid impression of the new world revealed....

This progression of cartography from the naive drawings of the traveller to the specialised work of the highly professional cartographic workshop of seventeenth century Europe, reflected a growing comprehension of the physical environment, and improved techniques in recording it. Among the features of the physical environment important to man, birds and beasts have commanded a special interest: as creatures closest to man, as a means of sustenance to him; if domesticated, a source of companionship; in the wild, source of danger. Hence, when man began to depict the environment in his drawings, animals were an inevitable feature of the scene. The cave paintings at Lascaux and at Altamira depict the animals of the chase. A narrative fresco in the Chien-Fo-Tung cave temples near Tunhuang in Kansu, of the seventh century AD, shows men, animals and landscape in a mural which is almost a map. (Panoramic maps had long been an established tradition in early Chinese and Japanese cartography, especially for coastal regions.) Animals of local husbandry, the horse and deer, appear in the Bronze Age cadastral maps of the Val Camonica in Europe. They were used very early as a form of conventional sign. A Greek coin bearing a map of Messina, dated ca. 500 BC, has a dolphin disporting itself in the bay, indicating the sea.

When travellers began to penetrate the distant regions of the earth in the Middle Ages and later, they brought back to their homelands both truly observed reports of the animals encountered and garbled versions. The great discoveries of the fifteenth and sixteenth centuries opened up huge territories with flora and fauna hitherto undreamt of. Artists such as John White depicted the animals and fishes seen in Raleigh's Virginia colony, 1585-1587, with a brilliant naturalism and animals gained an accepted place in the iconography of the continents.

Finally, with the beginnings of thematic cartography, aniamls appear as symbols of their distributions on J. M. Korabinsky's economic map of Hungary, 1697. It seems from this a logical step to Heinrich Berghaus's Physikalischer Atlas, 1845, in which scientific distribution maps of genera and species, showing the "animal kingdoms" and "provinces" with vertical diagrams to illustrate distribution by height. The marginal illustrations of the animals themselves are a striking feature of the English edition published by Alexander Keith Johnston in 1848. Cartography had now a new vocabulary, into which animals, men, and all natural phenomena with a spatial significance could be fitted.

In the nineteenth century it was common to decry medieval maps as fanciful, a demonstration of man's ignorance in the Dark Ages of knowledge. Only recently has the geographical content of such maps been truly interpreted, its language read without expectation of a literal accuracy, to reveal a remarkable conspectus of knowledge. Similarly the animals and "monsters" which adorn these and later maps reveal much zoological truth if they are studied with the eye of an expert. (George, p. 7-19)

Zoology, anthropology, archeology, geology, geography, English literature, mathematics--it would be tough to find a lesson that would not benefit from such study. Maps also have their place in the land of story. An English cartographer states it this way:

The scene was a North Country Inn, and a stranger was being given meticulous advice as to how to reach a certain place over the moors, but since he was so much a stranger that he understood little of their talk of "scars" and "grikes" and "becks" he was still hazy as to his route, until a certain old shepherd took him in hand.

The old man placed five beer mugs carefully on the table in an irregular line, and named them one by one, "Whitescar," "Yeates' Farm," and so on. Then, dipping his finger in a puddle of beer, he traced a wavy line amongst them; each turn referred to its landmark, the nearest beer mug, until a route map was completed, which indeed served its turn.

Now here was the very essence of all map-making, the beer mugs first with immense care, and then the line traced with reference to them. (Debenham, p. 3)

David Greenhood, another scholar and tale spinner, writes in Mapping:

Shut in one cold, rainy day in Scotland, a young man and a boy amused themselves by painting pictures--that is, the boy painted pictures. The young man, more boylike than his companion, drew a map of an island, one which he had never heard of or seen. But the longer he looked at it, the more real it became. Its story unfolded in his mind--Treasure Island! Stevenson's first novel was inspired by a map.

Many of the most inventive novelists draw maps while writing, so that they may keep before them the whole scene of the action and make their fiction as credible as history to the reader. In fact, the story "plot" is essentially a map idea. Navigators speak of "plotting" their bearings or courses on their charts.

A map need not be fanciful to stimulate our imagination. The most matter-of-fact maps, accurate down to the microscopic fraction of an inch, often do more for true map-musers than some of the pictorial maps with their sentimental overstatement and whimsical prettiness.

In contemplating maps, whether already made or about to be made, the imagination is a vital activity. And it leads to practical action. A map-musing Marlow must eventually do something to fill in those blank spaces. Thus maps breed more maps. For no map is ever quite complete, and instead of trying to be the map to end all other maps, an honest one that is performing its certain service well deliberately leaves need for further maps to use. There is also as much to understand about what a given map won't do as about what it does. Much of this further performance we may first imagine before we decide we need it; but in any event, once the need is apparent, our imagination as well as our reason must go to work solving the consequent problems.

The idea of such a thing as a map is at once one of the most primitive and the most civilized of human feats. It is both a yen and a conception, like such other old but ever new ideas as music and dance, myth and fiction, image and depiction, thought and symbol.

Every map is a tacit "as if" or, as children say, "Play like--" or "Pretend." This is absolutely necessary because the exact duplication of a place or area is obviously futile. Yet many people who are otherwise literate can't read maps simply because they expect such duplication; they just won't "play." They are like people who can't or won't, read a story unless they can be assured that it is "true," that it "really happened." Such people can't, or refuse to, understand that the truth itself is one thing and the process of showing it is necessarily something else. Or, less abstractly, let's say it's the difference between the fact of a river, which is if anything wet, and the wriggly line that symbolizes it on a map and has got to be dry. A map must therefore be a simile or metaphor if it is to tell us what we need to know. A map has as much right to be figurative as spoken or written language has; it too is language.

Actually, there are often many truths in a place or an area right before our eyes, and yet we're not aware of those truths (or features, or facts) until a depiction or a symbol or even a diagram shows them to us. That is one reason why we need maps not only of faraway places we've never seen but of the very regions we live in. Just as in the days of Sophocles and, centuries later, of Shakespeare people enjoyed the great plays all the more because they already knew the stories and wished to realize them anew for further satisfactions; maps have most to tell to people who already know some geography.

Map-making is almost as irrepressible in us as making gestures to bring out the full meaning of what we have to say. People who might back away from reading a map or diagram will lean forward to draw one for you rather than let you go away unimpressed. Restaurant owners have to tolerate the figuring and mapping done on their napkins and tablecloths by customers explaining various journeys, land-use projects, military strategies, etc. (Greenhood, p. I-XI)

Over and over again the cartographic scholars encourage the generalist, the information specialist, the teaching librarian to adopt "the idea of ... a map [as] one of the most primitive and civilized of human feats ... a yen and a conception like ... myth and symbol ... thought and symbol." Will you believe them in the name of Bibliographic Instruction and thus create another umbrella library literacy lesson?

Any human information need is fodder for library instruction. Such training, serving to transfer to all citizens the basic information processing skills of our M. L. S. education, supports the citizenry's desire to acquire their First Amendment Rights. Maps, both specific and metophorical, offer one universal teachable subject area.

A child can get his first truly geographic concepts in a sandbox with a few tiny toy cars, spools or small pieces of wood, and he alone knows what else, which, with his imaginative ingenuity, he will convert into veritable cartographic symbols. As he plays in this sandbox country of his he will discover by himself basic ideas of relative location, scale, elevation, and drainage. The more elaborately constructed terrain model his elder friends might be making in high school is the

> same wonderful lesson, with some materials and skill involved and a heritage of terms and attitudes applied. (Greenhood, p. 90)

Maps are the furrows of our feet and the valleys of our pillows. Awareness of this is a facet of consciousness worthy of teachers and learners. So that we, like Aldo Leopold, will understand our domains.

> Books or no books, it is a fact, patent both to my dog and myself, that at daybreak I am the sole owner of all the acres I can walk over. It is not only boundaries that disappear, but also the thought of being bounded. Expanses unknown to deed or map are known to every dawn, and solitude, supposed no longer to exist in my county, extends on every hand as far as the dew can reach. (Leopold, p. 41)

Chapter 17
Facts are not an End ⋯ but a Beginning!

Remember this also and be well persuaded of its truth: the future is not in the hands of Fate, but in ours.

Jules Jusserand

Contracts are paper images of human intentions. According to mine, this book was edited, rewritten, composed, and sent to the printer in the year 1984. Were 1984 and its companion, Brave New World, major societal signposts to be featured or merely noted? The first step was to re-read them (which I did as en route and bed-time reading for ALA San Antonio, 1983), and then mull. Result--none of us, Alvin Toffler, John Naisbitt, or CDCLM, see today and tomorrow as did Orwell or Huxley. But these interconnected visions offer some valid reflective guideposts! For example: it is a fact that in early 1983 a quarter of a million dollar grant from the Department of Housing and Urban Development was used by the Miami Beach Police to mount 120 camera boxes on poles on the streets of Miami Beach. Only some of these camera boxes hold real cameras, and volunteer monitors are the real vigilantes keeping watch over their own streets. The Big Brother telescreen of 1984 has become fact!

    A personal book offers a rare chance to speak--within the constraints of libel suits, good taste, and editorial suitability. Still, the range is wide and temptations are great. Like the after-dinner speaker who uses the cocktail hour to tailor his opening and closing remarks to his sense of the mood of the gathering, my Preface and final chapter are written last. For months, ideas arising from the pool of daily reading, talking, watching, listening, and generalized living are toyed with and forgotten. A Washington Post quote from an interview with John Naisbitt, "Catch a Rising Trend," together with the approaching manuscript deadline put pen to Chapter 17.

    My challenge is to match Naisbitts' "We are drowning in information, but starved for knowledge," with Boorstin's stand on the difference between the information industry and the knowledge industry and this statement from the AT&T 1982 Annual Report: "Today, about half the workers in the United States are engaged in generating, gathering, or otherwise handling information."

Fact Is Not an End

As generalized statistical facts, our national work force numbers 89 million and all "professional" librarians number 150,000. As information handlers we are outnumbered and, I'm afraid, on the banana peel of being surrounded. Naisbitt, with his book, Megatrends, joins the crowd who signal the change from a product-oriented to an information-oriented society. However, doesn't information itself become a product? It is generated, handled, packaged, transmitted, repackaged, and sold (technology)--or given away (libraries). Not that libraries are financed by heaven, but, once you have entered a family, qualified for and gotten a public library card, enrolled in a school, college, or university, or joined a firm, your library dues are paid and full access to the meta-knowledge therein contained becomes your right.

The Information Age technology profiled by AT&T is commercial--all the way. Teachers, journalists, consultants, "communicators," publishers, writers, secretaries, government workers all generate a word end-product. Words that are used to educate, inform, accredit, and achieve tenure become books, newspapers, periodicals, ephemera, and scientific and technical reports as they move from print to electronics, and often, back into print. With our pitiful portion of the "information pie," we knowledge professionals have a huge task before us.

A chronological table in Into the Information Age: A Perspective for Federal Action on Information, published by ALA in 1978, offers some clues as to how we got from there to here in our recent scientific-technical information past. The first section of "Characteristics of Three Information Eras," "discipline oriented," describes the growth of scientific disciplines from the 19th century onward when the motivation was growth of knowledge and the information systems mirrored the academic disciplines as seen in research libraries and the network of professional journals. The next chronology, "mission-oriented," peaking in the sixties covers the period from World War II to the present when the basic use of information was for huge and technology-based endeavors such as the Space Race. The third, "problem oriented," which overlaps with the second, begins at the end of the sixties, when the knowledge generated from information was being sought primarily for the solution of vital socio-technical problems such as housing, toxic waste disposal, and the nuclear maze, with the answers or solutions being judgments.

Under "content of system" we read first, "truth of

science ... dealing with physical systems;" second, "all of the above; also truth of science as it applies to technological objectives"; and third and very now, "all of the above; also wisdom and pragmatics which work in contexts of uncontrollable open systems that involve human as well as physical dynamics." (Guiliano, p. 21) Yes, in 1984 and beyond, we possess all of the above and plenty of high-tech more with which to create one information-age product, decisions.

As an example of the failure of librarians to highlight the marketplace value of information in decision making, Congressman Owens cites the tremendous long-term continuing effort of the County Agents as they pumped information into the ears and hands of America's farmers. Decisions made with the help of this technical government information support system are validated by the resulting vast productive capability of American agriculture. This example from special librarianship dramatizes the information management process as it services a societal need and delivers a product to fill that need.

What this adds to a discussion of "facts are not an End--but a beginning!" is Owens' emphasis on the relevance of libraries to the decision-making process. If decisions are not pure politics, thin air, Archie Bunker, whim, crystal ball, or "where is my intelligent machine?", they must follow the knowledge pyramid (see p. 21). Ever since Aristotle edited Plato by insisting that not just abstractions of the good, the pure, and the beautiful but everything is worthy of study, librarian keepers of the record have been in charge, but Owens thunders, "too quietly!" "Who owns government information?" he asks, referring to automated access to the Federal Register. This takes information management way beyond the implications of plagiarism in a term paper or balance in a Ph.D. thesis.

If we accept the reality of the hierarchical structure of fact, opinion, and value judgment processing as a sine qua non for rational, non-crisis management decisions, then we must also accept the reality of the librarian's historic, credentialed hold on knowledge--as a resource, a process, and a product. If we also observe the long-term failure of anyone to connect these two facts in the service of American democracy, then where can we look for our road that can "make all the difference?" What Toffler can add is this from his The Third Wave:

> The concept of "decision load" is crucial to any

Fact Is Not an End 335

> understanding of democracy. All societies require a certain quantity and quality of political decisions in order to function....
> In the preindustrial societies, where the division of labor was rudimentary and change was slow, the number of political or administrative decisions actually required to keep things running was minimal.... A tiny, semi-educated, unspecialized ruling elite could more or less run things without help from below, carrying the entire decision load by itself.
> What we now call democracy burst forth only when the decision load suddenly swelled beyond the capacity of the old elite to handle it. The arrival of the Second Wave, bringing ... a leap to a whole new level of complexity in society, caused the same kind of decision implosion in its time that the Third Wave is causing today....
> As industrial society developed ... its integrating elites, the "technicians of power" were ... continually compelled to recruit new blood to help them carry the expanding decision load.... It was this expanded need for decision-making that led to an ever-wider franchise and created more niches to be filled from below.... At any given time, however, there was a definite limit to how many additional people could be absorbed into the governing elites ... therefore, whole subpopulations were screened out on racist, sexist and similar grounds. Periodically ... the decision load swelled, the excluded groups would intensify their demand for equal rights, the elites would open the doors ... wider and the society would experience what seemed like a wave of further democratization....
> What all this ... suggests is that ... the very implosion of decision-making ... unlocks ... exciting prospects for a radical expansion of political participation." (Toffler p. 451, 452)

What cheer this offers me is the hope that today, anticipating tomorrow, may mark the "only connect" of a successful revival of library literacy in its true guise as the means for lifelong learning. John Lubans' phrase, "In Search of the Missing Link," connotes a "continuum in which library skills are integrated with other life skills in the service of survivorship decision-making."

One can flunk the Graduate Record Examination because

of an innate inability to make small, rapid distinctions that
are really just sortings. At the other end of the scale can
be placed these words about decisive emotion-in-action of the
distinguished Black educator, Kenneth Clark, "the highest
form of life ... involved struggling for such abstractions as
justice and decency. And always there has been a minority
of human beings engaged in that kind of struggle--people who
insist on being unrealistic, people who won't give up when
everything seems to indicate that they should." (Hentoff,
p. 72) Decision-ability is a fundamental keystone of the
knowledge pyramid. To paraphrase a proverb, For want of
a decision, the choice was lost. For want of a choice, that
opportunity was lost. For want of that opportunity, the battle
was lost. While the war of LLMLL can still be won, let's
translate that decision into emotion-in-action.

Searching for a literary figure brought me back to
1984, and its use of a paperweight as a metaphor.

> As Winston wandered toward the table his eye
> was caught by a round, smooth thing.... It
> was a heavy lump of glass, curved on one side,
> flat on the other, making almost a hemisphere.
> There was a peculiar softness, as of rainwater,
> in both the color and the texture of the glass.
> At the heart of it, magnified by the curved sur-
> face, there was a strange, pink, convoluted ob-
> ject that recalled a rose or a sea anemone.
> "What is it?" said Winston, fascinated.
> "That's coral, that is," said the old man....
> What appealed to him about it was not so
> much its beauty as the air it seemed to possess
> of belonging to an age quite different from the
> present one. The soft, rainwatery glass was not
> like any glass that he had ever seen. The thing
> was doubly attractive because of its apparent use-
> lessness, though he could guess that it must once
> have been intended as a paperweight.... The in-
> exhaustibly interesting thing was not the fragment
> of coral but the interior of the glass itself. There
> was such a depth of it, and yet it was almost as
> transparent as air. It was as though the surface
> of the glass had been the arch of the sky, en-
> closing a tiny world with its atmosphere complete.
> He had the feeling that he could get inside it....
> The paperweight was the room he was in, and the
> coral was Julia's life and his own, fixed in a sort

Fact Is Not an End

> of eternity at the heart of the crystal.... Winston was not trembling any longer.... One thing alone mattered; to keep still, and not give them a excuse to hit you!....
> There was another crash. Someone had picked up the glass paperweight from the table and smashed it to pieces on the hearthstone.
> The fragment of coral, a tiny crinkle of pink like a sugar rosebud from a cake, rolled across the mat. How small, thought Winston, how small it always was! (Orwell, p. 94, 95, 148, 224).

As Winston saw his world of escape caught and held within one of those wondrous pieces of crafted glass, so I can see our knowledge industry similarly reflected. Whether it is a home, public, school, or other institutional special library, its collections represent some part of the world's knowledge selected and organized for some special purpose. Each unit--the Children's Literature collection at LC (or a child's bedside bookshelf), Julia Child's collection of cook books (or my 12 inches of such)--holds some special part of the collective human brain--written, gathered, and shaped by people for people. A world as high and broad as our inexhaustible sky, complete in and of its carefully chosen, encased, organized self.

The coral "heart of it," fully revealed in __1984__ only by a blow from the Thought Police, is ourselves--the thought professionals. Very few paperweights center in coral. Most of the such inclusions are man-made, a garden or a menagerie of glass. But Orwell's natural heart sends a good message of the innate planetary rightness of humans at work helping others to daily increase the satisfaction and cultural power of their heritage of rationality. Indeed, one's mind would like to ignore Orwell's other point--that force was required to fully release the central focus.

Decision is the ultimate product of information processing. Related to the fact, opinion, value judgment pyramid is that other which illustrates the hierarchical relationship of decisions. From what entertainment to seek, to what career to pursue or whom to marry, personal decisions are hierarchical in import. So also with America! Public decisions range from where to locate a Stop Sign to whether to develop a first-strike nuclear arsenal and whether to pay for it from a reduction in social programs, or a tax increase. A vote for Jessica or Joe means a vote for their value judgments

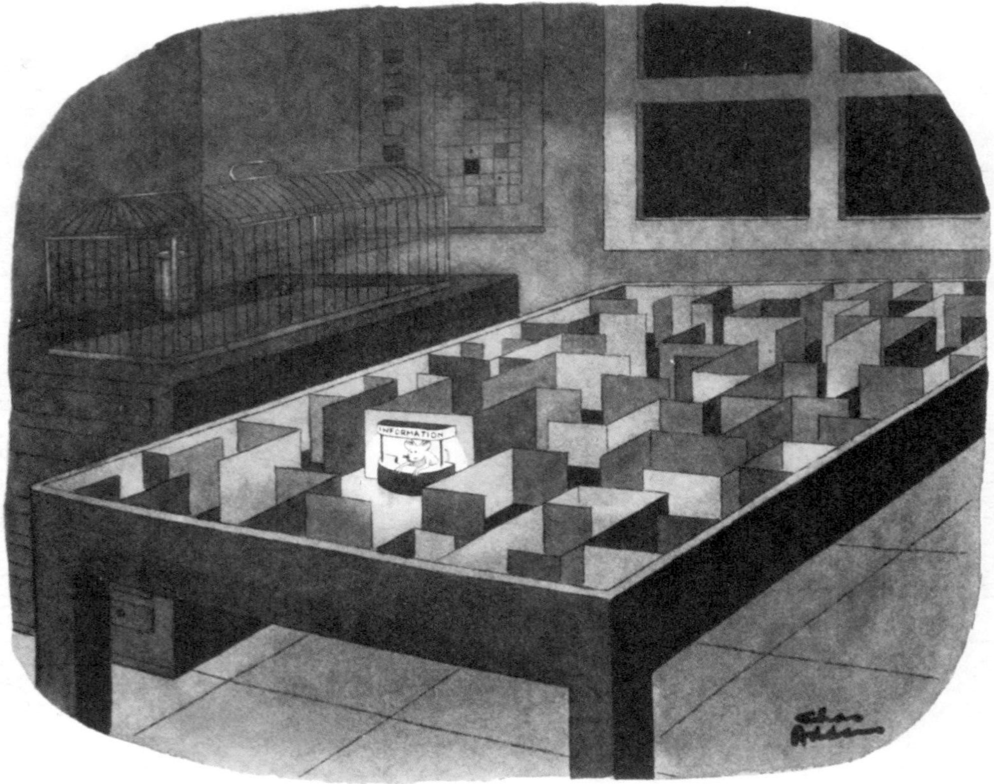
INFORMATION
Chas Addams

Fact Is Not an End

(and how they got there if anyone beyond their mirror is privy to this information).

> What we need ... is a knowledgeable citizenry. Information, like entertainment, is something someone else provides us. It really is a "service!" We expect to be entertained, and also to be informed. But we cannot be knowledged.... Knowledge comes from the free mind foraging in the rich pastures of the whole everywhere-past. It comes from finding order and meaning in the whole human experience. The autonomous reader is the be-all and end-all of our Libraries. (Boorstin, p. 116)

In 1961 in "Education for Decision," I commented, "The enlightened citizenship and the enriched personal life of each citizen exist only when expressed in responsible action--the decisions for which he must be educated." The question now for those of us who see "Teaching All" as the Missing Link between "Education for Decision" and the success of Toffler's "Expanding Elite," remains. Do public service librarians have a subject to teach and a mission to do so? Can <u>Library Literacy Means Lifelong Learning</u> become more than an alliterative icon?

The information industry is challenging our right to the arc of glass Boorstin calls our knowledge industry. Change doesn't just come. Power is not shared and chance favors the prepared mind. What will determine the outcome is the living inclusion in the paperweight, we advocates of library literacy who carry the fight at this turn of its historic wheel. Emerson encourages us with, "All our progress is an unfolding, like the bud ... first an instinct, then an opinion, then a knowledge."

BIBLIOGRAPHY

Abrams, M. H. A Glossary of Literary Terms. New York: Rinehart, 1957.

Adler, Mortimer J. How to Read a Book. New York: Simon & Schuster, 1940.

American Telephone and Telegraph Company 1982 Annual Report. Room 2615, 195 Broadway, New York, New York: 10007: AT&T, 1982.

Anglund, Joan W. A Friend Is Someone Who Likes You. New York: Harcourt Brace, 1958.

Arbuthnot, May Hill. Children and Books. Glenview, Illinois: Scott Foresman, 3rd ed., 1964.

Asheim, Lester, Baker, D. Philip, Mathews, Virginia H. Reading and Successful Living. Hamden, Connecticut: The Shoe String Press, 1983.

Ashton-Warner, Sylvia. Spinster. New York: Simon & Schuster, 1958.

_____. Teacher. New York: Simon & Schuster, 1963.

Beckson, Karl and Ganz, Arthur. Reader's Guide to Literary Terms, a Dictionary. New York: Noonday Press, 1960.

Bellow, Saul. Mr. Sammler's Planet. New York: Viking, 1970.

Benjamin, Harold. Saber-Tooth Curriculum: Including Other Lectures in the History of Paleolithic Education. By J. Abner Peddiwell, Ph.D. and several tequila daisies, as told to Raymond Wayne. New York: McGraw-Hill, 1939.

Berne, Eric. Games People Play. New York: Grove, 1964.

Berry, John, III. "Consciousness I, II, III," Library Journal, February 1, 1971, p. 429.

_____. "'Pilgrim's Progress' and 'The Bible'," Library Journal, April 15, 1981, p. 831.

Boorstin, Daniel J. Image: or What Happened to the American Dream. New York: Atheneum, 1962.

_____. "Remarks by Daniel J. Boorstin, Librarian of Congress, at the White House Conference on Library and Information Services," Special Libraries, February, 1980, p. 113-116.

Brinnin, John Malcolm. "Black and White in Redneck Country," The Washington Post, May 15, 1983.

Bromfield, Louis. Colorado. New York: Harper, 1947.

Bynner, Witter. Selected Letters. Edited by James Kraft. New York: Farrar, Straus, & Giroux, 1981.

Cabeceiras, James. The Multimedia Library. New York: Academic Press, 1978.

Capon, Robert F. Supper of the Lamb. New York: Doubleday, 1969.

Carlsen, G. Robert. Books and the Teenage Reader. New York: Harper & Row, 1967.

Carruth, Gorton, ed. An Encyclopedia of American Facts and Dates. New York: Crowell, 5th ed., 1970.

Cheney, Frances Neel. Fundamental Reference Sources. Chicago: American Library Assocation, 1971.

Churchill, Sir Winston. A Roving Commission, the Story of My Early Life. New York: Scribner's, 1939.

Clark, Kenneth. Civilization. New York: Harper & Row, 1970.

Clarke, Arthur C. Two Thousand and One: A Space Odyssey. New York: World, 1968.

Cox, Harry. Feast of Fools; a Theological Essay on Festivity and Fantasy. Cambridge, Mass: Harvard University Press, 1969.

Culbertson, Hugh M. "The Effect of Art Work on Perceived Writer Stand," Journalism Quarterly, 46:2 (Summer 1969), 294-301.

Current Index to Journals in Education. Semiannual cumulation (Jan. -June 1969). CEM Information Corp.

Daly, Lloyd W. Contributions to a History of Alphabetization in Antiquity and the Middle Ages. Brussels: Latomus, 1967.

Debenham, Frank. Map Making. London: Blackie and Son, 3rd ed., 1956.

DeFord, Miriam A. Who Was When; a Dictionary of Contemporaries. New York: Wilson, 2nd ed., 1950.

Delaney, Jack L. The School Librarian: Human Relations Problems. Hamden, Conn.: Shoe String Press, 1961.

Dewey, Melvil, Library Journal, Vol. 1, No. 1, Sept. 30, 1876.

Drake, Miriam A. "Information Management and Special Librarianship," Special Libraries. Oct. 1982, p. 225-37.

Duff, Annis. Bequest of Wings: A Family's Pleasure with Books. New York: Viking Press, 1944.

Dunkin, Paul. Tales of Melvil's Mouser. New York: Bowker, 1970.

Emrich, Duncan. Folklore on the American Land, Boston: Little, Brown and Co., 1972.

Erikson, Erik H. Childhood and Society. New York: Norton, 1964.

Fader, Daniel N. and McNeil, Elton B. Hooked on Books: Program and Proof. New York: Putnam, 1968.

Farley, Walter. Black Stallion. New York: Random House, 1944.

Foster, Genevieve. George Washington's World. New York: Scribners, 1941.

_____. World of Captain John Smith. New York: Scribners, 1959.

French, Arthur. "The Comprehension of Pictures," Visual Education, (June 1963), 6-8.

Friedman, Maurice. To Deny Our Nothingness. New York: Dell, 1967.

Fromm, Erich. Forgotten Language. New York: Holt, Rinehart & Winston, 1951.

Galvin, Thomas J. (ed.) with Brenda H. White and Margaret Mary Kimmel. Excellence in School Media. Chicago: American Library Association, 1980.

George, Wilma B. Animals and Maps. Berkeley, Calif.: Univ. of California Press, 1969.

Georgiou, Constantine. Children and Their Literature. Englewood Cliffs, N. J.: Prentice-Hall, 1969.

Gibbon, Edward. The Decline and Fall of the Roman Empire. London: Oxford, 1934.

Glasser, William. Reality Therapy. New York: Harper & Row, 1965.

Golding, William. The Hot Gates; and other occasional pieces. New York: Pocket Books, 1967.

Grahame, Kenneth. Wind in the Willows. New York: Scribners, 1933.

Granger, Byrd Howell. Arizona Place Names. Tucson, Ariz.: Univ. Arizona Press, 1983.

_____. "Folklore and Cultural Awareness in the Schools." Mimeograph. Tucson, Ariz.: Univ. of Arizona, 1971.

Greenhood, David. Mapping. Chicago: Univ. Chicago Press, 1954.

Gregory, Richard L. The Intelligent Eye. New York: McGraw-Hill, 1971.

Bibliography

Guiliano, Vincent, et al. Into the Information Age. Chicago: Arthur D. Little, 1978.

Haviland, Virginia. The Openhearted Audience. Washington, D. C. : Library of Congress, 1980.

Hearne, Betsy and Kaye, Marilyn. Celebrating Children's Books. New York: Lothrop, Lee & Shepard Books, 1981.

Hemingway, Ernest. The Snows of Kilimanjaro, and Other Stories. New York: Scribners, 1969.

Hentoff, Nat. "The Integrationist," New Yorker, 57 (August 23, 1982), 37-73.

Hendrickson, Paul. "Catch a Rising Trend," The Washington Post, May 3, 1983.

_____. "Picture Books for Older Children," Booklist, June 1983, p. 1,280.

Highwater, Jamake. Many Moons, Many Smokes. Philadelphia: Lippincott, 1978.

Holt, John. "Big Bird, Meet Dick and Jane," Atlantic, 227 (May 1971), 72-78.

Horovitz, Carolyn. "Fiction and the Paradox of Play," Wilson Library Bull., 44:4 (Dec. 1969), 397-401.

Houle, Cyril O. Continuing Learning in the Professions. San Francisco: Jossey-Bass, 1980.

Hutchins, Robert M. Great Ideas Today. Chicago: Encyclopaedia Britannica, 1966-1969.

_____ and Adler, Mortimer J., ed. Great Books of the Western World and the Great Ideas. Chicago: Encyclopaedia Britannica, 1952.

Hyman, Richard Joseph. Shelf Access in Libraries. Chicago: American Library Association, 1982.

Jewett, Sarah Orne. The Country of the Pointed Firs; and other stories. Garden City, N. Y. : Doubleday Anchor, 1954.

Joncich, Geraldine M. Psychology and the Science of Education: Selected Writings of Edward L. Thorndike. New York: Teacher's College Press, 1962.

Joos, Martin. The Five Clocks; a linguistic excursion into the five styles of English usage. New York: Harcourt Brace, 1967.

Kael, Pauline. "The Current Cinema, Numbing the Audience," New Yorker, 46 (October 3, 1970), 74, 80.

Keen, Sam. To a Dancing God. New York: Harper & Row, 1970.

Knowles, Malcolm. "Model for Assessing Continuing Education Needs for a Profession," First CLENE Assembly Proceedings, January 23-24, 1976.

Koestler, Arthur. Insight and Outlook: An Inquiry into the Common Foundations of Science, Art & Social Ethics. Bison, Nebr: Univ. Nebraska Press, 1965.

Koren, Edward. Don't Talk to Strange Bears. New York: Windmill Books, 1969.

Lange, Carl. J., "How ERIC Serves Higher Education," Educational Record, 51:2 (Spring 1970), 167-170.

Langer, William L. Encyclopedia of World History. Boston: Houghton Mifflin, 4th ed., 1968.

Learning Today. "Changing the Center of Gravity; A Q and A Discussion," 15: 2, Spring 1982.

LeGuin, Ursula K. A Wizard of Earthsea. Berkeley, Calif.: Parnassus Press, 1966.

L'Engle, Madeline, "Before Babel," Horn Book (Dec. 1966), 661-670.

Leopold, Aldo. Sand County Almanac, with other essays on conservation from Round River. New York: Oxford University Press, 1966.

Leopold, Carolyn C. "Education for Decision," Library Journal, January 1, 1961, p. 38.

Lewis, C. S. Four Loves. New York: Harcourt Brace, 1960.

_____. The Great Divorce. New York: Macmillan, 1946.

_____. The Lion, the Witch and the Wardrobe. New York: Collier, Macmillan, 1970.

Lindgren, Jon. "Seeking a Useful Tradition for Library User Instruction in the College Library," In Lubans, John, Jr. Progress in Educating the Library User. New York: R. R. Bowker, 1978.

Lorenz, Konrad Z. King Solomon's Ring. New York: Crowell, 1952.

Los Anglees County Public Library. "Story of the Dewey Decimal System." Duplicated. Los Angeles, Calif.: Los Angeles County Public Library.

Lubans, John, Jr. "Library Literacy," RQ, Spring 1983, p. 235-236.

_____. "Library Literacy" RQ, Spring, 1982.

_____, ed. Progress in Educating the Library User. New York: R. R. Bowker Company, 1978.

Marchant, Maurice P. "Faculty-Librarian Conflict," Library Journal, 94 (Sept. 1, 1969), 2886-2889.

Martin, Lowell A. 'The 1982 Bowker Memorial Lecture, The Public Library: Middle-age Crisis or Old Age?," Library Journal, January 1, 1983, p. 17-21.

May, Rollo. Love and Will. New York: Norton, 1969.

Mead, Margaret. Coming of Age in Samoa. New York: Dell, 1967.

Melville, Herman. Moby Dick. New York: Literary Guild, 1949.

Menninger, William C. Blueprint for Teenage Living. Eau Claire, Wis.: Hale, 1958.

Mitchell, Henry. "No Calories, No Answers: An Index of Modern Life," The Washington Post, September 26, 1980.

_____. "Blind Faith, to Remove Warts From the Soul," The Washington Post, May 13, 1983.

Naisbitt, John. Megatrends; 10 New Directions Transforming Our Lives. New York: Warner Books, 1982.

National Geographic Society. Everyday Life in Ancient Times. Washington, D. C.: National Geographic Society, 1968.

Norris, Carolyn G., "A Time of Discovery," Hornbook, 38: 2 (April 1962), 141-7.

O'Brien, Robert C., "Telepsyche: The Meeting of the Minds," Holiday, 41 (February 1967), 8-19.

Oksner, Robert M. Incompetent Wizard. New York: Morrow, 1965.

Orwell, George. Nineteen Eighty-Four. New York: Harcourt, Brace & World, 1949.

Ouspensky, P. D. The Psychology of Man's Possible Evolution. New York: Bantam, 1968.

Parker, Eleanor. I Was Just Thinking. New York: Thomas Y. Crowell, 1959.

Parkinson, C. Northcote. The Law of Delay. Boston: Houghton Mifflin, 1971.

Paterson, Katherine. Gates of Excellence; on Reading and Writing Books for Children. New York: Elsevier/Nelson Books, 1981.

Peter, Laurence J. and Hull, Raymond. The Peter Principle. New York: Morrow, 1969.

Pierson, Robert M., "Sorry--It's Charged Out," Wilson Library Bull., (May 1970), 951-956.

Powell, Lawrence Clark. The Alchemy of Books. Los Angeles: Ward Ritchie, 1954.

Raisz, E. Principles of Cartography. New York: McGraw-Hill, 1962.

Reich, Charles A. The Greening of America. New York: Random House, 1970.

Reik, Theodor. Listening with the Third Ear: The Inner Experience of a Psychoanalyst. New York: Farrar Straus, 1948.

Rodale, J. I. The Synonym Finder. Emmaus, Pa.: Rodale Books, 1967.

Ross, Ralph, Berryman, John and Tate, Allen. The Arts of Reading. New York: Crowell, 1966.

Ruesch, Jurgen and Kees, Weldon. Nonverbal Communication; Notes on the Visual Perception of Human Relations. Berkeley, Calif.: Univ. California Press, 1969.

Scanlon, T. Joseph, "Viewer Perceptions on Color, Black and White TV: An Experiment," Journalism Quarterly, 47 (Summer, 1970), 366-367.

Shales, Tom. "Merlin of the Media," The Washington Post, February 17, 1983.

Sheehy, Eugene P., and Murphy, Robert. How and Where to Look It Up. New York: McGraw-Hill, 1958.

Shores, Louis. Basic Reference Sources. Chicago: Amer. Library Assoc., 1954.

_____, Jordan, Robert and Harvey, John. The Library College: Contributions for American Higher Education at the Jamestown College Workshop. Philadelphia: Drexel Press, 1966.

Shostrom, Everett L. Man the Manipulator. Nashville, Tenn.: Abingdon, 1967.

Shute, Nevil. In the Wet. New York: Morrow, 1953

Silverberg, Robert. Nightwings. New York: Avon, 1968.

Stephens, James. The Crock of Gold. New York: The Macmillan Company, 1960.

Stewart, George R. Names on the Land. New York: Random House, Sentry Edition, 1967.

Taube, Mortimer. Computers and Common Sense; The Myth of the Thinking Machine. New York: Columbia University Press, 1961.

Taylor, Katherine Whiteside. Parents and Children Learn Together. New York: Teacher's College Press, 1967.

Toffler, Alvin. The Third Wave. New York: William Morrow and Company, 1980.

Tolkien, J. R. R. Tree and Leaf. Boston: Houghton Mifflin, 1965.

Tournier, Paul. The Meaning of Gifts. Richmond, Va.: Knox, 1963.

_____. The Strong and the Weak. Philadelphia: Westminster, 1963.

Townsend, Peter. Up the Organization. New York: Knopf, 1970.

Tway, Eileen. Reading Ladders for Human Relations. 6th ed. Washington, D.C.: American Council on Education, 1981.

U.S. Geological Survey. For maps east of the Mississippi, write to Branch of Distribution, U.S. Geological Survey, 1200 South Eads Street, Arlington, Virginia 22202; for those to the west write to Branch of Distribution, U.S. Geological Survey, Box 25286, Federal Center, Denver, Colorado 80225.

University of Chicago Press. A Manual of Style. 12th ed. Chicago: Univ. of Chicago Press, 1969.

Weiss, Paul. The Making of Men. Carbondale, Ill.: Southern Illinois Univ. Press, 1967.

Williams, Dennis A., et al. "Can the Schools Be Saved?" Newsweek, May 1983, pp. 50-58.

Yardley, Jonathan. "Hype and the Hitler Diaries," The Washington Post, May 9, 1983.

Yoder, Edwin. "The Problem With 'Perception,'" The Washington Post, November 4, 1982.

Index

Any simpleton may write a book, but it requires high skill to make an index.

--Rossiter Johnson. Quoted, by Anna L. Ward, in A Dictionary of Quotations in Prose.

"Terminological inexactitude."

--Winston Churchill

"Mirrors should reflect a little before throwing back images."

--Jean Cocteau

Probably a crab would be filled with a sense of personal outrage if it could hear us class it without ado or apology as a crustacean, and thus dispose of it. 'I am no such thing.' it would say; 'I am MYSELF, MYSELF alone.'

--William James

Index

A76, 4, 82
Adler, Mortimer, 12, 114-116, 119, 125, 247
  Quoted, 118-119
Administration
  Budget, 14, 17, 40, 52, 54, 59, 93
  Crisis, 14
  For materials, 57
  Housekeeping, 61, 94
  Influence on Bibliographic Instruction Program, 26-27
  Management, 61, 94
Advanced Placement Courses, 13, 25
Alexander, Lloyd
  Quoted, 266
American Council on Education, 8, 61, 100-101, 124, 180, 213-214, 236
  Kellogg Grant, 100
American Library Association, 5, 9, 11, 44, 61, 77, 78, 82, 96, 104, 108, 146, 250, 332, 333
American Telephone and Telegraph Co., 1982 Annual Report
  Quoted, 332
Anderson, Pauline
  Quoted, xvi

Banks, Julia, 92, 103
Bell, Terrell, 7
Bellow, Saul
  Quoted, 230
Berry, John
  Quoted, xvii, 16
Bibliographic Instruction, see Library literacy
Bibliographic network, 48
Bibliographies, 74
Body language, 127-128, 129
Book
  Arts, 218
  As information package, 214-223
  As vicarious experience, 146
  As voice beyond the grave, 208
  Collections, see Collections
  Discussion groups, 29

352

Index

Picture, 110, 112, 117, 179-180
Selection, 103
Boorstin, Daniel, 20, 34, 48, 332
   Quoted, 4, 33, 43, 339
Brinnin, John Malcolm
   Quoted, 270-271
Brown, Andrew Hutton, 92
Bruner, Jerome, 22-23
Bush, Barbara, 133
Butman, Robert, 291
Bynner, Witter
   Quoted, 293

Cabeceiras, James
   Quoted, 201
Carlsen, Robert
   Quoted, 268
Carnegie, Andrew, 17, 52
Carriers of knowledge
   History of, 220, 246-248
Cataloging, 47
   At the National Geographic Society, 93-94
   At the National Society Daughters of the American Revolution, 104-105
   Cutter Numbers, 87, 89
   Instruction in, see Library literacy
   Of multi-media, 71-72
   Subject, 87
Catalogs, 71-72, 224
   Divided, 234-235
Cathedral Church of St. Peter and St. Paul (Washington Cathedral), 128, 164
   Library of, 87
Catholic Library Association, 4, 28
Catholic University, 44, 85, 92, 163, 243, 277, 293
Clark, Kenneth
   Quoted, 336
Classification, 43-44, 71-72
   Instruction in, see Library literacy
   Term, 101, 104, 105, 236-237
Collections
   Balanced, 57, 87
   Building, 50, 56, 61
   Demand vs. balance, 269-271
   For Senior Citizens, 277
   Maintenance, 57
   Management, 57-59
   Order in, 60
   Policy for, 56-57
   Selection skills, 42, 44, 60, 92-93, 193-195

Size, 224
Traditional vs. electronic, 7, 9, 193
College and University Libraries, 81, 266, 269
College Board, "Project Equality," 21
Communication
  Book as, 208
  Cultural awareness as, 310
  Defined, 208
  Multi-media as, 138
  Narrative vs. picture as, 180-181
  Nonverbal, 128
  Person as, 151-152
  Picture as, 131, 195
  Reading as, 112-117
Computers, 4
  As information access, 37, 206
  As library material, 137
  For circulation, 10
  Human brain as, 22, 249, 275 illus., 23.
  Vs. secretaries, 3
Coolidge, Oliva, 141
Cooper, Martha A., 104
Council on Library Resources, 101
Creighton, William F., 237
Critical thinking, 20, 21, 22, 24, 31, 66, 104, 206
  As teaching librarian's subject specialty, 13, 50
  Fact, as part of, 12, 14, 20-21, 30-31, 35, 37, 218-219
  Opinion, as part of, 21, 47
  Problem-solving, as part of, 21, 22, 36, 104
  Value judgement, as part of, 20, 21, 273-275, 277-278, 284-285
Culbertson, Hugh M.
  Quoted, 175-176
"Cultural Awareness Project"
  Defined, 296, 298
Culture, 13, 16, 269, 301, 307
Curriculum development
  Libraries' role in, 28
  Reform, 21
Cutter, Charles, 67, 224
  Number Table, 89

Darling, Richard L., 96, 98, 99, 188
  Quoted, xvi
Daughters of the American Revolution, see National Society Daughters of the American Revolution
Debenham, Frank
  Quoted, 326-327
De Gennaro, Richard, 2, 4, 137
Delaney, Jack
  Quoted, 28-29

de Paola, Tomi
   Quoted, 178-179
Dewey Decimal Classification, 31, 79, 201, 205, 209, 224, 228, 236, 241, 243
   Chart of, illus. 227-228
Dewey, John, 17, 52, 252
Dewey, Melville, 52
   Quoted, 105-106
District of Columbia Library Association, 3, 296
Drake, Miriam
   Quoted, 39-40

Editorializing as anti-fact, 34
Emrich, Duncan
   Quoted, 309
Equal opportunity, 36, 173
ERIC, 58, 73, 74, 101, 102
Education
   Crisis in, 7, 9, 20, 221
   Defined, 24, 25,
   Independent Study, 25, 27
   Individualized Instruction, 25, 210
   Reform of, 7, 9, 256

Faculty
   As Bibliographic Instruction subject specialists, 229-230
   Relationship with librarians, 27, 30, 51, 210, 221, 256, 260
Fader, Dan, 210
Fairies
   Belief in as a way of testing people, 282-283
Fairy tales, 276, 279, 282
   And Jung, 280
Farley, Walter, 220
Fiction
   As vicarious experience, 289-290
   Science, in relation to that of the supernatural, 285-288
Folklore
   Defined, 297
   In relation to genealogy and local history, 296-297, 309
   Teaching with, 301-303
Footnotes
   In Bibliographic Instruction, 217
   Reasons for use, 46-47
French, Arthur
   Quoted, 177-178
Friedman, Maurice
   Quoted, 288-289

Generation gap
  Closing with people-lore, 300, 302-303, 307
George, Wilma
  Quoted, 322-326
Georgetown University, 137, 214, 241
Gerhardt, Lillian
  Quoted, 293
Golding, William
  Quoted, 95-96
Goodwin, Joseph, 219
Gorg, Sheila, 101
Granger, Byrd Howell, 296, 297, 318
  Quoted, 298-305, 308-309
Greenhood, David
  Quoted, 327-330
Gregory, Richard L., 131
  Quoted, 174-175
Guilano, Vincent
  Quoted, 333-334

Handicapped persons, 124, 132, 138, 189-190
  Blind, 155-156
  Sight impaired, 169, 242-243
Headmaster/Headmistress, 96
Hearne, Betsy
  Quoted, 179-180
Henne, Frances, 7, 61
Hickel, Wally J., 13-14
Highwater, Jamake
  Quoted, 311
Holt, John
  Quoted, 179
Holton-Arms School, 87, 109
Horowitz, Carolyn
  Quoted, 273-274
Hyman, Richard Joseph
  Quoted, 224

Illiteracy, 36, 113, 126, 133, 141, 155, 157
Imagination, 145, 280, 282
  In literature teaching, 157
Independent Schools, 9, 85, 86-92, 108-109
Information
  Access, 50
  Age, 2, 333
  Explosion, 53, 72-74
  Industry, 4, 7, 10, 11, 20, 44, 50, 332, 339
  Pyramid, see Knowledge pyramid
  Storage and retrieval, 5

Intelligence, 26, 163
  Defined, 122
  Non-verbal, 150-151
Invisible string, 94

Jewett, Sarah Orne, 116
Joos, Martin
  Quoted, 79
Jordan, Robert, 24

Kael, Pauline
  Quoted, 183-184
Keen, Sam
  Quoted, 220, 281-282
Kelloran, Marian, 220
Keppel, Francis, 7
Kipling, Rudyard
  Quoted, 105
Knowledge
  Defined, 43
  Industry, 4, 10, 17, 20, 44, 50, 339
  Pyramid, 21, 36, 38, 52, 53, 141, 148, 191-192, 206, 248, 252, 334, 336, 337; illus. 21, 334
Koestler, Arthur, 280
Kortendick, Father James J. 85, 92
Koren, Edward B. 112-113, illus. 113
Krayeski, Felix, 3
Kurzwell, Arthur, 297

Language, 22, 37, 133, 140, 209, 305
  As necessary for thought, 111
  Development, 166-167, 218
  Intimate, 79, 209
  Mathematics as, 126
  Music as, 126
  Native, 123, 310
  Object, 129-131, 306
  Symbolic, 283, 317
  And story, 266
Learning, 10, 22, 24, 66, 200, 206, 308, 314
L'Engle, Madeline
  Quoted, 222
Leopold, Aldo, 116
  Quoted, 330
Lewis, C. S., 115, 120

Librarian
   As teacher of "library," 7, 8, 13, 22, 24, 28, 31, 38, 50, 52,
      62, 106, 138, 206, 209, 211, 242
   In-service training, 85
   Personality requirements for, 29, 40, 44, 99
   School, 10, 26, 28, 292-293
   Teaching the "why," 225
Librarianship
   As a profession, 29-30, 44, 92, 102
   Paradoxes in, 38-39, 148
   Values of, 11
Library
   As network, 48, 69
   As physical entity, 86, 94
   As small business, 7, 26, 48-54
   As storehouse of knowledge, 53, 94
   As textbook for library literacy, 13, 28, 31, 34, 35, 48, 62, 242
   As textbook for teaching critical reading, 119-120
   Classes, scheduling, 91
   Crisis, 9, 14, 17, 40, 82
   Defined, 5, 42-44
   One person, 85-86
   Revolution, 12
Library literacy, Curriculum, 8, 24, 48, 64, 335, 339
   Alphabetization, 212-213
   As librarian's academic subject speciality, 23, 28, 35, 51, 204
   Book, 214-223, 268-269, 271
   Beyond "school," 251, 311
   Carriers of knowledge, 220
   Cataloging, 67-72
   Citation
      Book, 230, 232
      Periodical, 239-240
   Classification, 32, 71, 101, 225-234
   Components of, 258-259
   Dictionary arrangement, 213
   For Senior Citizens, 169, 251
   Government Documents, 238-239
   History of libraries, 246-248
   Materials, history of, 220-221
   Program, 60, 89, 94-95, 248
   Rationale for, 248-249, 252-253
   Reading skills, relationship to, 132-133
   Relationship to academic curriculum, 138, 211
   Skills necessary for, listed, 212
   Subject selection for "free" library classes, 89, 94, 169, 296,
      305, 307, 311, 314, 326, 329-330
   Telephone Directories, 237-238
   Testing
      Design of, 256-257, 260-262
      Psychology of, 257, 259
      Validation of, 262-263

Index

Library Literacy Means Lifelong Learning
   Defined, 64-67
Library College, 24
Library Instruction Round Table, 8, 146, 250
Library of Congress, 2, 3, 45, 56, 82, 103, 213, 290, 296, 336
Library of Congress Classification, 79, 209, 229, 235, 239, 241
Lifelong learning, 309, illus., 65
   Defined, 10, 37, 38, 53
   Library as textbook for, 64-67, 211
Lindgren, Jon
   Quoted, 81
Literacy, 37, 118
   Visual, 183-184
Literature
   Selectivity, artistic, 290-292
   See Fairy stories, Fiction, Mythology, Story, and Storytelling
Lowrey, Lois, xv
   Quoted, 307
Lubans, John, Jr.
   Quoted, 250, 335
Luce, Clare Boothe
   Quoted, xvi
Lurton, Sally, 90-91

Mapmaking
   History of, 322-326
Maps
   As end papers, 93
   Cadastral, 317
   Defined, 314-315, 320-321
   For children, 317-318, 329-330
   Less usual kinds, 321
   Scale, 315-317
   Teaching with, 314-315, 319-320, 322
   Topographic, 316
Manion, Esther Ann, 92, 103
Marchant, Maurice P., 221
   Quoted, 30
Maret School, 86
Marketing, 102, 253, 334
Martin, Lowell A.
   Quoted, 270
Master of Library Science (our credential) 13, 30, 38, 60, 72, 85, 208, 210, 271, 314, 329
   Continuing Education, 306
McDonald's, 49, 51, 102
McKenzie, Floretta Dukes
   Quoted, xvii-xviii
Media
   As technology, 160
   Checklist for selection of, 193-194

    Development of, 139-140
    Fakery in, 33
    Human being as media package, 166, 169
    In a post-literate society, 136
    Manipulation in, 190-193
    Mass, 9
    Multi-, 9, 136, 138, 187, 303-304
    Negative attributes of, 193
    Of sight
        Defined, 172-174
        Development of, 32-33
        Fact in, 181-183
        Personal, 189
        Skills for using, 173-174, 176-178
    Of sound
        Human voice as, 151-153, 167-170
    <u>See also</u> Recordings as instructional materials
    Teaching about, 140
        Embroidery, 186-187
        Halloween, 142
        Life in ancient Greece, 141
        Mathematics, 138, 140
        Mountains, 145-146, 185-186
        Oz, 143
        Seamanship, 138-140
        Spatial awareness, 141, 145-146
        Water, 143-145
Melville, Herman
    Quoted, 272
Men and fiction, 289-290
Minimarc, 5, 104
Mitchell, Henry
    Quoted, 16-17, 156
Mollegen, Albert T.
    Quoted, 34
Montgomery County, Md.
    Public Libraries, 10, 71
    Public Schools, 8, 62, 96-99, 187-188, 244
Moon, Eric, 11, 14
Morris, Wright
    Quoted, 195
Motivation, learner, 52, 62, 137, 148, 160, 201, 210, 302
Movies, 183-184, 189
    Vs. print, 219
Music in teaching and learning, 160-163
    Appreciation of, 95, 163-164
    As language, 126-127
    Canned, 160
    Chance, 164-165
    Development of a feeling for, 166-169
    Recipe for using recorded, 165-166

Mythology, 278-284
 And Jung, 280
 As early scientific history, 230

Naisbett, John
 Quoted, 332, 333
Naming, 151, 230, 279, 318
Nation at Risk, A, 8
National Geographic Society, 8, 15, 62, 64, 92, 93, 94, 102, 141, 190, 237, 243, 296
National Library Week, 36, 110
National Society Daughters of the American Revolution, 3, 48, 62, 64, 104-105, 124, 238, 251, 271, 296
Nemeyer, Carol, 82
Networking, 65-66, 248
1984, 12, 38, 54, 126, 312, 332
 Quoted, 336-337

Office of Personnel Management, Standards for Librarians, 14, 30, 82, 293
Offiesh, Gabriel D., 163
Online searching, 11, 67, 72, 103, 148, 206, 248
 Boolean Logic, illus., 11
"Only Connect," 64, 82, 105, 335
Orwell, George,
 Quoted, 336-337
Owens, Major R., 2, 3, 4, 334

Parents, 13,
 As Library patrons, 51
 Communication with, 300
 In the sixties, 13-14
 Role in language development, 166-167
Paterson, Katherine
 Quoted, 117
Patron
 Administrator as, 98
 As customer, 51-52, 53
 Ignorance, 8, 9, 61, 64, 79, 80-81, 201-202, 256
 Use, in schools, 9, 57
People-lore, For Teaching
 Cultural unity, 310
 Death, 299
 Divorce, 311
 English, 301, 303-305
 Holidays, 310-311
 Sexuality, 306-307

Weddings, 311
Witchcraft, 301-302
People skills, see Reference Service
Periodicals
   To illustrate fallacies of the "information explosion," 72-74
   Variant formats for, 74-75
   See also Library literacy
Pezzanite, Frank, 5
Pictures, reading, see Reading pictures
Pierson, Robert
   Quoted, 61
Photocopying, 74
Photographs, 33, 195
   Reading of, see Reading pictures
Plagiarism, 47, 80, 249, 334
Powell, Lawrence Clark, 46
   Quoted, ix-x, 121-122
Process vs. product, see Reference Service
Professionalism, sense of, 30, 80, 82, 102, 206
   The author's, 84-86, 91-92
Proverbs, 300, 303-304
Public Libraries, 8, 11, 48, 49, 51, 65, 169, 269, 271-272, 275, 276
Public Service, 11
   Circulation, 38, 94
   Librarians, 13, 17, 104, 209-210, 252, 339
Publishing
   Print vs. electronic, 2-5, 240
   Skills, 103

Raiz, E.
   Quoted, 315
Reader's Adviser, 45, 121-122, 272
Reading
   CRT screen, 132
   Critical, 267
   Defined, 110, 111, 113, 124
   For survival, 125
   In elementary schools, 24-25
   Learning how, 108-110
   Levels, 113-119, 258
   Librarian as middle man in, 122
   Lists, 45, 47, 80, 306
   Mathematics, 126
   Microforms, 132
   Music, 126-127
   Pictures, 174-176, 179
   Recreational, 267, 277
   Teaching, 110
   Vs. movies, 184
   Vs. television, 143

Index 363

Recordings as instructional materials
  As "show and tell," 159
  Disc, 156-157
  Tape
    As "show and tell," 159
    Dramatic, 158
    For foreign language, 157
    For Social Studies, 154, 159
    Of classroom lectures, 153
    Pupil production of, 154
    Sensitivity training with, 158, 160
    With the non-verbal person, 154
    With the verbal person, 153
  Video, 154
    Excerpts, 158
Records, storage
  Personal, 5-6
  Societal, 6
Reference books
  Appraisal, 76-77
  Encyclopedia, 76-77
  For "Action" issues, 147
  For teaching critical reading, 119-120
Reference Collection
  As subject for library literacy, 76-77, 242-246
Reference Service, 209-210
  As magic, 45
  Beyond K-Ph.D., 147
  Georgetown University, 137
  Interview, at NSDAR, 137
  Online vs. print delivery, 11
  Process vs. product, 8, 62, 64, 210
  Telephone, 124
Reich, Charles
  Quoted, xvii
Reid, Judith, 296
Research, library, 8, 103, 249
Reserve Books, 94
Roggenbuck, Mary June, 28
Ross, Ralph; Berryman, John; and Tate, Allen
  Quoted, 118
Ruesch, Dr. Jurgen
  Quoted, 128, 130-131, 238

Sagan, Carl, 7
Saint Albans School, 94-96
Scanlon, T. J., 178
Schoenfeld, Janet, 101
Scholarship as a blazed trail, 46-47, 147, 191, 247
School librarian, see Librarian, school
School Libraries, 7, 9, 10, 24, 26, 27-28, 80, 267-68

School Libraries Worth Their Keep, xv, xvi, 105, 296
Schools, 9, 24, 25, 92
Scott, Kathryn S., 104
Shales, Tom
    Quoted, 136
Sheen, Bishop Fulton John, 151
Shores, Louis, 24, 76
Silverberg, Robert
    Quoted, 286-288
Skills needed for library literacy
    Alpha, 200-202, 206
    Classification, 202-203
    Entry, 203
    Hierarchy, 205
    Listed, 199-200
    Reading, 199, see also Reading
    Subconscious, 198
    Subject discipline, 203-205
Special Libraries, 8, 39, 51, 59, 65, 87, 92-94, 100-101, 259, 334
Sputnik, 7, 20, 25
Staff size in relation to library instruction, 38
Stone, Elizabeth W., 85
    Quoted, x-xiv
Story, 220-221, 293, 326-329
Storytelling, 158, 222, 303
Subject
    Headings, 234-237
    Searching, 11, 70, 79
    Specialists, 24
    Tutor, 26
Symbol, 21, 174, 221

Tatnall, Dr. Lovisa
    Quoted, 155
Taube, Mortimer, 5
Tauber, Maurice, 3, 73, 99
Taylor, Katherine Whiteside, 279-280
Teacher, defined, 13, 209
Teaching, 9, 50, 208-209, 211
    For cultural awareness, 297-306
    Peer, 23
Technical Services, 45, 94
Television, 147, 178, 179, 184, 190-193
Term paper
    Lesson plan for teaching "how," 249-251
    Multi-media, 142, 210
Terry, Milton, 3
Theall, Father Bernard, 293
    Quoted, 277
Thorndike, Edward Lee
    Quoted, 200

Index

Toffler, Alvin, 270, 332
    Quoted, 334-335
Tolkien, J. R. R. 115
    Quoted, 273, 276, 279
Tournier, Dr. Paul, 116, 120
Track system, 26
Travers, P. L.
    Quoted, 82, 278
Truth, 12, 43, 52, 105
    Emotion vs. rationality, 32
    To establish, 273-275, 284

U. S. Geological Survey, 320

Value
    As emotion in action, 272
    As societal anchor, 12
    Defined, 36-37
    Judgment, 337
    Teaching with, 284-285
Van Doren, Charles
    Quoted, 47
Vertical File
    Of National Geographic Society Library, 93
    Processing and filing for, 77-79
    Subject headings for, 79
Video games, 147
Volunteers, use of, 23, 25, 50, 90

Warner, Sylvia Ashton, 218, 235
Weeding, 88, 97
Weiss, Paul
    Quoted, 280-281, 288
Wheatly, Katherine, 90
Women's special needs, 158

Yardley, Jonathan
    Quoted, 54
Yoder, Edwin M., Jr.
    Quoted, 192